亚洲文化遗产系列丛书
the Serie of Asian Cultural Heritage

QUFU, BIRTHPLACE OF CONFUCIUS

迈向可持续城市
Towards a Sustainable City

孔子故里·曲阜

林志宏　主编
Edited by Roland Lin Chih-Hung

同济大学出版社
TONGJI UNIVERSITY PRESS

目录

CONTENTS

序一

本书的内容来自2010年10月在同济大学举办的“空间，文明与可持续发展(Space, Civilization and Sustainable Development)”国际会议。这是一次跨文化活动：来自中外不同文化背景的国际同行，坐在一起讨论一座在中国传统文化中具有特殊意义的城市的保护与发展问题。这又是一次跨学科的活动：来自儒学、历史学的学者和来自建筑学、城市规划学的学者，坐在一起讨论城市的空间问题。这还是一次跨时间的活动：孔子故里、儒家圣地曲阜，代表着千年文明的城市空间，如何带着时代的烙印，拥抱一个可持续发展的未来？本书出版同时是为了表达欧洲及中国的一些学者朋友们对儒学大师汤一介教授（北京大学哲学系教授，1927年2月16日—2014年9月9日）的怀念。

曲阜具有非常典型的文化意义。这座具有特殊文化意义的历史文化名城，和数以千计的在时代滚滚洪流的冲击下与千百年文明历史渐行渐远的中国历史城市(镇)一样，同样无法抗拒不可阻挡的城市突变。城市空间的巨变和历史空间的延续成为当代中国最难解的一道难题。对于曲阜这样具有强烈文化象征意义的城市，自然历史文脉的传承和历史城市空间意向的延续是一个更容易引起全社会共鸣的话题。但即使如此，时代巨变的冲击仍具有毁灭性的危险。对于其他历史文化不那么悠久、不那么让人关注的城市，这种毁灭性的危险就更容易或者已经变成现实。随着中国经济的腾飞，那种因过度贫穷而产生的对时代巨变的渴望就渐渐变成了对记忆的怀念，乡愁越来越多地成为社会集体心态的主流。在经历了30年大拆大建后，大多数中国城市(镇)的大部分历史空间已面目全非甚至消失殆尽。但亡羊补牢，尤未为晚。哪怕历史已完全丢失，今天义将成为历史。只要真的拥有乡愁，就会懂得历史空间的价值，就会知道保护和延续城市历史空间的必要。当我们明白为什么要保护的时候，如何保护就成为主要问题。历史价值本身是需要研究才能理解的。这就需要更多跨

Foreword 1

The book is inspired by an International Conference on " Space, Civilization and Sustainable Development " held in Tongji University in October, 2010. This is a cross-cultural conference: experts from all over the world joined in the discussion of problems of a special city in traditional Chinese culture—its urban protection and sustainable development. This is a cross-disciplinary activity: scholars that specialize in Confucian studies, history, architecture or urban planning discussed related urban space issues. This is a cross-temporal gathering: the conference was rooted from the Qufu City, the hometown of Confucius and the sacred place of Confucian learning, which epitomizes urban space of millennial civilization and tells the story of having a sustainable future while preserving history. The book also serves, for scholars and his friends, to commemorate Yijie TANG (Professor of philosophy in Peking University, Feb 16, 1927—Sep 9, 2014), a master of Confucian studies.

Qufu City is famous for its cultural significance. As a historic and cultural city, like so many in China, Qufu stands the test of urban change. A dilemma persists in contemporary China—the change of urban space and the preservation of history, culture. The dilemma is more salient in Qufu with its cultural significance, and gets widespread attention. Even so, the impact of epochal change is devastating. For cities with less cultural significance, the impact is more keenly felt, or even has worked its way through. The boom of China's economy has propelled the need for epochal change, which in turns triggers fond memory of the past, or nostalgia. Nostalgia is on the mind of the vast majority. After 3 decades of mass demolition and construction, much of China's historical urban landscape has been eroded or has vanished out and out. Yet, there's still time to do something. Even when history is lost, today's experience will become history again. Once we have nostalgia, we will appreciate the value of historic space, hence the need to protect and sustain historic space of a city. When we know WHY, the next big question is HOW. Historic value must be studied before evaluated. Multi-disciplinary efforts are thus needed. Especially, historical research is needed for studying urban historic space and protecting built heritage. It is only with good research across disciplines that comes good protection measures.

The true mark of humanity is nostalgia, or more exactly the need for history. The need for a great future, like nostalgia, is the building humanity as a whole. The two needs should be balanced for the two parties involved, the planners and the architects. It's irrational to pursue the future while shelving the history and unreasonable to pursue the history while casting aside the future. The urban landscape and historic buildings, as built heritage, still live in the present moment. Adapting them into museums is unrealistic and unsound. Their very vitality, or the revival of it, hinges on the smart use and preservation of its historical value. For all

学科的研究。在城市历史空间和建成遗产保护领域，对于城市规划和建筑学科而言，尤其需要史学研究的加入。唯有此，保护工作才能真正做好。

乡愁，更准确地说是人类精神生活中对历史的需求，是人类文明成熟的标志，是人性的重要组成部分；同样，对未来美好生活的向往，也是人性中的重要组成部分。因此对于建成环境的参与者——规划师和建筑师而言，不可顾此失彼。为创造美好生活而不顾及历史延续是不理性的，为保护历史而不关注当下的生活也是不人道的。历史遗存下来的城市与建筑，作为建成文化遗产，大多数都仍然存活于当下现实生活之中。将建成遗产都采用博物馆式的保护是不现实也不合理的。在大多数情况下，其生命力在于如何合理使用，同时又不至于因为当下的使用而割断历史文脉的延续。这就使建成遗产的保护成为城市规划学和建筑学领域一个特别重要也特别具有挑战性的专业领域。这次会议将来自中外不同文化背景历史文化研究领域和城市规划领域的学者邀请到一起，使得会议主题得以拥有更为深刻的内涵。

与此同时，今天的城市发展和建设行为还要更多地顾及对未来的影响。我们不仅有责任将前人留给我们的遗产保护好、传下去，我们也要让我们今天所为更多地成为留给后人的遗产。更重要的是，我们不能因为今天的需要而断送了后代的发展，最终终断了人类文明。这就是可持续发展的真正本质内涵，也是当代人对自身需求主动约束的新境界。将历史文化遗产保护和可持续发展两个重要历史责任放在一起讨论——本书的特点，也正是中外城市文化界当下最值得讨论的话题。近 20 年来，联合国教科文组织也全力推动可持续发展理念下的建成遗产保护。本书的作者中有儒学、历史文化界的大家、巨擘，也有建筑与城市规划界的大师、泰斗，他们的观点，可以说代表了当下中外学术界对上述问题思考的最高水平。他们聚焦中国曲阜和由此延伸出来的世界性话题，共同探讨来自不同文化背景和不同学科背景专家的应对，相信他们的观点对于推动中国乃至世界当代城市的历史保护与未来发展，都具有很深远的理论意义和现实价值。希望本书能够引发更多的思考并因而引出更多更好的研究成果。

伍江
同济大学教授
同济大学常务副校长
法国建筑科学院院士
2018 年 1 月 12 日

the reasons and more, the protection of built heritage has become a special and challenging area of endeavor in urban planning and architecture. The International Conference pooled the wisdom of experts with various, relevant specialization, coming from home and abroad. Their smart words and insight brought the theme into life.

When it comes to urban development and construction, consideration should be given to the future. We're obligated to both inherit heritage from the past and create heritage for the future. More importantly, we won't sacrifice the future for the present, let alone history or culture. Such is the essence of sustainable development—to restrain when needed. The book is special in the juxtaposition of heritage protection and sustainable development, both being major historical responsibilities and heated topics of urban culture and history. The past two decades have witnessed the UNESCO promoting the protection of built heritage with a view to contributing sustainable development. Contributors to the book include Confucian studies scholars, masters of history or culture, mavens of architectural science and urban planning, who have most intensive academic reflections on these questions. With a focus on Qufu City and extended global topics, coping strategies considered across a wide spectrum of cultural or academic backgrounds have been given. Potentially able to balance protection and sustainable development for cities in China and worldwide, their thoughts and strategies will be valuable both in theory and practice. I hope that this book will inspire more reflections and researches.

WU Jiang
Professor
Executive Vice President of Tongji University
Academician at Academie d'Architecture, France
Jan 12, 2018

序二：曲阜，可持续之城？

曲阜市位于中国山东省的西南部，古为鲁国属地。孔子（又称孔夫子、孔圣，公元前 551—公元前 479）的故里就位于此，因此曲阜也成为了一种特殊的遗产。1994 年，联合国教科文组织将曲阜的三处遗产一同列入了世界遗产名录：孔子祠庙（孔庙）、孔子后裔所居之处（孔府）、孔子氏族之墓地（孔林）。这三处并称“三孔”。其中孔林是一座林木繁茂的大型墓地，安葬着孔子及其后代。曲阜，一座围绕着“三孔”慢慢形成的城市，就这样在历届政权的保护下，发展了两千多年。先贤生活的地方被其后代部分地行政化，在中国封建帝国中享有着特殊地位，实际已成为一处圣地。最初把此作为圣地的只有其家族成员和其一小部分弟子，到汉代（公元前 206—公元 220 年），汉帝国政权兴建孔庙，随后孔庙又被不断扩建重建，而孔子的后代直接被封官授爵，这样就通过政府的力量，确认了曲阜的圣地地位。20 世纪，在曲阜还没有被世界所普遍认识之前，它就被列入中国国家遗产。虽然在“文化大革命”（1966—1976）期间遭到重大破坏，但是国家从 1961 年起就对其采取诸多保护措施。1982 年，曲阜被中国政府纳入首批 24 个历史文化名城。

三大历史遗产使曲阜成为了一个令人印象深刻的例子：城市的建筑布局不仅能为伟人的传颂起到作用，并且能为一个社会的缔造做出贡献。圣人曾经居住的地方经过数个世纪的演变，成为了今天古老的孔庙。今天在孔庙里，我们还能看到曾经是孔子故居（孔子住宅）的一侧，有三处满载历史的古迹：孔子古井、诗礼堂、鲁壁。

孔子古井位于第二个庭院内，井旁立一石碑，上刻“孔子古井”四字，井的四周由明代的石头围成护栏，东侧叩之有脆响。很显然，古井已然不是当年的形态，但古井的存在，是孔子在此生活过的见证，当时的住户靠此井用水。此外，从古井里汲水，亦有“汲取灵感”之隐喻。我们总是能从前人那里得到自己思想和行为的指点。发出脆响的栏杆处于东侧就是一个暗示，因为东方是受人喜欢的方位。

Foreword 2: Qufu, Ville Durable?

Située en Chine au sud-ouest de la province du Shandong, dans l'ancien pays de Lu, Qufu est la ville natale de Confucius (nom latinisé de Kong Fuzi ou Maître Kong, 551-479 avant notre ère). Elle est constituée d'un patrimoine exceptionnel. En 1994, l'UNESCO a inscrit sur la liste du patrimoine mondial les trois monuments qui s'y trouvent réunis: le Temple de Confucius (*Kongmiao*), la Résidence de ses descendants (*Kongfu*), et le Cimetière de la famille Kong (*Konglin*), vaste nécropole boisée où sont ensevelis Confucius et ses descendants. C'est autour de ces trois lieux, devenus proverbialement en chinois « les Trois Kong » (*San Kong*),qu'une ville s'est constituée au fil des siècles et a connu au cours de plus de deux millénaires un développement quasi continu, souvent favorisé par la protection impériale. En effet, elle est devenue un lieu de pèlerinage, constitué des lieux où a vécut le maître, elle était en partie administrée par ses descendants et bénéficiait d'un statut particulier dans la Chine impériale. Cet héritage qui ne concernait au départ qu'une famille et un groupe restreint de disciples, a été reconnu par le pouvoir impérial, avec la refondation sous les Han (206 av. J.-C. – 220 apr. J.-C.) du temple de Confucius qui ne cessa par la suite de s'agrandir et connut plusieurs reconstructions. Plus tard, les descendants du sage furent anoblis. Au XXe siècle, l'ensemble fut pris en compte au sein du patrimoine national : après diverses mesures de protection à partir de 1961 et en dépit d'importantes dégradations au moment de la Révolution culturelle (1966-1976), Qufu a fait partie du premier groupe de vingt-quatre villes historiques et culturelles classées par le gouvernement chinois en 1982 avant d'obtenir, plus récemment, une reconnaissance au plan mondial.

Avec ses trois monuments principaux, la ville de Qufu constitue un exemple particulièrement frappant de la manière dont l'aménagement architectural peut contribuer, non seulement à célébrer une mémoire mais aussi à façonner une société. À l'intérieur du vieux temple de Confucius, édifié au fil des siècles sur les lieux mêmes où vécut le sage, on peut encore visiter la partie latérale est du temple, censée correspondre à l'ancienne demeure de Confucius (Kongzizhuzhai), un triple lieu de mémoire : l'Ancien puits de Confucius (Kongzigujing), la salle des rites et de la poésie (Shilitang), et la paroi de Lu (Lubi).

Dans la deuxième cour se trouve l'Ancien puits de Confucius, signalé par une stèle portant les quatre caractères de son nom, entourés d'une balustrade de pierre d'époque Ming dont le côté est, lorsqu'on le frappe, rend un son clair. Sa forme actuelle n'est évidemment pas d'origine, mais l'existence du puits est le plus sûr témoin que la demeure de Confucius se trouvait bien à cet endroit, là où ses habitants pouvaient s'alimenter en eau. En outre, il est la métaphore de la tradition dans laquelle on puise l'inspiration, comme on tire l'eau d'un puits. C'est cette traduction qui permet d'orienter correctement pensée et action. Le son clair rendu par sa balustrade du côté est (direction réputée favorable) en est le signe.

诗礼堂主导第一个庭院，相传其名字的由来，是孔子语录——《论语》中的一则故事。陈亢问于伯鱼曰："子亦有异闻乎？"对曰："未也。尝独立，鲤趋而过庭。曰：'学《诗》乎？'对曰：'未也。''不学《诗》，无以言。'鲤退而学《诗》。他日又独立，鲤趋而过庭。曰：'学礼乎？'对曰：'未也。''不学礼，无以立。'鲤退而学礼，闻斯二者。"孔子儿子在这个故事中展现了同样的对话如何反复发生在同一地点（此文中是在家族的庭院），且以同样的方式发生，这不仅仅是和问问题的人在交流，其本身也是一个隐喻，暗示经典诗书要反复研读。就是在这种反复中才能明白自己应该走的道路，而不是仅仅通过高人的指点，获得秘诀而一劳永逸。

井旁，一块石碑上书"鲁壁"二字，记载了一起关于中国思想史，关于古文流传的重大事件——公元前 213 年，秦始皇焚书坑儒，孔子的第九代传人孔鲋将儒学书籍藏匿于此墙中。这些书在秦灭之后，被汉朝的鲁恭王在拆墙建宫时偶然发现。虽然由于不恰当的拆墙方式，文书差一点全毁。但因此这些儒家经典才得以保存并传给后人。事实上，焚书之后，儒家思想是通过两种不同的渠道保存并流传的：其一，侥幸逃脱坑儒事件的文人的回忆和整理；其二，这些藏在墙中又重见天日的文本。孔庙作为孔子子孙保留的祭祖之地，地位十分重要，它与儒学传统紧密相连，这一传统影响了过去对知识教、传、习的根基。

这些地点背后丰富的内涵，以及汉代把儒家学说上升到意识形态的行为，阐述了历代政权对曲阜的保护，以及对圣地的政治利用。曲阜是古代的鲁国国都，孔子的故乡，于周朝（公元前 1050—公元前 221）始，囊括了广袤的区域；公元前 2 世纪，经由汉代的整治，曲阜城邦变为仅有当时的三分之一多一点大，在西南部围绕三孔而建；在之后的数世纪间，曲阜历经数次毁坏与重建；宋代（960—1279）宋真宗时期，又对曲阜进行了大规模的扩张和整改；明代（1369—1644），曲阜遭遇强盗洗劫，孔庙遭受火灾，城市和城墙又一次重建：这一切造就了今天的曲阜古城区。古城区作为曲阜的中心部分已经停止扩展。

明城墙（20 世纪又经历了一次毁坏与重建）的作用是保护两处至今依然贵为核心的建筑群：孔庙与孔府。孔庙和孔府在功能上完全不同，但其整体结构和内部构造又遵循着同样的设计原则。其中所使用的理念，经常被认为是儒家思想在建筑方面的具体表现。每个群建筑都围绕着位于主轴线上的一个中心展开。主轴线串起了主要建筑。进入庙府要一步一步、从南到北穿过数道门，最后才能到达最隐私的地方，它将在此的居住者和建筑群其他部分隔离。东西两条次轴线上分布着功能更为私密的建筑，但依然遵循着渐进的排列顺序，从南到北，直通主会客室，室内又分为数个相对私密的空间。孔庙和孔府的布置，遵循中国传统院落组织形式（四合院式，

La salle des rites et de la poésie (Shilitang), qui domine la première cour, renvoie quant à elle, par son nom, à une anecdote rapportée dans les *Entretiensde Confucius* (*Lunyu*, 16, 3). Quelqu'un ayant demandé à Confucius si son père ne lui avait jamais donné quelque enseignement exceptionnel, celui-ci répondit : « Non, jamais. Un jour, il était là, debout tout seul, et je traversais la cour à petits pas rapides (en signe de respect). Il me dit : « As-tu étudié les poésies (du Classique de la poésie *Shijing*) ». Je répondis : « pas encore ». Il dit alors : « Sans étudier la poésie, il est impossible d'apprendre à exprimer sa pensée. » Je me retirai donc pour étudier la poésie. Une autre fois, il était de nouveau là debout, et je repassais par la cour à petits pas rapides. Il me demanda : « As-tu étudié les rites ? » Je répondis : « Pas encore ». Il dit alors : « Sans étudier les rites, il est impossible de s'affermir le caractère. » Je me retirai donc seul pour étudier les rites. » Cette anecdote montre comment la fréquentation répétée des mêmes lieux (ici, la cour de la maison familiale), en fonction d'une étiquette précise, permet non seulement l'échange, mais est elle-même une métaphore de la manière dont il faut fréquenter les textes classiques. C'est cette pratique régulière qui montre la voie à suivre, et non une seule formule ou recette, imposée d'en haut, qui la résumerait et la figerait une fois pour toutes.

À côté, une stèle portant les deux caractères Lu Bi (Paroi de Lu) marque le souvenir d'un événement capital dans l'histoire de la pensée chinoise et de la transmission des textes classiques. Lorsqu'en 213 avant notre ère Qin shihuangdi, le Premier Empereur, fit persécuter les confucianistes et brûler leurs écrits, Kong Fu, le neuvième descendant du Maître, cacha dans un mur qui se trouvait à cet endroit les livres confucéens. Ces textes furent retrouvés par hasard sous la dynastie suivante des Han lorsque le prince Gong de Lu, pour agrandir son palais, fit démolir le mur. C'est ainsi, d'après la tradition, que ces textes sacrés furent conservés et livrés à la postérité. De fait, l'héritage confucéen fut sauvegardé et transmis par deux voies différentes après l'incendie des livres: d'une part, grâce aux lettrés qui, ayant échappé à la persécution, restituèrent de mémoire une partie de son contenu, et d'autre part grâce aux textes qui avaient été cachés et qui furent ainsi redécouverts, malgré une entreprise de destruction malencontreuse qui menaçait de tout faire disparaître. Le temple de Confucius, lieu de culte gardé par ses descendants est donc important car il est resté étroitement associé à l'histoire de la tradition textuelle confucéenne et au sens que cette tradition donne à l'étude xuede l'héritage du passé qui constitue la base de l'enseignement, de la transmission et de l'acquisition du savoir.

La richesse de signification de ces lieux, et la transformation sous les Han du confucianisme en idéologie d'État explique la protection dont la ville fit l'objet de la part des autorités imperials et les multiples tentatives, au cours de l'histoire, d'instrumentalisation de ce sanctuaire par le pouvoir. L'antique cité de Lu, capitale du pays de Confucius, englobait dès l'époque de Confucius, sous les Zhou (v. 1050-221 avant notre ère), une aire très vaste. Réaménagée sous les Han, au IIe siècle avant notre ère, la citadelle n'en occupait plus que le tiers environ, du côté du sud-ouest, recentrée autour des Trois Kong. La ville connut ensuite, au fil des siècles et des dynasties, plusieurs destructions suivies chaque fois d'une reconstruction, et bénéficia notamment d'une phase d'expansion et d'aménagement monumental sous l'empereur Zhengzong des Song (960-1279). Sous les Ming (1369-1644), suite à une attaque de brigands et à l'incendie du temple, la ville et sa muraille furent une nouvelle fois reconstruites : c'est cet ensemble qui constitue aujourd'hui la ville ancienne de Qufu, cœur d'une cité qui ne cesse aujourd'hui de s'étendre.

La muraille des Ming (encore une fois détruite puis reconstruite au XXe siècle) avait pour fonction de protéger les deux ensembles architecturaux qui constituent encore aujourd'hui le noyau : le Temple de Confucius et la Résidence de ses descendants. Ils avaient des fonctions bien distinctes, mais leur plan général et leur organisation intérieure obéissaient aux mêmes principes. Le type de plan adopté dans la maison comme dans le temple est souvent considéré comme l'expression concrète sur le plan architectural des idées confucéennes. Chaque ensemble est organisé autour d'un noyau central, situé sur l'axe principal, et qui constitue

即一个院子居中，建筑环绕四边而建），上文引文也有表述。孔庙的中心是祭祀的主大厅，先贤在这里接受所有来孔庙朝圣的人的祭奠。孔府的中心建筑不仅是孔子后人中的一家之主用来领导族内成员的地方，某些时期，这里更是管理全城居民生活和主持公道的地方。

曲阜的城市肌理围绕这些古迹而生，并在尊重古建的空间朝向和空间布局前提下不断更迭至今。这令曲阜成为了一个十分鲜明的案例：建筑和城市的整治是为了形成并传承一种社会组织形式和城市生活方式。曲阜市的古迹群，作为古代中国建筑和城市规划的重要见证，是值得被研究、被保护、被重视的遗产。在当今城市发展规划中，它也是值得被思考、被借鉴的。曲阜的未来该指向何方？正是需要到这些遗产不断寻访，研究它的过去，才能找到新的出路，从而让曲阜继续为中国及世界提供一个可持续发展的实例。这也是编写本书的中国及欧洲作者们致力研究的方向。近年来，作者们进行了积极交流，试图在这一系列问题上做出思考、达成共识。在这里，我谨向联合国教科文组织专员、巴黎索邦大学远东研究中心研究员林志宏博士致以特别的谢意，感谢其在这项研究工作及创建本系列书集中发挥的关键作用。本书是这个集子的开端，我们也希望这一切的努力能够持续下去。

顾乃安
法国巴黎索邦大学
考古艺术史系教授
2017 年 7 月 19 日

le point de rencontre le plus important. On y accède progressivement, en circulant du sud vers le nord et en passant plusieurs portes et cours. Derrière elles se trouvent des lieux plus privés isolant leurs occupants. De part et d'autre, le long de deux axes latéraux est et ouest s'organisent d'autres ensembles, secondaires en importance et de caractère plus intime, mais aménagés selon le même principe de progression, du sud au nord, vers une salle principale de réception qui précède elle-même une série d'espaces plus privés. Kongmiao et Kongfu sont donc tous deux aménagés selon des principes communs qui sont ceux de la maison chinoise traditionnelle organisée autour d'une cour intérieure (du type dit *siheyuan*, cour entourée de bâtiments sur ses quatre côtés), comme celle évoquée dans le texte cité plus haut. Au cœur du Kongmiao se trouve la principale salle de culte, où le Sage reçoit les hommages de tous ceux qui lui rendaient visite en son temple. Au cœur du Kongfu, la salle principale était le lieu où le chef de famille, descendant de Confucius, dirigeait non seulement le clan familial, mais était chargé à certaines époques d'administrer la vie des habitants de toute la ville et de rendre justice.

Le tissu urbain qui enveloppe ces monuments s'est toujours régénéré en respectant l'ancien bâti, son orientation et sa disposition dans l'espace. Qufu constitue un exemple particulièrement clair d'aménagement architectural et urbain dont la fonction est de façonner et de perpétuer un certain mode d'organisation de la société et de vie urbaine. Témoin important de l'architecture et de l'urbanisme chinois anciens, cet ensemble constitue un patrimoine digne d'être étudié, conservé et valorisé, ce qui de toute évidence doit être pris en compte dans les projets actuels de développement de la ville. Comment envisager son avenir ? C'est justement en fréquentant les lieux et en étudiant son passé qu'une voie pourra être trouvée, et qu'ainsi Qufu pourra continuer d'offrir à la Chine et au monde un modèle possible de développement durable. C'est à quoi se sont attachés les auteurs chinois et européens de ce livre, qui ont participé activement à nos échanges ces dernières années et à l'élaboration d'une réflexion commune sur ces questions. Je tiens à remercier ici tout particulièrement le Dr. Roland Lin Chih-hung, consultant auprès de l'UNESCO, spécialiste du patrimoine mondial, et membre associé du Centre de recherche sur l'Extrême-Orient à la Paris-Sorbonne (CREOPS), pour le rôle essentiel qu'il a joué dans cette entreprise, et dans la création de la présente collection, inaugurée par ce livre que nous espérons tout aussi durable.

Antoine Gournay
Professeur
Art et Archéologie de l'Extrême-Orient
UFR d'Art et d'Archéologie
Université Paris-Sorbonne
19 Juillet 2017

序三

曲阜是儒学的圣城，也是东方文明的一方胜地。很多的学者，无论是来自于哪里，都关注着这座城市所代表的文明及其时至今日的不断发展。大约 10 年以前，汤一介和我很高兴参与到一些来自欧洲和中国的朋友们在曲阜做的工作。这些工作发轫于欧盟一项国际间的城市合作项目，以空间遗产的保护为主要的议题，凝聚了一批对曲阜怀有深深敬意和浓厚情谊的中外朋友。之后，曲阜友谊协会的成立将这些中外朋友们对曲阜的关心凝聚起来，通过两届“相约曲阜”国际论坛，为曲阜所代表的儒家文明和古老城市空间的可持续发展献计献策，真正地体现了在平等交流中求同存异，在理解对话中追求创新的宗旨，成为中法跨文化交流的一段佳话。

古往今来，曲阜这座历史名城不断激发着创新。曲阜的孔庙和地理区域形成了一个人文空间，经孔子及其继任者改造，成了一方文明的胜地。几个世纪以来，中国及其他部分亚洲国家都打上了这种文明的烙印，社会和政治结构受到了很大影响，在哲学研究方式方面的影响尤其深远，正如同时代的希腊城市一样。但是古希腊的城市已不可寻，曲阜却依然留存着丰富的古代遗迹，城市空间的文化印记依然清晰而厚重。因此，古老的儒家文明和现代城市的可持续平衡发展之间的关联就显得更加凝重和深远。

儒家文化注重修身的功夫，讲修身、齐家、治国、平天下，“自天子以至于庶人，壹是皆以修身为本”，它不是要建立一种非常完整的知识体系，而是要建立一种提高自己境界或提高社会境界的学说。所以，我认为，中国哲学是以内在超越为特征的哲学，靠自己的修养摆脱自我的限制和环境的限制，靠自己的能力成圣成贤。那么，儒家文化影响下的古代城市谨严有序的空间秩序，在现代乃至未来的发展中，会以什么样的形式持续发挥着它潜在的文化影响，是否会和现代城市的可持续发展之间发生微妙的共鸣，实现稳定的平衡呢？这个问题是值得传统的儒家文化研究者

Foreword 3

Qufu is a sacred city where Confucianism originates and a famous site of oriental civilization. A number of scholars, wherever they come from, are looking at the city and its constant development, as well as the civilization and culture it represents. It was a great pleasure for Tang Yijie and me to get involved into some work carried out in Qufu by colleagues from Europe and China about ten years ago. Those efforts were a part of an international cooperation of European Union's programme, which gathered a group of Chinese and foreign friends interested in and respecting for Qufu to work together under the topics of space and heritage. The attentions and concerns led to the founding of the civil society organization "Friends of Qufu". The subsequent two sessions of international forums "Rencontres de Qufu" served as a platform to not only contribute to the sustainable development of both Confucian culture and the old urban space of Qufu, but also seek common grounds and innovative perceptions through equal dialogue and mutual understanding, and became a much-told story in the history of Sino-French communication.

As a historic city, Qufu has been a source of inspiration of all ages. The human space constructed by the temple of Confucius and the geographical setting has made the place a symbol of a distinctive culture through constant reconstructions by Confucius and the successors. Over the centuries, China and other Asian countries have been shaped and branded by this culture, with significant influences on their social and political systems, and the study of philosophy in particular. In this sense, Qufu is parallel to those contemporary counterparts in Greece. However, the ancient Greek cities have been nowhere to be found, while Qufu is still well preserved with diversified remains and relics, as well as visible and intense cultural traces in the urban fabric. Therefore, the correlation between century-old Confucian culture and the sustainable and balanced development of modern city is particularly significant.

Confucianism emphasizes the cultivation of one's mind, namely a theory of Self-cultivation, Family Harmony, State Governing and World Peace. "With self-cultivation at the center", Confucian culture aims to set up a system for the improvement of individuals or the society, instead of an ambition to establish a whole set of knowledge system. That is why I regard Chinese philosophy as a one featured with self-transcendence, which means to get rid of limitations imposed by oneself and the environment through self-nurturing and to become the man of wisdom and virtue based on one's own ability. Here comes the question: since these old towns possess a carefully-planned and orderly spatial layout as a result of the influence of Confucian culture, how will this pattern continue to exert its cultural influence in the modern and future development? And will it respond to the need of sustainable development of modern cities and contribute to the achievement of a stable balance between the two? This is a question for cultural scholars

深思，也需要来自于建筑、规划、社会、艺术等各领域的学者来共同凝心钻研的问题。这样的思考，对于曲阜尤为重要，且时不我待。

非常感谢这些来自欧洲和中国的朋友们始终记得汤一介和我的点滴工作。对儒家文明和古城曲阜的共同关注让我们有了很多的共鸣，这样的跨文化合作弥足珍贵，可以让曲阜这座历史城市在和世界的互联互动中展开新的一页。

乐黛云
北京大学教授
2017 年 7 月 20 日

of Confucianism and a question for colleagues from architecture, planning, sociology and arts as well. It is an urgent problem for us to contemplate and thus of great significance to Qufu.

I am grateful to those friends from Europe and China for memorizing the bits and pieces of work that Tang Yijie and I have been doing. We share common thoughts and concerns on Confucian culture and the old city of Qufu. The cross-cultural interactions are valuable to the city, and open a new chapter in its connection to the outside world.

YUE Daiyun
Professor of Beijing University
July 20, 2017

前言：曲阜历史文化名城的可持续发展：中欧合作欧盟亚洲城市复兴项目 Asia Urbs

林志宏

本书出版是为了表达欧洲及中国的一些学者朋友们和乐黛云教授对汤一介教授（北京大学哲学系教授，国学大师，1927 年 2 月 16 日 – 2014 年 9 月 9 日）的怀念。

引言

在本书中，欧洲及中国同行们在思考如何在保护亚洲历史城市的过程中运用可持续平衡发展城市策略，并对具体案例——曲阜，进行讨论、提出相关建议。最近几年，欧洲专家前往中国进行实地考察，反思都市化与曲阜的区域规划，与中国学者和有经验的建筑师进行交流，中国清华大学吴良镛教授和他的同事刘健教授提供了很多有益的建议。欧洲专家每次前往北京都与中国学术专家进行跨文化交流，使我们有机会与中国儒家文化学术专家（特别是中国北京大学汤一介教授、乐黛云教授以及他们的同事李中华教授）共同探讨与思考。上海同济大学历史城市保护团队和济南山东大学建筑系的年轻教授为我们提供了中国和曲阜有关城市和建筑保护方面的学术和实践支持。在此，除了感谢来自欧洲的建筑师和城市规划师同事们，还要感谢三名法国学者对我们的工作卓有成效的贡献：法国道德与政治科学学院玛丽亚娜 · 巴斯蒂德院士（Prof./Academician Marianne Bastid），法国纯文学和铭文学学院汪德迈通讯院士（Correspondant/Prof. Léon Vandermeerch）和法国马克 · 孟毅大使（Ambassador Marc Menguy）。

改革开放以来，“文化大革命”时期的批林批孔、反传统的风潮已成过去式，“重仁尚礼”的孔子儒家学说，再次被奉为传统中国文化的正统思想。近年来，中国国家领导提出了迈向小康及建设和谐社会的发展目标，中国教育部对外汉语办公室在世界各地设立“孔子学院”推动儒家文化，学习汉语逐渐成为世界潮流；联合国教科文组织配合中国政府于 2006 年 9 月底，在曲阜颁发了第一个以中国人名命名的联合国项目奖“孔子教育奖”。近年来中国大陆的经济高速增长，国际政治外交扩展，如何将中国传统文化推向全世界成为首要之急。反观全球，国际局势不稳定、恐怖活动频繁，西方文化发展至今，正面临着新的困惑。面对亚洲高速成长兴起的新世界时空观，欧

Introduction: Sustainable Development of Historic and Cultural City of Qufu: Sino-European Asia Urbs Programme

Roland Lin Chih-Hung

The publication of this book, initiated by a group of Chinese and European scholars and Professor Yue Daiyun, is dedicated to the memory of Professor Tang Yijie (1927–2014), a colleague and Professor of Philosophy and Master of Chinese Studies from Beijing University.

Introduction

In this book, our Chinese and European colleagues explore the issues and challenges concerning the implementation of a sustainable and balanced urban policy in the conservation of historic city context in Asia. They also specifically examine the case of Qufu and put forward some suggestions. In recent years, a number of European scholars have visited China and conducted fieldwork across the country. To draw lessons from the urbanization and regional planning process in Qufu, they have met and exchanged opinions with Chinese experts and experienced architects, amongst whom Professor Wu Liangyong from Tsinghua University and his colleague Professor Liu Jian generously offered many useful suggestions. During their various missions in Beijing, European experts always talked to Chinese academics and took the opportunity to discuss and exchange their views with Chinese scholars of Confucianism (in particular Professor Tang Yije and Professor Yue Daiyun from Beijing University and their colleague Li Zhonghua). The operational team for the preservation of the historic city at Tongji University (Shanghai) and young professors from the Architecture Department of Shandong University (Jinan) provided us with tremendous amounts of theoretical and technical support with regards to the urban and architectural conservation of both Qufu specifically and China in general. We are also grateful to our architect and urban planner colleagues from Europe. Moreover, we would like to acknowledge the support and contribution of three French scholars: Professor/Academician Marinanne Bastid from the Académie des Sciences morales et politiques (Academy of Humanities, Social and Political Sciences) of the Institut de France; Correspondant/Professor Léon Vandermeerch from the Academy of Inscriptions and Belles-Lettres of the Institut de France; and His Excellency Mr Marc Menguy, a former French Ambassador.

Since China's reform and opening-up, the anti-Confucian and anti-traditional campaign of the Cultural Revolution has long been buried in history and Confucian doctrines which emphasize the core values of Ren (benevolence and humaneness) and Li (rituals) have come back into mainstream culture in China. For the past few years, Chinese leadership proposed the development objective of building a moderately prosperous and harmonious society. The National Office for the Teaching of Chinese as a Foreign Language (Han Ban), a public institution affiliated with the Chinese Ministry of Education, has established Confucius Institutes around the world to promote Confucianism internationally. Learning the Chinese language has become trendy around the globe. At the end of September 2006, UNESCO, with the support of the

美国家不禁想要从中国的传统文化思想中去寻根溯源，孔子儒家学说再次被提起，其深远影响倍受重视。希望透过本书，我们可以从历史的发展进程走近这古老的城市，一起去了解正在进行的曲阜历史文化遗产保护发展概况，一同思考如何保护鲁国故里及儒家学术重镇的整体意含性的难题。

世界格局的演变、中国的政治决策走向，为孔子的故乡、儒学圣地曲阜的保护与发展，提供了绝佳良机。我自 2002 年开始至今，把参与曲阜的保护与发展视为要务，在巴黎、曲阜两地间往返不下十次，也数次安排曲阜市领导代表团赴欧洲访问及考察。为推动曲阜老城区的保护与发展，前法国大使马克 · 孟毅及我经由曲阜市规划局委托与欧盟接触，促成双边的合作意向。2004 年 10 月，曲阜市人民政府与两个欧洲合作城市——法国雷恩市、西班牙圣地亚哥市——签订了合作协议，2004 年末通过“中欧合作欧盟亚洲城市复兴项目”（Asia Urbs）计划，在欧盟 75 万欧元资助下，从 2005 年起为期三年（2005 年 1 月至 2007 年 12 月），就曲阜历史文化名城的可持续发展，在故城复兴、遗产保护、旅游振兴等方面进行合作。我一方面担任此项目的国际顾问，同时于 2005 年 9 月起接受了曲阜市人民政府委聘，成为曲阜市规划及城建国际顾问。近年来参与曲阜的保护与发展，我有幸能与中国北京大学汤一介教授、乐黛云教授、李中华教授及中国清华大学吴良镛教授、刘健教授，法国马克 · 孟毅大使、玛丽亚娜 · 巴斯蒂德院士、汪德迈通讯院士、法国建筑学院皮埃尔 · 克莱蒙院士、法国雷恩市、西班牙圣地亚哥市的专家们，以及前曲阜市规划局刘海涛局长和承办曲阜明故城保护规划的上海同济大学邵甬教授等人，多方探讨及论证，受益良多。为了推动在保护亚洲历史城市过程中运用可持续平衡发展城市政策，专家们认为，需要进一步加强中欧学者之间的交流，增加参与人员的数量。因此，欧盟资助在 2005 年发起中欧合作的“欧盟亚洲城乡合作计划”。以这个项目的名义，两座欧洲名城，法国的雷恩市和西班牙的圣地亚哥市，实质性地加入了与曲阜在持续发展背景下的遗产保护和调度方面的紧密合作。完成推动为期三年（2006 年至 2008 年）的“曲阜—亚洲城市项目” 程序后，我们继续成立了“曲阜友谊协会”，为中欧学者之间的交流提供了非常坚实的基础。（上述提及的中欧学者都是 2008 年成立的“曲阜友谊协会”的创始成员，在此特别感谢北京大学汤一介教授、乐黛云教授。曲阜友谊协会— Friends of Qufu：协会主席马克 · 孟毅大使以及作为协会秘书长的我本人负责所有参加者之间的主要联系。）

“曲阜友谊协会”举办了两届“相约曲阜”国际论坛（分别于 2008 年在曲阜和 2010 年在上海同济大学举办），探讨与思考文化遗产价值观和文化意义评价的问题、方法、原则，以及选择适当的方法（策略）和指导原则（工具、规划、任务 / 行动），以制定作为整合“文化发展规划”一部分的亚洲历史城市保护中运用的可持续平衡发

Government of the People's Republic of China, presented the first awards for the Confucius Prize for Literacy—named after a Chinese celebrity—in a ceremony held in Qufu. With the rapid economic growth and the increasing political and diplomatic influence of Mainland China, promoting Chinese culture across the world has become a top priority. In today's world, international political tensions and turbulences, along with increasing threats from terrorism, have caused new confusions to the Western world. In the wake of a new emerging world order, our Western counterparts cannot help but reach all the way back to the very traditional culture of China to understand this phenomenon. The philosophy of Confucius was brought back into the spotlight again, with its far-reaching influence and significance for Chinese culture. In this book, the editors hope to approach the centuries-old city Qufu through its historical development and to look at the ongoing process of conserving its historic and cultural heritage in modern times. More importantly, they call for a reflection on the means to protect this historic city and its legacy, which stretches from its time as the former capital of the ancient Lu State to the birthplace of Confucianism and beyond.

The transformation of the world and the reorientation of Chinese policies have provided good opportunities for the conservation and development of Qufu, the hometown of Confucius and sacred land of Confucianism. Since 2002, I have been placing the conservation and development of Qufu at the top of my personal agenda, travelling back and forth between Paris and China dozens of times and coordinating several visits of Qufu officials and delegations to Europe. In order to promote the conservation and development of Qufu, the City Planning Bureau has established contacts with European Union (EU) through former French Ambassador Mr Marc Menguy and me, and finally reached an agreement on bilateral cooperation. In October 2004, the People's Government of Qufu signed partnership agreements with two European cities: Rennes in France and Santiago de Compostela in Spain. By the end of 2004, with a grant of 750 000 Euros from the European Asia Urbs Programme, Qufu had launched a three-year cooperation programme (January 2005–December 2007) for the regeneration of the old town, heritage conservation and tourism development, aiming for the sustainable development of this historic and cultural city. I became an international consultant of the Asia Urbs Programme for Qufu, and was recruited as an international advisor for the urban planning and construction of Qufu in September 2005, at the invitation of the City Government. Since then, I have been more and more involved in the city's conservation and development process, and I was fortunate enough to work with a number of renowned experts from China and other countries and to benefit from their advice, notably Professors Tang Yijie, Yue Daiyun and Li Zhonghua from Beijing University, Professor Wu Liangyong and Liu Jian from Tsinghua University, H.E. Mr Marc Menguy, Academician Marinanne Bastid, Correspondant/Professor Léon Vandermeerch, Pierre Clément from the French Académie d'Architecture, experts from the cities of Rennes and Santiago de Compostela, and former Director of the Qufu Planning Bureau Liu Haitao, and Professor Shao Yong from Tongji University, whose team was in charge of the conservation planning for Qufu Ming City. The experts agreed that in order to promote the implementation of a sustainable and balanced urban policy, it is necessary to enhance the communication between Chinese and European scholars and to motivate more scholars. In this context, the EU financed and initiated the Asia Urbs Programme in 2005 to promote bilateral cooperation between China and Europe. In this programme, two historic cities in Europe—Rennes in France and Santiago de Compostela in Spain—officially established partnerships with Qufu to collaborate on heritage conservation and management for sustainable development. At the end of the three-year Qufu–Asia Urbs programme (2005–2007), we moved on to establish the civil society organisation "Friends of Qufu", a solid platform for exchanges between Chinese and European academics. (All of the experts mentioned above are founding members of the "Friends of Qufu". In this regard, I would particularly like to thank Professors Tang

展城市政策。2008 年 5 月 31 日至 6 月 1 日在曲阜孔子研究院召开了第一届“相约曲阜”国际论坛。论坛的主题是“文明与空间”，分为四场分论坛：①曲阜、空间和文明；②法律、宗教和空间；③曲阜：记忆的地方；④遗产与城市治理。本次论坛的成果已在北京大学主编的《跨文化对话》杂志“文化传统与空间发展”特别版块中整理发表（详见《跨文化对话》第 25 辑，“文化传统和空间发展”部分，2009:81-146.）2010 年 9 月 29 至 30 日，中国和法国的专家与学者，齐聚于由同济大学（中国上海）举办的“空间，文明与可持续发展”第二届国际论坛。第二届论坛除了在“城市研究中的文化反思与规划策略”的框架下继续讨论第一届论坛的内容，还试图以人类可持续发展的文化维度作为主题，分为三场分论坛：①人性化空间；②可持续发展的人类文化和文明维度；③文明作为一种工具能更好地理解城市化研究的跨文化思考和规划策略。第二届论坛中提出不应该忘记“文明与空间”的议题、“人居环境”及“人在可持续发展过程中的重要性”。论坛通过了《上海倡议书》，并在《中国名城》杂志整理发表（详见 2010 年 9 月在中国上海同济大学举办的中法论坛“空间，文明与可持续发展”，《中国名城》，北京编辑部和扬州编辑部，2011（3）：26-29.）我们希望通过启动为期三年的中欧合作欧盟亚洲城市复兴项目（Asia Urbs），以及在中国举办两届国际论坛，“曲阜友谊协会”可以继续作为一个智囊团，探讨和思考有关可持续平衡发展城市政策的问题、方法、原则。通过对曲阜的案例分析，我们了解到当前城市遗产政策对城市可持续发展有重要影响，特别是对四大核心战略和挑战的影响。四大核心战略是城市的公共控制，城市的平衡发展，城市中心的形象以及与公民的沟通。城市遗产可以作为平衡和可持续的工具来实现城市保护、更新和可持续发展。最后，为发展规划的需要，本人呼吁应成立一个跨学科的团队，由跨学科的城市研究领域的研究人员和专家参与，包括规划、交通、住房、领土研究、旅游、文化遗产保护、历史、社会学、经济、考古、建筑、人类学、博物馆学、艺术和美学研究等领域。可持续发展平衡城市政策必将使亚洲在历史城市保护上迈开新的一步。

《上海倡议书》

2010 年 9 月 29 日至 30 日，中国和法国的专家与学者，齐聚于由同济大学（中国上海）举办的“空间，文明与可持续发展”论坛，我们在此达成以下共识：

没有过去便没有现在；我们唯有充分地了解过去才可以享受现在与展望未来。我们的祖先所建构的历史承载着我们的文明，因此，保护历史遗产就是保护我们的个性和存在，意味着文明的延续。当今的世界性思潮已经证实了保持

Yijie and Yue Daiyun from Beijing University for their contributions. As President and Secretary-General respectively of the society Friends of Qufu, H.E. Mr Marc Menguy and I (Roland Lin Chih-Hung) are in charge of day-to-day contacts among members.)

Thanks to the Friends of Qufu, two international forums "Rencontres de Qufu" have been organized in 2008 in Qufu and 2010 at Tongji University, Shanghai, to discuss the issues, methodologies and principles regarding the assessment of cultural heritage values and cultural significance. These meetings also helped generate guidance to select appropriate methodologies (strategies) and principles (tools, plans, tasks/actions) in order to develop a sustainable and balanced urban policy applied to the conservation of historic Asian cities, as a part of the integrated "Cultural Value Led Development Planning". The first "Rencontres de Qufu" took place from May 31 to June 1, 2008, at the Confucius Institute in Qufu, China. The main topic was "Civilization and Space" with four sessions of presentations: (1) Qufu, Space and Civilization; (2) Law, Spirituals and Space; (3) Qufu: Memory of Place; (4) Heritage and Urban Governance. The outcomes of this meeting were analysed and published in the special section of "Cultural Tradition and Spatial Development" of the magazine *Transcultural Dialogues* (in Chinese) edited by Beijing University (See "Cultural Tradition and Spatial Development" section of *Transcultural Dialogues*, No. 25, 2009: 81-146.). The second "Rencontres de Qufu" was held from September 29 to 30, 2010 at Tongji University, Shanghai, on the theme of "Space, Civilization and Sustainable Development". Following the first forum focused on cultural reflections in urban studies and planning strategy, for this second forum, we tried to introduce the human/cultural dimension of sustainable development into our main topics, with three sessions of presentations and discussion: (1) Humanized Space; (2) Human/cultural dimension of sustainable development; (3) Civilization as a tool to better understand this transcultural reflection in urban studies and planning strategy. The participants also proposed that we should revisit the topic of "civilization and space" and other ones such as "living environment" and "the key role of humans in sustainable development". The "Shanghai Manifesto" was adopted at the meeting, and was analysed and published in the magazine *China Ancient City* (See 'Summary of the Sino-French Forum "Civilization, Space and Sustainable Development", International Forum, Tongji University, Shanghai, China, September 2010, in *China Ancient City* , Special Issue, Beijing & Yangzhou, 2011(3): 26-29.) It is hoped that, following the initial three-year Sino-European Asia Urbs programme and the two international forums held in China, the "Friends of Qufu" society can continue to explore issues, methodologies and principles regarding sustainable and balanced urban policy as a think tank. Through the case of Qufu, we have recognized that urban heritage policy presently has a great influence on sustainable development of the city, especially on the following four key strategies and challenges: urban public control, balanced urban development, the image of the urban centre, and communication with the citizens. Urban heritage can be taken as a balanced and sustainable tool to achieve urban conservation, urban renewal and sustainable development. The author emphasizes the necessity of an interdisciplinary approach to address the need for development planning, with the participation of researchers and specialists from a number of interdisciplinary areas such as city planning, transportation, housing, territory studies, tourism, cultural heritage preservation, history, sociology, economy, archaeology, architecture, anthropology, museum studies, art/aesthetic studies, etc. A sustainable and balanced urban policy will allow for a significant new step forward in the conservation of historic cities in Asia.

地区之间的差异与自身传统价值的珍贵。远离抽象的探讨，不同地区的文化多样性应当借由丰富的方式加以表述。

首先，为实现全球的可持续发展，人们自觉地反思技术进步、科学发展以及经济手段，积极而有效的政策和社会手段不胜枚举。然而对于新型社会的前景，我们仍尚未达成充分的认识，这就更需要我们重视未来文明的人文价值。

可持续发展不仅包括技术和经济方面，还应当包括文化的内容，而自然环境在文明的建设中也起着至关重要的作用。

现代性和传统是发展过程中应该得到同等重视的问题。空间、文明与可持续发展的概念，包含人类活动的三个方面。

空间

这是我们居住的地方。人类起源的大自然，被人类逐步地重塑为城市空间。而城市空间与环境也同时承载着社会的变革。我们应该遵守这样一个基本的原则：生存空间的改造，其本质首先是适应人的活动。

文明

人类最重要的需要之一是建构自己的文明和传统。文明倘若不能得以发扬和传承，就不可能存在历史与现代之间的交会。为了使各地区蕴含丰富历史宝藏的文明得以和谐发展并有能力展望未来，这个相会是至关重要的。

可持续发展

有鉴于资源的有限，可持续发展的理念为我们指明了采取行动的方向，涉及空间、技术和社会方面的诸多议题。国际领域的很多有益尝试已经开始影响更多的地区和居民。

为了整体意义上的人类可持续发展，与会的中国以及法国学者和专家共同呼吁国际社会在下列方面继续努力：

第一，将可持续发展的方式整合在一个更宽广的角度，塑造新的人文传统；

第二，在促进经济增长、改善民生的同时，应加强对文化遗产的保护力度，提高社会的文明程度；

第三，促使不同文明差异化发展和相互启发；

第四，发展科技以服务人民；

第五，在个体和和群体之间保持平衡的发展；

The Shanghai Manifesto

We, the Chinese and French experts and scholars gathered at the "Space, Civilization and Sustainable Development" Forum held at Tongji University, Shanghai (China), on September 29–30, 2010, agree on the following statements:

The present is a product of the past. We can live in the present and look into the future only based on a solid understanding of the past. Our civilization is rooted in the history that was created and handed down by our ancestors. Thus, by preserving cultural heritage, we preserve our identity and our existential status, which enables the continuity of our civilization. Currents of thought in the contemporary world have testified to the significance of maintaining regional diversity and the traditional values of each country. More concretely, the cultural diversity of each continent must be expressed in different ways.

First of all, the rise of awareness made it possible to envisage technical and scientific solutions and economic means for a global sustainable development. Numerous policies and social means are now available and have proven both positive and effective. However, few actions have been undertaken to sketch out new forms of society, which makes it even more necessary to initiate a reflection on the humanistic values of civilization for the future.

Sustainable Development has not only technical and economic aspects, but also a cultural dimension. In addition, the natural environment plays a major role in the development of civilizations.

Modernity and tradition should be given equal weight in the development process. Thus, the notions of Space, Civilization and Sustainable Development encompass these three dimensions of human activities.

Space

Space is the place we live in. Nature at the origin of humanity was gradually remodelled by man and converted into urban space. This new urban space and its environment represent various social changes in human history. We should observe the following fundamental principle: living spaces are reinvented, first of all, to adapt to the most basic needs of man and his activities.

Civilization

One of the most valuable needs for human beings is that to build civilizations and traditions. An encounter between tradition and modernity is not conceivable without the development and transmission of civilization from one generation to the next. This meeting is essential to make sure that civilizations of each region of the world evolve in harmony with their rich historical legacy and project themselves into the future.

Sustainable Development

In view of the limited resources, Sustainable Development sets a standard towards correct action for a number of spatial, technical and societal aspects. Positive national or international actions have been taken and began to influence regions and residents on a broader scale.

In order to promote a broad approach to Sustainable Development, we, the Chinese and French scholars and experts present at this meeting, call on the international community to work in the following direction:

第六，主动采取一种与自然之间和睦相处的态度。

结语

我们强调可持续发展应该是一个势在必行的行动，而不仅是一个简单的理论或设想：

“更好地维护过去的文明和更好地管理现在的空间与资源，期待建立一个有能力承载文明传统的可持续发展的人道社会。”

本《上海倡议书》（Shanghai Manifeste）由与会“空间，文明与可持续发展”论坛的三十位中国和法国的专家学者，于2010年9月29日至30日在中国上海共同通过。

一个跨文化主题：空间与文明之间的关系

很难找到比孔子的出生地更适合研究“空间，文明与可持续发展”的了。曲阜市前市长刘森在曲阜儒学文化与空间发展学术论坛（2008年5月31日至6月1日）的发言如下：

众所周知，曲阜以其5 000多年的文明史、延续3 000多年的城市建设史闻名于世，被称为中国城市发展的活标本；曲阜又因孔子而成为儒家文化的发祥地。曲阜是开展空间与文化交流活动的优良场所——曲阜作为孔子、孟子、颜子、鲁班等历史名人的故乡、黄帝诞生地、儒家文化的发源地，在国内外，特别是亚洲儒家文化圈具有巨大影响，被誉为“东方圣城”，在世界文化地理上具有独特的优势和影响力。历史上，儒家文化与空间发展关系紧密——孔子创立了以“仁”为核心的儒家学说。他的思想体系，既强调对个人的尊重，又强调建立社会秩序；既强调个人的自我修养，又强调与外界的和谐相处。在中国城市的空间布局、功能区划、建筑功能、单体设计上，明显地体现出社会组织关系，轴线对称布局更是中国儒家思想中等级观念及中庸思想物化的集中体现。在人与自然的关系上，儒家学说主张人与自然和谐相处，而这样的思想使中国人的艺术心境融于自然，“天人合一”思想成为中国古代设计师恪守的重要哲学。中国传统的城市与建筑空间布局、功能规则已然形成固有模式，成为中国传统社会“助人伦，成教化”的物质载体，使生活在其中的人们时刻感受到这种潜移默化。从某种角度看，儒学文化是中国空间发展的文化基因。在城市层面的

First, Integrate the Sustainable Development approach into a broader vision, to create new humanistic traditions;

Second, Extend efforts way beyond the mere production and accumulation of material wealth and into the preservation of cultural heritage, raising the level of civilization of societies;

Third, Encourage the unique development of civilizations and draw mutual inspiration from each other;

Fourth, Develop technology to serve people;

Fifth, Maintain a balanced development between the individual and the group;

Sixth, Adopt a harmonious attitude to live with Nature.

Finally, We declare that Sustainable Development is a matter of behaviour and practice rather than a theory or an idea.

We must "Better preserve the civilization of the past and better manage the space and resources of the present in order to build the future on a Sustainable Development with a new humanist civilization."

The present Declaration was adopted by thirty Chinese and French experts and scholars participating in the "Space, Civilization and Sustainable Development" Forum held on 29 and 30 September 2010 in Shanghai, China.

A Transcultural Topic: The Relationship between Space and Civilization

There is no other place in the world more suitable than Qufu—the birthplace of Confucius—when doing research on Space, Civilization and Sustainable Development. The former Mayor of Qufu, Mr Liu Sen, made the following speech during the international forum from May 31 to June 1 2006 in the city:

"Qufu is renowned around the world for its 5 000 years of civilization and 3 000-year old history of urban construction, and is known as a living specimen of Chinese town development. Qufu is also the birthplace of Confucianism, because it is the birthplace of the founder of the philosophy—Confucius himself. As the hometown of a number of historic figures such as Confucius, Mencius, Yan Hui and Lu Ban and the birthplace of the Yellow Emperor and Confucian culture, Qufu serves as an excellent place to conduct spatial and cultural exchanges. It has great influences at home and abroad, especially among Asian countries of Confucian culture, and is hailed as a "sacred city in the east" with a particular influence in cultural-geographical terms around the world. Confucianism had a lot to do with the spatial development of the society in history. Confucius created Confucian doctrines and principles centred on the core value of "Ren". Confucianism emphasizes both respect for individuals and the building of social order, and stresses both man's inner morality and his harmonious relationship with outside world. The social structure of China and its organization are vividly expressed in the spatial layouts, functional division, architectural functions and design and decoration of individual buildings in a city. One example is the symmetrical arrangement of the city along the central axis, which embodies the hierarchical concept and the doctrine of the mean in Confucian philosophy. In terms of the relationship of man and nature, Confucian principles highlight a harmonious one between the two, enabling an integrated aesthetics of artistic moods and nature, thus a "unity of man and nature" which has become the fundamental philosophy observed by traditional designers and

公共政策中，空间政策占很大的比重。在中国以往的城市管理实践中，儒学文化是很多公共政策的起源。不同文化的交流，可以最迅捷地表现在公共政策上。随着中国经济发展以及不同类型文化的交流融合，我们的空间政策，也在以人为本、可持续发展思路下深化，逐步转化为对空间发展的积极影响。

然而曲阜的长远历史促使我们思考，是否可以就此有理由做出如下的假设：在中国，其实城市规划理论产生于25个世纪之前的周朝，并且在这段长远的历史当中得到了进一步的发展？毫无疑问，孔子（公元前551—公元前479）出生在周朝，而这个朝代的城市规划以周礼的形式成为了中国城市规划的经典。第一座保留了曲阜痕迹的城市——鲁城，是周朝的一个都城，它显示了周朝城市的型制：方形，朝向，网格化，三条南北向和东西向的大道从城门穿越城市。曲阜显示了一种延续了2 500多年的城市规划延续性。在同一个地方相继有鲁、汉、宋、明等朝代建造城市。我们惊讶地发现曲阜这座城市并没有发展变大，其最大的10平方公里的鲁城范围包含了汉和明的城市范围。我们首先关注鲁城在于其世界城市规划历史上的科学价值：要知道2 500多年前规划一个10平方公里面积的土地，一个天然的基地，并不仅仅是简单保护建筑遗产，是无法想象的。鲁城的规划不仅要考虑城市规划的艺术，还要考虑到非常大的地域尺度和中国的特征，这种特征在现代的城市规划中已经丧失。事实上最近十年以来，我们有一种感觉，中国现今的城市发展只是考虑要占据最大的地域、修建新的道路而不是考虑现存的城市肌理密度。今天对于环境、空间经济、基础设施经济、能源、交通和公共设施的考虑难道不能提醒决策者对城市内部的肌理密度，甚至对现存的城市区域的布局进行考虑吗？曲阜作为城市规划延续的特殊案例，应被视为成功解读城市肌理密度空间问题的成功案例。这一解读建立在城市规划的基础之上；这一解读需要我们运用自我保护的模式及处理建筑、城市及景观等更大尺度问题的方法。

法国建筑学院皮埃尔·克莱蒙院士在同济大学（中国上海）举办的“空间，文明与可持续发展”第二届国际论坛会议的发言如下：

我们以曲阜作为案例出发，由此提出一些需要了解的关于中国城市规划的主要特点：

- 在一段较长的时期内建设同一块土地的能力，将之采用，将之改造，据此保证使用功能的连续性；
- 创造并建设新城的能力，常常是原址新建或者就近建设新城；
- 建立明确的或者暗含的、建筑方面的或者城市规划方面的、成为以后城

architects in China. The layout of a city, its architecture and the rules of functional zoning in Chinese history have shaped its own traditions and systems, a physical embodiment of the conventional thinking of "to restrain personal ethics and to educate the society" which seeks to enable an experience of this subtle change among the residents living in this environment. In a way, Confucian culture is the cultural gene that determines the spatial development of China. Spatial policy has been a big part of public policies in urban context. Confucianism was at the origin of a number of urban practices in the past, and the results of cultural exchanges are first and foremost reflected in public policy shifts. With the economic development of China and the fusion of different cultures, our spatial policy has been moving towards a people-centred approach and sustainable development, and has exerted a positive influence on the development of urban space."

The long history of Qufu leads us to consider the following assumption: urban planning theory in China started to take shape as early as 25 centuries ago in the Zhou Dynasty, and later has been constantly evolving in pace with China's long history. Undoubtedly, Confucius (551–479 BC) was born in the Zhou Dynasty, and the town planning of this period, influenced by the book of Zhou Li (Ritual of Zhou Dynasty), has endured as the classical point of reference in Chinese town planning history. The first town that the origins of Qufu can be traced back to is Lu City, the capital of the Zhou Dynasty and a vivid example of a city of its time, square and gridded with specific orientation rules. Three avenues run through the city from gate to gate on both south–north and east–west axes. Qufu also bears witness to a 2 500-year long continued history of urban planning. The city was later constantly reconstructed and expanded on its original site during the Lu, Han, Song and Ming dynasties. It is surprising to see that Qufu did not expand to a massive scale in the process of development, with the 10-km^2 Lu City being the largest and covering the area of both the Han and Ming cities. However, Qufu's greatest significance lies in its scientific value for the history of urban planning. It was first planned 2 500 years ago and the area as a completely natural site covered 10 km^2 of lands, which requires more than a focus on the conservation of its architectural heritage today. The planning of the Lu City takes into account not only the art of urban planning, but also the territorial scale and other unique characteristics of China, although these have gradually disappeared in the modern planning process. In recent decades, we have become increasingly aware that contemporary urban development places more and more emphasis on occupying large territory and constructing new roads instead of making use of the existing, dense urban fabric. Why can't our consideration of the environment, spatial economy, infrastructure economy, energy, transportation and public facilities remind decision-makers of the importance of a dense urban fabric and urge them to conceive planning based on existing urban layouts? A very special case in terms of urban planning, Qufu is supposed to be perfect to interpret and understand these issues. We have to link it in urban planning context, and apply self-conservation mode and various approaches to large-scale buildings, cities and landscapes.

Pierre Clément from the French Académie d'architecture made the following statement in his speech during the second "Space, Civilization and Sustainable Development International Forum" at Tongji University (Shanghai, China):

Based on the case of Qufu, we herein proposed a few characteristics of Chinese urban planning that request our attention:

- *The ability to construct a city on a same site over a relatively long period of time, and to ensure functional continuity through a series of duplications and renovations;*

市建设的参照的各种典范的能力；

• 从区域尺度进行城市建设思考的能力。超越了仅仅从建筑物尺度或城市规划中街区建设的尺度，从更广阔的区域尺度上整治和建设广泛的土地，同时也超出了仅仅围绕城市已建成空间的范围，包含为了城市将来发展的城市周边农业土地的建设、城市边界的保留；

• 空间结构的永久性和新建物的建设。

在都市化趋势不可遏制的今天，应该从传统街区保护与都市适度的更新案例来思考城市和谐性与历史文化名城的可持续发展，历史文化名城的保护应从现阶段对古建筑、遗产、环境等物质形态的保护转向对社会文明、经济生活和城市活力的整体保护，同时为居民创造舒适的居住环境。目前历史文化名城的规划发展，除了充分尊重城市的历史和现状，严格保护城市的格局和肌理，妥善地处理保护与开发利用、传承与发展的关系外，更要加强对历史文化的保护：不是一味地仿制和复原不可移动文物及文化遗产，其他包括口述、传说和表述、表演艺术、社会风俗、礼仪、节庆、传统的手工艺技能等非物质文化遗产都要有效地保护。更应关注社会生活，维护社会的稳定性和可持续发展。针对历史文化名城，不仅仅是保护古遗址、古建筑、近现代重要史迹及代表性建筑等不可移动文物及文化遗产，重点还是生活在历史文化名城内的人。不能为了保护而保护，而是应该体现以人为本的精神，保护的最终目的是为了居住、生活在其中的人。总结和提炼曲阜历史文化遗产的保护实践，有几点已经得到认可的经验值得特别指出，可以为国内的历史城市如何从单一的建筑保护桎梏中跳脱出来提供思路：

(1) 为了历史城市中心区的复兴，地方当局必须实施众多跨职能、跨地域的政策措施，并在地方城市的发展规划中体现出来，体现城市空间政策与各方面城市发展政策的融合。

(2) 空间是建筑、交通、景观等系统的结合，因此遗产保护不仅仅是对典型建筑物的技术性保存，更是与一般住房、道路交通与公共景观空间相包容的大系统。

(3) 有必要建立一个协调性的公共部门，在协商一致的前提下，强化其在城市规划实施方面所起的作用，将公共部门、私人部门以及普通公众的意愿融合到一起。

(4) 传统技术留存的必要。当前的传统建筑维修中经常遇到的一个难题是当代的建筑技术不适合原样重建古老的建筑构件，很多古老、精巧与富有特色的传统建筑技术都已经失传，专业技术培训的必要性在城市保护与复兴过程中不可忽略。

(5) 文化记忆的发扬是在传统建筑与景观保护基础上更深层次的历史保护工作。它

• *The ability to create and construct new cities, which were often reconstructed in situ or nearby;*

• *The ability to create various categories and examples of urban construction activities, explicitly or implicitly, in terms of architecture or urban planning;*

• *The ability to consider urban construction on a broader territorial scale, which goes beyond the buildings and districts in urban planning terms, and to include renovation and construction of lands in a more broader territorial setting, from built areas surrounding a city to peripheral agricultural lands reserved for future urban development and the retaining of urban boundary;*

• *The relatively constant spatial structure and the construction of new structures.*

In an era when urbanization has become a globally unstoppable trend, we should revisit cases in terms of the conservation of traditional blocks and urban renewal, in order to reconsider the relationship between the harmoniousness and the sustainable development of a historic city. Historic preservation needs a shift from the current conservation of physical objects (including historic buildings, tangible heritage properties and their settings) to a comprehensive protection of social cultures, economic activities and urban vitality, along with the creation of a liveable environment for residents. When planning and making development plans for today's historic and cultural cities, we have aimed to strictly preserve the organization and urban fabric of the city by taking into account the historical and current conditions of the place and carefully dealing with the balance between conservation and development. However, in addition to that, we should place a greater emphasis on the conservation of history and traditional cultures, which goes beyond the simple duplication and restoration of immovable properties and cultural properties to consider the effective conservation of intangible heritage such as oral traditions, legends and expressions, performing arts, social practices, rituals, festival events, and traditional craftsmanship. We should also pay more attention to social activities in order to ensure the stability and sustainable development of society. Except for immovable cultural properties such as ancient sites, historical buildings, historical and modern monuments and representative structures within a historic and cultural city, more importance should be attached to the people who live in the city. The act of conservation itself is not the ultimate objective, but for people who live in these places. The following are some of the lessons and experiences we have derived from the conservation practices of Qufu, which will provide a new perspective for Chinese practitioners to go beyond the single model of architectural conservation and explore more diversified approaches and philosophies:

(1) To regenerate historic centres, local authorities should apply an array of multi-functional and trans-regional policies and measures and include them into the planning and development process at the local level, enabling the integration of urban spatial policy and other urban development policies;

(2) Urban space is made up of various systems of buildings, transportation and landscapes, and heritage conservation, is therefore not simply a preservation technique for outstanding structures, but a more inclusive system of houses, transportation grids and public landscapes;

(3) It is necessary to set up a public coordinating department and to strengthen its role in implementing urban planning based on consultations and agreement, so as to integrate voices from the public, private and community sectors;

(4) It is important to preserve traditional techniques and skills. One of the problems occurring in the restoration of traditional building is the incompatibility of modern techniques with building components from the past. A number of long-standing and traditional skills are dying and/or lost, and thus technical training is essential and necessary in the process of urban conservation and regeneration.

深深地植根于普通大众的日常生活中，通过文化记忆的发扬，可以更好地为地方旅游业的发展提供充足的精神内涵，与物质遗产的保护相辅相成。

导读

本书针对曲阜历史沿革、空间与文明之间的关系及“曲阜历史文化名城的可持续发展”，以三部分作深入浅出的介绍。

第一部分“空间、文化与文明”，有三篇来自法国学者的文章：第一篇文章出自法国建筑学院皮埃尔·克莱蒙院士，《由曲阜的发展经验谈中国城市化的悠长传统》，文章从空间视角谈论曲阜；第二篇文章出自法国道德与政治科学学院玛丽亚娜·巴斯蒂德院士，《晚清时期欧洲游客眼中的曲阜及其文化遗产》，文章从文化的视角谈论曲阜；第三篇文章出自法国纯文学和铭文学学院汪德迈通讯院士，《通过齐鲁文化的起源探讨汉语“革命”的概念》，文章从中国文明的重要性视角谈论曲阜。

第二部分“保存、展示与规划”，有三篇来自中国学者的文章：第一篇文章出自清华大学建筑系吴良镛教授、刘健教授，《曲阜与济兖邹曲鲁文化城市群：区域视野中的曲阜城市空间发展》，文章指出曲阜规划的重要性，“作为一座特殊的宗教文化城市，曲阜围绕‘三孔’形成了十分独特的城市空间结构，在中国城市建设史上占有十分重要的地位”；第二篇文章《曲阜明故城的价值特征及其整体保护》，出自上海同济大学邵甬教授，提供了她对于曲阜明故城保护规划的深入理解和经验；第三篇文章《基于历史价值与现实条件的曲阜鲁故城遗址保护与展示》，出自清华大学建筑系郭璐博士后、清华大学刘健教授，文章基于历史价值与现实条件的曲阜鲁故城遗址保护与展示，强调规划与保护的原则对于曲阜考古公园展示要求的重要性。

第三部分“有生命力的活态城市，可持续发展与合作”，有三篇文章：第一篇文章出自林志宏教授，文章对《亚洲现有历史名城保护中城市政策可持续和平衡发展的新台阶: 中国曲阜案例研究》进行具体说明; 第二篇文章出自前法国大使马克·孟毅,《难忘的经历：2004—2010 在曲阜的欧洲人》，文章指出中欧应共同进行反思 ；第三篇文章出自西班牙的圣地亚哥·德·孔波斯特拉建筑师安杰·帕内罗·帕多，以他的文章《面对永续发展的挑战：西班牙圣地亚哥市与曲阜市的环境、建设施工技术、宜居性能源以及城市遗产保护与改善的日常平衡》作为本书的结束文章。

(5) Promoting cultural memory is a topic to be explored in more depth, based on the conservation of traditional buildings and landscapes. Rooted in people's daily life, cultural memory constitutes the spiritual dimension on which the local tourism industry is able to flourish, and brings added value to the physical dimension of heritage.

The Structure of this Book

This book provides a comprehensive overview of the historical development of Qufu, of the relationship between space and civilization, and of the sustainable development of Qufu as a famous historic and cultural city in China.

Section 1 deals with issues relating to Space, Culture and Civilization and contains three papers from French scholars: Pierre Clément's essay "Leçons de Qufu: La longue tradition de l'art urbain chinois" analyses the city from a spatial dimension; Marianne Bastid's essay "Qufu et son patrimoine aux yeux des voyageurs européens: de la fin des Qing" approaches Qufu from a cultural perspective; and Léon Vandermeersch's essay "La conception chinoise du geming: aux origines de la culture Qi–Lu" examines the old city with an emphasis on the significance of Chinese civilization.

Section 2 deals with Preservation, Presentation and Planning. Three articles from Chinese scholars are included: Professor Wu Liangyong and Professor Liu Jian from Tsinghua University co-authored the essay "From Qufu to Ji-Yan-Zou-Qu Lu-Culture City-Region: Spatial Development of Qufu in Regional Perspective", which identifies the importance of the planning of Qufu. "As a distinctive religious and cultural city, Qufu was constructed around the building groups of temple, cemetery and family mansion of Confucius, whose urban spatial structure is unique and important in Chinese city building history". Professor Shao Yong from Tongji University offers her in-depth insight and experience in the conservation planning of Qufu Ming City. The essay by Guo Lu, post-doctorate research fellow, and Professor Liu Jian from Tsinghua University first examines the conservation and exhibition issues of the ruins of Qufu Lu State from the perspective of its historical value and realistic conditions, and emphasizes the importance of planning and conservation to the display of Qufu archaeological park.

Section 3 deals with the Living city, Sustainable Development and Cooperation. Professor Roland Lin Chih-Hung provides his insights in the essay "A New Step for a Sustainable and Balanced Urban Policy in an Asian Living Historic City Conservation Context: the Case of Qufu, China". The essay of former Ambassador H.E. Mr Marc Menguy, "Une expérience inoubliable: des Européens à Qufu 2004–2010" calls for a reflection among both Chinese and Europeans academics. The last essay in the book "The Challenge of Retaining Permanent Change" by Angel Panero Pardo, the Spanish architect from Consorcio de Santiago of Spain, explores issues regarding environment, construction technology and liveability, and takes examples of Santiago de Compostela (Spain) and Qufu (China) to highlight the necessity of finding an everyday balance for the protection and enhancement of urban heritage.

第一章　空间、文化与文明

Section 1　Space, Culture & Civilisation

由曲阜的发展经验
谈中国城市化的悠长传统

皮埃尔·克莱蒙

曲阜是古城城址原址长期不变发展的典型案例，三千多年来，随着朝代的更迭（先后经历鲁、汉、宋、明）新的城镇在原地不断重建。由于曲阜并不像西安或者北京一样，是一座大都市，这些故城的遗迹在当代的城市景观中依然全面可循，因此，曲阜遗产的珍贵之处不仅仅在于它作为孔子家乡以及孔子纪念物的历史和文化价值，它也是中国城镇规划史上现代规划应当保护和重视的空间规划经验。

学习曲阜经验不仅对中国历史极为有益，它也是对世界城镇规划历史重要的贡献。

作为一项现代科学，西方城市规划诞生于19世纪下半叶，即依勒德丰索·塞尔（Ildefonso Cerda，1861—1876）为马德里和巴塞罗那成功设计城市版图之后，将具体理论归纳在其奠定城市化概念的著作《城市化概论》中[1]。

由此而言，我们是否可合理地进行推断，中国的城市化理论出现于25个世纪之前的周朝呢？吴良镛教授在其英文著作《中国古代城市化简史》[2]中的理论引导我们如是思考。

在西方国家中，W. C. 莫特（W. C. Mote）已提醒全世界关注城市化现象在中国的古老性，这个拥有悠长历史、辽阔地缘、众多人口的国家曾经建立了世界上最多的城市。R. 约翰斯顿（R. Johnston）则从具体的示例——平江，即中国13世纪时的苏州着手，研究当时出现的代表城市地图的一座两米余高石碑——该石碑雕刻于1229年，平江被摧毁后重修之时[3]。

此外，在20世纪的建筑师和城市规划师的努力之下，中国的古都历史遵循周朝开始的模型重新改写。曲阜，隶属于中国北方的富饶省份之一——山东省。大约25世纪之前，先师孔子的祖先决定定居于此地。公元前551年，孔子诞生于距鲁国都城东南部约25公里的地方，曲阜由此闻名。拥有30个世纪的发展历程，曲阜诠释了中国城市化的漫长历史以及城市化形式和建筑形式之间的关联。

公元前1121年，在周武王灭商后，武王封周公旦于河南鲁山一带。西周武王胞弟周公旦不断发展扩大都城领土，后由周公的儿子伯禽受封，在奄地曲阜营建鲁国，

Leçons de Qufu: La Longue Tradition de l'Art Urbain Chinois

Pierre Clément

Qufu is a very particular example of a long term occupation of the same site, at least 3000 years, where new towns were built when dynasties changed : Lu, Han, Song, Ming. As the town is not as big a metropolis, as Xi'an or Beijing, the remains of these different cities are still comprehensive in the contemporary landscape. So the heritage of Qufu is not only the historical and cultural values of the birth town of Kongzi and the Kongzi monuments, but also a spatial lesson about Chinese town planning history with which modern planning needs to deal, preserve and highlight.

Learning from Qufu is not only useful for chinese history but it's also a significant contribution for world's town planning history.

L'urbanisme en Occident est apparu comme discipline moderne, dans la deuxième moitié du xixe siècle, à la suite des travaux d'Ildefonso Cerda pour les plans de Madrid et de Barcelone, théorisés dans un texte fondateur : « la théorie générale d'urbanisme » [1].

Peut-on alors raisonnablement faire l'hypothèse que l'urbanisme en Chine serait né dès la dynastie des Zhou, il y aurait déjà plus de 25 siècles, comme le professeur Wu Liangyong, en particulier dans son ouvrage en anglais *A Brief History of Ancient Chinese City Planning* [2], nous inviterait à le penser.

En Occident, W. C. Mote attirait déjà l'attention du monde entier sur l'ancienneté du phénomène urbain en Chine et sur le fait que l'Empire chinois dans sa longue histoire, sur son vaste territoire et riche d'une population abondante, avait construit plus de villes que tout le reste du monde. R. Johnston ouvrait à son tour cette histoire sur une ville exemplaire, Pingjiang, la Suzhou du xiiie siècle, dont il nous est parvenu une stèle représentant le plan mesurant plus de 2 mètres de haut – pierre gravée en 1229 alors que la ville avait été détruite avant d'être reconstruite [3].

On connaît de plus, grâce aux archéologues et urbanistes chinois du xxe siècle, l'histoire des villes-capitales chinoises, retracée à partir du modèle de la dynastie des Zhou. La ville de Qufu, dans la province du Shandong, province riche de la Chine du Nord, est restée célèbre car, il y a quelques 25 siècles, la famille du maître Kong Zi (à savoir Confucius) décida de s'y installer. Confucius serait né en 551 av. J.C., à quelques 25 km au sud-est de la Cité de Lu. Développée sur une longue durée de quelques 30 siècles, Qufu peut nous servir à éclairer cette longue histoire de l'urbanisme chinois, et peut-être des rapports entre formes urbaines et formes architecturales.

La ville ancienne capitale du Royaume de Lu, de la dynastie des Zhou de l'Ouest, aurait été fondée en 1121 av. J.C. par le roi de Wu, victorieux des Shang, et développée par son frère, le duc de Zhou qui contrôlait un territoire équivalent à l'actuelle province du Shandong. Elle était alors une des villes importantes de la Chine orientale, capitale d'un royaume pendant 873 ans, sous trois dynasties : Zhou, Han occidentaux et Han orientaux, lesquels la relègueront au statut de chef-lieu de district [4].

领域范围与如今山东省面积不相上下。作为中国历史上拥有举足轻重地位的一个城市，曲阜经历了 873 年间的三朝换代：周朝、西汉和东汉，后者将曲阜降为县级都市[4]。

然而，关于曲阜的传说还要追溯得更为久远。一些人认为，曲阜是中国人文始祖——诞生于公元前 27 世纪末期的轩辕黄帝的诞生地，尽管这段传说颇具争议。此外，人们意图建立“黄帝墓”，陕西就在传言纷纷的黄帝墓穴处建立了一个陵墓。传说中，黄帝的儿子之一——少昊（公元前 2598—公元前 2514）——便是葬于曲阜。人们推测其坟墓位于曲阜东南部，鲁国古都之外，宋城以北。宋代时，1012 年在少昊逝世 3500 年后建立陵墓。公元前 17 世纪，商朝都城建立于鲁国古都之前，位于曲阜的东北部。

显而易见，中国擅长建立、修复城市和古迹。随着时间流逝，这些建筑物最终被“遗产化”了。

就我们而言，不仅要观察历史城市化的形式，即考古学者所见、所验证的各种迹象，还需要激发出当下城市保护和发展意识的当代城市化的形制。

我们将利用中国学者的历史研究，以及我们于 2002 年至 2008 年间在曲阜短暂停留期间的观察所得[5]——考察初衷为探讨建立新城市的相关问题，由此导向了对大曲阜的新版图规划研究，以及从两个尺度思考古迹的保护和价值重现问题：一是鲁国故城 10 多公里范围遗址上的土地及景观风貌，一是在城市和建筑尺度研究明故城的保护和发展。

因此，以曲阜为例关于城市发展的思考——它漫长的历史发展轨迹，现有的实践及未来的规划——是阐述中国城市发展展望，及经过漫长的历史演变，遇到发展、保护和历史价值重现问题的城市发展的不可多得的例子。之所以称其为不可多得，是因为曲阜一直是人口数量不多的小城，[6] 而且它作为朝圣古城，容纳着“活着与逝去”的居民、孔氏家族的后代以及中国最重要的儒家寺庙——孔庙[7]。目前，中国有 2 000 多座儒家寺庙遍布全国，这些寺庙在向国外（越南、韩国、日本……）传播中国文化，尤其在传统书法、文章等方面发挥的作用不容小觑。近年来，中国文化中心于世界各地成立“孔子学院”，证明了新政治群体对孔子思想的再次肯定。（图 1）

◎ 30 多个世纪在同一片土地的繁衍生息

许多其他的更大尺度的古都，诸如西安[8]（长安）、南京或是北京，尤其在近代都发生了翻天覆地的变化，使得我们难以研究其在漫长的历史进程中不同朝代的地域形态。然而曲阜尽管一直到现代，它的城乡大部分逃过了过度现代化，它的土地却面

Mais le mythe remonte, lui, plus loin encore puisque certains considèrent localement que Qufu aurait été la ville natale du fameux Empereur Jaune, *Huangdi*, père de la Nation, qui y serait né à la fin du xxviie siècle av. J.C., légende toutefois très contestée. On nous confiait de plus sur le terrain la volonté de construire « un tombeau pour l'Empereur Jaune », ce que la province du Shaanxi a réalisé en construisant un mausolée sur un site très contesté de son tumulus funéraire. La légende rapporte aussi que l'un des fils de cet Empereur Jaune mythique, Shaohao (2598 av. J.C. - 2514 av. J.C.) aurait été enterré à Qufu, comme le laisserait supposer son mausolée au nord-est du territoire de la municipalité, à l'extérieur de la Cité de Lu, au nord de la ville des Song, dynastie sous laquelle le mausolée existant fut toutefois édifié, près de 3500 ans après sa mort, à savoir en 1012. Une capitale de la dynastie des Shang aurait-elle aussi été implantée avant la Cité de Lu, au nord-est de Qufu, dès le xviie siècle av. J.C.

Il est clair que la Chine sait construire et reconstruire les villes et les monuments que le temps a fini par « patrimonialiser ».

Pour notre part, nous nous focaliserons sur quelques observations concernant les formes urbaines historiques qu'autorisent les traces, visibles ou attestées par les recherches archéologiques, mais aussi les formes urbaines contemporaines que révèlent aujourd'hui les intentions des projets de protection et de développement.

On utilisera les travaux historiques des chercheurs chinois et on les confrontera aux observations menées personnellement sur le site de Qufu de 2002 à 2008, au cours de quelques séjours professionnels malheureusement toujours trop brefs[5]. Ces séjours étaient orientés d'abord sur la question de la fabrication d'une ville nouvelle, conduisant à un nouveau plan directeur pour un Grand Qufu, puis sur celle de la protection et de la mise en valeur du patrimoine à deux échelles : celle territoriale et paysagère de la Cité de Lu, sur une superficie de plus de 10 km^2, celle plus urbanistique et architecturale de la protection et de l'évolution de la Cité Ming.

C'est ainsi que l'on s'autorisera une série de réflexions considérant l'exemple de Qufu – les traces de sa longue histoire, les pratiques actuelles et les projets futurs – pour illustrer cette mise en perspective de la ville chinoise sur une longue durée et les problèmes que posent son développement, sa sauvegarde et sa mise en valeur. Qufu est unique sans doute parce qu'elle est restée, ou devenue, une « petite ville »[6] de par sa population, mais aussi car elle est vénérée. C'est une ville de pèlerinage puisqu'elle abrite les habitations « des vivants et des morts », des descendants de la famille Kong et le temple confucéen *kongmiao* le plus important de Chine[7]. La Chine d'aujourd'hui compte plus de 2.000 temples confucéens répartis dans le pays et l'on sait l'importance qu'ils ont eu dans la diffusion de la culture chinoise à l'extérieur du pays (Viet Nam, Corée, Japon…), pour l'enseignement en particulier de l'écriture et des textes classiques. Cet héritage que le Maoïsme avait voulu rayer de la carte trouve dans la Chine d'aujourd'hui une nouvelle audience et le fait de baptiser, ces dernières années, les centres culturels chinois à travers le monde « Instituts Confucius » témoigne de cette réappropriation du Maître Kong Zi par les nouvelles autorités politiques.(Fig. 1)

◎ Un même site utilisé sur plus de 30 siècles

Plusieurs autres villes, plus importantes comme Xi'an[8] (Chang'an) ou encore Nankin ou Pékin, ont connu, et surtout à l'époque récente, des transformations qui rendent aujourd'hui plus difficile, sur le territoire lui-même, une lecture de leur occupation sur la longue durée et des traces de leur morphologie aux dif-

图 1. 孔庙
Fig. 1 Le kongmiao

临新的经济、区域、国家甚至是国际化开发的驱动和雄心需求。如林志宏[9]所言，"在以快速高效为主题的社会、政治背景下，合理地协调地域保护与经济开发，简直难于上青天"。

由曲阜的例子我们可总结出中国城市化的以下几点主要特征：

• 漫长时期内使用同一片地域，适应、改造它，保证土地利用延续的能力；

• 在同一地址或相近地区创建新城市的能力；

• 参考具体的或隐含的建筑或城市空间模型的能力；

• 合理掌控远超建筑和城市尺度的区域发展尺度的能力，合理分布及完善街区设置，便于在广阔的土地面积上分布及配置，不仅囊括建设区域，还囊括农用土地及发展预留区域，以利于后续发展；尽管建筑构建不断更新，空间结构依旧稳定持久的能力。

曲阜诠释了 30 个世纪中在同一片土地上，接纳不同时期城市方案的持续性。其于各个朝代不断更改的城墙轨迹便是最好的证明。至今我们仍可从中观察一二。1982 年，曲阜被列入中国首批 24 个"历史文化名城"；1994 年，孔子家族的遗址和墓穴所在地——孔府、孔庙、孔林，被列入世界文化遗产名录。曲阜还有 300 余处认证的文化保护点，其中 100 处被列为国家级重点保护对象。

férentes époques. Alors que « Qufu constitue jusqu'à présent un ensemble urbain et rural, en grande partie épargné par la modernisation », le territoire est aujourd'hui confronté à de nouvelles ambitions économiques, régionales et nationales, voire internationales qui interrogent sur « l'extrême difficulté de concilier préservation et développement économique, dans un contexte social et politique où la rapidité fait loi », comme le souligne Roland Lin Chih-Hung[9].

Nous mettrons donc en avant, à partir de l'exemple de Qufu, quelques caractéristiques majeures de l'urbanisme chinois à savoir :

· la capacité à utiliser un même site sur la longue durée, à l'adapter et à le transformer pour en assurer la continuité d'usage ;

· la capacité à créer des villes nouvelles, souvent sur le même site ou à proximité ;

· la capacité à élaborer des modèles spatiaux, explicites ou implicites, architecturaux ou urbanistiques, servant de référence ;

· la capacité à raisonner à une échelle territoriale qui dépasse largement les seules dimensions architecturales des bâtiments ou urbanistiques, la fabrication des quartiers pour aménager et équiper un vaste territoire, dépassant les seuls contours de l'espace bâti pour englober des terres agricoles, des réserves foncières pour les développements futurs ;

· la permanence des structures spatiales mais le renouvellement des objets construits.

Qufu illustre donc la permanence sur quelques 30 siècles de l'utilisation d'un même site pour accueillir des projets de ville qu'attestent sans doute les traces des enceintes, attribuées aux différentes dynasties, que nous pouvons encore aujourd'hui observer. Qufu fut d'ailleurs classée en 1982 sur la première liste de 24 « villes célèbres, historiques et culturelles » de Chine, avant de rejoindre celle du patrimoine mondial de l'Unesco en 1994, pour le temple de Confucius, le cimetière des Kong et la demeure de la famille Kong. Mais on y recense aussi plus de 300 sites culturels identifiés, dont 100 figurent sur la liste des sites classés.

La permanence du site et son importance n'est pas sans lien avec le rôle exceptionnel joué par la famille Kong, la mort et le culte de ces ancêtres a une place importante dans la société chinoise. En effet au nord, à l'extérieur de l'enceinte de la Cité de Lu, s'étend sur 200 ha boisés, c'est le cimetière de la famille Kong, « la forêt des stèles ». Il est peuplé de plus de 100.000 tombes et quelques 200.000 descendants, tous du nom de Kong, depuis près de 80 générations jusqu'à nos jours. Cette famille aurait encore quelques 3 millions de descendants vivants par le monde (dont 2,5 en Chine) et ce site est un exemple unique de sépulture familiale toujours « vivante » et vénérée sur 2.500 ans. Ce lien a largement contribué à la valeur symbolique du site, son entretien et son prestige ; il est exploité aujourd'hui sous toutes les formes possibles de valorisation touristiques et mercantiles.

Cette persistance à utiliser le même site sur une aussi longue période ne peut que conforter le bon choix des *fengshui xiensheng*, les géomanciens qui avaient dû interpréter ce site comme particulièrement favorable. Le *Taishan* Mont Tai, l'une des cinq montagnes sacrées les plus importantes, est au nord. C'est la montagne protectrice principale. Les rivières Wen et Si irriguent le site au nord, la rivière Si sert quant à elle à alimenter les douves de la Cité de Lu. La rivière Yi traverse au sud la plaine où Qufu peut encore se développer.(Fig. 2)

这种地域的持续利用及重要性与孔子家族的历史地位、对先人的崇拜不无关联。实际上，在鲁国都城围墙外的北部地区，延伸着 200 公顷林木，为孔子家族的墓穴所在地“孔林”。其中，有 10 万处坟墓，埋葬着约 20 万名孔氏家族后裔，至今已有将近 80 代孔氏传人下葬于此。如今，全世界约有 300 万（中国约 250 万）孔氏后人。这种家族与地域之间长久有序的关联正是 2 500 年间一处始终“活力十足”并受敬仰的孔氏家族圣地所系。这种关联提升了该地的象征意义及影响；如今已以各种形式被开发，以充分发挥其旅游、商业价值。

这种持续性，只能是验证了风水先生的判断，他们一定是断定了这片土地是一块风水宝地。中国五大名山之一——泰山，为北方提供了广大的庇护。汶河和泗河灌溉北部土地，泗河还为鲁国都城提供护城河水源。沂河穿越曲阜能朝其后续发展的南部平原。（图 2）

◎建立新的地域城市

自 1977—1978 年间起，在山东省考古研究所的努力下，鲁国都城的旧时版图得以清晰展现：呈东西 3.7 公里，南北 2.7 公里的矩形，面积为 10.45 平方公里。城市由城墙包围，护城河环绕，当时有 11 扇[10] 7 米至 15 米宽的城门。两扇于南面，另外三面（东、北、西面）各置三扇城门。城市由 10 条主要交通线构成。宫殿占据城市中心四分之一版幅，宫殿主轴线与城市南北主要交通轴线重合，市场位于城市北部。（图 3）

鲁国时期的曲阜诠释了周朝都城的模型规划——四方形，每边长 9 里（3.7 公里），由通往三扇城门的南北、东西三条主要交通轴线定向、分区、分级规划，宫殿位于中部，市场位于北部……周朝著作《周礼》第六部分的《考工记》中阐述了都城的城市规划，被认为是中国两千年前的城市规划思想的奠基之作[11]。（图 4）

汉朝时，曲阜丧失了其国都之称以及其相应的领导地位，被降为一个县级市；围墙被削减，仅限于西南一隅，面积为 3.75 平方公里，只占据鲁国城墙内面积的三分之一。

如今我们很难判断当年这些宽阔城墙内的建筑密度，但是我们知道南京或北京明朝时期的城墙内，直到几个世纪后的 20 世纪，城内才填满了建筑。

宋朝时，都城建立于鲁国城墙之外的东部地区。其体量看起来更像一个政治行政中心，远离当时城墙内的现有居民。

之后，农民起义占领祭拜孔子的孔庙，明朝决定加强对曲阜的保护，于其西南一隅竖立城墙，支撑于鲁国南部的部分墙垣之上。“明故城”面积缩小，仅 1.67 平方公里。

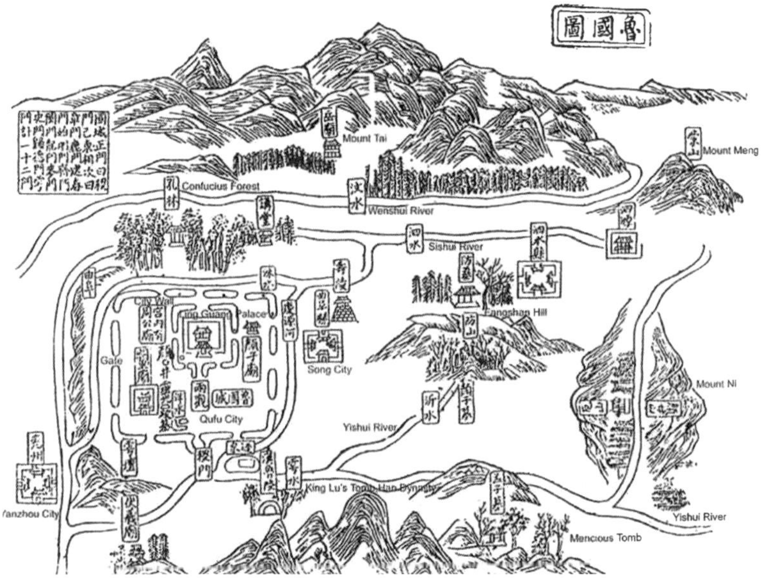

图 2. 金朝地图
Fig. 2 Carte de la dynastie Jin

◎ Création de villes nouvelles à l'échelle territoriale

C'est grâce aux travaux de l'Institut d'Archéologie du Shandong, menés dès 1977-78, que nous pouvons observer les traces et tracés de la capitale de Lu, et en dessiner le plan précis : rectangle de 3,7 km de long d'est en ouest, sur 2,7 km de large du nord au sud, pour une superficie de 10,45 km^2. La ville était entourée d'une enceinte, bordée de douves, percée à l'époque de 11 porte[10], de 7 à 15 m. de large, deux au sud, et trois sur chacun des trois autres côtés est, nord, et ouest. Elle était alors parcourue de 10 axes principaux. Les palais occupaient la partie centrale du rectangle sur le quart de sa surface, l'axe principal nord sud était celui du palais central, le marché était situé au nord. (Fig. 3)

La Cité de Lu de Qufu illustre alors la description du modèle de la capitale des Zhou – ville carrée, de 9 *li* (ce qui faisait à l'époque 3,7 km), orientée, quadrillée, parcourue par trois axes nord-sud et est-ouest aboutissant aux 3 portes, hiérarchisée, palais au centre, marché au nord… – que décrit, lorsqu'il traite des travaux d'implantation d'une capitale, le *Kaokongji*, sixième partie du *Zhouli*, le manuel de la dynastie des Zhou, considéré comme fondateur de la pensée urbanistique chinoise il y a quelques 2.000 ans[11].(Fig. 4)

La ville sous les Han perdra son statut de capitale, donc de son importance dans la hiérarchie des villes du pouvoir, pour n'être plus qu'un chef-lieu de district ; son enceinte fut considérablement réduite et concentrée dans l'angle sud-ouest, sur une superficie de 3,75 km^2, ne représentant plus qu'un tiers du territoire

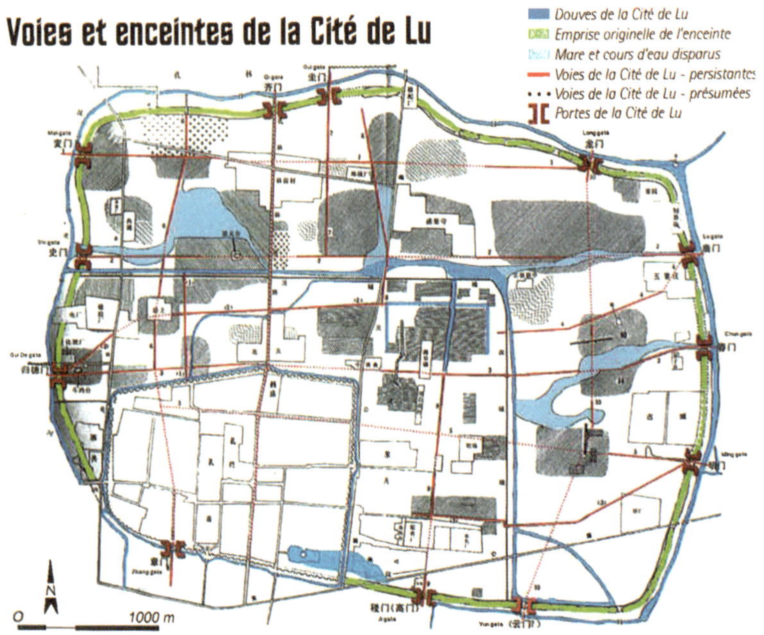

图 3. 鲁国古都
Fig. 3 Cité Lu

公元前 478 年，孔子逝世后第二年，周王室于其身前居所遗址建立孔庙，位于曲阜东南角，自鲁国起至今仍是该城市的中心所在。

我们也可以合理地质疑这种延续。它见证了同一片领土利用的历史连贯性，但也会由于特殊的嵌入现象而消减体量——如同俄罗斯套娃一般——在鲁国时期城墙面积内，从汉代的最为古老辽阔，及至明代时最为缩减。

不同朝代筑造的城墙都服从于新政权和建立新城市的需求，该行政中心城市必须得到新建立的城墙的保护。

不同于遵循同一个发展中心、不同时期城市同心圆发展的模式，我们观察到各个朝代都建立了新的地域结构，更甚者为显示政治决心，不惜摧毁前朝故城。自周朝起，掌控辽阔地域面积的雄心已很明显，也就是为什么鲁国古都的面积最为宽广（10.45 平方公里）；它囊括了汉代缩减到三分之一的土地面积（3.75 平方公里），后者又涵盖了面积为 1.67 平方公里的明故城。这种城墙内部的土地面积缩减不仅取决于历史上城市政治角色的演变，还在于将农用土地纳入城墙内的最为古老、最具雄心的城市化发展传统。

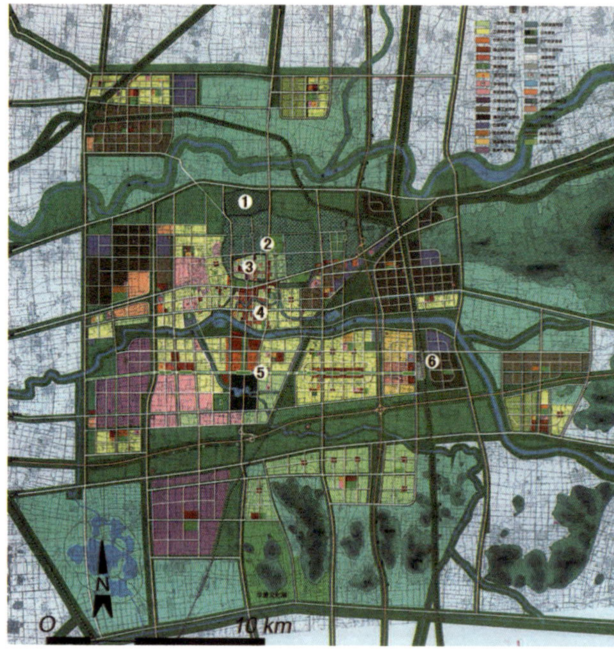

图 4. 不同时期城墙的嵌套及其面积
Fig. 4 Emboîtements des enceintes avec leurs superficies

enserré dans l'enceinte de la ville de Lu.

Il est toutefois difficile de dire aujourd'hui quel pouvait être le taux de remplissage de ces vastes enceintes, quand on sait que le Nankin ou le Pékin des Ming ne rempliront par le bâti le territoire à l'intérieur de leurs remparts que plusieurs siècles après leur fondation : seulement au cours du xxe siècle.

La ville des Song fut construite en dehors de l'enceinte de la Cité de Lu, à l'est. Par sa dimension, elle apparaît plus comme le siège d'un pouvoir politique et administratif qui se mit à l'écart des populations existantes.

C'est plus tard, à la suite d'une révolte de paysans qui occupèrent le Kongmiao, temple de Confucius, qu'il fut décidé par la dynastie des Ming de renforcer sa protection en érigeant l'enceinte ming, toujours dans l'angle sud-ouest, s'appuyant sur une partie des murailles sud de la Cité de Lu. La « ville Ming », dont la surface fut encore réduite, n'occupe plus alors que 1,67 km^2.

Il semblerait toutefois que le quartier du temple de Confucius, implanté en 478 av. J.C., juste après sa mort sur le site de sa maison, dans l'angle sud-est, aurait déjà été, même dès la Cité de Lu, le centre de gravité de la ville.

On peut légitimement s'interroger sur cette permanence qui témoigne d'une continuité historique de l'usage d'un même territoire, et qui se serait réduit, par un phénomène particulier d'emboitement – sur le modèle des poupées russes – à l'intérieur de l'enceinte de la dynastie de Lu : de la plus ancienne et la plus vaste à la ville des Han, puis enfin à celle des Ming, la plus petite.

就此而言，鲁国古都的发展对世界城市历史研究都具有科学研究意义。当下，问题在于一方面要管理、控制 10 平方公里多、拥有 40 000 居民土地的城市化，另一方面要策略性实施保护和重现景观风貌，并要重塑清晰可读的城市结构——除了已被认同、考证过的市内考古群体、建筑物等（如宫殿、居所、坟墓、作坊等），还有城墙，城门，护城河等 24 处城郊考古群，占据总面积约 15%。农业的发展一定程度保护了这些遗迹，可以等待最好的时机进行考古挖掘和重现遗址价值，但这些遗址群却不能承受城市的扩张。 鲁国古都为中国提供了一个思考大范围的地域尺度的城市保护、考古和景观风貌保护的契机。

◎大曲阜

这项规划旨在扩大城市面积，为北京—上海高铁提供站点。该规划的目的为建立一个“大曲阜”，囊括三大行政板块，即曲阜、兖州和邹城。后者是孔子最著名的弟子之一——孟子的诞生地，他出生于孔子逝世百年之后。新城区位于沂河以南，所占地域广阔，是之前曲阜市内面积的两倍，延续地域尺度四方形基础设施排布，拓展南北主要交通线。很快，大型基础设施工程得以实施，新的大学得以建立。（图 5）

2003 年，山东省颁发了《曲阜市城市总体规划（2003—2020）》，规划区达 900 平方公里，构成 30 × 30 公里的正方形。其中特别涵盖了南部新城市扩展规划。然而，20 世纪后半期，出于对环境、经济、设施、能源、交通、设备等因素的考虑，中国开始进行新的规划政策调整：不推动大规模新城扩张，而更加提倡在现有城市区域内提高建筑密度。

当然，还有其他很多闻名遐迩的城市也经历了这样漫长的历史进程：西安（长安）、北京……但是，最近几十年的飞速发展、史无前例的城市演变，相当程度地破坏了历史赋予我们的地域和景观的图景。1950 年，梁思成提出建议，希望在北京西面、历史古城旁建立一个新的行政城市，以服务于新成立的中华人民共和国。这项提议本可以保护世界最美丽城市之一的北京——这座纵横分布均匀、园林遍布的城市，但是过度的现代化使其不断地矿化、垂直化。

因此，曲阜成为唯一可以诠释中国城市化的空间发展历程的例子。不仅是从建筑、城市角度，而且还包括景观、土地规划等方面，它都引导我们对如何维持、开发城市化进行思考探究。我们将曲阜的例子与柬埔寨的吴哥进行比较。实际上，除了最负盛名的建筑（比如吴哥窟的寺庙），吴哥古迹——意指“王都”——首先是指七个世纪以来的系列城市遗迹。这些城市地域辽阔，具备许多重要景观：吴哥通城的围

Les enceintes attribuées aux différentes dynasties attestent chaque fois le besoin d'affirmation d'un nouveau pouvoir et de création d'une nouvelle cité, siège politique qu'il fallait protéger derrière une nouvelle enceinte.

Loin d'assister au développement radio-concentrique à partir d'un noyau originel qui aurait fixé le centre historique de la ville, nous constatons la mise en place de structures à l'échelle territoriale sous différentes dynasties, qui relève de décisions politiques n'hésitant pas à abandonner, voire détruire, les traces des dynasties précédentes. Dès l'époque des Zhou, l'ambition de maîtriser un vaste territoire est flagrante ; c'est ainsi que la première enceinte, celle de la Cité de Lu, est la plus vaste (10,45 km2) ; elle englobe la cité Han réduite au tiers de sa superficie (3,75 km^2), qui englobe à son tour la cité ming, ramenée à 1,67 km^2. Cette réduction de la superficie enserrée dans l'enceinte s'explique bien sûr par l'évolution du rôle politique de la ville à travers l'histoire, mais aussi par les traditions urbanistiques les plus anciennes, les plus ambitieuses, qui inséraient aussi dans les vastes enceintes des villes un important territoire agricole.

On retiendra à ce titre l'intérêt scientifique de la Cité Lu pour l'histoire mondiale de l'urbanisme. Se pose alors aujourd'hui la question de la maîtrise et du contrôle de l'urbanisation d'un territoire de plus de 10 km2, accueillant une population de 40.000 habitants, et de la mise en œuvre d'une stratégie de préservation, de conservation et de mise en valeur d'un grand paysage et de structures urbaines qu'il faut s'efforcer de laisser lisibles : murs d'enceintes, portes, douves, structure viaire, au delà des seuls ensembles archéologiques, architecturaux et urbains déjà identifiés (palais, habitations, tombes, ateliers…) correspondant à 24 secteurs *intra muros*, pour une superficie représentant quelque 15% du territoire. L'extension de l'agriculture avait permis d'attendre des jours meilleurs pour la recherche archéologique et la mise en valeur, le site par contre ne résisterait pas à l'extension urbaine. La Cité de Lu pourrait offrir à la Chine l'occasion d'engager une réflexion exemplaire sur l'art de la préservation et de la conservation archéologique et paysagère, à une échelle territoriale de très grande dimension.

◎ Le Grand Qufu

À l'époque contemporaine, la ville est sortie de ses limites pour se développer vers le sud, d'abord derrière les remparts des Ming, puis au-delà de la rivière au travers d'un projet de ville nouvelle élaborée en 2002.(Fig. 5)

Ce projet devait être une extension de la ville et accueillir la gare du train à grande vitesse Pékin-Shanghai. Il s'inscrivait dans la volonté de créer un Grand Qufu qui devait représenter les trois entités administratives des villes de Qufu, Yanzhou et Zhoucheng – ville célèbre aussi pour avoir vu naître Mencius, l'un des plus fameux philosophes héritiers de Confucius, né un siècle après la mort de son maître. Implanté au sud de la rivière, sur une très vaste emprise qui doublait le territoire déjà aménagé au cours des siècles, ce projet s'inscrivait dans une démarche territoriale qui reprenait la trame quadrangulaire des grandes infrastructures et prolongeait les grands axes symboliques nord-sud. Très vite, les travaux d'aménagement des grandes infrastructures furent lancés et de nouvelles universités installées.

Et en 2003 a été publié le plan du Grand Qufu (2003-2020), qui s'étalait généreusement sur les quelques 900 km^2 de la Municipalité, pour former un carré de 30 par 30 km, intégrant en particulier le projet d'extension de la ville nouvelle au sud.

Toutefois, dans le même temps, après le milieu des années 2000, s'opérait un revirement dans la politique

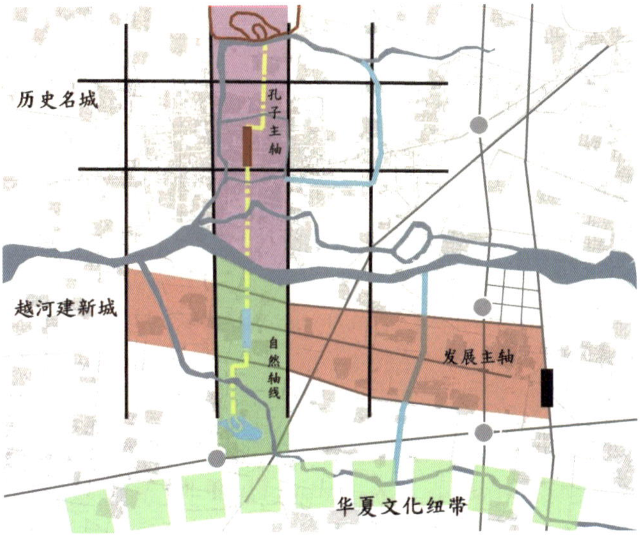

图 5：南部新城区
Fig. 5: Ville nouvelle du sud.
当代，曲阜摆脱了城墙限制，开始向南发展，先是扩展至明朝城墙以南，而后据 2002 年颁发的城市规划更是开始跨越沂河发展。

墙、土地及水利的地面构造、运河、护城河、池子（大型的容水池）。列入世界文化遗产名录的吴哥考古公园，面积达 400 平方公里，能够容纳 5 个巴黎古城区（intra muros），亦可囊括其周边农村区域。吴哥的例子，和曲阜一样，都说明了保护工作的复杂性和艰巨性，不仅要保护古迹建筑及环境，还要保护用于居住、生产、生活的土地。

◎明故城的“修复”问题

看起来中国的遗产保护法规，是在全国范围内为每一个历史文化名城定义其所代表的特殊朝代：唐朝的西安，宋朝的苏州，明朝的曲阜……实际上，除了保护鲁国古都的城市面貌及开发景观价值外，其政治目的是在新修复的城墙内建立一个理想化的明故城。

由此，我们以原始的方式来理解中国的传统建筑。中国的政治概念表现在其延续的空间构造当中——四方形，象征居住空间，同时也组成国家名字的“中”（中间的、中心的），大的四边形结构，方形嵌套，四方位导向，朝向南方……——建筑模式在数十个世纪中逐渐成型。这种模式的延续性使其不断再发展：这种格局也体现在不断

nationale d'aménagement, inspiré par des considérations environnementales, d'économie d'espace, d'infrastructures, d'énergie, de transport et d'équipement, qui remettait en cause ces grandes extensions nouvelles et plaidait pour une plus forte densification à l'intérieur même des villes existantes.

Bien sûr, il existe d'autres exemples célèbres de villes qui ont connu cette longue histoire : Xi'an (Chang-an), Pékin… Mais le développement fulgurant et les transformations sans précédent de ces dernières décennies ont largement troublé la vision que l'histoire aurait pu nous donner du territoire et du paysage. On se souvient du projet du professeur Liang Sicheng pour Pékin qui, en 1950, établissait à l'ouest, à côté de la ville historique ancienne, une nouvelle cité administrative pour la capitale de la nouvelle République, projet qui aurait pu permettre de sauvegarder ce qui était sans doute encore une des plus belles villes du monde, horizontale et végétale, riche de nombreuses cours-jardins, mais que la modernisation forcenée a minéralisée et verticalisée

Qufu doit donc être considérée à ce titre comme un exemple unique pouvant permettre la lecture spatiale sur le terrain de cette histoire de l'urbanisme et nous interroge sur les modes de préservation et de mise en valeur, non seulement architecturales et urbaines, mais aussi à l'échelle paysagère et territoriale. On peut comparer ainsi les problématiques rencontrées à Qufu de celles que connaît le site d'Angkor au Cambodge. En effet, bien au-delà du seul intérêt déjà majeur des monuments les plus célèbres (comme par exemple l'emblématique temple d'Angkor Vat), Angkor – dont le nom veut dire la *ville capitale* est avant tout le site d'une série de villes qui, pendant quelque 7 siècles, ont occupé un vaste territoire et l'ont marqué de traces paysagères importantes : d'enceintes comme celle de la ville d'Angkor Thom, mais aussi d'infrastructures, chaussées ou équipements hydrauliques, canaux, douves et *baray* (grands réservoirs d'eau). On est aussi à une échelle territoriale sans précédent et le périmètre du parc archéologique, inscrit également sur la liste du patrimoine mondial, s'étend sur quelque 400 km2, pouvant accueillir 5 fois le Paris *intra muros*, englobant aussi des villages et des terres agricoles. Cet exemple d'Angkor montre, comme à Qufu, la complexité et les difficultés à protéger non seulement les monuments, à savoir des éléments architecturaux bien identifiés et leur environnement, mais de vastes territoires habités, productifs et vivants, parcourus d'infrastructures elles aussi monumentales.

◎ La question de la « reconstitution » du tissu de la ville Ming

Il semble que la politique patrimoniale chinoise, définie à l'échelle nationale pour les villes célèbres d'histoire et de culture, ait décidé d'affecter à chacune d'elle une dynastie particulière de l'histoire qu'elle incarnerait : Tang pour Xi'an, Song pour Suzhou, Ming pour Qufu… En effet, à côté de la préservation du territoire de la Cité de Lu et de sa mise en valeur paysagère, la volonté politique était de reconstituer une ville Ming idéalisée à l'intérieur de l'enceinte Ming nouvellement reconstruite.

On touche là à une façon originale d'appréhender le patrimoine. La conception politique chinoise s'incarne dans des modèles spatiaux pérennes – rôle du carré, symbole de l'espace habité et forme du caractère qui donne son nom au pays *Zhong* (le milieu, la centralité), grandes trames quadrangulaires, emboitements de carrés, orientations cardinales, exposition au sud… – que les modèles architecturaux sont venus reproduire pendant des dizaines de siècles. Cette permanence des modèles conduit à leur reproduction : c'est ainsi que sur des trames urbaines anciennes des objets architecturaux nouveaux viennent prendre place.

Le défi posé à la coopération sino-européenne était pratiquement de valider la destruction de la ville

被新的建筑体量取代的老的城市格局中。欧亚曲阜合作面临的挑战在于，是否以重建一个以明代理想四合院模型为蓝本的历史城区，进而保护现有城市的肌理。（图6~图7）

上海同济大学[12]的研究证明，除了主要建筑物（闻名的寺庙或住所）之外，大部分建筑都只追溯到20世纪70年代之后。除一些重要建筑之外，城市构造、道路组织、城市尺度和脉络应该得到更多重视。制定这方面规章文件的主导思想是建立在构造"四合院"的基础之上，而不是推崇庭院式的明代模型上。建议采取当代模式，逐步向现代化理想型演变。这种不同的态度对社会和人口分布产生了重要的影响，值得我们重视：明故城大量的房主所有者，携家远离城内，居住在环城地带；古街区的拆除导致人口外流的迁移。我们都知道，历史悠久的城市中心的政治重建都伴随着社会变化和富裕人群的一些"高档化"。当城市中心重新充满吸引力时，中国也逃脱不了这种现象。但是，这些转变不可以从生硬的拆除开始、从明故城居民的离开开始。他们亦是人文遗产的一部分。较为缓和的旨在修复原本城市肌理上普通的房屋的实践已经开始。这些方法会成功么？

3 000年间针对于曲阜建立的不同城市的研究，以及近年来致力于其发展的城市规划项目，都诠释了中国人文空间发展思想的延续性。作为权利的载体，城市始终是全局土地规划视角下的政治计划目标。

对建立于不同朝代城墙的考证确认了根据政治需求而将领域内的生活圈与周期性建立的新城市之间进行隔断的思维。

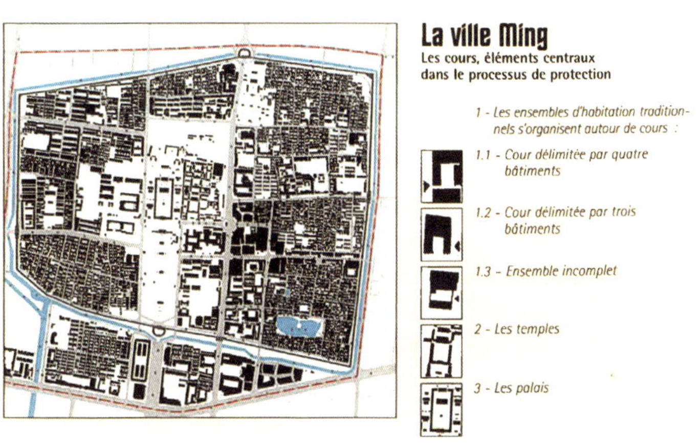

图6：明故城
Fig 6 La ville Ming

existante pour sa reconstruction neuve sur le modèle d'une maison à cour Ming idéalisée.(Fig 6~7)

Les travaux d'inventaire entrepris avec l'Université Tongji de Shanghai[12] ont montré que la majorité du bâti se révélait dater d'après les années 1970. Indépendamment des édifices majeurs (temples ou habitations prestigieuses), c'est la structure urbaine, ses réseaux de voies, son tissu, son échelle qui méritaient toute l'attention. La conception des documents réglementaires qui ont été élaborés, si elle repose bien sur le modèle présupposé d'organisation de l'espace urbain qui est celui engendré par « la maison à quatre ailes entourant une cour » (le *siheyuan*), refusait « de reconstruire » une ville sur un modèle Ming présupposé dont la maison à cour constituait la base, mais prônait d'adapter l'existant dans le temps et de faire tendre les transformations vers le modèle idéal. Cette attitude différente avait des conséquences importantes sur les plans sociaux et humains, qui méritent d'être soulignées et explicitées : de nombreuses familles, propriétaires des maisons de la Cité Ming, sont sorties de l'enceinte pour habiter des quartiers périphériques ; la destruction des quartiers anciens aurait entraîné *de facto* le déguerpissement des populations et leur remplacement. On sait bien que partout les politiques de réhabilitation des centres villes historiques s'accompagnent de transformations sociales et d'une certaine « *gentrification* », d'une concentration de populations aisées. La Chine n'échappera pas à ce phénomène quand les centres redeviendront attractifs. Néanmoins les opérations de transformations ne pouvaient pas commencer par des démolitions systématiques et le départ des populations de la Cité Ming qui en constituent aussi le patrimoine humain et vivant. Des expérimentations plus douces furent alors engagées pour réhabiliter des bâtiments du tissu ordinaire. Auront-elles réussi à convaincre sur la méthode ?

Les observations menées sur les différentes villes qui ont occupé le site de Qufu pendant près de 30 siècles, comme les projets à l'œuvre au cours de cette dernière décennie nous éclairent sur une continuité de la pensée chinoise sur l'espace humanisé. La ville, siège du pouvoir, fait l'objet d'un projet politique qui s'inscrit dans une vision globale d'aménagement du territoire à une très grande échelle.

L'identification des diverses enceintes attribuées aux différentes dynasties accrédite l'idée de ruptures

Le modèle idéal : le "siheyuan",
maison à quatre ailes entourant une cour

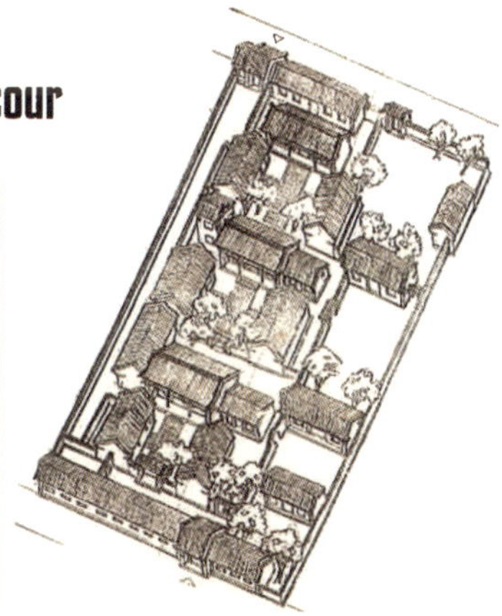

图片 7. “四合院”
Fig 7 Le « Siheyuan »

如今，已逐渐形成将曲阜的发展纳入到世界儒家思想革新及其带动的旅游文化潮流中的规划。

然而，这次展望并未单纯局限于遗迹的考古范围，而是拓展到土地面积的巨大规划中，以“古迹精神”规划曲阜，鉴于其在国际范围内的影响力，规划一个新的城市整体。1984年，曲阜建立了“第一家三星级酒店”，接待了104万中国游客，7 553名外国游客；2006年，曲阜接待了“来自中国大陆的550万名游客，以及222 000名来自海外、外国的游客”。[13]

1. I.CERDA. 城市化概论 . 贝桑松：Imprimeur 出版社，2005.

2. 吴良镛 . 中国古代城市化简史 . Urbs et Regio. Kassel: Gesamthochschubibliothek, 1986: 38(38).

3. R. Stewart Johnston. The Ancient City of Suzhou: Town Planning in the Sung Dynasty. The Town Planning Review, 1983, 54 (2): 194-222. 关于苏州石碑，还可参见：M. CARIER. 中国威尼斯的变化：苏州城及其版图 . Revue de la BN，1993(48): 2-9. 或 P. CLEMENT. 苏州：地势 . 历史古迹 . 1986（148）：15-17.

4. F.MAURET，刘海霞 . 曲阜城市历史 . // Heritage for Qufu 2005-2007，法国雷恩市 . 曲阜城市古迹的保护与开发，欧亚合作项目 Asia Urbs. 法国雷恩市出版社，2007：40-45.

5. 2002 年，我们受邀设计一座位于现存明故城南部的新城市。2005—2007 年，我们参与了 Rennes、曲阜以及 Saint-Jacques de Compostelle 三座城市之间的古迹合作研发项目。引自：Heritage for Qufu 2005-2007，2007.

6. 2007 年，曲阜扩张行政面积，达 895 平方千米（即将近 30×30 千米），人口达 640 000，人口密度较薄弱，为 7 人 / 公顷，但不可忽视其因地而异的多变性：由明故城城墙内的人口集中（167 公顷，10 200 人口，其中，孔庙及孔氏家族墓穴占据 38 公顷，人口密度为 61 人 / 公顷），至鲁国古都城墙内 21 个村庄的辽阔田地。

7. 1935 年，梁思成出版《曲阜孔庙建筑及其修葺规划》，旨在发展“修复历史古迹”理论。引自：张良 . 19—20 世纪中国古迹概念的诞生 . 巴黎：研究出版社，2003：253.

8. B. Fayolle-Lussac, H. Hoyem, P. Clément (dirs.). 西安，现代世界中的一座古城 . // 1949—2000 年城市化格局演变 . 巴黎：研究出版社，2007.

9. 林志宏 . 地域文化景观 . //Heritage for Qufu 2005-2007，2007：24-25.

10. 如今的地图显示为 12 扇城门，南面城墙的东门是假想的。

11. P.CLEMENT. 中国古都及其遗址 . // 从苍穹到大地，从花园到壁炉 . 巴黎：社会学高等学院出版社，1987：119-141.

12. 邵甬 . 明故城古迹保护与开发 . // Heritage for Qufu 2005-2007，2007：58-60.

13. 韩凤举，孔国栋 . 曲阜该走何种旅游发展之路？ // Heritage for Qufu 2005-2007，2007：7476. “相比较而言，1994 年吴哥仅接待游客 60 000 人次，而在 2012 年，接待 3 百万余人，其中包含 2 百万外国游客。”

dans le cycle de la vie du territoire et la création périodique, suivant les nécessités politiques, de villes nouvelles.

Ici, aujourd'hui, se matérialise le projet d'insérer Qufu dans le mouvement mondial de renouveau du confucianisme et du développement du tourisme culturel qu'il induit.

Mais au lieu de se circonscrire aux traces archéologiques de ce patrimoine, cette vision se projette dans un vaste projet d'aménagement du territoire, d'une nouvelle entité, « dans l'esprit patrimonial » de la ville mythique de Qufu, mais élargie aux dimensions mondiales que justifierait l'attrait de la ville pour la communauté internationale. Alors qu'en 1984, se construisait à Qufu « le premier hôtel trois étoiles » la ville accueillait 1,04 million de touristes chinois pour 7.533 étrangers ; elle accueillît en 2006 « 5,5 millions de touristes chinois continentaux et 222.000 touristes d'outre-mer et d'étrangers »[13].

1.I. Cerda, *La théorie générale d'urbanisation*, Besançon, Éd. de l'imprimeur, 2005 (préface de F. Choay)

2.Wu Liangyong, « A Brief History of Ancient Chinese City Planning », in *Urbs et Regio*, vol. 38, Kassel, Gesamthochschubibliothek, 1986.

3.R. Johnston, « The Ancient City of Suzhou: Town Planning in the Sung Dynasty », in *Town Planning Review*, vol. 54, n°2, p. 194222. Sur la stèle de Suzhou, voir aussi : M. Cartier, « Les métamorphoses imaginaires de la Venise chinoise : la ville de Suzhou et ses plans », in *Revue de la BN*, n°48, 1993, p. 29 ; ou encore P. Clément, « Suzhou : Plan en relief », in *Monuments Historiques*, n°148, 1986, p. 1517.

4.Cf. F. Mauret, Liu Haixia, « Historique de la ville de Qufu », in *Protection et mise en valeur du patrimoine urbain de Qufu, une coopération sino-européenne, programme Asia Urbs*, Ville de Rennes, 2007, p. 4045.

5.En 2002, nous avons été invités à dessiner une ville nouvelle au sud de la cité ming existante. De 2005 à 2007, nous avons participé à un programme de coopération sur le patrimoine de Qufu entre les villes de Rennes, Qufu et Saint-Jacques de Compostelle. *Cf. Protection et mise en valeur du patrimoine urbain de Qufu…, op. cit.*

6.En 2007, la Municipalité s'étendait sur un territoire administratif de 895 km² (à savoir approximativement 30 x 30 km) pour une population globale de 640.000 habitants. La densité globale, de 7 hab./ha, y est très faible, mais avec bien sûr des taux très variables, allant d'une forte concentration dans l'enceinte des Ming (10.200 hab pour 167 ha, dont 38 pour le Temple et la demeure historique des Kong, soit une densité globale de 61 hab./ha) à de vastes terres agricoles autour des 21 villages inclus dans l'enceinte de la Cité de Lu.

7. Dès 1935, Liang Sicheng publie *The Architecture of the temple of Confucius, Chu-fu, and plans for its restoration*, projet qui lui sert à développer « une théorie pour la restauration du monument historique ». Cf. Zhang Liang, *La naissance du concept de patrimoine en Chine, xixe-xxe siècles*, Paris, Éditions Recherches / Ipraus, 2003, p. 253.

8. B. Fayolle-Lussac, H. Hoyem, P. Clément (dirs.) *Xi'an, an ancient city in the modern world. Evolution of the urban pattern 1949-2000*, Paris, Éditions Recherches, « Les Cahiers de l'Ipraus », 2007.

9. R. Lin Chih-Hung, « Paysage culturel et mémoire des lieux », in *Protection et mise en valeur du patrimoine urbain de Qufu…*, op. cit., p. 2425.

10. Le plan en révèle aujourd'hui 12, la porte orientale de la muraille méridionale serait hypothétique.

11. P. Clément, « Les capitales chinoises et leur site », in *De la voûte céleste au terroir, du jardin au foyer*, Paris, Éditions de l'École des Hautes Études en Sciences Sociales, 1987, p. 119141.

12. Shao Yong, « Protection et mise en valeur du patrimoine urbain de la Cité Ming », in *Protection et mise en valeur du patrimoine urbain de Qufu…*, op. cit., p. 5860.

13. Han Fengju, Kong Guodong, « Quel développement touristique pour Qufu ? », in *Protection et mise en valeur du patrimoine urbain de Qufu…*, op. cit., p. 7476. Comparativement, Angkor n'avait accueilli en 1994 que 60.000 touristes et ils étaient en 2012 quelque 3 millions, dont 2 d'étrangers.

晚清时期欧洲游客眼中的曲阜及其文化遗产

玛丽亚娜·巴斯蒂德

19 世纪，由于陆地交通不便，来曲阜旅游的欧洲人非常少。即使是天主教传教士（他们的主教居住在济南），也不太愿意冒险来曲阜旅行。首批来到曲阜旅游的欧洲人中有苏格兰教会的牧师韦廉臣（Alexander Williamson），他在第二次鸦片战争之后来到曲阜。随后，当时的驻芝罘英国领事马安爵士（J. Markham）于 1869 年 3 月来到曲阜。他们两人都对当时曲阜这座城市及其周边的大致情况做了细致的描述，后者更是受到了年轻孔公的热情接待，年轻孔公甚至向他特别开放了孔庙。在这之后，多位德国游客也来到曲阜。法国汉学家沙畹（Chavannes）于 1890 年至 1892 年在华逗留期间曾来过山东，然而却是在 1907 年第二次来华登过泰山之后，才细致地游览了曲阜。正是他撰写了 1913 年的《马特罗列旅游指南：华北》（*Guide Madrolle: Chine du Nord*）旅游手册中的曲阜一章，并特别指出曲阜市及曲阜的圣庙是（山东省）主要的旅游景点。这些欧洲游客各式各样的见闻、相关的地图、建筑图纸和照片，都让人们能非常准确地追寻中国在过去半个世纪对这些地方的保护情况，让我们能够评估这段时期的生活水平发展和圣庙所起角色的变化。此外，这也让我们能了解这些欧洲人对于曲阜这个神圣地方的看法及受到的启发。

19 世纪中期，黄河河道的迁移，以及后来的太平天国运动和捻军起义，都对进入山东内陆的道路造成了极大破坏。少数意大利天主教方济各会的传教士在山东几个城市设立了方济各会——尤其是主教高（Mgr Cosi）和一个助理牧师在济南——设立了方济各会，但他们几乎不出门远行[1]。直至 1860 年，外国游客才走到山东各地，并来到曲阜。事实上，根据 1860 年的条约规定，外国游客只要具备中国当局颁发的护照，就能在中国境内自由活动。条约还向外国商贸开放了山东北部沿岸的芝罘港口（烟台市）。这里也成为日后地理探索者在内陆探索路线的起点。然而，截至 1900 年，来曲阜旅游的外国人数量仍然不多。1861 年 1 月，英国军人最先来到曲阜旅游。随后是苏格兰传教士韦廉臣（Alexander Williamson），他于 1865 年 10 月来到曲阜。在这段时期，这些来曲阜的欧洲人，他们要么是传教士，要么是外交官或军官，都是英国人或德国人。他们中很多人都写下了详细的文字介绍，并做了说明。他们因为不同的工作原因

Qufu et Son Patrimoine aux Yeux des Voyageurs Européens de la Fin dcs Qing

Marianne Bastid-Bruguière

Au XIXe siècle, en raison de la difficulté des communications par voie terrestre, le site de Qufu est assez rarement visité par les Européens. Les missionnaires catholiques, dont l'évêque résidait pourtant à Jinan, évitaient de s'y aventurer. Un des premiers voyageurs à s'y rendre est le Révérend Alexander Williamson, de l'Église écossaise, après la seconde guerre de l'opium. Il est suivi, en mars 1869, par J. Markham, consul britannique à Zhifu. Tous deux ont donné des descriptions très précises de l'état du site, de la ville et de ses environs. Markham a même été très cordialement reçu par le jeune duc Kong, qui lui a fait ouvrir spécialement le temple du Sage. Plus tard viennent divers visiteurs allemands. Le sinologue français Chavannes a sillonné le Shandong lors de son premier séjour en Chine en 1890-1892, mais c'est seulement lors de sa deuxième mission dans ce pays, en 1907, qu'il effectue une visite minutieuse à Qufu, après l'ascension du Taishan. C'est lui qui rédige le chapitre sur Qufu dans le *Guide Madrolle: Chine du Nord* de 1913, et signale la ville et ses sanctuaires comme une attraction touristique majeure. Les divers témoignages de ces voyageurs, les cartes, plans et photographies qui les accompagnent, permettent de suivre assez précisément l'état de conservation des lieux au cours du dernier demi-siècle de l'empire. On y apprécie également l'évolution de la vie et du rôle du sanctuaire à cette époque. Ils illustrent encore les différentes perceptions que ces Européens ont eues de ce lieu saint et la réflexion qu'il leur inspire.

Au milieu du XIXe siècle, les déplacements des cours d'eau du Huanghe 黄河 , suivis par les ravages des insurrections populaires des Taiping 太平 et des Nian 捻 ont causé des dommages considérables aux voie d'accès vers l'intérieur du Shandong. Une poignée de missionnaires franciscains italiens sont établis dans quelques villes, notamment un évêque, Mgr Cosi 高 , avec un vicaire, à Jinan 济南 , mais ils ne sortent guère de leur résidence.[1] Ce n'est qu'après 1860 que des voyageurs étrangers s'aventurent sur les routes du Shandong et se rendent à Qufu. En effet, les traités de 1860 autorisent désormais les étrangers à circuler à l'intérieur de la Chine à condition d'être munis de passeports délivrés par les autorités chinoises; d'autre part, ils ont ouvert au commerce étranger le port de Zhifu 芝罘 (ou Yantai 烟台) sur la côte Nord du Shandong, qui donne un point de départ à beaucoup d'explorations topographiques des côtes et des itinéraires terrestres. Le nombre d'étrangers qui se rendent à Qufu est cependant très faible jusqu'en 1900. Les premiers sont des militaires britanniques, en janvier 1861. Ils sont suivis par le missionnaire écossais Williamson, en octobre 1865. Dans cette période, ces visiteurs, tous européens, sont soit des missionnaires, soit des diplomates ou officiers, britanniques ou allemands. Plusieurs ont laissé des récits détaillés et illustrés. Ils viennent à Qufu sous des prétextes professionnels divers, mais animés d'une vive curiosité et en général très avertis de la littérature classique chinoise. Dans la seconde période,

来到曲阜，却被激发了极大的好奇心，而且普遍都对中国古典文学非常感兴趣。在第二段时期，即义和团运动晚期和1912年之间的那段时间，由于交通更为便利，曲阜的游客数量大增，游客的国籍和专业也更为多样化。正是在这段时期，法国汉学家沙畹（Chavannes）协同俄罗斯汉学家阿列克谢耶夫（Alexeev），于1907年在曲阜有条不紊地开展考古学研究。他们带来的文献和实物为我们从学术角度了解曲阜、解释曲阜的宗教特点带来了新的维度。同时，这些研究也让曲阜从此成为一个旅游景点，出现在环球旅行家的旅游指南中。清末的欧洲游客也逐渐将曲阜列入了面向公众的世界文化普及知识中。

◎ 1860 年后的信息

我所能做的研究发现，1861年前并非没有欧洲人来过曲阜。沿着中国大运河游览的荷兰和英国大使仅仅描述了沿线的城市风光，只字不提孔子的出生地。耶稣会会士描写了各个地方，但这些描述都来源于中文资料，而非根据他们的直接体验所写。对于这一点，传递最多信息的莫过于钱德明（Joseph-Marie Amiot，1720—1793）传教士。他不仅在第12卷的《北京传教士关于中国历史、科学、艺术、风俗、习惯的论文集》（*Mémoires concernant l'histoire, les arts, les sciences et les usages des Chinois*）中探讨孔子生平这个问题，并且提到其他19世纪初未经出版或未经欧洲汉学家考据的相关内容，同时也根据当时巴黎的皇家图书馆收到的有关曲阜及曲阜建筑的中国画藏品，传播了很多与曲阜相关的信息。钱德明从未到过曲阜，他的相关信息仅仅来源于阅读中文书籍和经常翻阅中文的公文信函[2]。纪尧姆·鲍狄埃（Guillaume Pauthier，1801—1873）在他的著作《现代中国》（*Chine ou description historique, géographique et littéraire de ce vaste empire, d'après les documents chinois*）中进一步丰富和明确了这些信息。该书于1837年面世，迅速被翻译成德语（1839年）和意大利语（1841年）。在很长一段时间，这本书都是鸦片战争之后在中国短暂生活的有文化的外国人所必备的书籍之一。鲍狄埃在书中详述了孔子的生活、儒家学说的要素，描写了孔子的葬礼、墓地、庙宇、祭礼以及孔子后裔享有的特权。除了对孔孟的描绘之外，鲍狄埃（Guillaume Pauthier）还根据皇家图书馆木版画陈列馆的《中国建筑》（*Edifices Chinois*）系列丝画上的地图，补充说明了孔子的墓地、庙宇和住所，充实了对孔子的介绍。鲍狄埃将曲阜描绘成一个宗教圣地，一个受到帝王、文人和民众尊崇的朝圣之地。[3] 鲍狄埃和钱德明一样，都对曲阜抱以极大的热诚和敬仰。鲍狄埃将其对曲阜的介绍总结如下：

“世界历史上无法找到一个可与这位伟大的中国哲学家相媲美的人物，他的学说

entre la fin du soulèvement des Boxeurs et 1912, les visiteurs sont plus nombreux car les communications deviennent plus faciles. Les nationalités et les personnalités sont plus variées aussi. C'est à cette époque que se situe l'exploration archéologique méthodique menée sur le site par le sinologue français Chavannes en compagnie du sinologue russe Alexeev, en 1907. Les documents et témoignages qu'ils ont rapportés de leur mission apportent des dimensions nouvelles à la connaissance savante du site et à l'interprétation de son caractère sacré. Ils contribuent aussi à en faire désormais un lieu touristique, décrit dans les guides de globe-trotter. Peu à peu, ces visiteurs européens de la fin des Qing ont fait entrer Qufu dans la culture universelle.

◎ L'information antérieure à 1860

D'après les recherches que j'ai pu faire, il ne semble pas que les Européen ait visité Qufu avant 1861. Les ambassades hollandaises et anglaises, qui suivirent le Grand Canal, décrivent seulement les villes le long de cet itinéraire et ne font nulle mention du lieu de naissance de Confucius. Les écrits des jésuites parlent du lieu, mais uniquement à partir de sources chinoises, non d'après une expérience directe. Celui qui a transmis le plus de renseignements sur ce sujet est le jésuite Joseph-Marie Amiot (1720-1793), non seulement par sa vie de Confucius publiée dans le 12e volume des *Mémoires concernant l'histoire, les arts, les sciences et les usages des Chinois* et par d'autres relations inédites publiées ou consultées plus tard par les sinologues européens du début du XIXe siècle, mais aussi par l'envoi à la Bibliothèque royale de Paris de collections de peintures chinoises représentant le site et les édifices de Qufu. Amiot n'avait jamais eu l'occasion de se rendre à Qufu, son information sur ce sujet lui venait uniquement de la lecture des ouvrages chinois et de la fréquentation des lettrés.[2] Cette information assez abondante et précise est reprise par Guillaume Pauthier (1801-1873) dans son ouvrage *Chine ou description historique, géographique et littéraire de ce vaste empire, d'après les documents chinois*, paru en 1837, aussitôt traduit en allemand (1839) et en italien (1841). Le livre resta longtemps un des bréviaire des étrangers cultivés qui séjournèrent en Chine après la guerre de l'Opium. Pauthier y relate en détail la vie de Confucius, les éléments de sa doctrine, décrit ses funérailles, son tombeau, ses temples, son culte, les privilèges accordés à ses descendants. Outre des portraits de Confucius et Mencius, des illustrations du tombeau, du temple et de la demeure de Confucius, gravées d'après les plans figuratifs peints sur soie conservés dans la série *Édifices chinois* du cabinet des estampes de la Bibliothèque royale ornent le récit.[3] L'auteur présente Qufu comme un lieu sacré, un lieu de pèlerinage révéré par les empereurs, les lettrés et le peuple. Très enthousiaste et admiratif, comme l'était aussi Amiot, il conclut ainsi son exposé :

"On ne trouverait pas dans l'histoire de monde une figure à opposer à celle du grand philosophe chinois pour l'influence si longue et si puissante que ses doctrines et ses écrits ont exercée sur ce vaste empire qu'il a illustré par sa sagesse et son génie. Et tandis que les autres nations de la terre élevaient de toutes parts des temples à des êtres inintelligents ou à des dieux imaginaires, la nation chinoise en élevait à l'apôtre de la sagesse et de l'humanité, de la morale et de la vertu; au grand missionnaire de l'intelligence humaine, dont les enseignements se soutiennent depuis plus de deux mille ans, et se concilient maintenant l'admiration et l'amour de plus de trois cents millions d'hommes."[4]

Dans la communauté étrangères des ports ouverts autour de 1860, les esprits cultivés qui s'intéressaient à l'histoire, à la littérature et aux arts chinois connaissaient l'existence des sanctuaires de Qufu, notamment à

和作品的影响力如此深远和强大，他用自己的智慧和天资在中国享有盛誉。尽管世界上其他国家都从教堂寺庙中培养不聪明的人或是臆造的神，中国人从中培养的是智慧和人道主义、伦理道德的使徒；培养了人类智慧的伟大传教士，他的教诲延续了两千多年，并且赢得了如今3亿多人的敬仰和尊崇。”[4]

1860年左右，生活在中国开放口岸的外国人中，对中国历史、文学和艺术感兴趣的知识分子都听说过曲阜的圣庙，尤其是通过孙嘉淦（1683—1753）的游记《南游记》中讲述的1721年的曲阜之旅。1867年4月，当时广州的传教士 W. R. 梅尔（W. R. Mayer）发表评论，指出了这本书的文学和文献价值。[5]此外，新教传教士和汉学家外交官都非常了解地方志和当时可以看到的中国地图。他们熟悉《大清一通志》（最终修正版发表于1842年）。当然还有1774年出版的曲阜地方志——《乾隆曲阜县志一百卷》，其流通范围非常广。

◎首批英国游客

首批来到曲阜的欧洲游客是否都是学识渊博者，这一点无法确定。我们这里要提到的是英军攻占北京后驻扎在天津的军队中的两位军官。他们其中一人在1861年9月28日的《北华捷报》（*North China Herald*）中匿名刊登了行车日志，其中提到1861年1月的曲阜之旅。[6]这篇日志似乎提到这两位军官来此的目的是确认是否能将军需经陆路从芝罘运往天津口岸，因为冬天的芝罘没有结冰，而此时的天津已被冰雪覆盖，外国军舰无法进入。1860—1861年的冬天尤为严酷。法英联军及他们的参谋部不得不等到融冰才能回到自己的国家。他们要忍受对他们而言少有的严寒，再加上补给不足和卫生条件不佳，增加了疾病和瘟疫的发生。此外，他们还要监察僧格林沁在济宁周边针对捻军和其他起义军的军事活动。行车日志的作者中文可能讲得很好，他非常了解中国经典文学作品、中国历史及当时最广为流传的汉学方面的文学作品。他主动与旅途中碰到的人交谈，自发地去参观庙宇和亭台楼阁。他和旅伴一起骑马旅行了1 200公里，时长近2个月，从1月9日至3月2日。之后，他们登上了一艘停泊在烟台的英国军舰，重返天津。

两位军官从天津出发后，沿着中国大运河的方向走。1861年1月25日，他们到达兖州，参观了兖州的七层塔楼，第一次见到了挂帆独轮车。第二天，即1月26日，他们到达曲阜。这样绕路而行看起来是这两位军官自己的想法，因为我们几乎看不到这与他们任务中的战略目标和后勤需要相关。从发表的日志中可以看出，他们本着当时英国上层社会普遍存在的好奇心、带着旅游的兴致来到曲阜。行车日记的作者非常尊

travers le journal de voyage de Sun Jiagan 孙嘉淦 (1683-1753), *Nan youji* 南游记 , qui relate une visite effectuée à Qufu en 1721. W. R. Mayer, alors missionnaire à Canton signalait la qualité littéraire et documentaire de l'ouvrage dans une note parue en avril 1867.[5] Mais surtout, missionnaires protestants et diplomates sinologues étaient bons connaisseurs des chroniques locales 地方志 et des cartes chinoises disponibles. Ils étaient familiers de *l'Encyclopédie géographique générale des* Qing 大清一通志 , dont la dernière révision datait de 1842. Ils n'ignoraient pas non plus la chronique locale de Qufu de 1774, *Qianlong Qufuxianzhiyibai juan* 乾隆曲阜县志一百卷 , dont les exemplaires étaient assez répandus.

◎ Premiers voyageurs anglais

Il n'est pas certain que les premiers visiteurs européens de Qufu aient été uniquement férus d'érudition. Il s'agit de deux officiers anglais appartenant au contingent stationné à Tianjin après la prise de Pékin. On connaît leur visite, effectuée en janvier 1861, par la publication anonyme du journal de route de l'un d'eux dans le *North China Herald* du 28 septembre 1861[6]. D'après le texte, il apparaît que ces deux officiers avaient pour mission de reconnaître la route terrestre de Tianjin à Zhifu pour voir s'il serait possible d'acheminer par terre des approvisionnements depuis ce dernier port, libre de glaces en hiver, pendant la période où le port de Tianjin, pris au contraire par les glaces, était inaccessible aux navires étrangers. En effet, l'hiver 1860-1861 se trouvait être extrêmement rigoureux. Les troupes franco-anglaises et leur état-major furent obligés d'attendre la fonte des glaces avant de regagner leur pays qui souffraient terriblement d'un froid inhabituel pour eux, aggravé par la médiocrité du ravitaillement et des conditions sanitaires précaires, qui multipliaient maladies et épidémies. Ils avaient également pour mission d'observer les opérations menées par Senggelinqin 僧格林沁 autour de Jining 济宁 contre les Nian 捻 et autres rebelles. L'auteur du journal semble bien parler le chinois et posséder une assez bonne connaissance des Classiques chinois, de l'histoire du pays et de la littérature sinologique la plus répandue à l'époque. Il converse volontiers avec tous ceux qu'il rencontre en chemin, visite volontiers les temples et les pagodes. Lui et son compagnon font entièrement à cheval les 1200 km de leur itinéraire, qui dure près de deux mois, du 9 janvier au 2 mars. Ils reprennent alors un navire anglais à Yantai 烟台 pour rejoindre Tianjin.

De Tianjin, les officiers suivent une route le long du Grand Canal. Ils arrivent à Yanzhou 兖 州 le 25 janvier 1861, y visitent une pagode de sept étages, observent pour la première fois des brouettes à voile. Le lendemain, 26 janvier, ils atteignent Qufu. Il semble bien que ce détour ait été leur propre initiative car on ne voit guère le lien avec l'objectif stratégique et logistique de la mission qui leur était confiée. Le récit publié manifeste qu'ils viennent à Qufu poussés par la curiosité et l'intérêt touristique fort répandus chez les jeunes gens de la bonne société britannique à l'époque. L'auteur est plein de déférence et de respect pour Confucius. Il explique que "ses écrits, ou ce qu'il en reste, sont pour les Chinois ce qu'est pour nous la Bible".

Les voyageurs observent qu'à Qufu tout le monde s'affaire à affûter, réparer ou fabriquer des épées et des lances car on attend une attaque des rebelles. Le mur d'enceinte a été rafistolé avec des planches. Du côté Ouest, on creuse un fossé profond de près de 8 mètres. Ils trouvent une auberge propre et vont voir aussitôt le temple de Confucius. La description donnée est précise. L'auteur indique, sûrement instruit par un gardien, qu'on a enlevé tous les livres par crainte d'une incursion des rebelles. Il ne mentionne pas non plus les vases précieux décrits par les voyageurs ultérieurs. Mais il indique les dimensions de la statue de Confucius,

崇孔子。他谈到“孔子的著作和留下的一切，对中国人而言就相当于《圣经》之于我们”。

两位军官注意到在曲阜，因为担心叛军来袭，大家都忙着磨尖、修理或制造剑和长枪。城墙的墙面是用木板马虎修理的。在曲阜西面，人们挖了深达近 8 米的坑。军官们找到了一家干净的旅店，并很快前去参观了孔庙。日志中对孔庙的描述非常细致。作者谈到（当然是孔庙看护人的转述），由于担心叛军入侵，人们搬走了孔庙中所有的书籍，更不用说后来的游客们所提到的珍贵的花瓶了。作者提到了孔子像的大小，它的细节和黄丝帷幔、家族石碑和题词碑文。当他看到一棵千年古树中长出了幼树时，感到非常震惊。一位孔子的后人在孔庙的一栋建筑中给两位军官奉上了茶水。之后，他们来到了颜庙的复圣殿，得知该庙由颜回的后人重建于 1841 年。他们又看到了一棵千年古树，看上去像黎巴嫩雪松。他们还看到了一口有盖的圣井。在主殿内，身着大型仪式服装的颜氏族长（颜回的第 75 代后人）接待了两位军官，而这位族长是一个 19 岁的年轻小伙儿。

第三天，即 1 月 27 日，军官们先后来到周公庙和少昊陵。日志中写道，他们在曲阜城东看到了周公采邑古城墙的遗迹，并讲述了守护人提供的历史介绍。这些遗迹被保护得很好。之后，他们还参观了孔子的陵墓，作者以非常细腻和崇敬的文笔叙述了这段旅程。他还明确指出，孔子坟头每三年修缮一次。他谈到，孔子后裔的族长年纪 40 岁，有爵位，但是没有任何实际权力。孔子的后裔多达 10 000 人，身份地位各不相同。孔氏家族的族长拥有 8 个村庄、6 个小村和 3 600 顷（24 000 公顷）土地，用于圣庙的维护和修缮。此外，军官们在走进驿站时感到非常惊喜，因为孔公招待了他们一顿有 120 道菜的餐饭。

第四天，即 1861 年 1 月 28 日下午，军官们前去拜访孔公。他们刚一到达，就受到了鞭炮还是小型步枪的欢迎：他们分不清二者的区别。在第二进院子的两侧，200 名仆人列队夹道欢迎他们。他们走进一幢满是“不怀敬意”的武器的楼房。在那里，作为家族和仆役首领的孔公把他们带到了一个大楼房左侧的小屋。孔公年约 40 岁，身高 1.6 米左右，为人特别亲切。他身着双层毛皮的衣服，佩戴玉饰和珊瑚饰。他看上去有些忧愁，向军官们询问了商贸事宜，想知道伦敦的实际大小。他拿出一块金表，和军官们核对了表上的时间。他说自己知道如何用工具每天校准时间，并且问军官们是否带着六分仪。军官们回到驿站时，中国人向他们购买自己带着的所有物件。

第五天，他们离开曲阜，前往兖州去拜访僧格林沁，但是后者早已离开走远。由于驿站内住满了士兵，一个当地显贵邀请两位军官下榻到自己家里。当得知当地居民以为他们是一支 800 人的英军部队的先遣士兵、要去协助僧格林沁打败起义军时，他们感到非常吃惊。

la détaille ainsi que les rideaux de soie jaune, les stèles généalogiques, les inscriptions. Il est frappé par la vue d'un arbre de mille ans dans lequel a poussé un arbre plus jeune. Un descendant de Confucius offre le thé aux deux officiers dans un pavillon du temple. Ils vont ensuite au temple de Yan Hui 颜回 (复圣庙), dont on leur dit qu'il a été reconstruit en 1841 par ses descendants. On leur y montre encore un arbre de mille ans, qui ressemble à un cèdre du Liban, et un puits sacré recouvert d'un toit. Dans le temple principal, le chef du clan Yan, un jeune home de 19 ans qui appartient à la 75e generation, les reçoit, revêtu de vêtements brodés de grande cérémonie.

Le lendemain 27 janvier, les visiteurs vont au tombeau du duc de Zhou 周公庙 , puis à la tombe de Shaohao 少昊陵 . Le récit signale qu'on voit des vestiges de l'ancienne muraille de la capitale du duc de Zhou au Nord-Est de Qufu et relate les explications historiques données par le gardien. Les monuments sont bien conservés. La visite continue par le tombeau de Confucius, décrit avec minutie et admiration. L'auteur précise que le tumulus est réparé tous les trois ans. Il relate que le chef des descendants a 40 ans, qu'il porte le titre de duc mais n'exerce aucune autorité. La descendance du sage compte plus de 10 000 personnes de toutes conditions. Le chef de la lignée possède 8 villages, 6 hameaux et 3600 *qing* 顷 (24 000 hectares) destinés à l'entretien des sanctuaires. Les officiers ont d'ailleurs l'heureuse surprise de trouver en rentrant à l'auberge un repas de 120 plats délicieux offert par le duc Kong.

Le lendemain, 28 janvier 1861, dans l'après-midi, les officiers vont rendre visite au duc Kong. Ils sont salués à leur arrivée par un feu nourri de pétards ou de petits fusils: ils ne savent faire la différence entre les deux. 200 serviteurs en rang de part et d'autre de la deuxième cour leur font une haie d'honneur. Ils pénètrent dans un bâtiment rempli d'armes "d'aspect désagréable". Là, le duc à la tête de sa famille et de sa domesticité les emmène dans un petit appartement dans l'aile gauche d'un grand bâtiment. Il semble avoir 40 ans, mesure environ 1,60 m., et parait très avenant. Il porte des vêtements doublés de fourrure et des ornements de jade et de corail. Il semble triste, interroge sur le commerce, veut savoir la taille réelle de la ville de Londres. Il sort une montre en or et compare l'heure qu'elle donne avec celle de ses visiteurs. Il dit qu'avec des instruments il sait mesurer l'heure chaque jour et demande si les officiers ont avec eux un sextant. Lorsque les voyageurs rentrent à leur auberge, les Chinois leur demandent à acheter tous les objets qu'ils ont avec eux.

Le lendemain, ils quittent Qufupour Yanzhou 兖州 afin de rendre visite à Senggelinqin 僧格林沁 , mais celui-ci a déjà avancé plus loin. Comme les auberges sont pleines de soldats, un notable les invite à descendre chez lui. Ils apprennent alors avec stupeur que les habitants pensent qu'ils sont les avant-coureurs d'une troupe de 800 soldats anglais qui vont aider Senggelinqin à vaincre les rebelles.

Cette première exploration de Qufu est intéressante par le climat de parfaite confiance et simplicité qu'elle reflète entre les deux cavaliers et la population tout au long du parcours au Zhili 直隶 et au Shandong. La description des monuments reste cependant relativement sommaire et s'appuie largement sur les renseignements fournis par les gardiens. Elle fut tout de suite oubliée, et lorsque Williamson vint à Shanghai en mars 1866 donner à la North China Branch of the Royal Asiatic Society une conférence sur sa visite d'octobre 1865 à Qufu, lui-même et tous ses auditeurs, dont plusieurs séjournaient en Chine depuis dix ans ou plus, considéraient qu'il était le premier voyageur européen en ce lieu saint. De même, Richthofen qui, entre 1868 et 1882, recensa très soigneusement, en Chine et en Europe, tous les renseignements et sources disponibles sur le Shandong, ne mentionne pas cette exploration anglaise de 1861.[7] Albert-Auguste Fauvel, fonctionnaire des Douanes impériales maritimes à Zhifu 芝罘 de 1874 à 1879, auteur d'une monographie sur le Shandong, l'ignore également[8].

这第一次的曲阜探险之旅非常有趣，两位军官和直隶及山东沿线民众之间的氛围是完全的信任而纯朴的。然而，他们对于当地文化遗产的描述相对简略。这些描述主要来源于遗迹守护人的讲述，而且很快就被忘记了。1866 年 3 月，韦廉臣（Alexander Williamson）传教士在上海面向皇家亚洲学会华北分会做有关他 1865 年曲阜访问之旅的演讲时，无论是他自己还是所有在场听众，其中包括很多在中国已经待了超过十年的人，都认为他才是第一个来到曲阜这片神圣土地的欧洲游客。此外，李希霍芬（Richthofen）于 1868 年至 1882 年期间，在中国和欧洲仔细审核了所有关于山东的现成资料，但他也没有提到 1861 年两位英国人的曲阜探险之旅。[7] 曾于 1874 年至 1879 年在芝罘担任皇家海关官员的艾伯特 - 奥古斯特 · 福威勒（Albert-Auguste Fauvel）也没有提到他们的这次旅行。[8]

◎捻军起义之后、义和团运动之前：外交官、传教士和地理学家

由于太平天国运动在中国北方所引发的紧张局势，没有一个外国人敢于踏入山东内陆，这样的情况持续了很多年。总理衙门拒绝签发通往山东的护照。甚至有谣言称曲阜的圣庙已被太平天国起义军破坏。然而，苏格兰传教士韦廉臣（Williamson，1829—1890）于 1865 年秋冒险再度来到曲阜，为我们提供了描述欧洲人在曲阜旅行的第一份详尽书面文稿。韦廉臣毕业于格拉斯哥大学（University of Glasgow）逻辑学、道德、哲学和神学专业，1855 年进入伦敦传道会（London Missionary Society），并且很快与妻子一起被传道会派往上海。由于他的身体状况无法适应上海的气候和他密集的研究任务，他很遗憾地于 1857 年被送回英国。1863 年，刚刚成立的苏格兰圣经会（National Bible Society of Scotland，由多个苏格兰宗教社团联合设立）推荐韦廉臣成为他们在中国的联络员。他因此很快带着妻子和独生女返回上海。1864 年，在山东海角的一次翻船事故之后，他便定居在了气候更宜人的芝罘。[9] 此后，他将自己装扮成中国人，开始在华北远途旅行。期间，他常常在市场、考场外布道或者以低于纸张造价销售经书和宗教宣传册甚至直接免费赠送。他首先来到满洲里和山东东部。他在民众当中受到热烈欢迎，大家争相来购买他的宣传册，尽管他们之间的言语交流并不多。[10] 本着好奇心和实用主义精神（他想增加捐赠人数量，资助苏格兰圣经会的活动），他专注于搜集他走过的地方的地理、动植物和天然产物的信息。[11]

受到成功的鼓励，1865 年秋，韦廉臣决定探索山东西部。[12] 在仅有的一位中国助理的陪同下，他于 1865 年 10 月 18 日出发，登上了中国大运河上的船只，前往通州。在大运河沿岸，他发现有很多伊斯兰教徒，自称是他的兄弟，看到他经过时友好地称

◎ Visites après les Nian et avant les Boxeurs : diplomates, missionnaires et géographes

Pendant plusieurs années, aucun étranger ne s'aventura plus sur les routes intérieures du Shandong à cause de l'extension vers le Nord des troubles liés à l'insurrection des Taiping. Le Zongliyamen 总理衙门 refusait les passeports pour la région. Le bruit courut même que les sanctuaires de Qufu avaient été détruits par les Taiping. Alexander Williamson (1829-1890), qui se risqua à nouveau dans la région à l'automne 1865 et nous procure le premier récit européen circonstancié d'un voyage à Qufu, est un missionnaire écossais. Diplômé en logique, morale, philosophie et théologie de l'Université de Glasgow, il était entré en 1855 à la London Missionary Society, qui l'avait aussitôt envoyé à Shanghai avec sa femme. Comme sa santé ne résistait pas au climat et à l'intense régime d'études qu'il s'imposait, il fut renvoyé en Angleterre, à son grand regret, en 1857. En 1863, la National Bible Society of Scotland, qui venait de se constituer par les efforts communs de plusieurs sociétés religieuses écossaises, lui proposa de devenir son agent en Chine. Il retourne aussitôt à Shanghai avec sa femme et sa fille unique. En 1864, après un naufrage au promontoire du Shandong, il s'établit à Zhifu, dont le climat est meilleur.[9] De là, déguisé en chinois, il commence des voyages lointains dans tout le Nord de la Chine, au long desquels dans les marchés, les foires ou à la sortie des examens, il prêche et distribue, gratuitement ou à un prix inférieur au coût du papier, des bibles et des brochures religieuses. Ses premières destinations sont la Mandchourie et la partie orientale du Shandong. Il trouve bon accueil parmi la population qui se précipite pour acheter ses brochures, bien que les conversions soient très rares.[10] Esprit curieux et pratique (il faut songer à multiplier les donateurs qui subventionnent l'action de la Bible Society), il s'applique à recueillir des renseignements sur la géographie, la faune, la flore et les productions naturelles des régions traversées.[11]

Enhardi par ses succès, à l'automne 1865, il décide d'explorer la partie occidentale du Shandong.[12] Il est accompagné seulement d'un assistant chinois. Il part de Pékin le 18 octobre 1865, va s'embarquer sur le Grand Canal à Tongzhou 通州 . Il note la présence de nombreux musulmans le long du canal, qui se déclarent ses frères et crient amicalement "mussulman" en le voyant passer. Il voyage en barque jusqu'à Linqing 临清 ,qu'il trouve en ruine, ravagée par les rebelles. Il quitte la ville le 2 novembre, en charrette tirée par des mules car le canal est impraticable. La route est très mauvaise et très encombrée. Williamson se cache à l'intérieur de la charrette car sa vue effraie les femmes qui cueillent le coton dans les champs. À un moment, la charrette se brise tant le terrain est défectueux. Impossible de la remplacer car les troubles ont saigné la région. Le missionnaire continue en brouette à voile jusqu'à Dongping 东平 . Là, bien que les rebelles soient proches et qu'on voie partout des villages brûlés, il se sent en terrain de connaissance. Il a avec lui le *Livre des histoires* 书经 et identifie les lieux historiques, retrouve les paysages décrits dans l'antiquité. Il passe par Wenchang 汶上 et parvient à Yanzhou 兖州 , en croisant une foule lamentable de réfugiés fuyant les zones infestées par les insurgés Nian 捻 . Il se rend ensuite à Zouxian 邹县 (Zoucheng 邹城), le lieu natal de Mencius, en notant chaque stèle le long de la route. La beauté du paysage de ce lieu l'enchante. Il détaille l'histoire de chaque montagne. Il visite le temple de Mencius, qu'il décrit minutieusement, ainsi que les temples voisins. Apprenant que le Duc, chef de la 70e génération, est chez lui, il remet sa carte et est reçu aimablement par cet homme d'environ 65 ans, en présence de son deuxième fils et de ses petits-fils. Le duc pose quelques questions sur l'Angleterre, fait quelques remarques sur le costume du visiteur et se retire. Williamson lui envoie en cadeau la bible, un ouvrage scientifique et plusieurs autres livres. En retour, il reçoit la copie de plusieurs inscriptions. Il visite ensuite la ville, qui lui paraît pauvre. Il y prêche, vend

呼他为“穆斯林”（mussulman）。他乘坐小船游览直至临清时，发现临清已经被起义军破坏，成为了一片废墟。11 月 2 日，由于大运河已经无法通行，他坐骡车离开临清。路况非常糟糕和拥挤。韦廉臣躲在骡车内，因为他的眼睛会让田间收割棉花的妇女感到害怕。有一次，地面凹陷太大以至于骡车都破裂了，但又没法替换，因为动乱已经让这个地方血流殆尽。韦廉臣传教士坐着挂帆独轮车继续他的旅程，一直到了东平。起义军离东平不远，这里的村庄也到处被烧毁，但是韦廉臣却感觉到这是一片知识的土地。他带着《书经》辨认历史古迹，找到了古人所描述的风景。他经汶上抵达兖州，途中遇到一群可怜的难民，他们正逃离被捻军起义者破坏的区域。随后，他来到孟子的出生地邹县（邹城），记录下沿途的每个石碑。邹县的美丽风景让他欣喜不已。他详述了每座山的故事，参观了孟庙（他对此作了详细描述）及临近的庙宇。当他得知孟子的第 70 代后人家主孟公在家时，便递上了自己的名帖，受到了年近 65 岁的孟公的友好接待，孟公的第二个儿子和最小的儿子也都在现场。孟公询问了几个有关英国的问题，评价了一番韦廉臣的服装，然后就走开了。韦廉臣将经书、一本科学类书籍和其他几本书作为礼物赠予孟公。作为回礼，他收到几个题词的复本。随后，韦廉臣参观了邹城。据他描述，这是座贫穷的城市。他在这里布道，把带来的所有宣传册都卖掉了。官府来人的时候，他就叫上一个向导去参观孟氏家族的墓园，并记下碑文。参观孟子墓可能会耽搁太久时间，他就没去。人们告诉他，孟子墓跟孟母的墓地很像，这种千篇一律让他失望了。而孟子的徒弟却指责他们的老师花了太多钱在母亲的葬礼上。之后，他就回到了曲阜。

韦廉臣在曲阜待了四天[13]，觉得这里比邹县更富裕、更有活力。他谈到，这里的南城墙有两扇门，面朝西的城门专为帝王而设，平时都是关闭的。韦廉臣否认到处都有破坏的声音，但他说起义军确实在靠近这座县城。当人们询问起义军是否会破坏孔庙时，他们说不会，但会杀死不公正的清朝官吏。当起义军知道曲阜的知县是孔子后人时，就离开了。然而，由于很多乡下人都逃难到了圣人的墓地、期望圣人的特点和四周的城墙能庇护他们，起义军可能会攻击和屠杀他们。

然而，在韦廉臣的描述中，丝毫没有提及近期有发生毁坏古迹遗址的事件。他最先参观了孔庙，并给了在他看来特别殷勤的看守人一笔小费。他说自己从未在中国其他地方看到过如此宏伟和绝妙的景色。他写道，孔庙“没有与我们的一等、二等大教堂相媲美的建筑构造，但其排列组合及整体效果更为庄严”。[14] 他细致地描述了孔庙的平面图、植被、建筑构造、雕像（尤其是孔子和孟子的雕像，陈列在西面的陈列馆中，且处于附属的位置，而不是陈列在东面陈列馆，让他觉着与它们的重要性不匹配）、古代物件（尧代的黏土花瓶、商代的青铜花瓶、周朝的铜像和香木桌）、石碑和碑文。

toutes les brochures qu'il avait apportées. Quand arrivent les émissaires de la police, il prend un guide pour aller voir le cimetière de la famille de Mencius, où il relève les inscriptions. Il renonce au tombeau de Mencius qui le retarderait trop. Il ressemble, lui dit-on, à celui de la mère de Mencius, qui le déçoit par sa banalité, alors que les disciples de Mencius avaient reproché à leur maître ses dépenses excessives pour les funérailles maternelles. Il gagne alors Qufu.

Il reste quatre jours à cet endroit.[13] Il trouve la ville plus riche et plus active que Zouxian. Il signale que la muraille comporte deux portes au Sud, dont celle située vers l'Ouest, réservée à l'empereur, reste fermée. Il dément les bruits de destruction qui ont couru. Il rapporte que les rebelles se sont effectivement approchés de la ville. On leur a demandé s'ils voulaient détruire le temple du grand sage. Ils ont répondu que non, mais qu'ils voulaient tuer les mandarins injustes. Apprenant alors que le sous-préfet descendait de Confucius, ils ont quitté la ville. Mais comme beaucoup de gens de la campagne s'étaient réfugiés dans les cimetières en croyant y trouver abri du fait de leur caractère sacré et des murailles qui les entouraient, les rebelles allèrent les y attaquer et les massacrer.

Cependant, le récit de Williamson ne signale aucune déprédation récente des monuments ou des sites. L'auteur visite d'abord le temple de Confucius, en donnant un pourboire au gardien, qui se montre très obligeant. Il déclare n'avoir rien vu de si grandiose et superbe ailleurs en Chine. Le sanctuaire, écrit-il, ne comporte "pas de construction comparable à nos cathédrales de premier ou même de second rang, mais la combinaison et l'effet de l'ensemble est plus imposant".[14] Il décrit minutieusement le plan du sanctuaire, sa végétation, ses architectures, les statues (notamment celle de Confucius et celle de Mencius, dont il s'indigne qu'elle soit dans le pavillon de l'Ouest, en position subalterne, et non dans celui de l'Est), les objets antiques (le vase d'argile datant de Yao 尧, les vases de bronze des Shang 商, les éléphants de bronze et la table en bois de rose datant des Zhou), les stèles et inscriptions. Il obtient du gardien des estampages des trois grands portraits de Confucius et des 120 scènes de sa vie gravées sur marbre noir dans le temple arrière. Il boit de l'eau du puits qu'utilisait Confucius et la trouve "excellente, bien qu'un peu douceâtre". Il examine soigneusement chaque édifice avec admiration.

Le but majeur de sa visite était cependant de rencontrer l'héritier de Confucius pour l'entretenir du christianisme et lui remettre de la littérature sur ce sujet et sur les sciences occidentales. Le jeune duc n'a alors que 16 ans, il est sous la tutelle d'un oncle. Williamson obtient seulement d'être reçu par des parents éloignés.[15] Sa prédication dans les rues de Qufu a plus de succès: les gens l'écoutent avec attention et lui achètent beaucoup de livres.[16] Il consacre ensuite tout son temps aux visites touristiques. Il se rend au tombeau de Confucius, au temple du duc de Zhou 周公, au tombeau de l'empereur Shaohao 少昊陵. Il est frappé par la pyramide de granit placée à l'arrière, sur laquelle a poussé un vieil arbre. Rapprochant cette forme, rare en Chine, des pyramides égyptiennes, il médite sur l'unité du genre humain. Ses observations, sans cesse étayées de citations du *Livre des Histoires* 书经, manifestent que l'état de conservation et d'entretien des sites historiques de Qufu est alors satisfaisant. Les statues sont bien peintes, les tuiles de céramiques sont entières, des fils de fer protègent les ornements des avant-toits du temple de Confucius contre les oiseaux. Williamson passe encore par les tombeaux de la famille de Yan Hui 颜回 (复圣庙), puis se dirige vers Sishui 泗水 où il visite le temple du disciple de Confucius Zilu 子路, absolument délabré. Il gagne ensuite Mengyin 蒙阴, Laizhou 莱州 et regagne Zhifu 芝罘.

L'émotion érudite de Williamson, tout à fait semblable à celle d'un Européen cultivé visitant les monuments de Rome ses classiques latins à la main, ne précipita pas les voyageurs étrangers vers Qufu. Dans les quatre ans qui suivirent, l'extension de l'insurrection des Nian rendit le Shandong trop dangereux. Les rebelles occupent encore Jinan 济南 et Taian 泰安 en décembre 1867. Le troisième voyage européen

他从看守人那里得来三幅很大的孔子像的拓印图和后殿中的黑色大理石上篆刻的 120 个孔子日常生活场景的拓印图。他喝了孔子曾经喝过的井水，觉得味道“非常棒，虽然有点淡而无味”。他带着崇敬之情仔细研究每幢建筑。

他参观的主要目的是与孔子后人见面，希望能谈论基督教教义，并将基督教文献和西方科学文献交托给他。年轻的孔公当时年仅 16 岁，由他的叔叔监护。韦廉臣因而只受到了其远亲的接见。[15] 他在曲阜街头的布道获得了更大成功：人们耐心听他讲道，还向他购买了很多书籍。[16] 之后，他就把所有的时间花在了旅游上面。他去到孔子的陵墓、周公的陵墓和少昊陵。他参观了少昊陵后面用花岗岩砌成的陵墓，陵墓上长出了古树。他很惊叹这个陵墓与埃及金字塔的异曲同工，也唤起了他对人类统一性的思考。他基于《书经》的观察研究，表明了当时曲阜的历史遗迹被保存和维护得非常好。雕像绘制得很棒，陶制瓦片非常完整，铁线保护了孔庙屋檐的装饰物不被鸟儿破坏。此外，韦廉臣也曾经到过复圣庙，并前去泗水参观孔子的弟子子路的庙宇（已被完全破坏），随后抵达蒙阴和莱州，并返回芝罘。

在之后的四年里，捻军起义的扩大让山东变得非常危险，尽管韦廉臣深入调研的热情与当年有学识的欧洲人参观古拉丁人用双手建造起来的罗马遗迹时的情怀是完全一样的，但是并没有唤起外国游客游览曲阜的热情。1867 年 12 月，起义军占领了济南和泰安。第三次有记录的欧洲人曲阜之旅是在 1869 年，仍然是韦廉臣，但是在当时芝罘的英国领事马安爵士（John Markham，1830—1872）的陪同下。这次旅行留下了两篇记载：其一是马安爵士于上海在《皇家亚洲学会华北分会报》上刊登的文章，他在 1870 年 2 月 28 日于伦敦举行的皇家地理学会会议上使用过。该学会在他们的刊物上发表了两个版本[17]；其二是韦廉臣在他于 1870 年出版的《华北、满洲及东蒙旅行记》（*Journeys in North China, Manchuria and Eastern Mongolia*）第 2 卷中穿插的内容。[18]

1853年，马安爵士作为学生翻译被派往广州。之后，他受聘于上海和福州的领事馆。1868 年 1 月起，他在芝罘担任领事。[19]1869 年初，他开始在山东旅行，考察捻军起义在前一年被清政府完全镇压之后山东的安全状况和经济活动。他急切地想要重新定位农业、手工业和矿业生产这些可能促进芝罘地区外贸的活动，尤其是当地的煤炭资源情况，因为如果当地煤炭资源足够，就避免了进口价格昂贵的英国煤炭去补给海军的蒸汽船。同时，他也非常关注道路和交通工具的情况，便于制定未来更佳的铁路线路。他很自然地与韦廉臣会合了，后者被认为是当时最了解山东的外国人。[20] 另一位传教士狄考文（Wilson）在青州碰到了他们两人。三人同路游览了一个多月，一直到邹县，韦廉臣和狄考文继续经由中国大运河前往南京，而马安爵士则在旅行 40 天后途经蒙阴、沂水、潍县和莱州，回到芝罘。

à Qufu dont on garde la trace fut effectué en 1869, encore par Williamson, mais en compagnie de John Markham (1830 -1872), consul britannique à Zhifu 芝罘 . On en possède deux récits : d'une part, un texte que Markham donna au *Journal of the North China Branch of the Royal Asiatic Society* à Shanghai, qu'il utilisa dans une conférence du 28 février 1870 à la Royal Geographical Society à Londres, et que cette société publia sous deux versions dans ses revues[17]; d'autre part, la relation de Williamson insérée dans le volume 2 de son livre de 1870, *Journeys in North China, Manchuria and EasternMongolia.*[18]

John Markham avait été envoyé comme élève-interprète à Canton en 1853. Il avait été ensuite employé aux consulats de Fuzhou et Shanghai. Il était consul à Zhifu depuis janvier 1868.[19] Il entreprend ce voyage à l'intérieur du Shandong au début de 1869 pour observer l'état de sécurité et d'activité économique de la région après la pacification définitive de la rébellion Nian annoncée par le gouvernement des Qing l'année précédente. Il est soucieux de repérer les productions agricoles, artisanales et minières qui pourraient alimenter le commerce étranger à Zhifu, en particulier les ressources locales en charbon qui permettraient d'éviter l'importation coûteuse de charbon anglais pour le ravitaillement de la marine à vapeur. Il prend soin également de s'informer sur les routes et moyens de transport pour définir le meilleur tracé de futures lignes de chemin de fer. Il s'adjoint tout naturellement Williamson, considéré alors le meilleur connaisseur étranger de la province.[20] Un autre missionnaire, Wilson, les rejoint à Qingzhou 青州 . Ils font route ensemble un peu plus d'un mois, jusqu'à Zouxian 邹县 , où Williamson et Wilson continuent vers Nankin par le Grand Canal, tandis que Markham rentre à Zhifu, après un total de quarante jours de voyage, en passant par Mengyin 蒙阴 , Yishui 沂水 , Weixian 潍县 et Laizhou 莱州 .

Williamson semble motivé surtout par le désir de compléter ses observations antérieures et de profiter de la présence du consul pour rencontrer enfin le descendant de Confucius. Du point de vue de la description monumentale de Qufu, les récits de ce voyage apportent peu à celle du précédent voyage de Williamson. Dans ses conférences, Markham en recopie même de nombreux passages. Les observations des deux voyageurs ajoutent cependant des précisions sur certains édifices et un témoignage sur l'état de conservation après les troubles des Nian 捻 .

Les voyageurs Anglais, escortés de quelques serviteurs chinois quittent Zhifu le 24 février 1869. Ils passent par Jinan, en étant reçus seulement par le trésorier provincial Pan Dingxin 潘 鼎 新 , qui était précédemment en poste à Zhifu. Ils rencontrent l'évêque catholique Mgr Cosi, qui compte 12 000 fidèles. Ils prennent la route impériale, en mauvais état, pour gagner Taian 泰 安 . Ils y croisent des cortèges de pèlerins de toutes conditions. Ils montent au sommet du Taishan 泰山 par les escaliers bordés tout au long de "mendiants hideux". Leurs descriptions de ces sites, dont la grandeur sacrée les impressionne très fortement, est minutieuse et intéressante.[21] Mais je ne m'y attarderai pas ici. Les voyageurs parviennent ensuite à Qufu, le 23 mars 1869, après la traversée de grands bourgs populeux où Williamson prêche et vend beaucoup de livres. Aux abords de Qufu, le sol leur paraît très fertile, couvert de nombreux mûriers.

Markham trouve la ville "propre et bien construite, mais sans force dans ses fortifications, sa grande sauvegarde est son caractère historique".[22] Les voyageurs descendent dans une auberge du faubourg Nord. Leur premier soin est de remettre leur carte au chef de la famille Kong 孔 , en sollicitant de lui rendre visite. La demande est aussitôt accordée. Markham y va en chaise, suivi par Wilson et Williamson à cheval. On les reçoit avec une grande cérémonie à la porte. Ils franchissent deux cours. Le duc les attend sur le seuil de la troisième avec son oncle et des parents. Il les conduit à la salle de réception, puis dans son petit salon privé, rempli de livres et d'objets antiques. Il place Markham sur le siège d'honneur à sa gauche, les deux autres à sa droite. Il pose des questions, le thé est servi et la conversation s'engage sur divers sujets. Les Anglais expliquent qu'ils viennent visiter la terre natale du Grand Sage et saluer son descendant. Ils

韦廉臣似乎很有动力，因为他期望能补充自己之前的研究，并借由领事出面最终见到孔子的后人。从曲阜的纪念性描述角度来看，此次旅行的叙述与韦廉臣前一次的旅行描述相比几乎没有什么新意。马安爵士甚至在自己做演讲时复制了很多段韦廉臣的文字记载，更描述了捻军动乱之后建筑的保护情况。

1869 年 2 月 24 日，英国游客在几位中国仆人的陪同下离开芝罘。他们途经济南时仅仅受到当时在济南任职、曾在芝罘任职的财政官员潘鼎新的接待。他们还见到了高大主教（Mgr Cosi），当时他有 12 000 名信徒。游客们走御道抵达泰安，但是路况糟糕，沿途碰到了各种各样的朝圣者。他们沿着两边都是“丑陋乞丐”的台阶登顶泰山。他们对这些地方的描述细致而有趣，从中可以看出宗教的伟大让他们叹为观止。[21] 然而，这方面我并不想在此提太多。这些游客穿过了韦廉臣曾经布道并卖过书的城镇，在 1969 年 3 月 23 日到达了曲阜。他们看到曲阜沿岸的土地被桑树所覆盖，非常肥沃。

马安爵士认为这座城市“干净，建造得很好，但是防御力度不足，它最大的保障是其历史特性”。[22] 两位旅行者下榻在一个北部郊区的驿站。他们首先关心的就是将自己的名帖递给孔氏家族的家主，恳请同意上门拜访。这个要求很快得到了满足。马安爵士坐着轿子前往，狄考文和韦廉臣则骑马跟随前往。孔府门口举行了隆重的欢迎仪式。他们三人穿过两个庭院之后，就看到孔公带着叔叔和父母在第三个院子门口等候。孔公将他们带到接待厅，之后又带他们去到自己的小型私人会客室，里面放满了书和古代摆件。孔公请马安爵士坐到自己左手边的尊席上，其他两人坐在右手边。孔公问了些问题，奉上了茶水，谈话涉及了很多不同主题。几位英国人解释说自己来游览孔圣人的出生地，并向他的后人致敬。此外，他们还提到很多他们的同胞都知道中国古典文学作品，并对中国人的智慧表示高度赞赏。他们感谢孔公同意接待自己，并向其担保，如果他或者他的家人来到芝罘，马安爵士将对他们表达最高敬意，这似乎也让孔公非常高兴。马安爵士向孔公讲述了同一时间由蒲安臣（Burlingame）带领的中国使节团访问美国时受到的隆重接待，并承诺如果孔公访问美国或英国，将受到同样的礼遇。孔公只需要登上新型蒸汽船穿越太平洋并乘坐火车就可前往。然而，从曲阜到北京只需要一天的想法让孔公及其随从都笑了。孔公挽留三位宾客，很明显跟他们交谈得非常愉快。他说三位是自己接待的首批外国人，但在这之前他从露台上看到过几个外国人。在宾客离开时，孔公将他们送到了第一进院子的门口。回到驿站之后，几位英国人收到了让他们多留几日的邀请，孔公也让知县派了守卫过来，防止好奇的民众打扰他们。

马安爵士和韦廉臣被这位年仅 20 岁的年轻人的魅力所折服。他是孔子的第 75 代后人，个子不高，身形有一点点走样，但是面相亲切，仪态舒适，感觉是个快乐、幸

ajoutent que beaucoup de leurs compatriotes connaissent les Classiques chinois et en apprécient la sagesse. Ils remercient de l'audience accordée, assurent le duc que si lui ou ses parents viennent à Zhifu, Markham les comblera d'égards, ce qui semble réjouir leur hôte. Markham lui raconte l'accueil fait en Amérique à l'ambassade chinoise menée par Burlingame au même moment et lui promet qu'il serait reçu de même s'il visitait les États-Unis ou l'Angleterre. Il est question des nouveaux navires à vapeur à travers le Pacifique et des chemins de fer. Mais l'idée qu'on puisse aller de Qufu à Pékin en une journée fait rire le duc et toute sa suite. Il retient ses hôtes, visiblement ravi de bavarder avec eux. Il dit qu'ils sont les premiers étrangers qu'il reçoit, mais qu'il avait vu déjà quelques étrangers depuis son balcon. À leur départ, il les reconduit jusqu'à l'entrée de la première cour. En rentrant à l'auberge, les Anglais trouvent une invitation à rester plusieurs jours et des gardes que le duc a fait envoyer par le sous-préfet pour éviter que la foule curieuse ne les importune.

Markham et Williamson sont sous le charme de ce jeune homme de vingt ans, chef de la 75e génération, petit, un peu déformé de corps, mais au visage avenant, très agréable de manières, gai, heureux, ouvert et d'une extrême vivacité intellectuelle.[23] Markham avoue qu'il ne s'attendait pas à ce que ce noble personnage daigne le recevoir. Il contraste le comportement du jeune duc et des siens avec celui des mandarins chinois dans le reste de son voyage et en général. Ses hôtes de Qufu "n'étaient nullement sur la réserve, ils semblaient avides d'information, et ceux qui nous ont ensuite accompagnés au temple nous ont questionné minutieusement sur tous les sujets relatifs aux pays étrangers." Williamson ajoute que dans cette conversation très animée, ils ont dit avoir lu des livres religieux et scientifiques étrangers, notamment un ouvrage de géographie. Au retour à Zhifu, les deux visiteurs envoyèrent donc en remerciement une caisse contenant des ouvrages scientifiques publiés en chinois par les étrangers, une bible, des années entières de journaux et revues en chinois de Shanghai et Canton.

Markham visite la tombe de Confucius, en signalant une table sculptée et une urne en pierre devant la stèle du sage. Le duc fait ouvrir le temple de Confucius pour les voyageurs, bien qu'il soit fermé ce jour-là en raison de l'anniversaire de la mort d'un des chefs de la famille. Devant la statue de Confucius, Markham note de superbes vases de cuivre émaillés de bleu, jaune et vert, ainsi que deux vaches de bronze, que Williamson ne signalait pas en 1865; mais pas d'éléphants. Il signale aussi que le temple a été rénové depuis le précédent passage de Williamson est qu'il est " dans un ordre magnifique, resplendissant de dorure, de peinture et de sculpture".[24]

La principale nouveauté monumentale par rapport au voyage antérieur de Williamson est la visite au temple de Yanhui 颜庙 , où les voyageurs admirent surtout un énorme pin argenté, dont le gardien assure qu'il a 10 000 ans.[25] Markham et Wilson se rendent au temple du duc de Zhou 周公庙 , sans avoir le temps d'aller au tombeau de Shaohao 少昊陵 , pendant que leur compagnon prêche au faubourg de l'Est un public attentif et lui vend bon nombre de brochures.[26]

Ensemble, ils se rendent ensuite à Zouxian 邹县 , en visitant d'abord les tombes de la mère de Mencius et de Mencius (ce dernier site n'avait pas encore été vu par Williamson), puis son temple. Les descriptions montrent un état des lieux satisfaisant. Markham ne peut rencontrer le chef des descendants de Mencius à la 71e génération car son père vient de mourir à 70 ans.L'héritier a plus de 40 ans et a un fils de 13 ans. Le consul juge la cité pauvre, bien que joliment située sur la route de Nankin à Pékin. Les rues sont étroites et très sales. Les auberges sont dans le faubourg Sud, qui est le seul quartier où il y ait un peu de vie et d'animation.[27] À Sishui 泗水 , Markham trouve le temple de Zilu 子路 à l'abandon et menaçant ruine.[28]

Le récit de Markham fournit des détails précis sur les conditions et le coût des moyens de transport et d'hébergement. On chemine à une vitesse moyenne de 10 *li* à l'heure (environ 5 km).[29] L'auteur est

福、心态开放且非常聪慧的人。[23] 马安爵士坦言，他没有想到这位贵主会惠予接待他们。在之后的旅程中，他将年轻孔公的仪态与中国满清官员的仪态相比较，认为曲阜的宾主们“毫不保留，看上去非常渴求信息，之后陪同我们参观圣庙的那些宾主还向我们仔细询问了有关外国的问题”。韦廉臣补充道，在这次非常热烈的谈话中，宾主们说他们看过国外的宗教和科学类书籍，尤其是看过一本地理书。回到芝罘之后，两位外国游客为表示感谢，给宾主们寄去了一箱由在中国的外国人出版的中文科学类书籍、经书，在上海及广州发行多年的完整版中文报纸和杂志。

马安爵士参观了孔子墓，特别提及了孔圣人石碑前的一张雕刻桌和石质骨灰瓮。虽然孔庙那天由于一位家主的忌辰而关闭了，但是孔公还是向几位游客开放了孔庙。在孔子像前，马安爵士注意到了非常漂亮的带有蓝、黄、绿三色珐琅的铜制花瓶，以及两个铜牛，这是韦廉臣在 1865 年的那次旅行中没有提到的，而且没有铜象。马安爵士还指出，孔庙在上次韦廉臣来过之后就翻新过，现在的孔庙“井然有序，镀金、画作和雕像都熠熠生辉”。[24]

跟前一次韦廉臣的曲阜之旅相比，这次具有纪念性的主要书面记载是参观了颜庙，几位游客都对颜庙里的一棵镀银松树特别推崇，看守人肯定地讲它有 10 000 多年了。[25] 韦廉臣在曲阜东部郊区向专心听讲的民众布道并售出数量可观的宣传册时，马安爵士和狄考文参观了周公庙，最后没时间去少昊陵。[26]

他们三人一起到达邹县，首先就去参观了孟母墓和孟子墓（韦廉臣没有来过孟子墓），然后参观了孟庙。从他们的描述中，我们可以知道孟庙、孟母墓和孟子墓保存状况良好。马安爵士没能见到孟子的第 71 代后人，因为他的父亲刚刚过世，享年 70 岁。这位继承人年逾 40，膝下有一个 13 岁的儿子。马安爵士认为邹县比较贫困，虽然地处从南京至北京的必经之处。道路狭窄且肮脏。旅店坐落在邹县南部的郊区，这也是唯一有些人气、比较活跃的区域。[27] 马安爵士在泗水发现了废弃的、即将变成废墟的子路庙。[28]

马安爵士的文字记载为我们提供了差旅条件和准确的价格。行走的速度为平均每小时 10 里（约 5 公里）。[29] 让他觉得沮丧的是，最初建设得非常好的道路交通系统很久以来都无人照管，没有做任何维护。他因而又找到了一项在他那个时代官吏行事荒谬的证据。[30] 他强调，在自己的整个旅程中，除了满清官吏之外，他碰到的人都“彬彬有礼”。尽管他们是以官方名义来旅行的，除了济南财政官员和曲阜的孔子后人之外，其他满清官吏对他们都完全冷漠且没有礼貌，甚至蛮横无理。商人都非常友好；在很多城市，有威信的商人前来拜访过他，向他咨询很多有关铁路、蒸汽航海和国外发明的问

consterné que le réseau routier, à l'origine remarquablement construit, soit laissé à l'abandon depuis très longtemps, sans le moindre entretien. Il y trouve une preuve de plus de l'ineptie du mandarinat de son temps.[30] Il souligne que tout au long de son voyage, il a rencontré chez tout le monde la "plus grande civilité", sauf de la part des mandarins. Hormis le trésorier provincial de Jinan et les descendants de Confucius à Qufu, ceux-ci l'ont traité avec totale indifférence et impolitesse, voire avec parfaite insolence, bien qu'il ait voyagé à titre officiel. Les marchands étaient très aimables; dans plusieurs villes, les marchands influents lui ont fait visiter et ont posé beaucoup de questions sur les chemins de fer, la navigation à vapeur et les inventions étrangères, en exprimant un vif désir que ces perfectionnements étrangers soient introduits en Chine. Dans les grandes foires qu'il a traversées, où étaient réunies de grandes foules de gens dont la plupart n'avaient probablement jamais entendu parler des étrangers ou en voyaient pour la première fois, il n'a entendu qu'une fois une épithète malveillante à leur égard. Bien sûr, poussés par la curiosité, les gens s'agglutinaient volontiers autour de lui et de ses compagnons, mais sans jamais leur manquer d'égards.[31]

Dans le livre de Williamson, la description de Qufu est ornée de deux gravures. L'une représente le portique 牌楼 et l'allée conduisant au tombeau de Confucius; l'autre, la stèle funéraire de Confucius avec devant la table et l'urne de pierre. Williamson indique que ces gravures ont été faites d'après les photographies prises par M. Baker, en possession du Docteur Carmichael à Zhifu.[32] Le docteur Carmichael était un médecin de la London Missionary Society. Il est vraisemblable que ce Baker, que je n'ai pas pu identifier, mais qui pourrait être un officier chargé des relevés topographiques activement menés par le commandement militaire anglais à l'époque, a pris ces photos peu après le passage de Markham et Williamson, en tout cas avant 1870, date de la parution du livre à Londres.

En effet, à partir de 1869, les routes étant plus sûres et les ambitions commerciales ou ferroviaires européennes toujours plus vastes, les voyageurs étrangers fréquentent davantage le Shandong. Ils s'appliquent à dresser des cartes. L'Anglais Ney Elias a fait l'hydrographie de l'embouchure du Fleuve Jaune en 1867[33], Albert-Auguste Fauvel la vérifie en compagnie de *Bei Jinquan* 贝锦泉, capitaine du navire de guerre *Wannianqing* 万年青.[34] En 1871, l'astronome russe Hermann Fritsche (1839-1913) effectue la mesure de l'altitude du Taishan et corrige par des mesures astronomiques la position de 22 villes de la carte dressée en 1711 par les jésuites Régis et Cardoso, qui servait de base aux cartes chinoises et européennes.[35] Il a fait l'excursion de Qufu, sans en laisser de récit, mais en mesurant exactement la position de la ville.[36] En revanche, Richthofen qui se rend de Zhenjiang 镇江 à Zhifu 芝罘, entre le 13 mars et le 30 avril 1869, ne visite pas Qufu ni le Taishan. "J'étais alors trop novice pour y penser", écrit-il avec regret dans son chapitre sur le Shandong.[37] Il apprend le voyage de Markham et Williamson en rencontrant le consul à son arrivée à Zhifu. Le géographe allemand a emprunté le Grand Canal jusqu'à Huaiyin 淮阴, puis a voyagé par route de terre car la voie du canal est asséchée, en passant par Suqian 宿迁, Yizhou 沂州 (aujourd'hui Linyi 临沂), Mengyin 蒙阴 et Jinan 济南, sans faire non plus l'ascension du Taishan 泰山.[38] Il est occupé à des relevés géologiques, pour lesquels il se guide sur les explorations pratiquées par le géologue américain Raphaël Pumpelly (1837-1923) en 1863-1865, lequel n'avait prêté aucune attention aux antiquités chinoises.[39] Dans ses ouvrages, l'évocation de Qufu emprunte à Williamson et Markham, comme le font d'ailleurs couramment les voyageurs qui visitent le lieu à leur suite.[40] Mais la carte du Shandong qu'il publie en 1885 dans son *Atlas von China*, en couleurs, avec tous les derniers perfectionnements typographiques est désormais la référence de tous les voyageurs étrangers.

Entre temps, deux illustres missionnaires sinologues ont pris ensemble la route de Qufu: JamesLegge (1814-1897), le célèbre traducteur des Classiques chinois, et Joseph Edkins (1823-1905). Tous deux appartiennent à la London Missionary Society. Legge, qui était posté à Hong Kong depuis 1843, est venu faire un

题，同时表达了想让这些国外改良设施引进到中国的热切期盼。马安爵士穿过大型市集，那里聚集了大量人群，其中很多人可能从未听说过外国人，或是第一次见到外国人。但就是这样，他也只听过一次他们对他不够友善的修饰语。当然，出于好奇心，人们会自发地聚拢到他和他同伴的身边，但从来都不会不尊重他们。[31]

韦廉臣在他的书中用两个镌版的图来描述曲阜：其一，通向孔子墓的牌楼和小巷；其二，孔子的墓志铭及其墓碑前的桌子和石质骨灰瓮。韦廉臣指出，这些镌版的图是根据 M. 贝克尔（M. Baker）拍摄的照片来制作的，这些照片归芝罘的卡迈克尔（Carmichael）医生所有。[32] 卡迈克尔医生是伦敦传道会（London Missionary Society）的医生。这位贝克尔很有可能（我也无法鉴别）是当时英军委派前来负责记录地形的军官，他可能是在马安爵士和韦廉臣走后不久拍摄的照片，总之是在 1870 年前（该书在伦敦出版之时）。

事实上，从 1869 年开始，由于道路更为安全、欧洲人在商业或铁路方面的野心更大，国外游客越来越多地来到山东。他们专注于拟定自己的地图。1867 年，英国人内伊 · 伊莱亚斯（Ney Elias）对黄河河口做了水道测量。[33] 福威勒（Albert-Auguste Fauvel）与贝锦泉（清朝万年青号战舰舰长）一起做了核实。[34]1871 年，俄罗斯天文学家弗里切（Hermann Fritsche，1839—1913）测量了泰山的海拔高度，并通过天文学测量纠正了 1711 年由耶稣会会员雷居（Régis）和卡多佐（Cardoso）绘制的地图上 22 座城市的位置，这个地图在当时被用作绘制中国和欧洲地图的基准。[35] 他游览了曲阜，没有留下文字记录，却准确测量了曲阜的位置。[36] 相反，1869 年 3 月 13 日至 4 月 30 日期间从镇江前往芝罘的里希特霍芬（Richthofen），没有到曲阜游览，也没去泰山。“我当时刚来不久，没有想到这一点”，他在山东一章中不无遗憾地写道。[37] 里希特霍芬抵达芝罘见到马安爵士之后，得知了他和韦廉臣的旅行。这位德国地理学家借道大运河抵达淮阴，然后经陆路旅行（因为大运河已经干涸），途经宿迁、沂州（如今的临沂）、蒙阴和济南，也没有登泰山。[38] 他使用了美国地质学家庞培勒（Raphaël Pumpelly，1837—1923）在 1863—1865 年间做的地质测绘，但当时庞培勒没有关注中国历史遗产。[39] 他的作品中对曲阜的回忆源自韦廉臣和马安爵士，正如其他旅行者追随这两人的脚步游览曲阜一样。[40] 但是，他于 1885 年发布在《中国地图集》（*Atlas von China*）一书中的彩色山东地图却带有最新的排版印刷修缮，从此成为了所有国外游客的参考。

在此期间，两位著名的汉学家传道士一起来到了曲阜：知名的中国古典名著翻译家理雅各（James Legge，1814—1897）和艾约瑟（Joseph Edkins，1814—1897）。他们俩都隶属伦敦传道会（London Missionary Society）。理雅各从 1843 年起定居香港，想在回伦敦前来华北旅游。艾约瑟 1863 年起定居北京，他也要回英国了。1873 年 5 月 16

tour dans le Nord avant de regagner Londres. Edkins est installé à Pékin depuis 1863 et doit aussi retourner en Angleterre.Ils visitent Qufu, en venant de Taian 泰安 , du 16 au 18 mai 1873. Le récit de leur excursion à Qufu fait l'objet d'une conférence donnée par Edkins, dès le 2 juin 1873 à Shanghai, à la North China Branch of the Royal Asiatic Society, publiée l'année suivante dans la revue de la société.[41] Legge semble n'avoir rien publié sur cette visite, mais il est possible qu'on en trouve une trace écrite dans ses papiers inédits conservés à Londres, à la School of Oriental and AfricanStudies, que je n'ai pas pu aller consulter.

Le récit d'Edkins ignore superbement les voyageurs antérieurs, sauf une brève allusion à Williamson, mais il est imprégné de la lecture des Classiques : les Entretiens de Confucius 论语 et le *Mencius* 孟子 sont évoqués à chaque instant, devant les paysages, les arbres, les noms inscrits sur les stèles, comme dans un pèlerinage littéraire. Edkins n'énumère pas les objets et le mobilier à l'intérieur des sanctuaires, mais il donne des détails nouveaux sur les particularités archéologiques de l'architecture, et surtout une description précise du rituel des sacrifices offerts chaque mois au temple de Confucius.

En arrivant à Qufu, à quelques kilomètres, les deux missionnaires sont frappés par la vue du premier champ d'opium qu'ils aient rencontré depuis Pékin. Mais de là sur 500 km vers le Sud, cette culture est pratiquée partout, dit Edkins. Aucun voyageur précédent n'avait observé ce fait, mais il est vrai qu'ils étaient venus en hiver ou au début du printemps.

Après avoir franchi la rivière Si 泗河 , qui n'a que 30 cm d'eau, Edkins et Legge aperçoivent une plantation de cyprès. On leur dit qu'il s'agit de l'Académie de la Zhu et de la Si 洙泗书院 , instituée pour préserver l'enseignement de Confucius, avec l'idée de relier la patrie du sage à la Si qui coule juste derrière l'enclos, la Zhu étant la petite rivière qui traverse l'enclos de sa tombe à 800 mètres au Sud-Ouest. Les voyageurs ne voient que des ruines. Les bâtiments avaient été construits sous les Yuan. Il restait quelques grandes stèles de pierre, l'une datée des Yuan, deux autres des Ming et des Qing.[42]

Les deux pèlerins visitent ensuite le tombeau de Confucius, dont Edkins donne l'appellation chinoise, "forêt de Confucius" 孔林 . Il note que la *Zhu* 洙水 a très peu d'eau, rougeâtre, et que son nom pourrait être traduit "ruisseau rouge", selon le sens du caractère zhu 洙 . Il souligne le caractère unique de ce cimetière où sont enterrées plus de soixante-dix générations. Il prétend, à tort, qu'aucun étranger n'est jamais entré dans l'enclos des tombes des descendants, situé derrière celui de la tombe de Confucius, mais n'y pénètre pas lui-même. Il commente les six figures de pierre qui ornent l'allée du tombeau de Confucius, en donnant leurs désignations chinoises et leur description. Il note que bien que les Qing ne reconnaissent plus Confucius ni comme "roi" 王 , ni comme "empereur" 帝 , à la différence des Ming, on n'a pas réaménagé le cimetière, si bien que le tombeau conserve les statues des deux "premiers ministres" 丞相 . Des pins, des acacias et un arbre au feuillage luisant appelé *shuijingshu* 水晶树 (arbre de cristal)poussent sur le tumulus, qui semble donc plus boisé que dans les descriptions antérieures. Edkins ajoute des indications sur l'emplacement des tombes du fils et du petit-fils de Confucius et sur les dégâts fréquents occasionnés par les inondations de la Si 泗河 .[43]

Entré en ville, Edkins trouve la cité "petite, tranquille et propre". Un descendant de Confucius avec lequel il était lié à Pékin lui avait donné une lettre de recommandation pour son frère qui occupait un poste important sous le duc Kong à Qufu. Ce frère se montre près prévenant.[44] Les deux voyageurs sont d'abord conduits au temple de Yan Hui 颜回 (复圣庙). Edkins indique que le quartier Est de la ville où il est situé, et où résident les descendants de Yan Hui, porte le nom de *louxiang* 陋巷 (humble quartier), inscrit sur une arche qui enjambe la rue à cet endroit, en souvenir du passage du *Lunyu* 论语 où Confucius loue son disciple pour sa frugalité. Il commente aussi les piliers du temple. Le matériau de ceux de marbre provient de carrières à 5 km au Sud de la ville. Ces piliers sont d'une pièce, ornés d'un travail de sculpture en camée

日至 18 日，他们从泰安来到曲阜旅游。1873 年 6 月 2 日期，艾约瑟在上海给皇家亚洲学会华北分会做演讲时，讲述了他们两人的曲阜之旅。第二年，故事还刊登在学会的会刊上。[41] 理雅各似乎没有发表有关此次旅行的文章，但是伦敦的东方和非洲研究院保存着的他未经发表的文稿中可能会找到一些蛛丝马迹（我无法查阅这些资料）。

艾约瑟的叙述中极大地忽略了之前来过曲阜的旅行者，除了简略提到韦廉臣。他沉浸在阅读中国古典文学中：他的作品中每时每刻都会提到《论语》和《孟子》，比如在看到风景、树木和石柱上篆刻的名字时，他的文字像是一次文学的朝圣。艾约瑟没有列举圣庙内的物件和家具，而是给出了有关建筑考古特性的新细节，尤其详述了孔庙每月举行的祭祀大典。

两位传教士到达曲阜时，在距离曲阜几公里的地方看到一片鸦片种植田，感到非常吃惊，这是他们自北京以来看到的第一片鸦片种植田。然而，从这里往南 500 公里，鸦片种植田随处可见。之前没有一个来曲阜的游客注意到这一点，但确实之前的游客来的时候要么是冬季，要么是初春。

在穿过泗河（水深仅 30 厘米）之后，理雅各和艾约瑟发现了一片柏树，据说这是洙泗书院的古柏。建立洙泗书院是为了保护孔子曾经讲学的地方，并将孔子的故乡与书院围墙后面的泗河连接起来。洙水曾是一条小溪，在西南方向 800 米的地方穿过孔子墓的墙围。现在游客只能看到一片废墟。书院的楼宇建于元朝，现存元、明、清三个石碑。[42]

两位朝圣者随后参观了孔子墓，艾约瑟还给了它中文名字“孔林”。他提到，洙水的水量很少，河水呈浅红色，因而可以将其翻译为“红溪”，这也符合“洙”字的含义。他强调这片墓地的特别之处，在于它埋葬着七十多代人。他说没有一个外国人曾踏入孔子后人墓园的墙围（位于孔子墓的后方），这是错误的，他自己也没有深入研究。他评述了孔子陵墓的林荫道上矗立的六座石像，给出了他们的中文名称，并做了描述。他指出，清朝并没有像明朝那样封孔子为“王”或“帝”，这片墓园也没有被重新布置，因而还保留着两个“丞相”的雕像。坟头长有松树、洋槐和一棵树叶发光的水晶树，这样看起来孔林的绿化要比前人描述的更为繁茂。艾约瑟还增加了对孔子的儿子和孙子墓地的描述，谈到了泗河经常泛滥所造成的墓园损坏。[43]

进入曲阜之后，艾约瑟发现这座城市“很小，但很安静和干净”。一位他在北京时就有过接触的孔子后人给他写了一封介绍信，将艾约瑟介绍给他的一位在曲阜孔公之下担任要职的兄弟。这位兄弟非常亲切友好。[44] 两位传道士首先被带到了复圣庙。艾约瑟提到，他们所在的曲阜市东区居住着颜回的后人，称为“陋巷”。“陋巷”之名刻在跨越东区的拱门上，以此纪念《论语》中讲到的孔子夸奖其弟子简朴。艾约瑟

noir et blanc appelé en chinois *chunhuashizhu* 醇化石柱 . Le teck des piliers intérieurs vient de Birmanie. Les édifices ont été construits à l'époque où la conquête mongole avait ouvert les échanges avec cette région. Edkins signale encore un arbre, qui aurait été planté par Confucius, mais n'est plus qu'une racine desséchée et un tronc.[45]

La visite du temple de Confucius s'effectue sous la conduite du frère de son ami pékinois et d'un autre administrateur du site, chargé du cimetière, dépêché par le duc Kong. Edkins note que l'édifice de l'Autel de l'abricot 杏坦 vient d'être repeint en rouge, vert et or: il resplendit. Il s'émerveille devant les dix piliers de marbre du temple, souligne que c'est une particularité de ce sanctuaire du Shandong, due évidemment à la proximité des carrières. On ne trouve rien de tel à Pékin, seules certaines villes du Sud présentent quelques exemples de ce type. Les piliers de teck massifs sont moins grands que ceux du temple de Yongle 永乐 aux tombeaux des Ming. Il trouve une influence bouddhiste dans l'image et les représentations de Confucius.[46]

À la grande déception des voyageurs, au dernier moment, une affaire urgente empêche le duc Kong de les accueillir, alors que les préparatifs de leur réception étaient déjà faits. Ne pouvant prolonger leur séjour à Qufu, les voyageurs quittent la ville.

Edkins ajoute des informations sur la famille Kong tirées des propos de deux de ses voituriers, qui appartiennent à la famille, et de ses guides à Qufu. On lui confirme l'information rapportée par Williamson sur les propriétés foncières du duc Kong. Elles sont trois fois plus étendues que le don originel de 24 000 hectares concédés par les empereurs Yuan. Avec un rapport de 1 taël 银两 par mu 亩 , le duc dispose d'un revenu annuel de 340 000 taëls, soit 120 000 £. Il possède aussi sept ou huit grands bateaux qui font le commerce sur le Grand Canal. Edkins s'indigne que malgré ces ressources, il n'existe aucune école charitable pour les enfants pauvres du clan. "L'établissement d'une université ou d'un système d'éducation pour les pauvres serait peut-être un meilleur moyen d'honorer le Sage que d'accumuler la richesse sur une petite portion du clan Kong".[47]

Son récit se termine par une description précise du rituel des sacrifices mensuels et annuels pratiqués au temple de Confucius.[48] Il ne cite aucune source. Il semble probable qu'il s'était renseigné à Pékin par la lecture d'ouvrages sur les rituels et en consultant son ami Kong. Il a ensuite vérifié et complété son information en interrogeant ses guides lors de la visite du temple de Confucius. Il explique la place des différents musiciens, le nombre de chaque instrument, l'ordre suivi. Il décrit les 50 danseurs, leurs costumes à l'antique et leurs mouvements, en accompagnant son texte de diagrammes figurant la chorégraphie. Il traduit les paroles des chœurs qui sont chantés lors des offrandes de viande, puis de fruits, puis de vin, et enfin lorsqu'on retire les viandes et que l'esprit retourne là où est conservée la tablette. Il donne le détail du costume moderne que portent le duc et ceux qui assistent au sacrifice.

En quittant Qufu par la porte Sud, ses voituriers montrent à Edkins l'autel de la pluie, marqué par une grande stèle portant les caractères *wuyuntan* 舞云坦 , où le sous-préfet vient toujours sacrifier en cas de sécheresse.

À la suite de Legge et Edkins, d'autres Anglais encore sont venus à Qufu : fonctionnaires des douanes comme Chalmers[49], et autres missionnaires comme Alexander Armstrong.[50] Le Français Albert-Auguste Fauvel, fonctionnaire de la douane à Zhifu 芝 罘 de 1874 à 1879, s'y rend aussi, mais sa description très succincte recopie Williamson.[51]

Un effet indirect des observations de Richthofen au Shandong est l'implantation d'une mission catholique allemande dans le Sud de la province. Anzer, prêtre de la Société de Steyl, constituée de catholiques allemands installés en Hollande, arrive à Jinan en 1880. L'évêque italien lui fait étudier la langue et les mœurs chinoises pendant deux ans, puis le charge ainsi que son collègue Freinademetz du soin des

还评述了复圣庙的石柱。制成石柱的大理石石料是从距离曲阜市南面5公里的采石场运来的。这些石柱来源于同一块石料，饰有黑白色浮雕玉石，中文称之为醇化石柱。复圣庙内部石柱的柚木产自缅甸。这些建筑建于蒙古人入侵而迫使曲阜开放对外交流的这段时期。艾约瑟还特别提到了一棵可能是孔子本人栽种的树，这棵树现在仅剩干枯的树根和树干了。[45]

艾约瑟北京朋友的兄弟和一位孔公派来的、掌管墓园的管事陪同参观了孔庙。他提到，杏坛的祭坛刚被刷成红、绿和金三色，熠熠生辉。他对孔庙的十个大理石柱啧啧称赞，强调说这是山东圣庙的特色，这样说显然是因为他们职业相似。北京就看不到这样的景色，只有中国南方的几个城市才有这类例子。巨大的柚木柱没有明陵中的永乐帝的庙（即长陵）那么高大。此外，他还发现孔子的形象和描述受到佛教的影响。[46]

让两位传道士失望的是，在最后时刻，孔公因急事无法接待他们，尽管招待他们的准备工作都已经做好了。他们无法延长在曲阜逗留的时间，因此就离开了。

艾约瑟还附加了从他的两位车夫（隶属孔氏家族）和向导那里听来的关于孔氏的信息，确认了韦廉臣关于孔公土地财产的消息是正确的。孔公名下的土地是明朝皇帝最初赏赐的24 000公顷的三倍。按一亩地一两来计算，孔公的年收入达340 000两，即120 000英镑。此外，孔公还有七八艘在中国大运河上开展贸易的船。让艾约瑟生气的是，孔公家财丰厚，却没有为家族的贫困孩童专设一所慈善学校。“为穷人建立大学或设立教育体系，可能是向孔圣人表达敬意的更好方式，而不是在孔氏家族小部分的财富之上累积财富。”[47]

最后，艾约瑟还详细描述了孔庙每月和每年举行的祭祀大典。[48]他没有提到任何资料来源，看起来可能是他在北京时阅读有关仪式的书籍，以及咨询他的孔姓朋友才知道的。在参观孔庙时，他还就这些自己知道的信息，向向导验证了一番，并做了补充。他详述了每位乐师的位置，每种乐器的数量和排列顺序。他提到了50位舞者，描写了舞者的古代服装和动作，还用文字图解了舞蹈动作。他翻译了献祭肉品、水果、酒和最后撤下祭祀用的肉品及灵魂回归到祭桌时所吟诵的祭祀歌的歌词。他细致描述了孔公穿着的现代服装，以及协助祭祀的人们。

从南门离开曲阜后，车夫指给艾约瑟看了求雨的祭台，即一个刻有“舞云台”的大石碑。一旦发生干旱，曲阜知县就会来此祭祀求雨。

在理雅各和艾约瑟之后，其他英国人也来到曲阜：海关官员查尔穆斯理（Chalmers）[49]，其他像亚历山大·阿姆斯特朗（Alexander Armstrong）这样的传教士。[50] 1874至1879年间，芝罘的海关官员法国人艾伯特-奥古斯特·福威勒（Albert-Auguste Fauvel）也来到曲阜，他非常简短的描述抄袭了韦廉臣的文字记载。[51]

chrétientés du Sud-Ouest de la province, qui comptaient seulement 158 fidèles. La société de Steyl envoie d'autres missionnaires. En 1885, le Saint-Siège érige le Sud du Shandongen vicariat apostolique confié exclusivement à la mission de Steyl. Il comprend les préfectures de Yanzhou 兖州 , Yizhou 沂州 , Caozhou 曹州 et Jining 济宁 , avec Anzer comme évêque : Qufu, où il n'y a d'ailleurs aucun chrétien, se trouve englobé dans le vicariat. La présence permanente de ces Allemands, qui dès 1891 dénoncent le protectorat français sur les missions catholiques pour demander la protection de l'empereur Guillaume II, conduit l'Allemagne à faire agir son consul à Tianjin 天津 . Ce consul, von Seckendorff se rend fréquemment à Yanzhou 兖 州 , où des incidents éclatent dès 1889, à cause du militantisme brutal de l'évêque, qui veut installer le siège de l'évêché dans la ville au lieu de le laisser dans une paroisse rurale éloignée. Von Seckendorff visite Qufu.[52] Divers visiteurs allemands font de même. Ces excursions se multiplient après l'occupation allemande de Jiaozhou 胶州 en novembre 1897. Les récits qui en restent sont surtout touristiques et anecdotiques, sans intérêt particulier par rapport à leurs prédécesseurs, sauf qu'ils insistent sur le caractère "sacré" du lieu. Je signalerai seulement celui du diplomate écrivain Ernst von Hesse – Wartegg (1854-1918), paru en 1898, qui a visité Qufu et le Taishan accompagné d'un photographe professionnel. Les photographies reproduites sont intéressantes.[53]

◎ Après 1900 : amateurs et savants

De 1899 à 1901, l'extension de l'insurrection des Boxeurs interrompt les voyages. Ils reprennent activement ensuite, d'autant que la construction des chemins de fer facilite en partie les déplacements. La voie ferrée de Qingdao 青岛 à Jinan 济南 est achevée en 1904, le Pékin-Hankou 京汉 en 1906. Les jeunes diplomates anglais se précipitent : Litton en 1902, Garnett en 1906.[54] Les Allemands sont nombreux aussi à sillonner le Shandong pour des raisons commerciales ou purement touristiques, mais de plus en plus les deux se mêlent. Parmi ceux qui publient une description de leur itinéraire, on peut citer le jeune géographe Walter Anz (1874-1938). Il a visité le 30 décembre 1902 le temple de Mencius à Zouxian 邹县 . Il trouve la ville endormie et le temple paisible. Le 3 janvier 1903, il arrive à Qufu, adresse sa carte au duc Kong en demandant la permission de voir le temple de Confucius. Le duc accepte aussitôt et lui envoie un guide. La description du voyageur ne signale rien de particulier par rapport à ses prédécesseurs. Lorsqu'il sort du sanctuaire, un personnage âgé de la famille Kong vient à sa rencontre, entouré de nombreux serviteurs, et le reconduit à la sortie. Anz explique que le chef de la famille actuel est un autre, plus jeune. Il ajoute qu'un des plus riches membres de la famille est un ami de la culture occidentale et veut introduire à Qufu la gestion forestière sur le modèle allemand. Le renseignement vient sans doute du guide qui l'a accompagné. Il ne fait pas mention d'autres lieux visités à Qufu, mais il signale à une journée de marche de la ville les ruines d'un palais et des stèles abandonnées à Quanlinzi 泉林子 . Il est allé au Taishan 泰山 et reproduit une vue panoramique chinoise de ce lieu de pèlerinage.[55]

Le missionnaire américain Charles Alfred Stanley Junior publie aussi, dans une revue de Shanghai, un récit d'une excursion au Taishan et à Qufueffectuée en avril 1905.[56] C'est le fils d'un missionnaire, né en Chine, parlant parfaitement la langue et familier du pays. Il est alors stationné dans le Nord-Ouest du Shandong, à Pangzhuang 庞庄 . Il voyage avec un collègue en charrette, empruntant des routes en mauvais état. En arrivant à l'auberge, c'est au sous-préfet 知县 qu'il fait porter sa carte en demandant l'autorisation de visiter le temple et le tombeau de Confucius, et en le priant de lui donner un guide. Le sous-préfet en-

里希霍芬（Richthofen）还间接发现了德国天主教布道团在山东省南部负责布道。1880年，德国圣言会（Société de Steyl，由在荷兰的德国天主教徒设立）教士安治泰（Anzer）到达济南。圣言会的意大利主教让他用两年时间学习中文，了解中国的风俗习惯。之后还让他和圣福若瑟（Freinademetz）一起负责管理山东西南部的基督教社团，社团只有158名信徒。德国圣言会还派了其他传教士。1885年，教廷将山东南部视为宗座代牧区，独家委托给德国圣言会，包括兖州、沂州、曹州和济宁，由安治泰担任主教：从没有过基督徒的曲阜也就包含在了代牧区内。这几位一直出现的德国人从1891年起宣布放弃法国保护领地授予的天主教使命，而向德国皇帝威廉二世（Guillaume Ⅱ）寻求庇护，德国因而委派了驻津领事。这位驻津领事司艮德（von Seckendorff）经常来兖州。1889年，兖州爆发了几起事件，起因是主教激烈的斗争，想要将主教管辖区从偏远乡下的教区教堂迁移到市中心。司艮德游览了曲阜。[52] 很多德国游客也陆续前来。1897年11月，德军占领胶州后，来曲阜旅游的德国人更多了。留存的文字记载主要是旅游性质或是趣闻，与在他们之前游览曲阜的德国人的兴趣点不同，除了一点：他们都认为曲阜带有“神圣”的特性。我这里只想提到作为外交官和作家的海司（Ernst von Hesse-Wartegg，1854—1918）于1898年发表的文章。他曾在一位专业摄影师的陪同下游览曲阜和泰山。再现的照片具有重要意义。[53]

◎ 1900年之后：业余爱好者与专业学者

1899—1901年期间，义和团起义大规模爆发，西方传教士无法出行。然而当时开始修建铁路，旨在便利交通出行。1904年，青岛至济南段铁路完工，京汉（北京至汉口）铁路于1906年竣工。[54] 两名年轻的英国外交官员，列顿（Litton，1902年）、加内特（Garnett，1906年）投身其中，见证了这段历史。与此同时，怀揣着商业目的或单纯的游历愿想，众多的德国人也开始在山东留下了他们的足迹，随着时间的推移，商业动机与游历因素已密不可分。在记载他们出行的资料中，有一名年轻的地理学家沃尔特·安兹（Walter Anz，1874—1938），于1902年12月30日参观了邹县的孟庙。据其形容，邹县安详宁静，孟庙平和安静。1903年1月3日，他抵达曲阜，会见当地县令，请求获准参观孔庙。县令欣然应允，并为其安排了一名陪同向导。与前人相比，他的游记描述并无特别之处。当他踏出庙宇时，一位孔氏家族年长的后人在众多仆人的簇拥下，前来接见了安兹，并陪同其一直到出口。安兹在记载中解释道，孔氏一族当时的领袖另有其人，是一位较为年轻的人士。他还补充道，这个家族中有一位非常富有的族人是西方文化的拥护者，他曾计划将德国的森林管理模式引入到曲阜。这些讯息

voie deux serviteurs du *yamen*. L'opinion de l'Américain est que le temple de Confucius ressemble à tous les autres temples chinois. Il est loin d'être le plus grand. Mais "il y a un un certain air de respectabilité, une certaine atmosphère héritée du passé qui font impression".[57] Sa description est très sommaire. Elle note cependant que dans la petite salle qui contient de nombreuses stèles, à l'arrière de la salle principale, les 120 stèles représentant la vie de Confucius sont illisibles tant on a fait d'estampages. Heureusement, quelques uns des dessins originaux ont été restaurés et il est désormais interdit de pratiquer des estampages. L'état général de conservation du bâtiment principal lui semble satisfaisant. Il ne parle que de tables diverses devant la statue de Confucius, pas de vases ni d'objets. Il rapporte que le "prince Kong", chef de la famille, vient accomplir le rituel quatre fois par an. Deux fois par an seulement, à la deuxième et à la huitième lune, on exécute le rituel compliqué en entier. Dans les autres occasions, la forme du rituel n'est pas aussi complète.[58] Lors de la visite au tombeau, il remarque la présence de nombreux arbres à fleurs qu'il ne connaît pas. Ses guides lui disent qu'ils poussent dans la région, mais sont plus abondants dans le cimetière qu'ailleurs. Lorsqu'il se rend ensuite au tombeau de Mencius à Zouxian, il le trouve dans un complet abandon. Il a beaucoup de peine à se faire indiquer le bon tumulus. Il n'y a pas de mur d'enceinte et les paysans d'alentour y viennent ramasser l'herbe et le bois, sans aucun souci des tombes.[59] Quatre photos prises par l'auteur ornent le récit: la tombe de Confucius, celle de Mencius (qui ne semble pas en si mauvais état), les piliers de marbre du temple de Confucius et l'allée d'arbres conduisant à sa tombe.

Toutefois, dans cette période où les voyages européens à l'intérieur de la Chine deviennent chose banale, sinon vraiment aisée, une visite à Qufu mérite une attention spéciale, celle qu'effectue en 1907 le sinologue français Édouard Chavannes (1865-1918), accompagné du jeune sinologue russe Vassili MichaelovicAlexeev (1881-1951). Il s'agit en effet de la première exploration archéologique méthodique pratiquée par des savants étrangers.

Chavannes a alors 41 ans, il est professeur au Collège de France 法兰西公学院教授 , membre de l'Institut 法兰西学院院士 . Il est probablement le plus remarquable sinologue européen de l'époque. Il a obtenu une mission du ministère français de l'Instruction publique 法国教育部 pour effectuer des recherches archéologiques en Chine du Nord. Un premier itinéraire, du 23 avril au 14 mai 1907, le conduit à travers le Nord-Est, en passant par Shenyang 沈阳 , jusqu'en Corée. C'est au cours de son second itinéraire, du 29 mai au 4 novembre 1907, à travers le Zhili, le Shandong, le Henan, le Shaanxi et le Shanxi, qu'il va visiter Qufu, après l'ascension du Taishan et avant de retourner à Jiaxiang 嘉祥 revoir les temples funéraires de la famille Wu 武氏祠 , qu'il avait étudiés lors de son premier séjour en Chine. Lors de sa première visite à Jiaxiang 嘉祥 , en janvier 1891, il était passé à Jining 济宁 , mais ne s'était pas rendu à Qufu, ni d'ailleurs au Taishan 泰山 .

Alexeev a 26 ans. Après ses études à la Faculté orientale de Saint Pétersbourg, il a effectué un séjour d'études en Europe occidentale, au cours duquel il a suivi les cours de Chavannes à Paris. Depuis l'automne 1906, il séjourne à Pékin pour préparer sa thèse. C'est là qu'il rencontre Chavannes par hasard, sur la muraille de la ville et, apprenant son projet de voyage, lui demande de l'accompagner. Le sinologue français l'accepte volontiers. Le jeune Russe parle très bien chinois, tandis que Chavannes, qui ignore les tons, arrive difficilement à se faire comprendre. Alexeev rassemble avec passion l'épigraphie "quotidienne"et les images de Nouvel An 年画 en vue de ses propres travaux sur la religion et les coutumes populaires. Le sujet intéresse Chavannes et complète ses investigations personnelles, d'autant qu'Alexeev a acquis déjà une certaine compétence pour interpréter ces textes et cette iconographie ignorés des livres et des lettrés chinois.

L'objet du voyage de Chavannes était l'étude de la sculpture, des sépultures et de la religion anciennes. Qufu n'était pas prévu dans son plan scientifique initial. Cette visite est marginale par rapport à son but

无疑源自当时陪同他的向导。在记载中，他没有提及曲阜的其他地方，但记录了某天在一处废弃宫殿和泉林子石柱旧址的所见所闻。他还去了泰山，在作品中重现了这处朝圣之地的宏观景象。[55]

在一本上海杂志中，美国传教士查理·阿尔弗莱德·斯坦利·朱诺（Charles Alfred Stanley Junior）发表了一篇其于 1905 年 4 月在泰山和曲阜的游记。[56] 他是一位出生于中国的传教士的孩子，精通汉语。他暂住在庞庄，庞庄位于山东的西北部。他与一名同事一起，在条件恶劣的道路上，坐着小推车出行。到达驿站时，他会见了当地知县，请求参观孔庙及孔子墓，并希望能安排一名陪同向导。知县指派了两名衙役陪同其前往。这位美国传教士认为，孔庙和其他中国的庙宇相比并无不同，亦不是最大的庙宇。但是，“庙宇中弥漫着某种庄重肃穆的气氛，某种源自过去的历史气息，让人印象深刻”。[57] 他对于庙宇的描述十分简洁。记录中指出，在主厅之后的小厅堂里，有许多石碑。其中记载了孔子生平的 120 个石碑已经模糊不清，无法辨认，不可进行拓印。幸运的是，有些原始图画已被修复，但是禁止进行拓印。据其描述，庙宇的主厅保存得非常完好。他只提到了孔子塑像前的各式桌子，没有花瓶，也没有其他物件摆设。他指出，孔氏家族的领导者“孔氏殿下”每年四次来孔庙举行祭拜仪式。一年仅有两次，即二月和八月时，他们会完整地举行复杂的典礼仪式。除此之外，其他仪式的形式都不完整。[58] 当他参观墓址时，注意到许多他不认识的开花树种。据向导解说，这种树木在当地普遍生长，但在墓穴中比其他地方更为茂盛。参观邹县的孟庙时，他认为那里则是一片荒凉，很难辨认正确的孟子墓所在。没有围墙，村民们并无顾忌，肆意践踏墓穴周围的草地，砍伐树木。[59] 作者拍摄了四张照片加以描述：孔子墓，孟子墓（照片上看起来保存状况并非太糟），孔庙的大理石柱及通往其墓穴的林荫小道。

此段期间，欧洲游客来中国旅游变得非常普遍容易。其中一段曲阜游历格外值得关注，即 1907 年法国的汉学家沙畹（E. Chavannes，1865—1918）与年轻的俄国汉学家阿列克谢耶夫（V. M. Aleksee，1881—1951）一起完成的曲阜之行。实际上，这是历史上国外专家学者组织的首次系统性的考古勘察。

沙畹当时 41 岁，任职法兰西公学院教授，是法兰西学院院士。他可能是当时欧洲最著名的汉学家。法国教育部命其前往中国北部进行考古勘察研究。1907 年 4 月 23 日至 5 月 14 日期间，他完成了第一次游历，穿越了中国东北部，经过沈阳，直抵朝鲜。1907 年 5 月 29 日至 11 月 4 日期间，他进行了第二次游历，途经直隶（今河北省）、山东、河南、陕西、山西，攀爬泰山之后，他参观了曲阜，而后返回嘉祥，拜访了他第一次游历中国时勘察过的武氏祠。1891 年 1 月，他第一次抵达嘉祥时，曾经路过济宁，但并未前往曲阜，亦没有去过泰山。

principal. Il n'en a publié qu'un très bref récit, qui figure dans le texte d'une conférence donnée le 27 mars 1908 au Comité de l'Asie française.[60] En revanche, il s'est chargé d'écrire le chapitre sur Qufu et Zouxian (et aussi celui sur Taian et le Taishan) pour la deuxième édition du guide touristique Madrolle *Chine du Nord, Corée*, parue en 1911.[61] Le récit très sobre de Chavannes est heureusement complété par le journal de voyage tenu par Alexeev, un texte très riche et très vivant. Il a été publié en russe en 1957. Ne lisant pas le russe, j'ai utilisé la traduction allemande, ornée de nombreuses photographies rapportées par l'auteur.[62]

Accompagnés d'un estampeur et d'un photographe chinois, ainsi que d'un domestique chinois, les deux sinologues quittent Pékin. Ils rejoignent Tianjin en train le 30 mai. Là, ils louent une jonque et suivent le Grand Canal. À Yangliuqing 杨柳青 , ils visitent les ateliers de fabrication des images de Nouvel An et en achètent d'énormes quantités. Leurs arrêts sont très fréquents, pour explorer temples et marchés. À Dezhou 德州 , ils louent une charrette pour gagner Jinan 济南 . C'est affreusement inconfortable, la chaleur est accablante. À Jinan, le gouverneur du Shandong les fait chercher dans leur auberge pour les loger au *yamen*. Il leur fait rencontrer les meilleurs lettrés de la ville. Alexeev est invité à leur faire une conférence. Le gouverneur recommande aux voyageurs d'aller voir à Weixian 潍县 la remarquable collection d'antiquités de la famille Zhang 张 , pour laquelle il leur donne une lettre d'introduction. Chavannes et Alexeev y vont en train, sont chaleureusement accueillis et photographient les pièces les plus remarquables. Ils repartent de Jinan le 14 juin en charrette. Le 18, ils sont à Taian 泰安 . Après l'ascension du Taishan, ils repartent le 25 juin en brouette, faute d'avoir pu trouver une charrette. Mais, ne pouvant supporter de voir peiner un homme à les transporter, ils font la route à pied par une canicule épuisante. La rivière Wen 汶河 est complètement asséchée.

De ce dernier trajet, Chavannes conserve un souvenir pénible. Il avertit les touristes : de Taian à Qufu, "il n'y a pas de route de voiture; il faut donc, soit aller à cheval, soit, si on ne trouve pas à louer de chevaux à T'ai-ngan-fou 泰安 , avoir recours à la brouette, mode de transport lent et incommode".[63] Sur le logement en route, il ajoute: "l'auberge est fort misérable et, si on n'a pas pris la précaution de se munir d'un lit portatif, on devra coucher sur la terre battue recouverte d'une natte crasseuse".[64] "Terre âpre et rocheuse… région austère", écrit-il encore.[65] "Que des pierres, des pierres… Toujours le même spectacle: du sorgho, du sorgho", renchérit Alexeev.[66] On est loin du paysage riant dépeint trente ou quarante ans plu tôt par les voyageurs anglais : en dehors des sanctuaires, les arbres semblent disparus et les conditions de vie des habitants plus dures.

Peu avant Qufu où ils parviennent le 26 juin 1907, les deux voyageurs visitent l'Académie de la Zhu et de la Si 洙泗书院 , en payant un pourboire au portier. À l'interieur, écrit Alexeev, "c'est sale et vide". Dans de grands bâtiments d'habitation récents, il y a du foin par terre et de la lessive qui sèche sur les dalles de pierre. Devant pousse un arbre gigantesque. Les voyageurs traversent ensuite la rivière Si 泗水 , qui a juste assez d'eau pour que le jeune Russe y prenne un bain. Il parvient à convaincre Chavannes de remettre au lendemain la visite au tombeau de Confucius.

À l'auberge, on leur sert des mets végétariens 素菜 car toute la ville jeûne pour supplier le Roi Dragon 龙王 d'envoyer la pluie. Alexeev observe et commente les processions, qu'il suit à travers la ville. Trois jours plus tard, la pluie commence à tomber, quand ils rentrent du tombeau de Shaohao 少昊 . Les tambours des villages voisins redoublent :" Ça y est", dit Chavannes.[67] Dans leurs échanges avec la population locale, ils n'ont aucun contact avec la famille Kong, ne songent pas à lui remettre leur carte ni à visiter leur résidence 孔府 . Ils se présentent seulement au jeune sous-préfet, originaire de Pékin, titulaire de la licence 举人 , qui les accueille avec beaucoup d'amitié et a avec eux plusieurs longs entretiens sur les problèmes culturels et politiques de la Chine dont il est très préoccupé. À leur départ, il fait cadeau aux deux sinologues d'une très

阿列克谢耶夫当时 26 岁，结束其在圣彼得堡东方学院的学习之后，他前往西欧进行短暂进修，听取了沙畹那当时在巴黎所开设的课程。从 1906 年秋天起，他暂住北京，为论文做准备。他在长城偶遇沙畹，在得知其游历计划后，要求与其一起同行。沙畹欣然应允。年轻的阿列克谢耶夫中文口语水平极佳，而沙畹则无法辨认汉语声调，很难与当地人进行沟通交流。阿列克谢耶夫热衷于收集中国的“日常”碑铭作及年画，旨在研究民间宗教与风俗习惯。他的研究主题引起了沙畹的极大兴趣，丰富了他的个人研究，况且阿列克谢耶夫已具备某些被中国书籍及文人所忽视的文字与肖像的解读能力。

沙畹的游历目的是研究中国的古代雕塑、墓穴及宗教。曲阜并不在他最初计划的学术参观之列。因此，此次游历与其主要目标相比，略显不值一提。他仅仅在 1908 年 3 月 27 日举办的亚洲—法国委员会议上发表过一篇非常简短的叙述文章。[60] 但是与此同时，他负责为马特罗列（Madrolle）1911 年第二次出版的旅行手册《中国北方，朝鲜》撰写关于曲阜与邹县（以及泰安和泰山）的章节。[61] 幸运的是，阿列克谢耶夫用一篇内容生动丰富的旅游日记完善了沙畹（E. Chavannes）极其简单乏味的描述。1957 年该书出版。因为我不擅俄语，只好参阅了德语译文版，内有作者拍摄的大量照片。[62]

在一名括画者、一位中国摄影师以及一名仆人的陪同下，两名汉学家离开了北京。1907 年 5 月 30 日，两人乘火车抵达天津。在当地，他们租用了一艘帆船，沿大运河而行。在杨柳青，他们参观了年画的制作作坊，购买了大量画作。前行途中，为参观庙宇和市场，他们停靠颇为频繁。在德州，他们租用了一辆小推车，以此前往济南。旅途颠簸不适，酷暑难耐。在济南，山东知府县令前往其所住驿站，接待他们前去衙门暂住。他为两位汉学家引见了当时城中最著名的文人雅士们。阿列克谢耶夫受邀为他们举办讲座。县令建议二位前往潍县，参观拜访著名的张氏家族的古代收藏，并为他们开具了介绍信。沙畹和阿列克谢耶夫乘坐火车前往，受到了热情款待，拍摄了大量著名藏品的照片。6 月 14 日，他们坐着推车离开济南。18 日，两人抵达泰安。攀登泰山之后，由于无法找寻到推车，他们于 6 月 25 日乘坐两轮车再次离开。但是他们不愿意看到车夫为此受苦，两人在极其炎热的天气下选择步行。当时汶河完全呈现干涸状态。

最后这次游历对于沙畹而言，苦不堪言。他告诫游客：“从泰安到曲阜，没有车路；因此需要骑马前行，如果无法在泰安租到马匹，只好求助于两轮手推车这种缓慢又不适的交通工具。”[63] 至于沿途住宿，他补充道：“客栈条件十分恶劣，如果我们没有提前准备好便携式床铺的话，我们就只好睡在肮脏的草席上面。”[64]“坚硬多石的地面……条件艰苦的地区。”他又写道。[65]“石头，还是石头……永远都是一副景象：高粱，高粱。”亚历弗补充道。[66] 与三四十年前英国传教士所描述的美好景象大相径庭：

bonne photo de la statue de Confucius, prise sans l'ombre des rideaux de soie jaune, et de photos des vases les plus célèbres du temple.[68]

Accompagnés par un serviteur du *yamen* du sous-préfet, Chavannes et Alexeev se rendent deux fois au temple de Confucius 孔庙 . Les dix vases de bronze donnés par Qianlong en 1771 ne sont alors pas exposés dans le temple 大成殿 , mais conservés chez le duc Kong. On voit seulement cinq vases qui passent pour dater del'an85 de notre ère, et d'autre part des brûle-parfums, deux chandeliers et deux vases à fleurs en métal émaillé datant de 1732. La description des édifices donnée par Chavannes est très méthodique et soucieuse d'exactitude, beaucoup plus complète et précise que toutes celles de ses prédécesseurs. Elle est accompagnée par la reproduction d'un plan chinois du sanctuaire.[69] Alexeev ajoute que les mauvaises herbes envahissent les cours et qu'il règne une affreuse puanteur à l'intérieur du grand temple à cause de la fiente des oiseaux qui y nichent. Les stèles qui portent la généalogie de Confucius sont en si mauvais état qu'on les a recouvertes d'une enveloppe.[70] Chavannes fait prendre de nombreuses photos, en distribuant des pourboires d'un air mécontent.[71] Dans la partie Sud-Est de l'enceinte du sanctuaire, un bâtiment neuf de style étranger abrite une école moderne. L'intérieur est "vide et sale". C'est la période des vacances, admet Alexeev. Aux murs, on voit des cartes de type européen et des tableaux noirs: "la Chine Nouvelle pénètre l'ancienne jusque dans son cœur", ironise le jeune homme. À la vérité, il est plus enthousiasmé par la boutique d'images du Nouvel An qu'il découvre juste à côté du temple.[72] La description archéologique de Chavannes mentionne des cérémonies avec danses et musique deux fois par an seulement.[73] Il semble bien que l'entretien et la vitalité du sanctuaire soient alors en déclin par rapport à la situation vingt ans plus tôt.

Au temple de Confucius, "imposant et majestueux", Chavannes préfère le tombeau, "autre lieu de pèlerinage, non moins sacré aux yeux des lettrés", qu'il dépeint ainsi : "dans un bois aux épais ombrages où l'on accède par une avenue bordée de statues en pierre d'hommes et d'animaux, le plus grand homme de la Chine est enseveli et sa sépulture est d'une rigoureuse simplicité; derrière un brûle-parfum et un autel de pierre se dresse, devant le tumulus, une stèle de dimension moyenne sur laquelle on lit 'Tombe du roi parfait, absolument saint, propagateur de la civilisation'".[74] Sa description archéologique précise les noms des édifices, leur fonction, leur date ainsi que celle des stèles les plus remarquables.[75]Alexeev rapporte que Chavannes et lui ont l'idée qu'il faudrait fouiller la tombe de Confucius pour tirer au clair beaucoup d'énigmes du personnage, mais que les habitants ne l'accepteraient sans doute pas.[76]

La notice de Chavannes sur Qufu comporte une description détaillée du temple de Yan Hui 颜庙 .[77] Pourtant, il n'en parle pas dans sa conférence et Alexeev ne mentionne pas cette visite. En revanche, les deux sinologues se sont assurément rendus au temple du duc de Zhou 周公庙 et au tombeau de Shaohao 少昊陵 , où ils ont vu des offrandes et où Chavannes s'est précipité sur les inscriptions[78], bien que sa notice ne mentionne que très brièvement ces deux sanctuaires.[79] Après Qufu, les deux voyageurs sont allés à Zouxian 邹县 , mais sans visiter le tombeau de Mencius, qui est mentionné sans autre commentaire dans la notice de Chavannes. Alexeev déclare que le temple de Mencius est dans un état lamentable, avec de l'herbe partout, des excréments d'oiseaux, des déchets, des cadavres d'animaux qui jonchent le sol, dans une odeur pestilentielle. Il relève quand même beaucoup d'inscriptions mongoles intéressantes. Chavannes observe que " le parc ombreux serait un séjour délicieux si les cadavres des corbeaux crevés qui jonchent le sol n'exhalaient une odeur insupportable".[80]

Pendant leur séjour à Qufu, Chavannes et Alexeev voient apparaître à l'auberge un Japonais, qui voyage à pied, au grand étonnement des Chinois, suivi par un serviteur qui porte son bagage. Il semble chercher un hébergement, mais disparaît très vite, si bien que tous le prennent pour un espion.[81] Après les deux sinologues, les voyageurs de toutes nationalités se succèdent à un rythme plus soutenu jusqu'à la Révolution

庙宇之外，树木好像都消失了，居民的生活条件也十分恶劣。

1907年6月26日抵达曲阜前不久，给了看门人一笔小费，两人一道参观了洙泗书院。据阿列克谢耶夫描述，里面“肮脏而且空旷”。在附近的高大的居民住所里，地上摆放着草垛，石盘上晾晒着衣物。前面有一棵参天大树。他们穿越了泗水，水量丰沛，年轻的俄国汉学家在河里洗了个澡。他成功劝说沙畹次日一起去参观孔子墓。

在驿站，他们吃素菜，因为整个县城都在斋戒向龙王求雨。阿列克谢耶夫观察并解释了祭祀的队列，并跟随队列穿过了这个县城。三天后，当他们从少昊陵返回时，开始下雨了。邻村的鼓声更迭起伏，“终于到了！”沙畹（Chavannes）说道。[67] 他们在与当地民众交流时，完全没有和孔氏家族的人接触，没有想过向孔公递上名帖，或是去孔府拜访。他们只是前去见了年轻的知县（北京人，是位举人）。知县友好地接待了他们，并就他特别关心的中国文化和政治问题与他们进行了多次长时间的会谈。在他们离开时，知县还将一张孔子塑像的照片和孔庙内最著名的花瓶照片赠予两位汉学家。照片上的孔子像没有被黄丝帷幔的阴影覆盖住。[68]

沙畹和阿列克谢耶夫在一个曲阜衙役的陪同下，两次参观孔庙。他们参观时，1771年乾隆御赐的十个铜制花瓶没有陈列在大成殿，而是由孔公保管。大成殿内只看到五个公元85年制造的花瓶，还有一些香炉、两个烛台和两个1732年的搪瓷花瓶。沙畹对建筑物的描述非常有条理和精确，比前几位的描述都要完整和精确。他还重新绘制了孔庙的中文平面图。[69] 阿列克谢耶夫补充提到，孔庙的庭院中杂草丛生，殿内由于鸟儿筑巢产生的粪便，散发着阵阵恶臭。刻有孔子家谱的石碑状态糟糕，其上已经覆了一保护层。[70] 沙畹让人拍了很多张照片，并且不甚高兴地给了小费。[71] 在孔庙围墙的东南角，有一幢外国风格的新楼，里面是一所现代的学校。其内部“又空又脏”。阿列克谢耶夫坦言，当时正值假期。学校墙面上，我们看到欧洲风格的画作和黑板，“新中国渗透进了旧中国的心脏。”他讥讽道。实际上，更让他兴奋的是孔庙旁边的年画店。[72] 沙畹在他考古研究里提到一年两次的载歌载舞的祭孔大典仪式。[73] 孔庙的维护和活跃度相比二十年前呈下降趋势。

相比“庄严雄伟”的孔庙，沙畹更欣赏墓园孔林——“另一个朝圣地，在文人眼中同样神圣”，他是这样描述的：“我们穿过一条两旁都是人和动物石像的林荫道，进入绿荫浓密的树林中。中国最伟大的人埋葬于此，他的坟墓却异常简朴；坟头前的香炉和石质骨灰瓮后面，有一块中等大小的石碑，上刻‘大成至圣文宣王墓’。”[74] 他考古研究里详细记录了孔林里建筑的名称、作用、建造年月，还有孔林里的著名石碑。[75] 阿列克谢耶夫谈到，他和沙畹觉得应该挖掘孔子墓，从而解答很多人类未知的谜团，但是当地居民肯定不会同意。[76]

de 1911. Les quelques récits publiés ont moins d'intérêt documentaire.[82]

Ces témoignages européens égrenés dans le temps sur le site de Qufu n'apportent évidemment aucune nouveauté par rapport aux sources chinoises sur la connaissance de l'architecture, de l'épigraphie ou de l'iconographie des monuments. En revanche, ils donnent des renseignements utiles sur l'état de conservation, puis de dégradation progressive des sanctuaires. La restauration a été immédiate après le passage des Taiping et des Nian. Mais après les troubles des Boxeurs, l'entretien semble beaucoup plus négligent. L'appauvrissement général de la région paraît aussi évident, et les sanctuaires en souffrent autant que la population locale, qui confie sa misère à Alexeev dans la cour de l'auberge. On relève aussi qu'à partir de 1905, c'est au sous-préfet et non plus à la famille Kong qu'on s'adresse pour visiter les sanctuaires. Le rôle de la famille Kong s'efface tout à fait pour les visiteurs. Il en va de même pour les descendants de Mencius à Zouxian. Ce fait correspond avec un net relâchement dans l'entretien des monuments. Cela semblerait indiquer que les ressources de ces familles sont en déclin, ainsi que leur pouvoir local.

Très frappante aussi dans tous ces récits est l'absence totale de visiteurs chinois, alors que les pèlerins se pressent en foule au Taishan, même en période troublée. À Qufu, les voyageurs européens sont toujours suivis par une nombreuse foule de curieux dans tous leurs déplacements, mais la population se montre tout à fait accueillante et prête à bavarder et questionner.

En 1911, malgré le chemin de fer jusqu'à Jinan, l'excursion à Qufu reste encore un exploit sportif pour voyageurs jeunes et en bonne santé. Cependant, au fil des années, les visiteurs européens, beaucoup plus que les missionnaires américains qui s'y aventurent davantage par curiosité exotique et paradoxale, ont construit l'image d'un pèlerinage aux sources de l'histoire et de la civilisation chinoise. Devant la majesté des sanctuaires, par une sorte de transfert, la formation classique gréco-latine qui les imprègne les conduit tout naturellement à inscrire Qufu parmi les hauts lieux de la culture universelle et de la vie de l'esprit.

---

1. L'évangélisation du Shandong avait débuté en 1636, avec le séjour du jésuite Nicolas Longobardi à Jinan 济南, où il avait converti quelques lauréats de l'examen de licence 乡试. La mission avait été continuée en 1650 par des franciscains espagnols, qui s'y maintinrent jusqu'en 1797. Depuis la création d'un évêché à Pékin en 1690, la province du Shandong dépendait de ce diocèse. Après la mort du dernier Espagnol, la chrétienté du Shandong n'eut plus de missionnaire étranger permanent jusqu'en 1839. À cette date, en conséquence du retour des jésuites en Chine, le Saint-Siège décida de redistribuer la responsabilité des missions entre les différentes congrégations religieuses en donnant à chacune un terrain exclusif, pour éviter les querelles. La région du Shandong fut alors séparée du diocèse de Pékin et constituée en vicariat apostolique confié aux franciscains italiens. Il y eut d'abord deux missionnaires seulement, résidant à Jinan, dont l'évêque. Les troubles récurrents les tenaient enfermés dans la ville : en 1861, le P. Molino avait été tué par les Taiping et les attaques de bandits étaient incessantes. En 1862, un troisième missionnaire fut installé à Zhifu 芝罘, auprès de la communauté étrangère.

2. Sur la vie et les travaux de Joseph Amiot: Yves Lenoir, Nicolas Standaertdir., *Les danses rituelles chinoises d'après Joseph-Marie Amiot*, Bruxelles/Namur,

沙畹对曲阜的文字记载中包含了对颜庙的细致描述。[77] 然而，他没有在演讲时提起这一段，阿克谢列耶夫也没有提到参观颜庙的故事。然而，两位汉学家去过周公庙和少昊陵，他们在这里看到了祭品，沙畹则急着去看碑文[78]，尽管他的文字记载中只对这两个圣地做简单介绍。[79] 参观完曲阜，沙畹的记载中提到两位汉学家前往邹县，但却没有做任何评论，也没有去参观孟子墓。阿列克谢耶夫称，孟子庙的情况非常糟糕，野草遍地丛生，鸟类的粪便、垃圾、动物的尸体遍地都是，像是要发生瘟疫的样子。他还抄录了一些有趣的蒙古语碑刻。沙畹说，"如果不是遍地都是的乌鸦尸体而发出令人难以忍受的气味，那么这个小花园会是个很好的驻足之地"。[80]

沙畹和阿列克谢耶夫在曲阜逗留期间，在驿站中见到过一个徒步旅行的日本人，后面跟着一个提行李的随从，这让中国人非常吃惊。日本人像是在寻找住宿，却很快消失了，以至于所有人都把他当成了间谍。[81] 在两位汉学家之后，来自各个国家的游客相继来到曲阜旅游，一直到 1911 年的辛亥革命。这些旅客发表的几篇文章的文献价值就不是很大了。[82]

相比中国在建筑、碑铭学或古迹肖像学方面的资料，这些欧洲人从前在曲阜的零散见闻显然没有任何新意。然而，这些见闻却为我们了解圣庙的保护情况及损毁程度提供了有用信息。太平天国运动和捻军起义之后，圣庙很快就得到修复。然而，义和团起义之后，保护工作似乎大不如前了。曲阜的总体贫困也更明显，圣庙也难逃此劫，人们在驿站的庭院中向阿列克谢耶夫吐露了他们所遭受的的苦难。我们也注意到，从 1905 年起，参观圣庙要与曲阜知县联系，而非与孔氏家族联系。对游客而言，孔氏家族的角色已被完全抹去。邹县孟子的后人也同样如此。这就解释了为何古迹的维护会完全懈怠下来，似乎也说明了这些家族的财富在减少，在当地的权力在下降。

让我深感震惊的也包括：所有的文字记载中，对中国游客只字不提。此时中国的朝圣者们正成群结队前往泰山，即使在动乱时期也是如此。在曲阜，欧洲游客们无论走到哪里，都会尾随一群好奇的当地人。但当地民众完全是欢迎的态度，并随时准备好与他们交谈、回答他们的问题。1911 年，尽管铁路已直达济南，身强力壮的年轻游客仍然会将去曲阜旅行当成一项体育运动。随着时间的推移，来曲阜的欧洲游客要比美国传教士多得多，他们更多是带着对异国的奇特好奇心来曲阜探险，并建立起来曲阜旅游是朝圣中国历史文明的这样一种形象。在庄严的神庙前，在希腊 - 拉丁古典教育中浸淫已久的欧洲游客，以一种移情的方式，很自然地将曲阜列入了世界文化圣地和精神之旅的行列中。

1. 山东的福音传教始于 1636 年，是耶稣会会士龙华民（Nicolas Longobardi）在济南逗留期间开展的。他成功地让几位乡试举人皈依天主教。之后，1650 年，几位西班牙方济各会修士接替了他的工作，直至 1797 年。自从主教府于 1690 年在北京设立之后，山东就隶属于这片主教管区。最后一位西班牙传教士死后，一直到 1839 年，山东的基督教社团就一直缺少常驻的外国传教士。当时，由于耶稣会会士重返中国，圣座（Saint-Siège）就决定将职责重新分配给各个宗教修会，给每个修会划分一块专属的地区，以避免发生争执。山东也就脱离了北京的主教管区，作为宗座代牧区移交给意大利方济各会修士管理。最初只有两名居住在济南的传教士，其中一人是主教。循环往复的动乱把传教士们困在了城市里：1861 年，P. Molino 被太平天国起义军杀死，匪徒的攻击从未停止。1862 年，第三位传教士定居芝罘，住在外国人修会附近。

2. 钱德明（Joseph Amiot）的生活经历和作品：Yves Lenoir，钟鸣旦（Nicolas Standaert）. 钱德明对中国礼仪舞蹈的研究（*Les danses rituelles chinoises d'après Joseph-Marie Amiot*）. 布鲁塞尔 / 那慕尔（Namur）：那慕尔大学出版社，Lessius 出版社（Éditions Lessius），2005.

3. 纪尧姆·鲍狄埃（Guillaume Pauthier）. 现代中国（*Chine ou description historique, géographique et littéraire de ce vaste empire, d'après les documents chinois*）. 巴黎：Firmin Didot 出版社，1837：120-185.

4. 同上，183 页。1837 年，鲍狄埃也出版了《大学》的翻译版，并于 1840 年出版《四书》的翻译版。

5. N.B. Dennys (ed.). Notes and Queries on China and Japan. Hongkong：Charles A. Saint, 1867(4): 41.

6. 我在此感谢狄瑞景（Régine Thiriez）提醒我注意这篇文章。文章出现在第 583 期的《北华捷报》（*North China Herald*）上，出版于 1861 年 9 月 22 日，155 页。这篇日志还占据了这一期报纸“增刊”的一整页。

7. 李希霍芬（Ferdinand von Richthofen）. 中国：我的旅行成果和基于旅行的研究（*China: Ergebnisse eigener Reisen und darauf gegründeter Studien*）. 柏林：Reimer，1877—1912 年，5 卷。关于山东的一章出现在第 2 卷，1881：173-266.

8. 福威勒（A.A. Fauvel）. 中国山东省：地理和自然历史（*La province chinoise du Chan-toung: géographie et histoire naturelle*）. 布鲁塞尔：Imprimerie Polleunis et Centerick 出版社，1892：6-8，93-98. 这项研究分为历史和贸易数据两部分，是赫德爵士（Sir Robert Hart）命令两位海关职员分别撰写的，希望出版后能增加海关收入。但他最终放弃了这个计划。只有被赫德爵士于 1884 年因中法战争而解职的福威勒通过自己的方式出版了手稿。

9. 这些传记类信息源自法思远（Robert C.Forsyth）对韦廉臣的注解：中国圣省山东（The Sacred Province of China in some of its Aspects）. 上海：基督文学社，1912：220-222. 韦廉臣是当时主要的耶稣会传教士。他用中文编写了流传度极高的几本书，如《格物探原》（*Natural Theology*）和《基督实录》（*Life of Christ*）。他致力于推广高质量的通用知识和接触精英人士，于 1877 年联合中国的耶稣会会士，共同创立了“学校和教科书委员会”（School and Textbooks Committee）并担任会长。1890 年，他成为中国教育协会（Educational Association of China）成员。1884 年，他设立了学校教科书委员会 (School and Textbooks Committee)，1887 年委员会更名为广学会，主要在科学知识领域起作用。他让卫理公会传教士林乐知 (Young Allen) 和德国传教士花之安（Faber）之间的合作更为牢固，后者出版了多本科学教育方面的中文书籍，并在韦廉臣死后负责管理广学会。广学会拥有一台现代打印机，向文人阶层刊发科学类书籍和图画书。

10. 关于这些宣传册广受欢迎的原因，李希霍芬在他的日记中提到了一位在济南的意大利籍基督教主教好心提供的有趣解释：大家之所以急着去买耶稣会的宣传册，是因为它的纸张价格要比制作中国鞋底所必需的纸张价格更低。

11. 韦廉臣除了向专家学者学会讲述他的几次旅行、并将其刊登在学会会刊上之外（这些我们在后文都会提到），还于 1870 年出版了关于他旅行所有内容的书籍。在天津大屠杀之后，英国政府考虑禁止英国传教士居住在开放口岸以外的地方，以避免发生事故，详见：Alexander Williamson. Journeys in North China, Manchuria, and Eastern Mongolia. London: Smith, 1870, two volumes.

12. 韦廉臣在两次讲座中都提到了这段从北京到芝罘途经曲阜的路程：1866 年 3 月 13 日和 4 月 16 日在上海，分别面向皇家亚洲学会的当地分部，并以“从北京到芝罘途经中国大运河、Yan-Chow-fou 等的摘要记录”（Notes of a journeyfromPeking to Chefoo via Grand Canal, Yan-Chow-fou etc）为标题发表于：Journal of the North China Branch of the Royal Asiatic Society, 1866(3): 1-25. 韦廉臣将这次旅行中的部分内容拿出来，补充了一些学识渊博的人和趣闻后出版，详见：Alexander Williamson, 1870, vol. I: 193-235.

13. 对曲阜的描述参见注释 12 中提到的文章的第 16-22 页，以及：Alexander Williamson, 1870, vol. I: 223-235.

14. Alexander Williamson, 1870, vol. I: 225.

15. Alexander Williamson, 1866: 19.

16. Alexander Williamson, 1870, vol. I: 225.

17. 马安爵士（John Markham）. 山东省摘要记录，从芝罘到 Tsiuhsien，孟子的县城（“Notes on the Shantung province, being a journey from Chefoo to Tsiuhsien, the city of Mencius”）. Journal of the North China Branch of the Royal Asiatic Society，第 6 卷，1869—1870 年（1871 年出版），1-29 页。另见：山东之旅摘要记录（“Notes on a journey through Shantung”）. 伦敦皇家地理学会会议记录（Proceedings of the Royal Geographical Society of London），第 14 卷，第二期，1869—1870：137-144. 其缩略版本，是 1870 年在伦敦演讲的文稿：山东之旅摘要记录（“Notes on a journey through Shantung”）. 伦敦皇家地理学会会议记录（Proceedings of the Royal Geographical Society of London），第 40 卷，1870 年：207-240. 此文与在上海发表的是同一篇，但其中包含一张很大的山东彩色折叠地图，上边标有他的旅行路线，最后添加了他自己的一些思考。马安爵士还向外事办公室（Foreign Office）递交了一份相关的官方报告。

18. 文字记载在第 2 卷，第 14 章，239-264 页。

19. Lo Hui-min，Helen Bryant. 英国在中国的外交和领事机构（British Diplomatic and Consular Establishments in China）. 台北：SMC 出版公司，1988，2：68.

20 E. Tiessen (ed.). Ferdinand Freiherr von Richthofen's Tagebücheraus China. 柏林：Reimer，1907, 1: 13-14.

21. 对泰山顶的 80 多个建筑的评述列表详见：Alexander Williamson, 1870, vol. II：252-258. 在 1867 年 3 月的另一次旅行中，他就已经登上过泰山，文字记载参见：Alexander Williamson, 1870, vol. I: 408-428.

22. John Markham, 1871: 21.

23. 同上，17-18. Alexander Williamson, 1870, vol. II：259-263.

24. John Markham, 1871: 20.

25. 同上，21.

26. Alexander Williamson, 1870, vol. II：263-264.

27. John Markham, 1871: 24.

28. 同上，25.

29. 同上，26-28.

30. 马安爵士（J. Markham）. 山东摘要记录（Notes on the Shantung province）. 伦敦皇家地理学会会刊（Journal of the Royal geographical Society of London），1870，40：227-228.

31. 马安爵士（J. Markham），“山东摘要记录”（Notes on the Shantung province），28-29 页。

32. Alexander Williamson, 1870, vol. I: X. 雕刻参见：vol. I: 228, 230.

33. 在皇家亚洲学会华北分会的要求下，测量于 1867 年 11 月至 12 月展开，报告发表在他的杂志上：内伊·伊莱亚斯（Ney Elias）. 黄河新航道探索报告（"Report of an exploration of the new course of the Yellow River”）. 皇家亚洲学会华北分会报告，1868，5：259-279.

34. 艾伯特奥古斯特·福威勒（A.A. Fauvel）. 中国的山东省（La province chinoise du Chan-tong）. 36 页。

35. 同上，第 74 页。Ferdinand von Richthofen. China. vol. I: 714；vol. II：179.

36. 弗里切（H. Frietsche），Geographische, magnetischeundhypsometrischeBestimmungenvon 27 imnordöstlichen China gelegenenOrten，圣彼得堡

Presses universitaires de Namur, Éditions Lessius, 2005.

3. G. Pauthier, *Chine ou description historique, géographique et littéraire de ce vaste empire, d'après les documents chinois*, Paris, Firmin Didot, 1837, pp. 120-185.

4. Id., p. 183. En 1837, Pauthier publiait aussi une traduction de *La Grande étude* 大学 et en 1840 une traduction des *Quatre livres* 四书 .

5. *Notes and Querieson China and Japan*, 30 avril 1867, p.41.

6. Je remercie Régine Thiriez d'avoir eu l'obligeance de me signaler cet article. Il figure dans le n°583 du *North China Herald*, daté du 28 septembre 1861, p. 155. LE récit occupe encore les deux pages d'une feuille de "Supplément" ajoutée à ce numéro.

7. Ferdinand von Richthofen, *China: Ergebnisse eigener Reisen und darauf gegründeter Studien* (Chine: résultats de mes voyages et des études fondées sur eux), Berlin, Reimer, 1877-1912, 5 volumes. Le chapitre sur le Shandong figure dans le volume 2, pp. 173-266, paru en 1882.

8. A.A. Fauvel, *La province chinoise du Chan-toung: géographie et histoire naturelle*, Bruxelles, Imprimerie Polleunis et Centerick, 1892, pp. 6-8, 93-98;. Cette étude, complétée par une partie historique et une partie commerciale et statistique rédigées par deux autres employés de la douane, avait été commandée par Sir Robert Hart en vue de la publication aux frais de la Douane d'un livre sur la province du Shandong. Mais il abandonna le projet. Seul Fauvel, que Hart avait obligé à démissionner en 1884 en raison de la guerre franco-chinoise, publia son manuscrit par ses propres moyens.

9. Ces éléments biographiques sont tirés de la notice sur Williamson dans Robert C. Forsyth, *Shantung. The Sacred Province of China in some of its Aspects*, Shanghai, Christian Literature Society, 1912, pp. 220-222. Williamson fut une figure majeure des missions protestantes de l'époque. Il écrivit en chinois plusieurs ouvrages très diffusés, dont *Natural Theology*, et *Life of Christ*. Très soucieux de diffuser des connaissances générales de bonne qualité et de toucher les élites, il fut le fondateur et secrétaire du School and TextbooksCommittee, créé en 1877 par l'effort conjoint des missions protestantes en Chine, et absorbé par l'Educational Association of China en 1890. En 1884, il fonda la Chinese Book and Tract Society, qui devint en 1887 la Society for the Diffusion of Christian and General Knowledgeamong the Chinese 广学会 , dont le rôle scientifique et intellectuel fut considérable. Il s'était assuré la coopération du missionnaire méthodiste Young Allen et du missionnaire allemand Faber, auteurs de nombreux ouvrages en chinois sur les sciences et l'éducation, qui dirigèrent la société après sa mort. La société possédait une imprimerie moderne et publiait des ouvrages scientifiques et des livres illustrés à l'intention de la classe lettrée.

10. Sur la faveur que connaissent ces brochures, Richthofen rapporte dans son journal une explication pittoresque que lui donne charitablement l'évêque catholique italien de Jinan: les acheteurs se précipitent car les brochures protestantes fournissent à moindre coût le papier nécessaire à la confection de la semelle des chaussures chinoises.

11. Outre des conférences sur plusieurs de ses voyages devant des sociétés savantes qui en ont diffusé le texte dans leur revue, comme on le verra plus loin, Williamson a publié un livre d'ensemble sur ses voyages, en 1870, au moment où, à la suite du massacre de Tianjin, le gouvernement anglais envisageait d'interdire à ses missionnaires de résider hors des ports ouverts, afin d'éviter les incidents : *Journeys in North China, Manchuria and EasternMongolia: withsomeaccount of Corea*, Londres, Smith, 1870, 2 vols.

12. Cet itinéraire de Pékin à Zhifu par Qufu est relaté par Williamson dans deux conférences données le 13 mars et le 16 avril 1866 à Shanghai, devant la section locale de la Royal Asiatic Society, et publiées sous le titre " Notes of a journeyfromPeking to Chefoo via Grand Canal, Yan-Chow-fou etc. ", *Journal of the North China Branch of the Royal Asiatic Society*, n°3 (December 1866), pp. 1-25. Le récit est partiellement repris, avec des ajouts érudits et pittoresques, dans le livre de Williamson, *Journeys in North China*, vol. 1, pp. 193-235.

13. La description de Qufu occupe les pages 16-22 de l'article mentionné note 12, et les pages 223-235 du volume 1 des *Journeys*.

14. A. WIlliamson, *Journeys*, vol. 1, p. 225.

15. A. Williamson, "Notes of a journey", p. 19

16. A. WIlliamson, *Journeys*, vol. 1, p.225.

17. John Markham, "Notes on the Shantung province, being a journeyfromChefoo to Tsiuhsien, the city of Mencius", *Journal of the North China Branch of the Royal Asiatic Society*, n°6, 1869-1870 (paru en 1871), pp. 1-29. Id., "Notes on a journeythrough Shantung", *Proceedings of the Royal Geographical Society of London*, vol. 14, n°2, (1869-1870), pp. 137-144: il s'agit d'une version abrégée, qui est le

科学学会，气象学索引，第3卷，第8期，1873年。这些结果被译为法语，参见：1867—1894年间在亚洲和欧洲开展的509个磁场观察，圣彼得堡，1897年。

37. Ferdinand von Richthofen. China. vol. Ⅱ：195.

38. 他在RichthofensTagebücher一书中描述了旅行路线，第1卷，146—211页。近期出版的李希霍芬（Richthofen）再版旅行日志（Entdeckungsreisen in China，1868—1872年，由Klaus Dietrich Petersen编辑，斯图加特，1984年）遗憾没有将他这次的山东之旅包含进去，只收录了他在1870至1872年间的旅行。

39. Ferdinand von Richthofen. China. vol. I: 707-708. 前面引用的书，98页。庞培勒（Raphaël Pumpelly）没有去山东，根据在中国的观察研究，他发表了：中国地质研究，蒙古和日本（Geological Researches in China, Mongolia and Japan）. Washington: Smithsonian institution, 1866.（Smithonian Contributions to Knowledge，第202卷）；穿越美国和亚洲（Across America and Asia）. 纽约，1870年。

40. Ferdinand von Richthofen. China. vol. Ⅱ：195, 255-257；同上，Schantung und seine Eingangspforte Kiautschou，柏林：Reimer，1898：143.

41. 艾约瑟（J. Edkins）. 参观孔子的城市（A visit to the city of Confucius）. 皇家亚洲学会华北分会会刊，第8卷，1874：79-92.

42. 同上，80.

43. 同上，80-82.

44. 同上，85.

45. 同上，82-83.

46. 同上，83-84.

47. 同上，86.

48. 同上，87-91.

49. 参见上方第8个脚注：他没有发表任何文章，福威勒（Fauvel）提到的手稿可能保留在海关的档案中，或与赫德爵士（Robert Hart）的手稿放在了一起。

50. 他出版了两本著作，但是我在巴黎没有找到：《山东》（Shantung），上海，1891年，里面包含曲阜之旅的所有文字记录；《乘苫子前往儒家圣地的旅行》（In a Mule Litter to the Tomb of Confucius），伦敦：J. Nisbet and Co，1896年，插入共计148页，是他曲阜之旅的文字记录。

51. 艾伯特—奥古斯特福威勒（A.A. Fauvel），《中国的山东省》（La province chinoise du Chantong），96页。

52. 年轻沙畹（E. Chavannes）的一封信函，1891年1月28日，保存在巴黎的外交部档案中，讲述了他刚在济宁的客栈碰到的这位德国领事的一次旅行。我（M. Bastid）和M.C. Bergère, J. Chesneaux一起发表了这封信函，《中国2》（La Chine 2），巴黎：Hatier，1972：43-44. 在扬州，这位德国领事拿到了招贴广告，号召他两天后赴死，当地政府对平息骚乱已经无能为力了：环境已经不像马卡姆（Markham）二十年前来的时候那么好了。

53. 海司（E. von Hesse-Wartegg）. Schantung und Deutsch-China. Von Kiautschou ins heilige Land von China und vomJangtsekiangnach Peking imJahre 1898. 莱比锡：Weber，1898：294.

54. 列顿（Litton）的报告发表于1902年的《英国议会文件》中；加内特（Garnett）的报告发表于1907年《英国议会文件》一号中国特刊中。这些文件并非保存在巴黎，因此我无法参阅它们。

55. 沃尔特·安兹（Walter Anz）. Eine Winterreise durch Schantungund das nördliche Kiang-su", Petermann's Mitteilungen. 1904，50：131-140.

56. 查理·阿尔弗莱德·斯坦利·朱诺（Charles Alfred Stanley Junior）. 泰山与孔子墓穴. 东亚期刊，1905，4（4）：301-309.

57. 同上，306.

58. 同上，307.

59. 同上，308-309.

60. 沙畹（E. Chavannes）. 满洲与中国北方考古之旅. 亚洲—法国委员会议报告，85号文件. 1908：135-142. 这份报告包含一份孔子墓穴照片

texte de la conférence donnée à Londres le 28 février 1870. Id., "Notes on a journeythrough Shantung", *Journal of the Royal geographical Society of London*, vol. 40, (1870), pp. 207-240 : ce texte est le même que celui paru à Shanghai, mais il comporte une grande carte dépliante en couleurs de la province, où est figuré l'itinéraire suivi, et quelques réflexions générales supplémentaires à la fin. Markham adressa aussi un rapport officiel circonstancié au Foreign Office.

18. Le récit est dans le volume 2, chapitre 14, pp.239-264.

19. Lo Hui-min, Helen Bryant, *British Diplomatic and Consular Establishments in China: 1793-1949*, Taipei, SMC Publishing Inc., 1988, vol. 2, p. 68.

20. Quand Richthofen arrive en Chine en septembre 1868, il s'arrête d'abord à Shanghai pour réunir l'information nécessaire à ses voyages d'exploration géologique, puis il passe une journée à Zhifu, le 21 septembre, pour consulter Williamson sur la Chine du Nord où ce dernier a beaucoup voyagé, et note dans son journal qu'"en peu de temps il a pu me donner plus de renseignements sur le pays que tous les étrangers de Shanghai réunis"; les cartes précises qu'il a dressées avec l'indication des mines et de l'extension des cultures agricoles lui semblent particulièrement intéressantes. *Ferdinand Freiherr von Richthofen'sTagebücheraus China*, édité par E. Tiessen, Berlin, Reimer, 1907, volume 1, pp. 13-14.

21. Williamson, *Journeys*, vol. 2, pp. 252-258, donne la liste commentée de plus de 80 édifices du sommet. Il a déjà fait l'ascension du Taishan au cours d'un autre voyage en mars 1867: le récit se trouve dans *Journeys*, vol. 1, pp. 408-438.

22. J. Markham, " Notes on the Shantung province ", p. 21.

23. Id., pp. 17-18. Williamson, *Journeys*, vol. 2, pp. 259-263

24. J. Markham, " Notes on the Shantung province ", p. 20.

25. Id., p. 21

26. Williamson, *Journeys*, vol. 2, pp. 263-264.

27. J. Markham, " Notes on the Shantung province ", p. 24.

28. Id., p.25.

29. Id., pp. 26-28.

30. J. Markham, "Notes on a journeythrough Shantung", *Journal of the Royal geographical Society of London*, pp. 227-228.

31. J. Markham, " Notes on the Shantung province ", pp. 28-29.

32. Williamson, *Journeys*, vol. 1, p. X. Les gravures sont vol.1, p. 228 et 230.

33. L'expédition effectuée en novembre-décembre 1867, à la demande de la China Branch de la Royal Asiatic Society à Shanghai, fait l'objet d'un rapport dans sa revue: Ney Elias, "Report of an exploration of the new course of the Yellow River", *Report of the North China Branch of the Royal Asiatic Society*, vol. 5, 1868, pp. 259-279.

34. A.A. Fauvel, *La province chinoise du Chan-toung*, p. 36.

35. Id., p.74. Richthofen, *China*, vol. 1, p. 714; vol. 2, p.179

36. H. Frietsche, *Geographische, magnetischeundhypsometrischeBestimmungen von 27 imnordöstlichen China gelegenenOrten*, Académie des sciences de Saint-Pétersbourg, Répertoire de météorologie, vol. 3, n°8, 1873. Ces résultats sont repris en français dans: Observations magnétiques sur 509 lieux faites en Asie et en Europe pendant la période de 1867-1894, Saint Pétersbourg, 1897.

37. Richthofen, *China*,vol. 2, p. 195.

38. Il décrit l'itinéraire dans *RichthofensTagebücher*, vol.1, pp.146-211. La récente réédition du journal de voyage de Richthofen (*Entdeckungsreisen in China, 1868-1872*, édités par Klaus Dietrich Petersen,Stuttgart, 1984) n'inclut malheureusement pas ce voyage au Shandong. Elle ne comporte que les voyages de 1870 et 1872.

39. Richthofen, *China*, vol. 1, p. 707-708. Fauvel, *op. cit.*, p.98. Pumpelly n'est pas allé au Shandong, sur ses observations en Chine, il a publié: *GeologicalResearches in China, Mongolia and Japan*, Washington, 1866 (*Smithonian Contributions to Knowledge*, n°202), et *Across America and Asia*, New York, 1870.

40. Richthofen, *China*, vol. 2, p. 195, 255-257; id., *Schantung und seine Eingangspforte Kiautschou*, Berlin, Reimer, 1898, p. 143.

41.J. Edkins, "A visit to the city of Confucius", *Journal of the North China Branch of the Royal Asiatic Society*, vol. 8, 1874, pp.79-92.

42. Id., p. 80.

43. Id., pp. 80-82.

44. Id., p.85.

45. Id., pp. 82-83.

46. Id., pp. 83-84.

及一张游历行程地图。在《通报》（1908 年，9 号刊，系列 2）中，他再次引用了该文章，并申明希望吸引更多的读者。他发表的游历任务学术报告《中国北方的考古之旅》（1909 年，卷 2）中，并没有关于曲阜的内容。

61. 关于曲阜与邹县的内容参见：马特罗列（Madrolle）. 中国北方与黄河河谷，朝鲜 . 第二版 . 巴黎：Hachette 出版社，1911：139-148. 第一版于 1904 年出版，其中仅有少量关于山东的内容

62. 阿列克谢耶夫（V. M. Aleksee）. 1907 年的中国(China im Jahre 1907: Ein Reisetagebuch). 由 S. Behrsing 翻 译；M.V. Bankovskaja, B.L. Riftin, Leipzig/Weimar, Gustav Kiepenheuer 合作发表《俄国汉学家亚历弗与他的中国行》，1989 年。

63. 马特罗列（Madrolle），1911：139.

64. 同上，140.

65. 沙畹（E. Chavannes)，1908：136.

66. 阿列克谢耶夫（V. M. Alekseev），China im Jahre 1907，139 页。

67. 同上，164.

68. 同上，149，153-155，152-164.

69. 马特罗列（Madrolle），《中国北方》（Chine du Nord），142-145 页。

70. 阿列克谢耶夫（V. M. Alekseev），1989：153.

71. 同上，157 页。沙畹（Chavannes）的文章里仅有一张曲阜的照片：孔子墓及其石碑。其他照片保存在法国巴黎吉美博物馆（Musée Guimet）的图书馆照片档案中。

72. 同上。

73. 马特罗列（Madrolle），1911：144.

74. 沙畹（E. Chavannes)，1908：137.

75. 马特罗列（Madrolle），1911：145-146.

76. 阿列克谢耶夫（V. M. Alekseev），1989：156.

77. 马特罗列（Madrolle），1911：145.

78. 阿列克谢耶夫（V. M. Alekseev），1989：156，164.

79. 马特罗列（Madrolle），1911：141.

80. 马特罗列（Madrolle），1911：148；阿列克谢耶夫（V. M. Alekseev），1989：167.

81. 阿列克谢耶夫（V. M. Alekseev），1989：162.

82. 比如，模勒氏（A.C. Moule）的旅行，《皇家亚洲学会华北分会会刊》，1912（43）.

47. Id., p. 86.

48. Id., pp. 87-91.

49. Voir plus haut note 8: il n'a rien publié, le manuscrit mentionné par Fauvel se trouve peut-être encore dans les archives de la Douane ou parmi celles de Robert Hart.

50. Ce personnage a publié deux ouvrages que je n'ai pas pu trouver à Paris: *Shantung*, Shanghai, 1891, qui contient des notes sur un voyage à Qufu; *In a mule litter to the tomb of Confucius*, Londres, J. Nisbet and Co, 1896, un livre illustré de 148 pages, qui est le récit de son voyage à Qufu.

51. A.A. Fauvel, *La province chinoise du Chan-tong*, p. 96.

52. Une lettre du jeune Chavannes, du 28 janvier 1891, conservée aux Archives du ministère des Affaires étrangères à Paris, raconte un des voyages du consul allemand qu'il vient de rencontre à l'auberge à Jining 济宁 . J'ai publié cette lettre dans M. Bastid, M.C. Bergère, J. Chesneaux, *La Chine 2*, Paris, Hatier, 1972, pp.43-44. À Yanzhou, le consul a été accueilli par des affiches appelant à le mettre à mort dans les deux jours, les autorités ont grand mal à calmer l'émeute : l'atmosphère n'est plus à la bienveillance rencontrée par Markham vingt ans plus tôt.

53. E. von Hesse-Wartegg, *Schantungund Deutsch-China. Von Kiautschouinsheilige Land von China undvomJangtsekiangnachPekingimJahre 1898*, Leipzig, Weber, 1898, 294 p.

54. Le rapport de Litton a été publié dans les *British ParliamentaryPapers en 1902*; Celui de Garnett est paru dans British ParliamentaryPapers, China n°1, 1907. Ces documents ne se trouvent pas à Paris, je n'ai pu les consulter.

55. Walter Anz, "EineWinterreisedurchSchantungunddasnördlicheKiang-su", Petermann'sMitteilungen, vol. 50, 1904, pp.131-140.

56. C. A. Stanley, Junior, "T'aishan and the Tomb of Confucius", The East of Asia Magazine, vol. 4, n°4, décembre 1905, pp. 301-309.

57. Id., p. 306.

58. Id., p. 307.

59. Id., pp. 308-309.

60. E. Chavannes, "Voyage archéologique dans la Mandchourie et dans la Chine septentrionale", Bulletin du Comité de l'Asie française, n°85, avril 1908, pp. 135-142. Cette publication comporte une photographie de la tombe de Confucius et une carte de l'itinéraire suivi. Chavannes a reproduit l'article tel quel dans le T'oung-Pao, série 2, n°9, 1908, pp. 503-529,en indiquant qu'il serait ainsi accessible à un plus grand nombre de lecteurs intéressés. La publication des résultats scientifiques de sa mission, intitulée Mission archéologique dans la Chine septentrionale, Paris, 1909, 2 volumes, ne comporte rien sur Qufu.

61. Madrolle, Chine du Nord et vallée du Fleuve Bleu, Corée, 2e édition mise à jour, Paris, Hachette, 1911 : sur Qufu et Zouxian, voir pp. 139-148. La première édition du guide datait de 1904, avec peu de renseignements sur le Shandong.

62. V. M. Alexeev, China imJahre 1907. EinReisetagebuch, traduit du russe par S. Behrsing, avec un essai "Le sinologue russe Alexeev et son voyage en Chine, par M.V. Bankovskaja et B.L. Riftin, Leipzig/Weimar, Gustav Kiepenheuer, 1989.

63. Madrolle, *Chine du Nord*, p. 139.

64. Id., p. 140.

65. E. Chavannes, "Voyage archéologique", p. 136.

66. V. M. Alekseev, China imJahre 1907, p. 139.

67. Id., p. 164.

68. Id., pp. 149, 153-155, 162-164.

69. Madrolle, *Chine du Nord*, pp. 142-145.

70. V. M. Alekseev, *China imJahre 1907*, p. 153.

71. Id., p. 157. L'article de Chavannes comporte une seule photo de Qufu: la tombe de Confucius avec sa stèle. D'autres photos sont conservées parmi les archives photographiques de la bibliothèque du Musée Guimet à Paris.

72. Id.

73. Madrolle, *Chine du Nord*, p. 144.

74. E. Chavannes, "Voyage archéologique", p. 137.

75. Madrolle, Chine du Nord, pp. 145-146.

76. V. M. Alekseev, China imJahre 1907, p. 156.

77. Madrolle, *Chine du Nord*, p. 145.

78. V. M. Alekseev, *China imJahre 1907*, pp. 156, 164.

79. Madrolle, *Chine du Nord*, p. 141.

80. Id., p.148 ; V. M. Alekseev, *China imJahre 1907*, p. 167.

81. V. M. Alekseev, *China imJahre 1907*, p. 162.

82. Par exemple le voyage de A.C. Moule, Journal of the North China Branch of the Royal Asiatic Society, vol. 43, 1912.

通过齐鲁文化的起源探讨汉语“革命”的概念

莱昂·汪德迈

“* 革命”一词，在现代意义上（本文中，笔者在这一词前加 * 时，即指现代意义上的革命。以此避免与以往意义上的革命产生任何混淆）是一个西方的政治概念，指“人民通过暴力手段推翻政治政权”。这一意义源于西方，仅始于 18 世纪。一开始是一个纯宇宙学术语，指天体绕其轨道完整运行一周。后转变为政治术语。汉语里，“革命”的本意是纯政治的，指“政权（朝代）更迭”，即此朝代被彼朝代所取代；相反地，这个政治概念，最初是指变更那个超越一切的万能力量——“上帝”授予的使命。后来词义又演化，因为万能的“上帝”遵循纯宇宙学中必然的规律，推动世界万物在五个阶段里往复轮转。其五个阶段的主导，称为“五元素（五行）”。这个概念属于中国哲学中的“阴阳五行”，解释了朝代因天命而进行的历史更迭。这种把历史归于天命的做法基于中华文化里特有的占卜科学（占卜学）。占卜学完全成型于殷代末期，当时一种编排好的六行图示（数字卦）已代替了甲骨裂纹（兆璺），数字卦写在占卜用的片状物（占卜片）上，预兆《易经》里的卦。这就是为何“革命”这一汉语里的宇宙学概念，会最初与周推翻殷有关。而谋划灭殷的后来的文王，被尊为《易经》中六行卦图的发明者。文王将伏羲的三行卦图（伏羲八卦）排列叠加，变为六行卦，用“数字卦”取代了“兆璺”。而实质上，文王仅仅是革新占卜术的一个推力。伏羲发明三行卦图的神话，和文王通过六行卦图对其做的发扬，实则皆由周朝人一手造出。因周人恶殷，故以此掩盖文王支持的蓍草占卜（占蓍）与殷代发明的龟甲占卜（卜龟）本质上的血缘关系。因此，数以万计的殷代的占卜片（殷时代占卜甲骨几万片）被历史彻底遗忘了四千年，直到 1890 年才开始重新被发现。

在汉语中，“革命”一词从 19 世纪末开始，才有了“通过群众暴力行为倾覆政权”的含义。这一含义由日本翻译家于日本明治时期从西方著作中引入，用来翻译“revolution”（后文中称为“* 革命”）[1] 一词在近代西方的含义，正如其汉语同义词“革命”（后文中称为“革命”）的新概念通常指朝代的倾覆。在西方，“革命”一词的概念出现得也相对较晚：直到 18 世纪才出现。值得注意的是，在西方语言和汉语中，该词从一个含义转变为第二个含义是互不干扰平行发生的，而含义转变的顺序则相反。

La Conception Chinoise du Geming aux Origines de la Culture Qi-Lu

Léon Vandermeersch

Le terme *geming au sens moderne (pour éviter toute confusion avec les sens anciens je l'écrit précédé de * tout au long du texte) est un concept politique occidental signifiant "renversement d'un régime politique par le peuple et dans la violence". Cette signification apparait en Occident que du XVIIIe siècle, et provient d'un détournement politique du sens premier du mot, le sens purement cosmologique de tour complet d'un astre sur son orbite. En chinois, le sens propre de geming est purement politique, à savoir le sens de «changement de mandat (dynastique)» rend légitime le renversement d'une dynastie par une autre ; mais inversement ce concept politique, d'abord compris comme celui d'un mandat décerné par une toute-puissance transcendante désignée comme Shangdi, a évolue en s'approfondissant par conversion de la toute-puissance du Shangdi en nécessité purement cosmologique du passage du cosmos d'une phase à une autre dans la succession des cinq phases de prédominance cosmique de chacun des cinq éléments(wuxing). Cette conception s'inscrit dans la philosophie chinoise du yingyangwuxing, qui explique les changements historiques de dynastie par des raisons cosmologiques. Cette cosmologisation de l'histoire est fondée sur la science divinatoire (zhanbuxue) propre à la culture chinoise, dont la complète formation s'achève à la fin de l'époque Yin par la substitution, sur les pièces divinatoires (占卜片), d' hexagrammes chiffrés (shuzigua 数字卦), préfigurant les hexagrammes du Yijing , aux configurations de craquelures augurales (zhaowen 兆璺). C'est pourquoi le concept cosmologique chinois de geming est rapporté originellement au renversement des Yin par les Zhou, fomenté à cette époque par le futur Wenwang 文王 , réputé inventeur des hexagrammes du Yijing par redoublement des trigrammes de Fuxi (伏羲八卦), mais en réalité simplement promoteur de la divination rénovée par shuzigua substitués aux zhaowen. Le mythe de l'invention des trigrammes par Fuxi et de leur perfectionnement en hexagrammes par Wenwang est une histoire inventée par les Zhou, pour occulter la filiation effective de la divination par l'achillée (zhanshi 占蓍), patronnée par Wenwang, à la divination par la tortue (bugui 卜龟), inventés par les Yin , que les Zhou détestaient. Si bien que des dizaines de milliers de pièces divinatoires d'époque Yin (殷时代占卜甲骨几万片) sont tombés dans l'oubli pendant quatre mille ans, avant d'être redécouvertes seulement à partir de 1890.

En chinois, le terme geming n'a pris la signification de renversement d'un régime politique par la violence populaire que depuis la fin du XIXe siècle. Cette signification a été introduite par les traducteurs japonais d'ouvrages occidentaux du début de l'ère Meiji pour traduire le concept occidental moderne de révolution (ci-après *geming [* 革命]) [1], comme sens nouveau du concept chinois homonyme (ci-après geming [革命]) classiquement appliqué aux renversements dynastiques. En Occident aussi le concept est relativement tardif : Il ne date que du XVIIIe siècle. Ce qui est remarquable, c'est que la modification de signification de ce mot, du premier sens au deuxième sens, est parallèle dans les langues occidentales et en chinois, mais en sens inverse, comme nous l'allons voir.

我们接下来会谈到这个问题。

在中国和西方概念之间，无论是中国思想中的“革命”，还是欧洲思想中的“*革命”，在第二个纯政治性的含义出现之前，平行论都在于指出其第一个含义是宇宙学的，涉及“一个循环的宇宙性动作”。[2] 其实，在汉语中，《易经》就谈到“天地革而四时成，汤武革命顺乎天而应乎人”。因此，“革命”的第一个含义指的是四季循环往复的天则，而“阴阳五行家”则将其理论化，形成了“五行相生相克”的理论。在西方，拉丁语的“révolutio”（欧洲语言中 revolution 这个词都来自于这个拉丁词）出现在 1190 年左右，同汉语一样指的是“循环的宇宙行为”，但此时在西方语言中指一个天体重新回到它所在轨道的起始点，这与“五行”这一纯中国的概念完全不相关。[1] 在欧洲，从 18 世纪思想家（法国启蒙时代的思想家们）之后“*革命”一词的含义才开始引申为“政治倾覆”。“*革命”的这第二个含义最初被运用于 17 世纪英国革命中，尤其是在 1688—1689 年英国二次革命——被称为“光荣革命”的时期，但只是以隐喻的方式。直到这个词被运用在 1789 年法国大革命，其词汇方面的隐喻才形成了一个新的概念，在政治倾覆的引申含义上，增加了“群众暴力”的含义；卡尔·马克思将这一概念进行了理论化。

回到汉语中“革命”一词古老的概念。从这个词的起源开始，其宇宙学意义就与“朝代倾覆”这一政治含义联系在一起。前文中我们也谈到过，根据宏观—微观—宇宙学感应原则，“革命”一词在《易经》中被运用于指成汤覆灭夏朝和周武王倾覆商朝（殷朝）。这一概念应该是于周朝初期出现在中国人思维中的。与此同时，宗教层面的“上帝”被形而上学的“天”所替代。“革命”一词建立在这一新的概念上，用来论证商周的朝代更迭不是宗教使然而是宇宙天命。先前夏商的朝代更迭，又对这一理论加入了其普遍性。这一研究用比宗教原因更有说服力的“科学”原因来解释周朝覆灭殷（商）朝这一事件，进而发展出了汉语中“革命”的概念。

“科学”原因？其实，如果认为朝代的变迁遵循着季节变换的准则，就是将偶然的无规律的历史事件归入了规律而客观的科学自然现象中。这种归纳法使得汉语语义中的特例历史事件有了普遍的自然宇宙规则（通常用“天命”这类宗教般的方式来解读）。这种归纳法与西方词汇的演变相反，西方词汇在解释历史必然事件时，将其完全脱离出自然环境和宇宙运行规则。

中国人把历史特殊事件上升到宇宙客观规律的思想，使他们把所有事件的变革都记录为天地运行的结果，如同西方所说是上帝的强大意愿所致。这种转变与玄学、预言学或占卜学的进步密切相关，是通过分析诸多记录于“甲骨文”上的预言一点一点建立起来；形而上的元素不同的组合是如何影响大事件的结果，如何通过占卜时龟壳

Entre la conception chinoise et la conception occidentale, le parallélisme tient à ce que, aussi bien pour geming dans la pensée chinoise que pour *geming dans la pensée européenne, avant le sens second , purement politique, le sens premier est cosmologique, référant à un mouvement cosmique circulaire. En effet, du côté chinois le Yijing indique que « Le Ciel et la Terre changent, et les quatre saison en résultent ; de Tang à Wu le Mandat [céleste] a changé (geming), par résonance du Ciel chez les humains»[2] . Ainsi, geming au sens premier désigne le principe céleste du mouvement circulaire des saisons, théorisé par le yinyangwuxingjia en transformation les uns dans les autres des cinq agents-éléments (commandant les phases cosmiques) (五行先生相克). Or du côté occidental, le mot latin révolutio (d'où viennent tous les mots signifiant révolution dans les langues européennes) est apparu vers 1190 pour désigner, comme en Chine, un mouvement cosmique circulaire, sauf qu'il s'agit cette fois du mouvement par lequel un astre revient sur son orbite à son point de départ[1], mouvement qui n'a rien à voir avec celui des wuxing, de conception purement chinoise. En Europe ce sont par la suite les penseurs du XVIIIe siècle, ceux de l'Époque des Lumères, qui ont commencé de prendre le mot *geming au sens figuré de renversement politique. Dans ce deuxième sens, *geming a d'abord été appliqué aux révolutions anglaises du XVIIe siècle, en particulier à celle de 1688-1689, la deuxième, qualifiée de glorious revolution, mais de façon encore simplement métaphorique. C'est quand le mot a été appliqué à la Révolution française de 1789 que la métaphore s'est cristallisée lexicalement en un nouveau concept, ajoutant à la signification figurée de renversement politique la connotation de violence populaire ; et c'est ce concept qui a été théorisé par Karl Marx.

Revenons à l'ancien concept chinois de geming. Son sens cosmologique est, dès l'origine du mot, associé au sens politique de renversement de dynastie, comme nous venons de le voir dans le Yijing qui applique le terme aux renversements de la dynastie des Xia par Tang le Vicioreux (成 汤) et de la dynastie des Shang (devenus Yin) par le roi Wu (武　王), selon le principe des correspondances par résonance (ganying 感应)macro-micro-co smique. Ce concept a dû apparaître dans la pensée chinoise au début de l'époque Zhou, en même temps que la représentation religieuse du souverain d'en haut (上帝) était recouverte par une conception nouvelle du Ciel (天), suprasensible (形而上). Le terme de geming a été construit sur cette base conceptuelle nouvelle, pour légitimer non plus religieusement mais cosmologiquement le renversement des Yin par les Zhou. La référence additionnelle au renversement des Xia par les Shang, regardé comme un précédent, a été évidemment greffée a posteriori, par généralisation ultérieure du principe. C'est la recherche, pour expliquer le renversement des Yin par les Zhou, d'une raison quasi-scientifique, plus solide que les raisons de croyance religieuse, qui a conduit au concept chinois de geming.

Raison quasi-scientifique ? En effet, interpréter les renversements dynastiques comme obéissant aux mêmes lois que les changements de saison, c'était ramener la singularité hors norme d'événement historiques à la normalité objective, scientifique, des phénomènes naturels. Mais cette induction, qui commande l'évolution du sens du terme chinois de l'idée d'une historicité singulière (expliquée religieusement par une volonté divine donnant des ordres [ming]), à l'idée d'une loi cosmique naturelle, procède à l'inverse de l'évolution du terme occidental, qui, au contraire, a détaché de son contexte naturel la normativité des lois astronomiques pour en appliquer l'irrésistibilité à des événements purement historiques hors normes naturelles.

Le saut de la pensée chinoise, de la singularité historique à la normativité cosmologique, marque la conversion de la représentation des événements, quels qu'ils soient, comme voulus par la puissance divine du Shangdi, en représentation des événements, quels qu'ils soient, comme résultant des changements naturels du Ciel et de la Terre. Cette conversion est liée aux progrès de la science des devins, science divinatoire ou manticologie (zhanxue 占学), qui établit peu à peu, en analysant un grand nombre de div-

不同的卦象获得天机：首先是火烧（龟甲裂纹），然后是抽签（易卦）。这些卦象的科学价值得到了极大的认可，因而《易经 · 系辞》向我们证实了重大技术发明是如何从卦象中孕育而出的：从 30 号卦发明了渔网和捕鱼工，从 42 号卦发明了犁的犁铧，而从 59 号卦则发明了船等。[3] 准确地来讲，占卜学趋于精细化的过程发生在殷朝到商朝的转折期，这也标志着《易经》中卦的产生。这时，虽然宗教仪式作为加强社会关系的最佳方式仍然进行着，但宗教信仰却不再在中国智者的思想里流传。这就是《礼记》在谈到周人时说“周人尊礼……事鬼敬神而远之”所要表达的。[4] 如同仪式因礼节的原因被保留了下来，把“命”当术语来释宇宙之“理”的含义也被保留了下来。此时这个用语的这种含义仅仅是隐喻，一直等到“文言”文慢慢成熟，这一表达法才真正形成。新的表达方式最终出现在驺衍的文章中，用于表述朝代的改变是宇宙运行的规律：但这些改变不再与“命”相关，而是与“五行相生”或“五行相克”相联系。

在中国人的思想中，这种“生”或“克”的实质是一个万有引力场，每个元素都有其在宇宙运行规律中的“德”。把这一中国理念运用到革命中，革命就是天道推动改变宇宙的状态。这和欧洲历史唯物主义理论相对应，按这一理论，是“历史潮流”推动了历史事件的发生。不论如何，改朝换代的“革命”或“* 革命”都有顺应民心的暴力事件；在西方的“* 革命”中，暴力事件来自民众，而中国“革命”的暴力事件来自天灾（革命先兆往往是地震或其他自然灾害）。西方思想抽象出宇宙运行规则中的不可抗性，来解释人民的力量在革命中所起的作用；中国的思想却抽象出人类的良好道德品质来解释天道的运行规律。这里把宗教的价值观变为了宇宙价值观：精神的力量如同宗教品行，是上天给予其真命天子的，如果他变成逆天命而为的暴君，也就会失去这些力量。这一力量的分配和天地中阴阳变换和五行相生相克密切相关，如果政权违背这些规律，就会招来革命的灾祸。

在汉语的“革命”中，天的力量就是五行相生而非相克。五行相生的变化顺序如下：木→火→土→金→水（五行相生）。

违背其运行规律，相生变为相克。五行相克的变化顺序如下：

木→金→火→水→土（五行相克）。[5]

中国朝代变更史某种程度上可以简化为一部宇宙五行的循环史。古代中国占卜行为频繁，并用其解释行星共线现象（尤其是日月蚀），占星术很可能就是这么产生的。在殷朝的统治时期，占卜曾为国家行政部门之一，为王权所服务；然而先周占卜变得非常强大，从发现的刻有占卜文字的钱币都出自先周足以说明这一点。因而，张守节在对《史记》的评论中提到，文王还仅仅是西伯侯时，就在“岁在鹑火”的天兆后自称为王，[6] 这一点并不令人惊讶。虽然当时的文献已经失传，这一记载出现在很晚的

inations enregistrées en jiaguwen, comment les événements résultent de combinaisons de forces supra-sensibles (xingershqng), que la divination découvre en les rendant visibles sous forme de configurations produites d'abord par brûlage, en craquelures sur des écailles de tortue (龟甲裂璺), puis par tirage au sort, en *hexagrammes du Yijing* (易卦). La valeur scientifique de ces configurations est si bien reconnue que le Xici du Yijing nous indique comment les grandes inventions techniques ont été conçues à la lumière des hexagrammes : les filets de chasse et de pêche à la lumière de l'hexagramme n° 30, les socs de charrue à la lumière de l'hexagramme n° 42, les bateaux à la lumière de l'hexagramme n° 59 etc[3]. C'est précisément à l'époque du tournant des Yin aux Zhou que les progrès de la science divinatoire ont porté cette science au niveau de sophistication que marquent les hexagrammes du Yijing. À ce niveau, les croyances religieuses n'ont plus cours dans la pensée savante chinoise, même si les cérémonies du culte continuent d'être rituellement pratiquée parce qu'elles sont le meilleur moyen de renforcer les liens sociaux. C'est ce que veut dire le Liji quand il rapporte que les Zhou, tout en respectant les rites de la tradition religieuse, *se sont éloignés des esprits*[4]. De même que les cérémonies sont maintenues, mais désormais seulement rituellement, de même se maintient la formule d'un commandement (命) pour exprimer des raisons (理) cosmologiques; mais la formule désormais n'est plus que métaphorique, en attendant que la lente maturation de la langue graphique (文言) aboutisse à la mise au point d'une terminologie appropriée à la cosmologie. La nouvelle formulation apparaît finalement chez Zou Yan (驺衍), dans les termes d'une théorie des changements de phases cosmiques entraînant les renversements dynastiques : ces changements ne sont plus rapportés à un commandement (命) mais à une genèse(生) des cinq agents-éléments les uns par les autres (五行相生), ou à une force dominante (克) qui les renverse les uns sous les autres (五行相克).

Dans la pensée chinoise, la nature de cette genèse (生) ou de cette force dominante (克) est une sorte de champ gravitationnel propre à chaque agent-élément qualifié de vertu (德) au sens cosmique du mot. Appliquée au geming par la théorie chinoise, cette notion d'une sorte de vertu gravitationnelle cosmique entraînant les changements d'état de l'univers est l'homologue de ce qui, dans la pensée européenne du *geming, est le "*sens de l'histoire*" entraînant les événements selon les lois du matérialisme historique. D'un côté comme de l'autre, le changement politique du *geming* ou du **geming* est empreint de violence populaire; mais dans le **geming* occidental la violence est populaire, tandis que dans le *geming* chinois elle est pour ainsi dire météorologique (les prodomes du *geming* chinois sont des tremblements de terre ou autres météores). La pensée occidentale abstrait du mouvement cosmique son irrésistibilité pour l'appliquer à la force populaire en œuvre dans le **geming*; la pensée chinoise abstrait de la *vertu* éthique son sens moral pour l'appliquer à la *vrtu* cosmique. Ici se retrouve la cosmologisation des valeurs de la religion : la force d'âme que la mentalité religieuse concevait comme conférée par le *Shangdi* aux Saints rois(圣王) des dynasties régnantes, mais que perdaient les tyrans contrevenant à son *commandement* (命), est requalifiée en termes de conduite parfaitement en phase avec le dynamisme cosmique du *yin*, du *yang* et des *wuxing* du Ciel et de la Terre, et c'est le déphasage cosmique des actes du souverain qui, par une politique contraire au sens des choses, provoque la catastrophe du *geming*. Dans le *geming* chinois, la violence du Ciel n'est autre que la conversion en *force dominante* (克), de la *genèse* (生), purement organique et donc non-violente des cinq agents-éléments les uns dans les autres. L'ordre organique, non-violent, des changements naturels des cinq phases cosmiques, est le suivant :

bois → feu →terre → métal → eau (五行相生).

Le déphasage de l'ordre cosmique provoqué par une conduite non conforme à la *raison des choses* (理) entraîne la conversion des successions organiques non-violentes en successions violentes dans un ordre différent, l'ordre du renversement des agents-éléments chacun par son antagoniste :

bois → métal → feu → eau → terre (五行相克).[5]

唐代史书中（公元 9 世纪），但毫无疑问这段历史是存在的。如果周朝的天道为火，那么朝代创始者在仍为西伯侯时就通过占卜知道了“岁在鹑火”是火的象征，是他获得皇权的标志。中国占卜的哲思就是这样由占星术扩展为宇宙学，从而演化出“革命”的汉语意义。

正如在所有中国古代思想的思辨性发展中，思想本身的理性占有主导地位，这种理性受到中国占卜学这一特有科学的支撑。从殷朝甲骨文的发明开始，占卜学有了决定性的发展，这一发展延续到商朝初期有了超越以前的新成就：龟甲裂璺变成标准化的“卜”形，这导致在龙山文化最后时期龟甲替代了胛骨。生活在当今郑州附近的商人很大程度上吸收了这种当时在山东盛行的占卜文化。在他们移民到殷（即如今的安阳）之后，通过卜璺化将占卜学继续合理化。就是借助其邻国商人丰富占卜文化，周人才诞生了其“革命”（周朝替代商朝）中最重要的历史人物之一——姜子牙，即师尚父，别名“太公望”。后来的文帝任命他为自己的谋士。太公望当时是个穷困移民，没有谋生之技，但他却是东夷丰富文化的传承人，因而不会被忽略，最终成为未来君主身旁最有影响力的人。起初，太公望软硬皆施成功将殷朝的支系部族收入了周国旗下；随后，也正是太公望在文帝宾天之后，指导文帝的儿子周武王获得了牧野之战（根据最近的年代计算，牧野之战发生于公元前 1046 年）的胜利。牧野之战终结了殷朝最后一代君主纣王（帝辛，后世人称纣王）的统治。牧野之战结束后，太公望甚至在周武王的亲弟弟周公旦之前，第一个受到封赏。太公望被授予齐国的封地，并最终以姜太公之名建立齐国；而周公旦则受封鲁国。这两个封地并不仅仅是两个皇室封地，他们后来成为周文化的两个策源地：鲁国是孔子的诞生地，而齐国则在不久后成立了中国历史上第一所高等学府的摇篮——稷下学宫。

回到周文王的话题上。文帝的名字被孔子援引为周文化的象征：“文王既没，文不在兹乎？天之将丧斯文也，后死者不得与于斯文也。”[7]

孔子肯定是因为要和其所在时代用词习惯相符，才会在这里将文帝的“文”以“文化”的意思来解读，认为“文”这个字在周文王时期就是这个意思。那么当“文”被用作周朝两位建立者中第一位的周文王的名号时，它究竟有什么含义呢？对应周朝另一位奠基者周武王，因为其用武力赢得了牧野之战的胜利，所以后人顺理成章地将象征武士的武字作为其名号，因为牧野之战的事迹使他配得上武士这个称号，那么周文王又有什么事迹让他配得上自己的名号呢？在文帝生活的殷朝末期，他的名号只存在于甲骨上的占卜学文字中。因而，文帝是因为其精通占卜学文字才有“文”这个名号的。通常我们认为“阴阳”重卦是由重叠伏羲发明的八卦而来。然而，我们应该对伏羲发明八卦的传说表示怀疑。在《易经》之前没有任何关于八卦占卜的考古结果。1899 年，

Telle est la théorie de la réduction de l'histoire des dynasties chinoises au cycle des *cinq vertus cosmiques*. Dans la Chine archaïque, qui pratiquait intensément la divination et l'appliquait aux conjonctures astrales (notamment aux éclipses), elle a vraisemblablement germé d'une divination de cette sorte. Sous les Yin, la divination était une fonction de l'administration d'État réservée à la royauté; mais *la Maison prédynastique des Zhou* (先周) est devenue assez puissante pour s'en octroyer la pratique, nous le savons depuis la découverte de pièces divinatoires inscrites ne pouvant être attribuées qu'à cette Maison. Il n'est donc pas surprenant que le commentaire de Zhang Shoujie du *Shiji* rapporte que le futur roi Wen, alors qu'il n'était encore que Comte de l'Ouest (西 伯), s'auto-proclama roi « quand la planète Jupiter entra dans la palais méridional de l'Oiseau de feu ».[6] Si tardif que soit ce commentaire (du IXe siècle), il repose certainement sur des sources aujourd'hui disparues mais encore accessibles sous les Tang, qu'il n'y aucune raison de mettre en doute dans ce passage. Il en ressort que si la vertu cosmique des Zhou a été identifiée à celle du feu, c'est que le fondateur de la dynastie, quand il n'était encore que comte de l'Ouest, a su, assurément par divination, que l'entrée de Jupiter dans la constellation de l'Oiseau rouge, signe astrologique du feu, était le signe de sonaccès à la royauté. Voilà comment la spéculation divinatoire chinoise a conduit au concept chinois de *geming* par élargissement de l'astrologie en cosmologie.

Comme dans tous les développements spéculatifs de la pensée chinoise ancienne, règne ici la rationalité propre à cette pensée, appuyée sur la science *manticologique* (占 卜 学) spécifiquement chinoise. Les progrès décisifs de cette science à l'époque Yin, à partir de l'invention des *jiaguwen*, prolongent la remarquable avancée que représente, au début des Shang, la standardisation en " 卜 " des craquelures divinatoires d'écailles de tortue (龟甲裂璺变成标准化的"卜"形的分裂) intervenue après la substitution de ces écailles (龟甲) aux omoplates d bovidés (胛骨) au cours de la dernière période de la culture de Longshan (龙山). Les Shang ont largement absorbée cette culture, qui régnait sur le Shandong à l'époque où ils étaient, eux, installés sur le site de la ville actuelle de Zhengzhou, dans une proximité immédiate. Ils en ont ensuite prolongé les avancées, continuant de rationaliser *la divination par la tortue* (卜龟办法) après leur migration à Yin (aujourd'hui Anyang). C'est précisément de ce riche milieu culturel du voisinage des Shang qu'est issue l'une des figures historiques les plus importantes du *geming* des Zhou, la figure de Jiang Zi Ya (姜子牙), *alias* Shi Shangfu (师尚父), surnommé Taigongwang (太公望), que le futur roi Wen choisit comme son conseiller personnel. Pauvre immigrant en quête d'emploi, mais porteur de cette riche culture des Yi de l'Est (东夷), Taigongwang n'a pas manqué de devenir le plus influent des membres de l'entourage du futur roi. Pour commencer, il réussit à coaliser sous l'autorité Zhou, de gré ou de force, toutes les ethnies tributaires des Yin; puis c'est lui qui, après la mort du Roi Wen, conduisit son fils, le roi Wu, à la victoire de Muye (牧野 , en 1046 avant notre ère selon les plus récents calculs chronologiques), qui entraîna le renversement du dernier souverain Yin, le roi Zhou 紂 (de nom liturgique posthume Di Xin 帝辛). Après la bataille, il en fut récompensé le tout premier, avant même, le propre frère du roi Wu, le duc Dan (公旦), par l'octroi d'un fief à Qi dont il est ainsi le fondateur sous le titre de grand duc Jiang (姜太公), tandis que le duc Dan recevait le fief voisin de Lu. Ces deux fiefs sont devenus par la suite, bien plus que la métropole royale, les deux foyers de la culture Zhou : celui de Lu, devenu la patrie de Confucius, et celui de Qi, devenu peu après le berceau de la première université de l'histoire de la Chine, le Palais des études établi à Qixia (稷下学宫).

Revenons au Roi Wen, dont le nom est invoqué par Confucius comme symbole de la culture Zhou: « Le roi Wen est mort, mais son "*wen*" n'est-il pas toujours de ce monde? Si le Ciel avait voulu la perte de ce "*wen*", comment l'aurait-il confié à quelqu'un (moi) postérieurement à cette mort!»[7].

Ce ne peut être que par anachronisme que le"*wen*" du Roi Wen est ici pris par Confucius avec le sens de *culture*: le mot ne pouvait avoir ce sens à l'époque de ce roi. Quel sens pouvait-il donc avoir, quand il a été ajouté comme épithète honorifique au titre du premier des deux fondateurs de la royauté Zhou, le Roi

成百上千的标记着殷朝占卜文字的牛胛骨和龟壳被发现，这证明了甲骨文占卜是当时人们使用的唯一占卜形式。在殷朝末期周文王生活的时代，有什么新的占卜文字呢？由于数字卦对文字的创新，尤其是刻在占卜钱币上的占卜文字使得其他新的占卜文字形式的案例并不多。我们应当如何解读这些新的占卜文字呢？肯定不能用纯属传说的伏羲八卦做参照；因而只能用当时的占卜行为做解读，占卜钱币通过火烧产生璺，璺被作为预言的代码而需要被破译。很明显璺上的预言的代码替代了璺本身。产生这种替代的原因在于璺经过标准化成为了“卜”，多样的“卜”被减少成了五到六个规则横线组成的图案，具有创造力的占卜者把“卜”编号用于抽签。这要比通过火烧产生卦象方便很多。替代占卜璺的数字卦如今被所有专家认为是《易经》中卦的原型。我们完全可以认为周文王在自封为王前十分热衷于占卜，并将占卜作为其战略核心——前文我们提到过先周在其大殿里占卜——周文王曾在羑里监狱里研究数字卦，通过已经在《易经》中理论化的阴爻和阳爻的代数卦为数字卦的完善作出了贡献。但这一占卜学研究的真实性完全被伏羲画八卦演生《易经》的传说所掩盖。

为什么这一传说会掩盖周文王对发明占筮所作出的贡献？因为占筮的发明很好地解释了这一占卜术对前朝殷占龟术的沿袭。由于对殷人的憎恨，周人抹去了所有他们的前辈是令他们羞耻的殷人的痕迹。

这种憎恨起初源于殷朝末帝纣王臭名昭彰的暴政，随后由于殷朝百姓对新的周朝皇权的反抗而扩大到了所有殷朝百姓。周武王在牧野之战胜利之后，将殷朝国土分为三块封地，一块给了纣王之子武庚（或称禄父），让他负责俾守殷祀；其他两块封赏给了协助监管周朝的周成王的两位叔叔——管叔和蔡叔。“三监”后来利用周武王之子周成王年幼进行叛乱；叛乱被周公旦所镇压，周公旦作为已故周武王的兄弟而摄政。周公旦是周武王的亲信，为了确认“革命”胜利，将所有标志殷朝皇权荣耀的东西都没收了，包括仪式用的铜器和玉器。考古学家已在周诸侯的不同墓穴找到了许多他们当初受赏的殷朝皇家器具。叛乱平定之后，周公旦又对根除前朝旧势力做了很多事情。他处决了武庚，流放了周成王的两位叔叔；之后，他将武庚的封地封赏给了纣王的庶兄微子启，让他归附周朝。微子启是商王帝乙的长子，和纣王同母，是其母在未成为妃时所生。启在殷朝时建立了微国（商朝故都，如今的商丘），而他再次受封也是在这里，但是封地名称变成了宋。

从这以后，商朝祖先的祭祀就在宋国举行。然而在殷朝故都（如今的安阳，黄河的另一边，距离宋国西部 200 多公里的地方），殷墟王陵遭到了蓄意破坏，近期新的考古学发现证明了这一点。[2] 考虑到在中国古代社会中葬礼祭祀的重要性，对殷朝陵墓的毁坏标明周朝百姓对这些陵墓的憎恨程度。随着这些陵墓遭到彻底毁坏，殷朝和

Wen? Un sens symétrique à celui de l'autre épithète honorifique, celle *wu* (*guerrier*) ajouté au titre de l'autre fondateur, le Roi Wu (武王). Symétriquement *au fait d'armes* de la victoire de Muye, qui valut au Roi Wu son épithète de guerrier, ce doit être un *fait de lettres* que consacre l'épithète du titre du Roi Wen. Quel fait de lettres? À l'époque, celle de la fin des Yin, il n'existe de *lettres* qu'en l'espèce des *formules divinatoires* (占卜学的文字) *des inscriptions écailles de tortue* (*jiaguwen*). C'est donc en tant que *savant en lettres divinatoires* que le Roi Wen a mérité l'épithète *wen* ajoutée à son titre. De fait, la tradition le crédite de l'invention des hexagrammes (*chonggua* 重卦) du *Yijing*, par duplication des trigrammes (八卦) réputés inventés par Fuxi (伏 羲). Cependant, il faut se garder de prendre Ici au comptant la légende de Fuxi inventeur des trigrammes. Il n'y a aucune trace archéologique de trigrammes divinatoires avant le *Yijing*, alors qu' ont été découverts depuis 1899 des dizaines et des dizaines de milliers de fragments d'omoplates de bovidés et d'écailles de tortue porteurs de marques divinatoires d'époque Yin, représentant manifestement la seule forme de divination pratiquée à l'époque. Qu'est-ce qui est nouveau à la fin de l'époque Yin, du vivant du futur Roi Wen? Ce sont des exemples peu nombreux parce que très innovants *d'hexagrammes numériques* (*shuzi gua* 数字卦), découverts gravés notammant sur des pièces divinatoires. Comment les interpréter ? Surement pas par référence à de supposés trigrammes de Fuxi, purement légendaires; donc seulement par référence à la seule divination alors pratiquée, en les rapportant aux craquelures (璺) produites par brûlage sur les pièces divinatoires comme significatives des pronostics à déchiffrer. Il est clair que les chiffres des hexagrammes numériques sont des substituts à ces craquelures. La substitution a pu avoir lieu parce que les craquelures étaient standardisées en forme de " 卜 ", dont les variantes se réduisaient à cinq ou six différences du dessin du trait latéral prises pour pertinentes, que des devins inventifs ont eu l'idée de numéroter pour les tirer au sort, ce qui était bien plus facile que de les produire réellement par brûlage. Les hexagrammes chiffrés ainsi obtenus à la place des craquelures divinatoires sont aujourd'hui reconnus par tous les spécialistes comme prototypes des hexagrammes du *Yijing*. Il y a tout lieu de penser que le futur Roi Wen, féru de divination — fondement de tout projet stratégique à l'époque et en usage dans la Maison prédynastique Zhou (先周) nous l'avons vu —, a contribué, en y réfléchissant dans sa prison de Youli (羑里), au perfectionnement de cette innovation des hexagrammes numériques en hexagrammes algébriques en *yinyao* (阴爻) et *yangyao* (阳爻) — ceux qui sont théorisés dans le *Yijing*. Le problème est que la nature de aa véritable invention manticologique a été complètement occulté par la légende qui rapporte à Fuxi l'origine du *Yijing*.

Pourquoi cette occultation par la légende au lieu du souvenir de la véritable contribution du Roi Wen à l'invention de la divination par l'achilée (占筮) ? Parce que cette invention ne s'explique historiquement que comme appuyée sur la culture Yin de la divination par la tortue (占龟), et que, par haine des Yin, les Zhou ont effacé toute trace de ce qu'ils devaient à la culture de ces prédécesseurs honnis.

Cette haine, vouée d'abord à la tyrannie tristement célèbre du dernier roi Yin , le Roi Zhou(纣), s'est élargie à tout le peuple Yin du fait de son insoumission persistante à la nouvelle royauté Zhou, à laquelle, "peuple obstiné" (顽民), il est resté rétif. Le Roi Wu, après sa victoire, répartit le territoire Yin en trois fiefs, attribués l'un au fils du roi Zhou, Wugeng (武庚 , alias Lufu 禄父), chargé d'entretenir le culte de ses ancêtres, (俾守殷祀) et les deux autres à deux de ses oncles cadets, Guanshu 管叔 et Caishu 蔡叔 , chargés de l'aider à surveiller le pays. On sait comment ensuite ces trois autorités de surveillance (三监) profitèrent de la minorité du fils du Roi Wu, le Roi Cheng, pour se rebeller; et on sait comment les rebelles furent écrasés par le Duc Dan, exerçant la régence comme frère du Roi Wu décédé. Il avait suffi au roi Wu, pour consacrer le *geming*, de confisquer toutes les marques de prestige de la royauté Yin, bronzes et jades rituels, dont l'archéologie a retrouvés de nombreuses pièces dans divers tombeaux de seigneurs féodaux Zhou (周 诸 侯) qui les avaient reçus en récompense. Après la rébellion, le Duc Dan est allé beaucoup plus loin dans l'éradication de l'ancien pouvoir renversé. Il fit exécuter Wugeng et bannir ses

周朝文化一直到其文化核心的前后联系也被完全抹去——周朝的文言和殷朝的甲骨文的前后联系以及周朝的占筮源于殷朝的占龟。随着野草再次将殷墟完全覆盖，和伏羲发明重卦、中国文字来源于卦的传说的流传，《易经》中的中国象形文字真正起源于殷朝的事实完全被掩盖了。孔子本身也从宋国移民到鲁国，是帝乙和微子启的后代（微子启替代纣王的子孙，选择归附周朝，成为了宋国的建立者）。孔子也是《易经》汇编的发起人，这是儒家学说的第一准则。在这一准则最有权威性的评论中，《系辞》给出了伏羲发明重卦，文言起源于卦的依据。而四千年后的1899年，人们发现在一味名叫“龙骨”的药上的神秘图案，之后历经半个世纪的深入研究，终于了解及恢复了中国文化的真正渊源，而周朝的“革命”是让殷朝真正的渊源完全消失的根本原因。

1. “革命”现在的用法，是从日本语来的。旅美学人陈建华，在1998年的《读书》上写过一篇文章，指出晚清王韬的《法国志略》（1890年）第一次使用了现代语义的“革命”“法国革命”，而王韬这个用法，和他这本著作的很多地方一样，取自日本人冈千仞的《法兰西志》和冈本监辅的《万国史志》。

2.《周易·革卦·彖传》：“天地革而四时成，汤武革命顺乎天而应乎人。”

3.《周易·系辞下传》，第二章。

4. 详见《礼记表记》，第12-13章：“周人尊礼……事鬼敬神而远之。”

5. 这一由其相克元素颠倒了的顺序应用在了后来朝代（正统）的推演中，在汉朝引起了许多论战性探讨。一些理论学家曾想过依靠“革命”的有机排序来克服这个问题，而没有考虑到这样做的话，宇宙学基础很有可能引发朝代的更替。

6. 张守节《史记正义》引《帝王世纪》云：“文王即位四十二年，岁在鹑火，文王更为受命之元年，始称王矣……”

7.《论语·子罕》第九篇：“文王既没，文不在兹乎，天之将丧斯文也，后死者不得与于斯文也。”

参考文献：

[1] Alain Rey. LE ROBERT Dictionnaire historique de la langue Française. PARIS, 1992.

[2] 何毓灵．殷墟王陵早期被盗年代研究．考古，2014（6）：97-98.

deux oncles cadets; puis il inféoda à la place de Wugeng le frère aîné illégitime de son père Zhou(纣), rallié contre celui-ci aux Zhou : un des fils de Di Yi (帝乙) nommé Qi (启), né de la même mère que Zhou(纣) et avant lui, mais aussi avant que celle-ci ne reçoive le titre de reine. Ce Qi avait été établi sous les Yin à Wei (微 , site d'une ancienne capitale des Shang, aujourd'hui Shanqjiu 商丘), et c'est ce territoire qui lui fut réattribué en fief, mais sous un autre nom, le nom de Song (宋).

C'est désormais à Song que fut entretenu le culte des ancêtres des Shang, tandis que dans l'ancienne capitale Yin (aujourd'hui Anyang 安阳 , de l'autre côté du fleuve Jaune et deux cents kms plus à l'Ouest), les tombeaux des Rois et des aristocrates de l'ancienne dynastie furent délibérément détruits, comme de nouvelles explorations archéologiques ont permis récemment de l'établir.[2] Compte tenu de l'importance du culte funéraire dans la société chinoise archaïque, la destruction des tombeaux des Yin donne la mesure de la radicalité de la haine que les Zhou portaient à ceux-ci. De même que furent de fond en comble détruits ces tombeaux, de même fut effacée complètement toute filiation à la culture Yin de la culture Zhou, jusque, au cœur même e ces deux cultures, la filiation de la *langue graphique* (文言) Zhou aux *jiaguwen* (甲骨文) Yin et la genèse de la divination Zhou par l'achillée (占筮) à partir de la divination Yin par la tortue(占龟) . Ainsi, de même que les herbes sauvages recouvrirent entièrement l'emplacement des tombeaux Yin détruits, de même la légende de Fuxi, inventeur des trigrammes, et la légende de la genèse des caractères chinois à partir des trigrammes, ont entièrement recouvert la véritable origine Yin de l'idéographie chinoise des hexagrammes du *Yijing*. Confucius lui même, immigré à Lu venu de Song et descendant de Di Yi comme Qi, le fondateur de Song par substitution à la lignée du Roi Zhou (纣), proclame comme Qi qu'il choisit les Zhou (周). Et Confucius encore, initiateur de de la compilation *Yijing*, premier de tous les canons du confucianisme, dans le plus magistral des commentaires explicatifs de ce canon, le *Xici* (系辞), donne force d'authenticité aux légendes de Fuxi inventeur des trigrammes et de la genèse de la langue graphique (文言) à partir des trigrammes. Au point qu'il a fallu attendre quatre mille ans, jusqu'à ce que la surprenante découverte en 1899 de graphismes énigmatiques sur des "os de dragon", pour qu'ensuite un demi-siècle de recherches érudites restituent les véritables origines de la culture chinoise que le *geming* des Zhou avait fait complètement disparaître.

1." 革命 " 现在的用法，是从日本语来的。旅美学人陈建华，在 1998 年的《读书》上写过一篇文章，指出晚清王韬的《法国志略》（1890 年）第一次使用了现代语义的 " 革命 "" 法国革命 "，而王韬这个用法，和他这本著作的很多地方一样，取自日本人冈千仞的《法兰西志》和冈本监辅的《万国史志》。

2.Voir《周易 · 革卦 · 彖传》：" 天地革而四时成，汤武革命顺乎天而应乎人。"

3. Pour plus de détails, voir：《周易 · 系辞下传》，第二章。

4. Pour plus de détails, voir:《礼记 · 表记》, 第 12-13 章: " 周人尊礼 …… 事鬼敬神而远之。"

5.L'application de cet ordre antagonistique à la déduction de la légitimité des dynasties successives (zhengtong 正统) a suscité, dès l'époque des Han, beaucoup de discussions polémiques, que certains théoriciens ont pensé surmonter en appuyant le geming plutôt sur l'ordre organique, sans se rendre compte que, ce faisant, ils faussaient complètement les fondements de la conception cosmologique des changements dynastiques.

6. Voir: 张守节《史记正义》引《帝王世纪》云：" 文王即位四十二年，岁在鹑火，文王更为受命之元年，始称王矣 ……"

7.Voir《论语 · 子罕》第九篇：" 文王既没，文不在兹乎，天之将丧斯文也，后死者不得与于斯文也。"

第二章　保存、展示与规划

Section 2　Preservation, Presentation & Planning

曲阜与济兖邹曲鲁文化城市群：区域视野中的曲阜城市空间发展

刘健、吴良镛

城市发展的区域化是当今世界城市发展的重要趋势之一。曲阜所在的鲁西南地区，济宁、兖州、邹城、曲阜四座城市在空间上密集分布，在交通上联系便利，在经济上各有侧重，在社会上关系紧密，具有城市发展区域化的优越条件；鉴于四座城市均有深厚的鲁文化渊源，故可称为“鲁文化城市群”。在中国城市化快速推进、社会经济转型发展的背景下，济兖邹曲四座城市的人口规模不断增长、城市空间不断扩大，面临着从相对独立的城市发展向相互关联的区域发展的转变。在此过程中，在曲阜高铁车站建设带动下的区域交通条件的进一步改善，以曲阜和邹城两座国家级历史文化名城为节点的历史轴线的不断强化，以京杭大运河申遗为契机的运河文化轴线的初步建立，以及针对煤炭挖掘造成的塌陷地区的生态环境治理，都将成为促进济兖邹曲鲁文化城市群整合发展的重要媒介及其特色所在。而曲阜作为其中的重要结点，其空间发展应在加强历史遗产保护的基础上，充分发挥独特的历史文化特色，重视建设富有人文精神、文化特色和地方风貌的城市空间结构，塑造新型城镇化政策背景下的城市发展典范。

当前，人类社会已然步入城市时代，城市发展的区域化亦已成为世界城市发展的重要趋势之一；在全球化背景下，任何一座城市的发展都比以往更加紧密地与其所在的地区联系在一起，成为区域城市发展的重要组成部分。曲阜隶属济宁市管辖，地处山东西南，是中华文明的重要文化分支之一——齐鲁文化中的鲁文化发源地。在济宁市管辖的两区三市七县当中，济宁市区以及兖州、邹城和曲阜三座城市，在空间上分布密集，在交通上联系便利，在经济上各有侧重，且自古以来即在社会、文化等方面关系紧密，形成了以鲁文化为基础的城市地区，即鲁文化城市群，曲阜的城市发展则是该地区城市发展的重要组成部分。

◎一、区域发展理念的提出

早在1990年代初期，就有山东社会科学院的学者撰文指出，“应正视鲁南城市群开发建设”，建议把济兖邹曲四座城市作为一个城市群来研究；此后，这一区域发

From Qufu to Ji-Yan-Zou-Qu Lu-Culture City-Region: Spatial Development of Qufu in Regional Perspective

LIU Jian and WU Liangyong

The regionalization of urban development is one of the important trends of the world's urban development in the contemporary time. In the southwest of Shandong Province where Qufu is standing, the four cities of Jining, Yanzhou, Zoucheng and Qufu are densely distributed in terms of space, closely interlinked in terms of communication, comparatively diversified in terms of economy, and broadly interweaved in terms of society, all of which give them the inherent advantages for regional development. In view that the four cities are all historically rooted into the Lu-Culture, the culture of the Lu State in the West Zhou Dynasty, the Ji-Yan-Zou-Qu City Region can also be called as Lu-Culture City Region. Under the circumstances of China's rapid urbanization and socio-economic transformation, the four cities have seen the continuous increase of urban population and the sustained expansion of urban areas, making them face the transition from respective urban development to integrated regional development. From that viewpoint, the improvement of the region's transportation system based on Qufu High-speed Railway Station, the development of the region's historical axis based on the historic and cultural cities of Qufu and Zoucheng, the establishment of the region's new cultural axis along the Grand Canal, and the ecological restoration of the coal mining subsidence lands at the center of the region can all be taken as catalysis for promoting the development of Lu-Culture City-Region. Qufu, as one of the key nodes of that city region, should make further efforts to better protect its historic heritages, while, by making full use of its unique historic and cultural resources. Due attention should be paid to the construction of the new spatial structure full of humanism spirit, cultural identity, and local features, which could be taken as a good example of urban development in the context of new type of urbanization.

Nowadays in an urbanizing world, the regionalization of urban development has become one of the significant trends of the world's development. Meanwhile, under the circumstance of globalization, the development of a city is more closely related than ever before to the region where it is located, and it is becoming an important part of the regional development. Qufu, a city in the southwest of Shandong Province and under the jurisdiction of Jining Municipality, is the birthplace of the Lu Culture, an indispensable component of the Qi-Lu Cultures which is one of the key branches of Chinese culture. Among the two urban districts, three county-level cities, and seven counties under Jining's jurisdiction, the cities of Jining, Yanzhou, Zoucheng and Qufu (referred to as Ji-Yan-Zou-Qu hereinafter) are densely distributed in terms of layout, closely interlinked in terms of communication, comparatively diversified in terms of economy, and broadly interweaved in terms of society and culture, forming a city region based on the Lu Culture which can be called as Ji-Yan-Zou-Qu Lu-Culture City Region, thus the urban development of Qufu can hardly be independent from the development of that city region.

◎ 1. Origin of the concept of Ji-Yan-Zou-Qu Lu-Culture City Region

The idea of developing the four cities of Ji-Yan-Zou-Qu into a city region was firstly put forward by

展理念逐渐被各方接受。1994年《济宁市城市总体规划》提出，“应该把济兖邹曲四个城市建设成为一个统一的复合经济中心，作为地区的一级中心”；《山东省21世纪前十年经济社会发展战略》关于“城市化和区域协调发展问题”的研究报告建议，“尽快扩大济宁的城市规模，增强辐射带动功能，形成济宁—兖州—邹城—曲阜复合中心，对于拉动鲁西南地区经济增长、优化全省经济布局、促进区域经济的协调发展都有着重要的战略意义”。2001年，北京大学周一星教授主持完成《济宁—曲阜都市区发展战略规划》，首次提出“济宁—曲阜都市区”概念，建议将其建设成为鲁西南地区的区域性中心城市，通过引入都市区协调机制解决跨行政区的城市发展问题；该规划还提出都市区“绿心”概念，建议在济兖邹曲四座城市环绕的采煤塌陷区的中央，建设都市区的绿心，设立煤炭主题公园、鲁国民俗文化村等旅游开发项目，在进行生态治理的同时，带动区域城市发展。2008—2009年，清华大学吴良镛教授及其研究团队在进行《区域文化视角下的曲阜城市发展构想及城市中轴线城市设计研究》和《济宁城市湿地系统规划研究与洸府河湿地公园概念设计》研究时，则进一步提出了以济兖邹曲四座城市为核心，将鲁西南地区建设成为鲁文化城市群的概念。

上述区域发展理念的出现及其被广泛接受，在很大程度上得益于济兖邹曲地区所特有的、有利于区域城市发展的各种条件。首先在空间上，济兖邹曲四座城市呈四边形布局，平均距离为28千米，两两之间的距离最短仅15千米（兖州—曲阜），最长不过43千米（济宁—曲阜），空间分布十分密集。其次在交通上，伴随区域交通基础设施的建设发展，济兖邹曲四座城市之间均有高速路或快速路作为联系通道，平均车程时间不超过半小时，人员与货物往来十分便利。再次在经济上，济兖邹曲四座城市的既有主导产业各有不同，且互补性强；其中，济宁是全市的政治中心和地区最大的经济中心，在金融、煤炭、制造等领域实力强劲；兖州是鲁西南地区重要的铁路交通枢纽，经济发展以机械制造、煤炭开采等作为支柱；邹城是兖济煤田的开发基地，拥有火力发电中心等重要企业，旅游业也十分发达；曲阜是闻名全国的旅游城市，旅游和制造是其经济发展的重要组成。最后在文化上，济兖邹曲四座城市同处鲁文化核心区域，历史悠久、文化深厚，又有各自的独特之处；其中，济宁是省级历史文化名城，作为历史上的全国漕运管理中心，享有“运河之都”的美誉，是运河文化的重要代表；兖州古为九州之一，素有“九省通衢、齐鲁咽喉”之称，汉唐以来文风盛行，文人荟萃；邹城是国家级历史文化名城，作为孟子故里、儒学胜地，既有“四孟”（即孟庙、孟府、孟林、孟母林）等历史遗迹，又有“四山”（即铁山、岗山、葛山、尖山）和九龙山、峄山等风景名胜；曲阜同为国家级历史文化名城，是儒家文化的起源之地和鲁国文化的代表城市，拥有孔庙、孔府、孔林等世界文化遗产以及鲁国故城、

some scholars from Shandong Academy of Social Sciences in the early 1990s in an article entitled "Due Attention Paid to the City Region Development in Southwest Shandong", which was broadly accepted by various parties of the society afterwards. In 1994, the *Jining City Master Plan* stated to build the four cities of Ji-Yan-Zou-Qu into a unified and complex economic center which would function as a regional center of Shandong Province. In the late 1990s, the research report on *Urbanization and Coordinated Regional Development*, as part of the *Socio-Economic Development Strategies of Shandong Province in the First Decade of the 21st Century*, proposed to enlarge the city scale and strengthen the radiating influence of Jining Municipality, so as to facilitate the formation of Ji-Yan-Zou-Qu complex center as a significant strategy for promoting the economic growth of southwest Shandong, optimizing the economic layout of the whole province, and encouraging the coordinated development of regional economy. In 2001, in the *Strategic Plan for the Development of Jining-Qufu Metropolitan Area* chaired by ZHOU Yixing, professor of geography of Peking University, the concept of Jining-Qufu Metropolitan Area was advocated, in hope of turning it into a regional city in southwest Shandong through cross-boundary urban development by introducing the mechanism of metropolitan coordination. The Plan also proposed the construction of a green area in the coal mining subsidence area at the center of the region as the "Green Heart" of Jining-Qufu Metropolitan Area, where some tourism projects, such as Coal Mining Theme Park and Lu Folk Culture Village, could be developed to promote both regional development and ecologic restoration. From 2008 to 2009, when chairing the Conceptual Planning for *Qufu's Urban Development in Regional and Cultural Perspectives and Urban Design for Qufu's Central Axis and the Planning Study on Jining's Urban Wetland System and Conceptual Design for Guangfu River Wetland Park*, WU Liangyong, professor of architecture and planning of Tsinghua University, further put forward the idea of building the Lu Culture City Region in southwest Shandong Province based on the urban development of the four cities of Ji-Yan-Zou-Qu.

The popularization of the concept of regional development in southwest Shandong should be mainly attributed to the advantageous conditions of the four cities of Ji-Yan-Zou-Qu for regional development. Firstly, in terms of spatial layout, they are densely distributed in a quadrangular shape, with an average distance among them of 28 km, the shortest distance between Yanzhou and Qufu of 15 km, and the longest distance between Jining and Qufu of 43 km. Secondly, in terms of communication, they are, with thanks to the sustained construction of regional transportation infrastructure in the past decades, conveniently linked with each other via either highways or expressways, with an average distance of less than half an hour's drive. Thirdly, in terms of economy, they have different leading industries respectively which are complementary with each other. In details, as the political center of the municipality and the biggest economic center of the region, Jining is strong in finance, coal mining, and manufacturing; as the key rail transport hub in southwest Shandong Province, Yanzhou is strong in machine manufacturing and coal mining; as the development base of Jining-Yanzhou coal field, Zoucheng is strong in thermal power generation and tourism; and as a well-known tourism city, Qufu is strong in tourism and manufacturing. Last but not the least, in terms of culture, they are all historically rooted into the Lu Culture, with a long history, rich traditions, yet unique cultural characters. For example, being a historic and cultural city of provincial level and the seat of China's old canal authority, Jining is appraised as "the Capital of Canals" and taken as the representative city of the canal culture; being one of the nine states of ancient China, Yanzhou is boasted as "the gateway to nine provinces and the key to the Qi and Lu States" and has been experiencing the prosperity of literature and the gathering of talents since the Han and Tang Dynasties; as historic and cultural city of national level, Zoucheng is the hometown of Mencius and well-known for both rich historic heritages, in particular the Temple, Mansion, Cemetery of Mencius, and the beautiful natural heritages, such as Tie Mountain, Gang Mountain, Ge Mountain, Jian Mountain, Jiulong Mountain, and Yi Mountain; also as a historic and

颜庙、周公庙、少昊陵等众多历史遗迹，被誉为“鲁国故都、儒学圣城”。

◎二、济兖邹曲鲁文化城市群发展面临的挑战

过去十多年里，正是基于上述各种有利条件，济兖邹曲鲁文化城市群在中国城市化进程快速推进、社会经济转型发展的背景下，伴随四座城市的持续发展而不断壮大，逐渐形成规模；尤其是区域交通条件的改善、国内旅游市场的增长以及国家大型重点项目的实施，为该地区的区域化城市发展创造了良好机遇。在区域交通方面，位于嘉祥的济宁曲阜机场于 2008 年建成并投入使用，辐射济宁、泰安、枣庄、菏泽、商丘、濮阳等鲁、豫、苏、皖四省八市 3 000 余万人口，将济兖邹曲与北京、上海、广州等国内重要城市通过空中航线直接联系在一起；京沪高速铁路于 2010 年建成通车，并在曲阜设立客运车站，将济兖邹曲与北京和上海的时空距离缩短到 2 个小时左右。在旅游发展方面，基于国民经济高速发展、生活水平迅速提高的社会大环境，我国旅游业已经进入快速发展阶段，《山东省旅游总体规划（2001—2020）》做出了 2006 年至 2010 年为山东旅游国际国内市场起飞阶段、2011 年至 2020 年为成熟发展阶段的战略部署，人文和自然旅游资源丰富的济兖邹曲鲁文化城市群无疑在其中扮演着重要角色，游客数量和旅游收入连年增长。在重点项目方面，南水北调东线工程一期主体于 2013 年年底完工并正式通水，济宁作为该项工程的重点地区，过境长度达 198 千米，对沿线地区的城市发展产生重要影响；始于 2008 年的运河申遗直至 2014 年终于尘埃落定，处于京杭大运河中段的济宁段运河，因为水利设施众多、运河文化浓厚，特别是以南旺为代表的一系列水利工程，在运河申遗工作中意义重大，对运河文化遗产的保护勘察、考古发掘和规划利用，为城市空间整合、文化旅游发展、生态环境建设，以及在此基础上发展地区文化特色、重塑地区整体形象、提高地区文化声誉创造了重要契机。

与此同时，济兖邹曲鲁文化城市群的发展也开始面临巨大挑战。一方面，济兖邹曲四座城市均是鲁西南经济比较发达、人口比较密集的地区，并且同时处于城市化加速发展阶段，普遍呈现人口规模增长和空间规模扩大的发展态势，规划中四座城市的建设用地分布几乎完全连在一起。另一方面，作为当地主导产业的煤炭开采导致大范围的地面塌陷，加剧了土地资源紧缺的问题（图 1）。此外，考虑到传统资源依赖型产业的转型发展以及旅游业作为新兴产业的迅速增长，四座城市均面临整合自然和文化资源、开发建设新型城市空间的课题。凡此种种，都需要从区域的角度，对济兖邹曲鲁文化城市群的空间发展进行统筹安排。

cultural city of national level, Qufu is the birthplace of Confucianism and the representative city of the Lu Culture, being praised as the Holy City of Confucianism and famous for the World Culture Heritages of the Temple, Mansion, and Cemetery of Confucius, as well as numerous historic heritages including the relics of the old capital city of Lu State, the Temple of Yan Hui, the Temple of Zhou Gong, and the Mausoleum of Shaohao.

◎ 2.Challenges faced by Ji-Yan-Zou-Qu Lu-Culture City Region

With thanks to the above-mentioned advantageous conditions for regional development and along with the respective development of the four cities of Ji-Yan-Zou-Qu under the circumstances of China's rapid urbanization and socio-economic transition, the Lu-Culture City Region developed fast in the past decade. In particular, the improvement of regional transportation, the development of tourism industry, and the realization of a number of large-scale projects have brought about favorable situations for the sustained development of the region. As regards regional transportation, firstly, the Jining-Qufu Airport in Jiaxiang put into use in 2008 has directly linked the region to China's primary cities, including Beijing, Shanghai, and Guangzhou via airlines, serving a population of more than 30 million in eight municipalities of the four provinces of Shandong, Henan, Jiangsu, and Anhui; secondly, the High-speed Railway between Beijing and Shanghai with a station in Qufu which was completed in 2010 has remarkably shortened the time distance between the region and both Beijing and Shanghai to about 2.5 hours. For tourism development, in view that China's tourism industry has stepped on the track of rapid development along with the fast growth of national economy and the outstanding increase of living standard, the Tourism Master Plan of Shandong Province (2001-2020) enacted the strategies of initiating both domestically and internationally the tourism markets in the period of 2006 to 2010 and maturing the tourism industry in the period of 2011 to 2020, with thanks to which the region, possessing a large number of humanism and natural heritages, has seen a continuous increase in terms of both tourist volume and tourism income, playing a significant role in the tourism development of Shandong Province. Regarding large-scale projects, firstly, the construction of the first phase of the South-North Water Transfer Eastern Line Project was finished at the end of 2013, 198 km of which is within the administrative boundaries of Jining, influencing remarkably on the urban development of the areas along the line; secondly, the Grand Canal was finally nominated by UNESCO as World Culture Heritage in 2014 after six years of application, for which Jining, standing at the middle section of the Grand Canal, played a significant role due to its outstanding hydraulic facilities and unique canal culture, and the protective investigation, archaeological excavation, and utilization planning for the cultural heritages distributed along the Grand Canal have created some hard-won opportunities for the areas concerned to integrate urban constructions, develop cultural tourism, and improve ecologic environment, as well as to highlight regional identity, reshape regional image, and upgrade regional prestige.

However, at the same time, the development of the Lu-Culture City Region is facing huge challenges. On the one hand, being the comparatively developed areas in southwest Shandong with a higher population density, the four cities of Ji-Yan-Zou-Qu are all in the period of accelerating urbanization, and have underwent sustained increase of both population and land-use with the planned construction areas being completely connected with each other. On the other hand, the activities of coal mining, which is the leading industry of the region, have resulted in a large area of subsidence lands, making the shortage of land resources even more serious (Fig. 1). Moreover, taking into consideration the transition of traditional

◎三、围绕“绿心”的济兖邹曲鲁文化城市群空间结构构想

2009 年，吴良镛先生曾带领研究团队，进行了济宁城市湿地系统规划研究与洸府河湿地公园概念设计研究，从区域文化和地域生态的角度，对济兖邹曲鲁文化城市群的文化发展、生态改善与城市建设进行了深入、系统的探讨，提出重点开展以区域“绿心”为主题的生态建设，塑造围绕“绿心”的“葡萄串”城市群空间结构，并且挖掘多样的地方文化，以文化复萌为契机，推进济兖邹曲鲁文化城市群的整体发展。

就区域结构而言，济兖邹曲鲁文化城市群拥有良好的自然环境和悠久的历史文脉，自然与人文资源丰富，以此为依托，可以形成自然与人文相融合的独具特色的区域整体空间结构。即：在地区中部，依托黄河、泰山、曲阜和邹城形成传统的“山水圣人文化轴”；在地区西部，依托京杭运河形成“运河文化带”；在地区东部，依托九龙山、尼山、峄山等山体林地形成“山林文化带”；在地区中心，依托泗水、洙水等河流水系形成“洙泗文化轴”。其中， 山水圣人文化轴、运河文化带和山林文化带由横贯区域“绿心”的洙泗文化轴联系在一起，相互依存、相得益彰，构成“两轴两带”

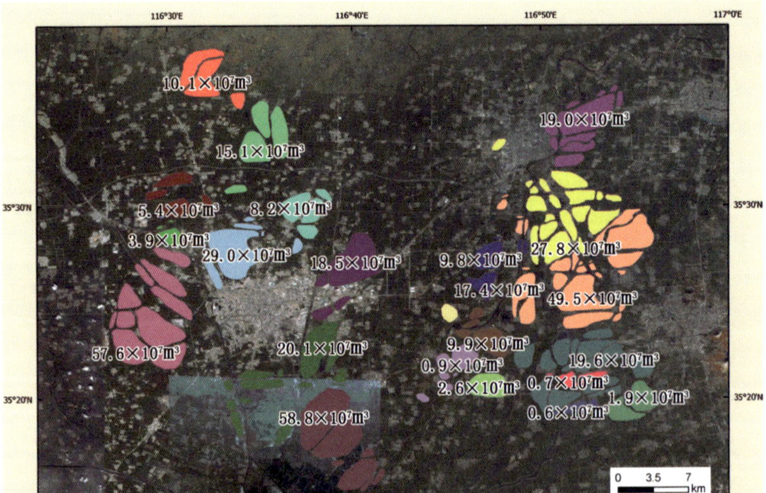

图 1. 济兖邹曲鲁文化城市群煤炭开采导致地面塌陷的范围与体积模拟
Fig.1 Scope and volume simulation of the coal mining subsidence lands in the Ji-Yan-Zou-Qu Lu-Culture City Region

resource-based industries and the uprising of tourism as emerging industry, it is necessary for all the four cities to integrate region-widely the natural and cultural resources and build new urban areas in a regional perspective. All these mentioned above imply the necessity of restructuring the spatial development of the Lu-Culture City Region in an overall way.

◎ 3. Spatial Structure of Ji-Yan-Zou-Qu Lu-Culture City Region Centering on A Green Heart

In 2009, while carrying out the Planning Study on *Jining's Urban Wetland System and Conceptual Design for Guangfu River Wetland Park*, WU and his team made a systematic analysis from the perspectives of regional culture and ecology, focusing on the cultural development, ecologic restoration, and urban construction of the Lu-Culture City Region. They proposed to restore the regional ecology through the construction of the "Green Heart", restructure the regional space through the shaping of an "urban cluster" spatial pattern centering on the "Green Heart", and strengthen the regional integrity through the development of various local cultures amid cultural renaissance.

In view of the advantaged natural environment and rich historic heritage of the Lu-Culture City Region, a regional spatial structure composed of two cultural axes and two cultural belts was proposed which is characterized by the combination of nature and humanism, that is the cultural axis of mountain-water-sage in the middle of the region which, from north to south, links the Yellow River, Mount Tai, Qufu and Zoucheng—the Zhu-Si cultural axis going through the "Green Heart" at the center of the region from east to west along the river system including the Zhu River and Si River, the canal cultural belt along the Grand Canal in the west of the region, and the cultural belt of hills and woods linking the Jiulong Mountain, Ni Mountain, Yi Mountain, and so on in the east of the region (Fig. 2). The cultural axis of mountain-water-sage—the canal cultural belt and the cultural belt of hills and woods that go through the region longitudinally are connected by the latitudinal Zhu-Si cultural axis, complementing with each other to form the key tourism routes of the region.

In view of the ecologic diversity of the Lu-Culture City Region dotted with rivers and hills, as well as the new requirements for ecological development following the construction of the south-north water transfer project and the water management of the coal mining subsidence area, an ecological zoning was proposed which, in line with the principle of giving priority to ecologic restoration and taking into consideration the regional spatial patter of two axes and two belts and the distinctions of the local natural conditions, divides the region into three ecologic zones, i.e. low mountains and hills in the east, subsidence lands and wetlands in the middle, and lakes and canals in the west (Fig. 3). Differentiated measures could be taken to foster, develop and protect the ecology of the three zones, so as to promote the sustainable development of the region's ecological environment to support the tourism development of the region.

In view of the rich local cultures of the Lu-Culture City Region, such as the Confucian culture represented by the heritages related to Confucius, the canal culture represented by the Grand Canal, and the natural culture represented by hills and rivers, as well as the emerging ecologic culture represented by the ecologic restoration of coal mining subsidence lands, a cultural zoning was proposed which, following the principle of integrating local cultures and taking into consideration the distribution of various cultural heritages, divides the region into three cultural zones in a concentric pattern, i.e. historic city circle, natural and humanism circle, and ecologic wetland circle (Fig. 4). Due attention would be paid to the exploration

的区域整体空间格局，同时也是当地文化旅游线路的重要依托（图 2）。

就地区生态而言，济兖邹曲鲁文化城市群水网密布，山丘连绵，生态环境类型多样，南水北调工程建设和采煤塌陷以及随之而来的水环境治理，为当地生态建设提出新的要求。遵循“以生态修复为先”的发展理念，结合“两轴两带”的区域空间格局，同时考虑自然条件的差异，可将济兖邹曲鲁文化城市群由东向西划分为低山丘陵、塌陷湿地和运河湖泊三个生态分区，分别采取不同措施，有针对性地进行生态环境的培育、建设和防护，促进地区生态环境的可持续发展，构成当地旅游业发展的本底（图 3）。

就地域文化而言，儒家文化、运河文化以及以天然山体、河流为载体的自然文化赋予济兖邹曲鲁文化城市群丰富的文化资源，而以采煤塌陷治理为代表的生态文化萌

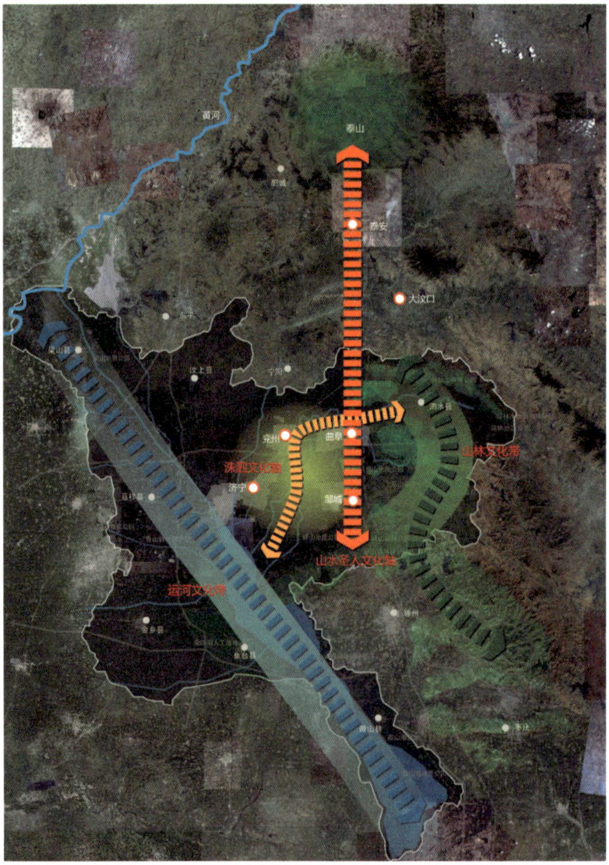

图 2. 济兖邹曲鲁文化城市群空间结构构想
Fig.2 A conceptual spatial structure of the Ji-Yan-Zou-Qu Lu-Culture City Region

and development of other traditional or modern local cultures besides those mentioned above, such as coal culture, poem culture, fishing culture, gourmet culture, etc., so as to promote the prosperity of various local cultures to become a new resource for both urban and tourism development of the region.

In view of the natural geography of the Lu-Culture City Region which is characterized by a dense distribution of rivers and water surfaces and a large area of hilly lands, as well as the potential direction of urban expansion and the functional zoning of the four cities of Ji-Yan-Zou-Qu, a spatial pattern of urban clusters was proposed which, in accordance with the principle of Transit Oriented Development, advocates the concentration of residential, industrial and service facilities to certain areas along the transportation arterials of either highway or railway, so as to form a number of mixed-use urban clusters, the functions and size of which could be fixed according to actual demands and local conditions. Thus, along with the extension of the highway and railway networks, more mixed-use urban clusters could be built up accordingly to form an urban corridor centering on the "Green Heart", being separated from each other by a series of green wedges which are connected to the "Green Heart" (Fig. 5).

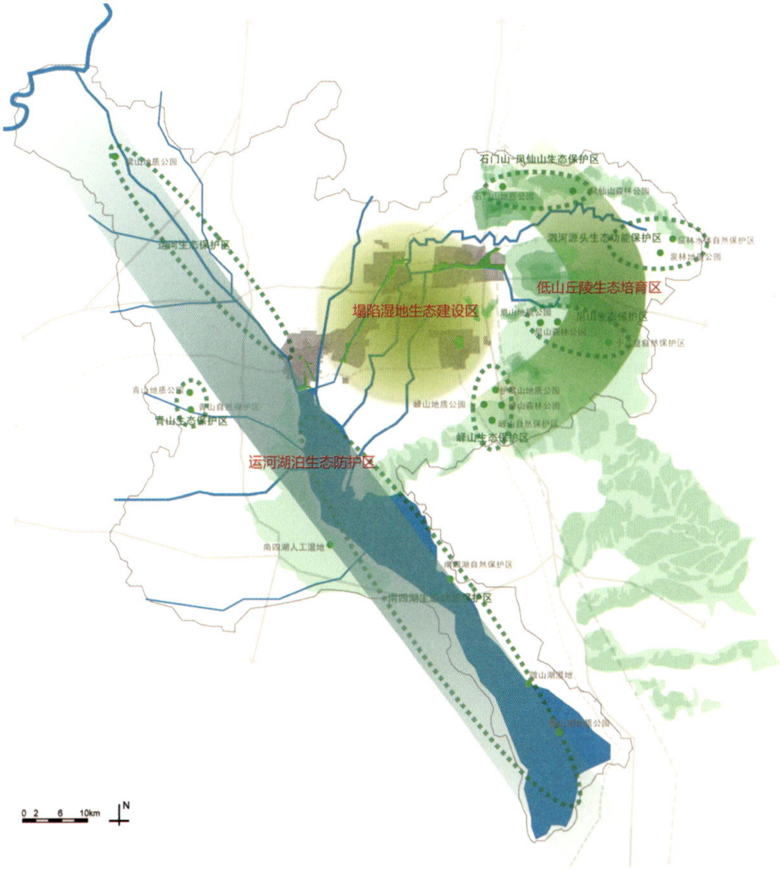

图 3. 济兖邹曲鲁文化城市群生态分区构想

Fig.3 A conceptual ecological zoning of the Ji-Yan-Zou-Qu Lu-Culture City Region

芽使得既有丰富的文化资源得到进一步发展。遵循“融合地区文化”的发展理念，结合不同文化资源的空间分布特点，可对济兖邹曲鲁文化城市群进行文化圈层的划分，形成由历史城市文化圈、自然人文文化圈和生态湿地文化圈组成的圈层式文化空间格局，并且在儒家文化、运河文化和自然文化的基础上，深度挖掘各地的其他传统和现代文化，包括煤炭文化、诗歌文化、渔家文化、祭祀文化、餐饮文化，等等，促进多元的传统文化与现代文化的和谐共荣，成为旅游产业和城市发展的新资源（图 4）。

就空间形态而言，济兖邹曲鲁文化城市群拥有众多自然水系，四座城市也各有特定的自然格局，有必要也有可能立足本地条件，结合城市发展方向、功能分区和自然山水，构建组团式城市空间形态，即：结合公路和轨道交通建设，采取以交通为导向的 TOD 发展模式和带状城市的组织方式，在主要交通干线的适当地点，集中布局居住、工业、服务等设施，形成功能复合的城镇组团，并且根据实际需要，合理确定城镇组团的大小和内容，最终沿交通线路形成“葡萄串”式的城镇走廊，围绕“绿心”布局，

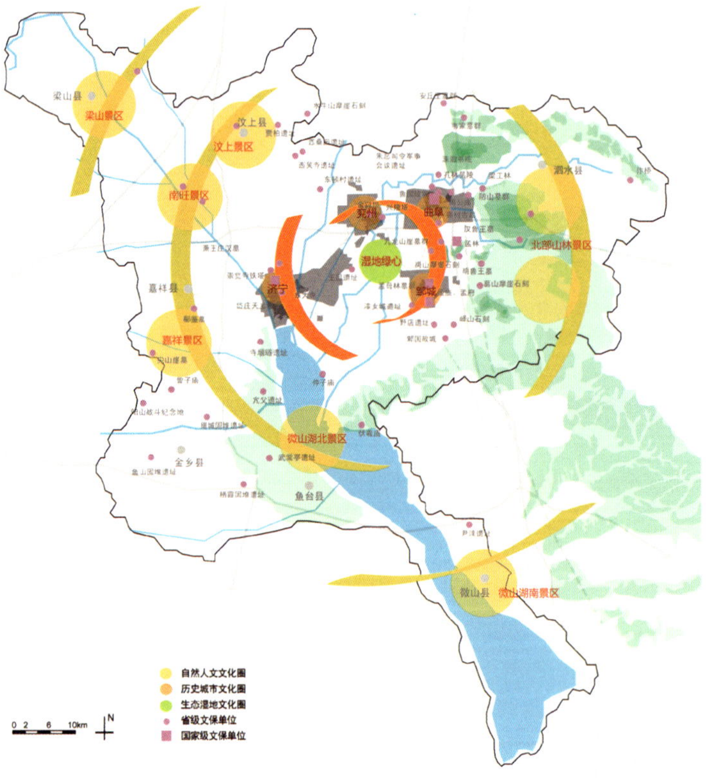

图 4. 济兖邹曲鲁文化城市群文化分区构想
Fig.4 A conceptual cultural zoning of the Ji-Yan-Zou-Qu Lu-Culture City Region

In some sense, the improvement of the regional transportation system based on Qufu High-speed Railway Station, the development of the regional historical axis based on the historic and cultural cities of Qufu and Zoucheng, the establishment of the new cultural axis based on the Grand Canal as World Culture Heritage, and the ecological restoration of the coal mining subsidence lands at the center of the region can all be taken as catalysis for promoting the urban and tourism development of the Lu-Culture City-Region, as well as the unique characters of that region.

◎ 4. Spatial Development of Qufu from the perspective of Ji-Yan-Zou-Qu Lu-Culture City Region

Being the capital city of Lu State before the Qin Dynasty, Qufu is the place of origin of the Lu Culture, as well as one of the cradles of traditional Chinese culture. With a history of more than 5,000 years, it can be boasted as one of the oldest and greatest cultural holy land of the world. As a typical representative city of the Lu Culture, it is famous for being the hometown of Confucius, a great thinker and educator of ancient China and the founder of Confucianism, being appraised as "the home of Confucius and Mencius" and "the state of rite and courtesy". It possesses a great number of cultural resources of various periods and forms, including World Culture Heritages, national historic and cultural cities, cultural protection sites of various levels, and historic relics of various periods. The long history and rich culture give it a unique situation in the spectrum of both Chinese culture and Chinese cities.

In the past decade, Qufu has seen an unprecedented development of regional transportation facilities. Firstly, both the highway between Beijing and Fuzhou and the high-speed railway between Beijing and shanghai, as key component of the transportation arterial along the eastern coast of China, go through Qufu longitudinally with an interchange and a station respectively there. Secondly, the highway between Rizhao and Heze also goes through Qufu in a latitudinal way, directly linked to the longitudinal highway between Beijing and Fuzhou. The construction of all these regional transportation facilities has remarkably improved the communication of Qufu to other parts of China and dramatically changed its role in the Lu-Culture City Region, giving it more potentiality to become the new gateway city of the region and welcome new urban growth at the intersection of the two transportation arteries. This will inevitably play a significant influence on its future spatial development. Taking that into consideration, WU Liangyong and his research team put forward some ideas on the spatial development of Qufu from the perspective of Ji-Yan-Zou-Qu Lu-Culture City Region when carrying out the project of Conceptual Planning for Qufu's Urban Development in Regional and Cultural Perspectives and Urban Design for Qufu's Central Axis in 2007 and 2008.

Firstly, in view of the unique role of Qufu in Chinese culture spectrum and Chinese city system, as well as the objective of "rejuvenating Chinese nation in the new era" set by the Chinese government, it is possible and necessary as well to develop Qufu into a world-class cultural city based on its long history and rich cultural resources. It means that the spatial development of Qufu should be firmly rooted into its cultural identity and closely related to the renaissance of the regional culture, with due attention to the strict protection of various historic and cultural heritages, the active exploration of various local cultures, in particular the Lu Culture, and the great development of Confucian culture.

Secondly, being a key member of the Lu-Culture City Region, the spatial development of Qufu should be closely integrated into the spatial development of the region. Among the two axes and two belts of the

各城镇组团之间建设楔形绿地，并与“绿心”相连（图5）。

在此过程中，在曲阜高铁车站建设带动下的区域交通条件的进一步改善，以曲阜和邹城两座国家级历史文化名城为节点的历史轴线的不断强化，以京杭大运河申遗成功为契机的运河文化轴线的初步建立，以及针对煤炭挖掘造成的塌陷地区的生态环境治理，都将成为促进济兖邹曲鲁文化城市群发展，特别是基于地域文化的旅游产业发展的重要媒介，也将成为济兖邹曲鲁文化城市群的特色所在。

◎四、区域视野中的曲阜城市空间发展

曲阜是先秦时期的鲁国故城、鲁文化的发源地，也是中国古代传统文化的发祥地之一，迄今已有五千年历史，堪称世界上最古老、最伟大的文化胜地之一。作为鲁文化城市群的典型代表，它以中国古代伟大的思想家、教育家、儒家学派的创始人——孔子的故乡而闻名于世，以“孔孟之乡”“礼仪之邦”而蜚声中外，拥有不同历史时期、多种空间形态的大量文化资源，包括世界文化遗产、国家级历史文化名城、各级重点文物保护单位以及各种历史文化遗迹，因为悠久的历史和丰富的文化而在中国文化和中国城市中占据特殊地位。

近十多年来，曲阜的区域交通设施建设得到空前发展。一是我国东部沿海南北向交通主轴线的重要组成部分——京福高速公路和京沪高速铁路——都在曲阜境内通过，并且分别建有出入口和车站；二是横贯济兖邹曲的日荷高速公路也在东西方向上从曲阜境内通过，并与京福高速公路相交。上述区域交通设施建设极大改善了曲阜的对外交通联系，同时也极大改变了曲阜在济兖邹曲鲁文化城市群中的地位，赋予其发展成为该地区新的交通门户的潜力，以及在东西、南北两个方向的交通通道相交之处出现新的城镇生长点的可能，进而对其空间发展产生深远影响。2007年，吴良镛先生领导的研究团队进行了《区域文化视角下的曲阜城市发展构想及城市中轴线城市设计研究》，针对新形势下曲阜城市空间发展提出了以下构想。

首先，鉴于曲阜在中国文化和中国城市中的特殊地位，以及中国政府在新时期提出的“中华民族伟大复兴”的发展目标，曲阜应该也有可能基于其悠久的历史文脉和丰富的文化资源，发展成为世界级的文化城市。这意味着，曲阜的城市发展必须立足于自身的文化特点，在严格保护各类历史文化遗产的基础上，大力挖掘鲁文化的地域特色，积极发扬儒家文化的内在精神，自觉地将城市建设发展与地域文化复兴统一在一起。

第二，曲阜作为济兖邹曲鲁文化城市群的重要一员，其城市空间发展必须纳入该地区整体发展的空间框架。在济兖邹曲鲁文化城市群“两轴两带”的区域空间结构中，

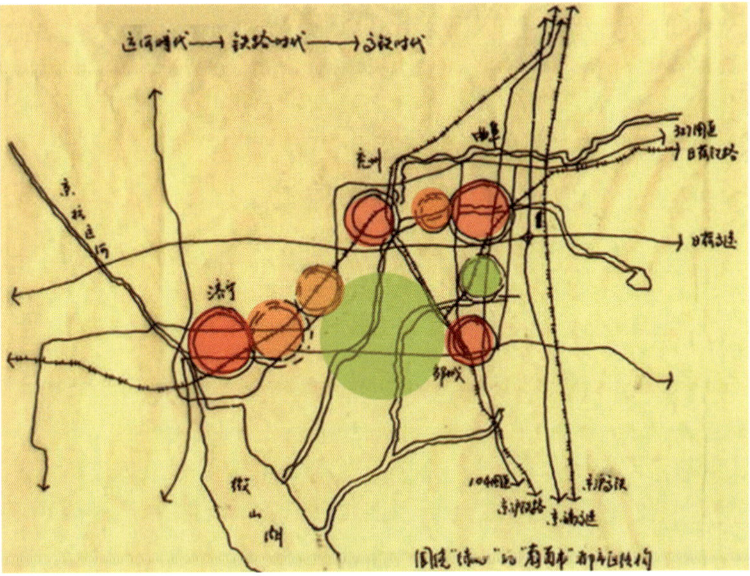

图 5. 吴良镛先生关于济兖邹曲鲁文化城市群城市形态的构想
Fig.5 A conceptual spatial pattern for urban development in the Ji-Yan-Zou-Qu Lu-Culture City Region proposed by WU Liangyong
资料来源：图 1~5：清华大学建筑学院，《济宁城市湿地系统规划研究与洸府河湿地公园概念设计》，2009.
Source: Fig.1~5: School of Architecture, Tsinghua University. Planning Study on Jining's Urban Wetland System and Conceptual Design for Guangfu River Wetland Park, 2009.

region's spatial structure, the cultural axis of mountain-water-sage is the most important component of the cultural matrix of Shandong Province, which starts from the Yellow River in the north, passes by Mount Tai in the middle, and ends at Qufu and Zoucheng in the south. By linking two national historic and cultural cities, i.e. Qufu and Zoucheng, and a great number of historic and cultural heritages, including the temples, mansions and cemeteries of both Confucius and Mencius, it actually forms an axis of Confucianism which is the core of the cultural axis of mountain-water-sage (Fig. 6). Obviously, the development of this Confucian axis should become the theme of Qufu's spatial development.

Thirdly, in view that the Qufu City Master Plan approved in 2003 structured the spatial development of Qufu into one central area composed of two sectors respectively to the north and south of the Dayi River and two new areas composed of four clusters, the future spatial development of Qufu could be further integrated into a structure of "one core in the middle, two wings respectively to the east and west, and one central axis extending southwards". It means that the northern and southern sectors of the existing central area should be taken as a whole to form the core urban area of the city centering on the central axis, while new urban development should be more guided to the east and west of the central axis to form the new urban wings in the pattern of urban clusters (Fig. 7). In practice, potential urban growth should be oriented southwards along the central axis, as well as eastwards and westwards to the new urban wings. Due attention should be paid to the development of the central axis as a key demonstration area of urban and cultural identity, which links from north to south the traditional Confucian area, the new Confucian area,

“山水圣人文化轴”是山东区域文化格局中最重要的一环，它北起黄河，途经泰山，向南先后进入曲阜和邹城境内，串联起曲阜和邹城两座国家级历史文化名城，以及从“三孔”到“三孟”的一系列历史文化遗产，天然地形成了一条“儒学文化轴线”，成为“山水圣人文化轴”的核心内容。显然，彰显“儒学文化轴线”应该成为曲阜城市空间发展的主脉（图 6）。

第三，基于 2003 年《曲阜城市总体规划》确定的“一城，两区，四组团”的总体布局（即以大沂河为界，中心城区分为“北城区”和“南城区”，东西分别发展开发区、高铁、时庄、陵城四个城市组团），未来曲阜城市空间结构可进一步整合，将“北城区”和“南城区”视为整体，围绕城市中轴线统一规划建设，同时在其东西两翼进一步细分城市组团（图 7）。在城市空间发展的时序上，则应强调“中轴南进，两翼展开”，即以城市中轴线向南拓展作为重点，进而向东西两翼展开，城市中轴线

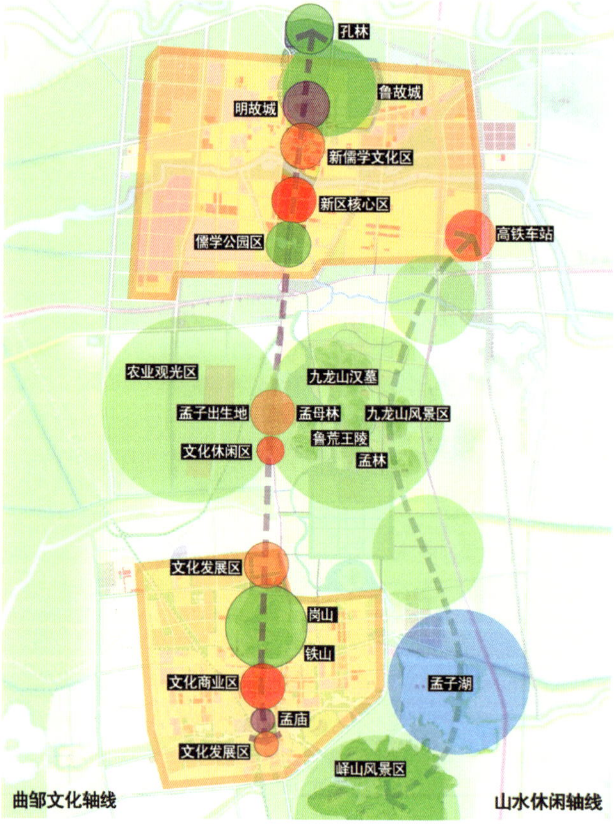

图 6. 曲阜—邹城儒学文化轴线发展构想
Fig.6 A conceptual spatial structure of the Qufu–Zoucheng Confucian axis

and the planned Confucian New City.

Fourthly, in order to fully play the cultural identity of Qufu as the Holy City of Confucianism and create as much as possible the happy sense of Holy Land through the construction of physical environment, due attention should be paid to shaping an artful framework for its spatial development by taking into consideration the spatial patterns of the old city and the natural environment. From north to south, the traditional central axis starting from the Temple of Confucius links successively along the Dacheng Avenue—the traditional Confucian area, the new Confucian area, and the planned Confucian New City, forming a spectacle scroll of Confucian culture in terms of both time and space, which can be appraised as an axis of courtesy culture to demonstrate the order and grandness of Qufu's spatial development; meanwhile from east to west, the Dayi River, as an important branch of the Zhu-Si river system featured by a long history and many beautiful views, meanders through the city as a key landscape corridor, which can be appraised as an axis of pleasure culture to demonstrate the natural and easy aspects of Qufu's spatial development (Fig. 8).

Last but not the least, close attention should also be paid to the creation of a better cultural environment in Qufu amid its spatial development based on the strict protection of listed cultural heritages of all kinds and all levels, so as to integrate the cultural heritages into modern life and integrate the cultural heritage protection with the contemporary urban construction through "active protection and holistic creation". Particularly, for the historic protection areas, careful studies should be carried out to reasonably delimitate the protected zone and buffer zone of a certain cultural heritage and describe the regulations on the height, volume and style of new buildings surrounding it, so as to guarantee a harmonious and orderly physical environment in its surrounding area. Regarding the relics of the old capital city of Lu State, the protection measure of landscaping for great sites could be applied to fuse the cultural heritages into the pastoral scene of the countryside, turning the site into another important base for Qufu's development of cultural tourism. For instance, the relics of its city walls and city moats could be built into a landscape ring, the axis of which would link the Temple and Cemetery of Confucius into a sequence of public spaces full of the sense of pilgrimage, the ruins of the Temple of Zhougong into a relic park featured by the mood of grief, and the east-west axis of the city into a tourism route demonstrating the historic evolution of the city.

NOTE: The research team of School of Architecture, Tsinghua University for the project of "Conceptual Planning for Qufu's Urban Development in Regional and Cultural Perspectives and Urban Design for Qufu's Central Axis" includes WU Liangyong, LIU Jian, LI Liang, ZHANG Yue, GUO Lu, LI Yunjing, CAO Wen, WU Xiao and YIN Xiao.

The research team for the project of "Planning Study on Jining's Urban Wetland System and Conceptual Design for Guangfu River Wetland Park" includes WU Liangyong, LIU Jian, LI Liang, LIN Wenqi, GUO Lu, LI Mengying, WU Xiao, YIN Xiao, and FAN Dongyang.

Reference

[1] School of Architecture, Tsinghua University. Conceptual Planning for Qufu's Urban Development in Regional and Cultural Perspectives and Urban Design for Qufu's Central Axis, 2008.

[2] School of Architecture, Tsinghua University. Planning Study on Jining's Urban Wetland System and Conceptual Design for Guangfu River Wetland Park, 2009.

[3] KIM SeokChul, WU Liangyong, and LIU Jian. *Qufu Urban Proposal*. Archiban, Seoul, Korea, 2006.

[4] Department of Urban and Environmental Sciences, College of Environment, Beijing University. Strategic Planning for the Development of Jining-Qufu Metropolitan, 2001.

[5] LIU Jian. The Cultural City of Qufu: Its Past, Present & Future. *China City Planning Review*, 2007, 16 (2): 69-72.

由北向南串联起“三孔”历史文化区、新儒学文化区和儒学文化新城，作为城市文化特色集中展示区。

第四，为彰显曲阜作为“儒学圣城”的文化特色，曲阜城市空间发展应在尊重传统城市格局和自然山水格局的基础上，重视城市空间“艺术骨架”的构建，通过体型环境建设创造“欢乐的圣地感”（图 8）。例如，在城市南北方向上，始于孔庙的传统城市轴线沿大成路由北向南依次联系“三孔”历史文化区、新儒学文化区和儒学文化新城，堪称儒学文化在时间和空间上的画卷，可视为曲阜城市空间结构中体现庄重礼仪的“礼文化”轴线；在城市东西方向上，大沂河蜿蜒而过，作为洙泗水系的重要支流，不仅历史渊源深厚，并且沿线景色宜人，通过多年的景观建设，已然成为曲阜城内重要的景观轴线，可视为曲阜城市空间结构中体现轻松自然的“乐文化”轴线。

此外，曲阜城市空间发展应在严格保护各级法定历史遗产的基础上，致力于围绕历史遗产的文化环境的创造，努力做到“积极保护、整体创造”，从而将历史遗产保护与当代城市建设统一起来；尤其在历史保护区内，要通过合理划定保护区和缓冲区以及对新建建筑高度、体量、风格等的规定，一方面严格保护历史遗产本身，另一方面整体创造历史遗产周边环境的空间秩序，同时结合文化旅游发展，使历史遗产与当代生活紧密联系在一起。其中，针对鲁故城所覆盖的历史文化区范围，可采用大地景观的手法进行大遗址的保护与展示，最终形成历史遗产与田园风光交相辉映的局面，作为曲阜发展文化旅游的另一重要基地。例如，依托鲁故城城墙城河遗址可建设形成环城景观带，依托孔庙孔林轴线可建设形成具有“朝圣”之感的开放空间序列，依托周公庙及其轴线遗址可建设形成具有“黍离之悲”的遗址公园和景观通道，依托鲁故城东西轴线可建设形成串联多个历史遗迹的览古之路，等等。

附：清华大学《区域文化视角下的曲阜城市发展构想及城市中轴线城市设计研究》课题组成员包括吴良镛、刘健、李亮、张悦、郭璐、李韫静、曹雯、吴霄、般宵等。

清华大学《济宁城市湿地系统规划研究与洸府河湿地公园概念设计》课题组成员包括吴良镛、刘健、李亮、林文祺、郭璐、李梦颖、吴霄、般宵、范冬阳等。

参考文献：

[1] 清华大学建筑学院 . 区域文化视角下的曲阜城市发展构想及城市中轴线城市设计研究 . 2008.

[2] 清华大学建筑学院 . 济宁城市湿地系统规划研究与洸府河湿地公园概念设计 . 2009.

[3] 金锡澈，吴良镛，刘健 . 曲阜城市设计提案 . Archiban，韩国汉城，2006.

[4] 北京大学环境学院城市与环境资源系 . 济宁—曲阜都市区发展战略规划 . 2001.

[5] LIU Jian. The Cultural City of Qufu: Its Past, Present & Future. China City Planning Review, 2007, 16 (2): 69-72.

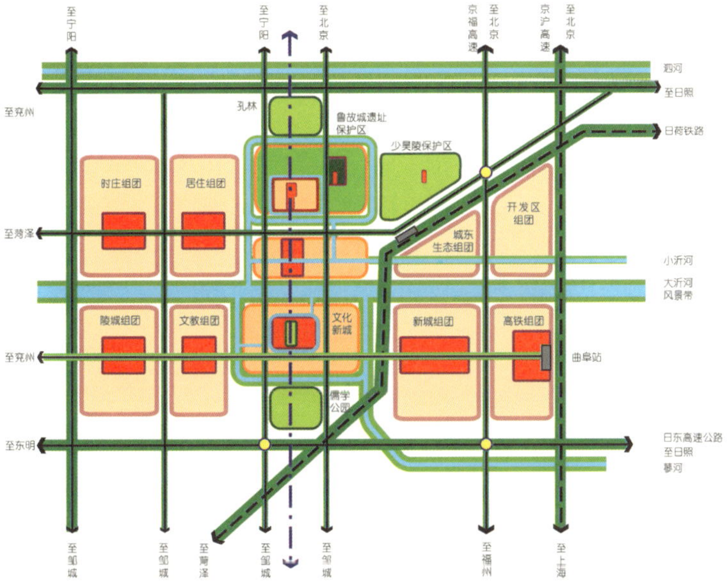

图 7：曲阜“一体两翼、中轴南进”的城市空间布局构想

Fig.7 A conceptual spatial structure of Qufu composed of one core, two wings and a central axis extending southwards

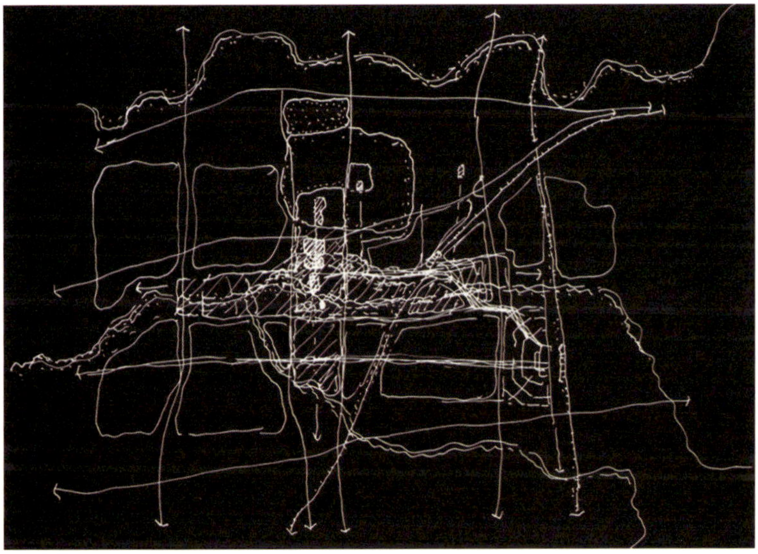

图 8：吴良镛先生关于曲阜城市空间“艺术骨架”的构想

Fig.8 An artful framework for the spatial development of Qufu proposed by WU Liangyong

资料来源：图 6~8：清华大学建筑学院，《区域文化视角下的曲阜城市发展构想及城市中轴线城市设计研究》，2008.

Source: Fig.6~8: School of Architecture, Tsinghua University. Conceptual Planning for Qufu's Urban Development in Regional and Cultural Perspectives and Urban Design for Qufu's Central Axis, 2008.

曲阜明故城的价值特征及其整体保护

邵甬

曲阜是具有悠久历史的中国历史文化名城，是鲁国的都城，孔子的故乡，儒家思想的诞生地，被称为“东方圣城”，同时曲阜至今还是一个活着的城市，具有文化、生活、旅游等多重功能。本论文从自然基底、历史渊源、城市与建筑特征等几个方面试图阐释曲阜明故城的价值特征，同时提出对其整体保护的建议。

曲阜在人们的印象中是一个“圣城”，因为它孕育了孔子及其所倡导的儒家文化。但是为什么曲阜能够成为“圣城”？或者是否仅仅只是“圣城”？它的价值特征到底有哪些？今日的曲阜明故城还有哪些遗存？应该如何保护？要回答这些问题必须从曲阜明故城的历史文化和价值特征的研究中寻求答案。本论文希望从自然基底、历史渊源、城市与建筑特征等几个方面诠释曲阜明故城的整体价值，同时强调对其整体保护的重要性。

◎一、曲阜明故城的自然基底

我国古代山水交融，复杂多变的地理环境决定了各地文化的多样性，而在人工建设能力极其有限的条件下，自然环境与聚落的选址、形态、规模以及地域文化形成都有着紧密联系。

曲阜地处鲁中山区和鲁西南平原的交界处，属于泰、沂、蒙山前冲积扇的中上部。东、南、北三面环山，丘陵起伏，为鲁西南平原的东北角。

风水上来看，曲阜北依玄武泰山，南引朱雀峄山，东连沂蒙群山为青龙，西俯千畴平原为白虎。地势东青龙高，而西白虎低，正好符合中国人的环境风水格局（图 1）。而其更有独特之处，境内泗河、沂河均自东向西流淌，并在境内汇合而成怀抱之势，形成了较为理想的微观环境，这是曲阜历代城市在此选址的重要前提。

Qufu Ming City: the Attributes of the Values and Its Comprehensive Conservation

Shao Yong

Qufu, as the capital of Lu State, the birthplace of Confucius and his belief system and known as a "sacred city", is a famous historic and cultural city in China. It is also a living city with multiple functions of culture, living and tourism. The author hopes to give an overall picture of the value of Qufu Ming city from its natural setting, historical development and its city and architectural characters, and to highlight the significance of a comprehensive conversation of the city.

Qufu, as the birthplace of Confucius and his belief system, is known as a "sacred city" among people. How can Qufu be sacred, or is it just a sacred city? Where are its attributes of value? What still remains in the old Ming-era walled city of Qufu? How can it be well preserved? To answer these questions, we have to look at the history, culture and the attributes of values of the city area. The author hopes to give an overall picture of the value of Qufu Ming city from its natural setting, historical development and its city and architectural characters, and to highlight the significance of a comprehensive conversation of the city.

◎ 1. The Natural Setting of Qufu Ming-era Walled City

The complex and varied geographical conditions in ancient China, with blending of mountainous and water landscapes, determines the cultural diversity of the country in different areas. Due to limited construction ability of human society, the location, form, size of settlements and the development of local culture are always closely linked with their natural settings.

Qufu is located at the border of the middle mountainous area and the flat lands in the south-western part of the province, as a middle-upper part of the alluvial fan in the front area of Tai, Yi and Meng mountains. Surrounded on three sides by mountains in the east, south and north, the area with rolling hills is in the north-eastern end of the flat lands.

According to Fengshui theory, Qufu is geographically embraced by four guardian animals, with Tai Mount as a black turtle in the north, Yi Mount as a red phoenix in the south, Yimeng Mountains as a blue dragon in the east and Qianchou plains as a white tiger in the west. High in the east and low in the west, the site is a perfect example of the Fengshui landscape of China (Fig.1). Besides, Qufu is embraced by Si River and Yi River, both flowing from east to west and joining each other in the area. The unique condition

图 1. 曲阜大山水格局（上海同济城市规划设计研究院）
Fig. 1 the landscape pattern of Qufu (Shanghai Tongji Urban Planning and Design Institute)

◎二、曲阜明故城的历史渊源和城市建设

根据史料记载和考古挖掘，曲阜在明故城建成之前还有五次成规模的城市营建活动，包括封鲁之前的“少昊之墟”（《史记 · 鲁周公世家》）、周鲁故城、汉鲁故城、北魏石城和宋仙源城，而其中周鲁故城和汉鲁故城与明故城在地层上形成叠压之势，而周鲁故城的形成背景及其建设对鲁故城又有着非常重要的影响。（图 2）

1．周鲁故城建设与“孔庙初立”

曲阜在商代（公元前 16 世纪至公元前 8 世纪）为奄国，是商王朝在东方的重要属国，是商第十八王南庚的都城，到第二十王盘庚由奄迁都于殷（河南安阳小屯村）。公元前 11 世纪，周武王灭商，建都镐京，为了建立和巩固国家的统治，在全国范围内进行了大分封。周武王将其胞弟、王国辅臣周公旦封到这里，国号鲁。周公长子伯禽成为第一代鲁君。曲阜成为鲁国的都城，历时长达 873 年，经历了周、春秋、战国三个时期。东汉应劭曰“曲阜在鲁城中，委曲长七八里”，故名曲阜。鲁君凭着自己的优越地位及带来的大量周王朝的礼器、典籍，使鲁国在政治、经济、文化等方面得到了迅速的发展，为建设鲁故城打下了基础。

西周成王为了推行西周的宗法分封政体，指导当时的建设活动，以便更好地把城邑建设纳入宗法分封政体的轨道，特制订了一套城邑建设制度——营国制度。《周礼 · 考工记》中对于都城建设规划制度有明确要求：“匠人营国，方九里，旁三门。国中九

has facilitated to develop an ideal microenvironment, an important prerequisite when the site was selected to build the city by different dynasties.

◎ 2. The Historical Development and Urban Construction of Qufu Ming city

According to historical records and evidence of archeology, Qufu had undergone another five large-scaled urban construction activities before the Ming-era city was built, including "remains of Shaohao Kingdom" (*Records of the Grand Historian: House of Lu zhougong*), Zhou Lu City, Han Lu City, Shi City in the Northern Wei Dynasty and Xianyuan County in the Song Dynasty. The ancient Han Lu city was built upon the layering of the Zhou Lu city, thus the latter had a significant influence in the development of the former (Fig. 2).

2.1 The Development of Zhou Lu City and the Establishment of the Temple of Confucius

Known as the State of Yan during the Shang Dynasty (16th Century BC to 8th Century BC), Qufu was an important state in the east during the Shang Period, and was established as the capital city during the reign of Nangeng, the 18th King of the Shang Dynasty till the reign of the 20th King Pangeng, who removed the capital to Yin (Xiaotun Village in Anyang, Henan Province). In the 11th Century BC, the King Wu of Zhou overthrew the Shang Dynasty and founded capital in Haojing. In order to consolidate the power, he established a number of feudal states under his brothers and clans, among whom Ji Dan, his younger brother, was appointed Duke of Zhou to administrate the territory that was titled Lu. His eldest son, Bo Qin became the founder of the State of Lu. For more than 873 years, Qufu had been the capital city of the State of Lu all the way through the dynasty of Zhou, the Spring and Autumn Period and the Warring States Period. Ying Shao, a famous scholar in the Eastern Han Dynasty, said "several-mile long hills winding across the city of Lu", thus the city was named Qufu (crooked hills). With its advantageous geographical location and a number of ritual vassals, ancient books and classics, the State of Lu had been politically, economically and culturally developed, which laid a foundation for the construction of the city.

In order to carry out a political system of patriarchal clans and fiefdom and to bring city constructions into the system, King Cheng of Zhou started to guide the building activities by establishing a set of regulations: regulations on city planning. *Zhou Li Kao Gong Ji (Records of Inspection of the Craftsmen)* specified the requirements in the construction of the capital city — "the design of the city shall be a walled square with three gates at each side, partitioned into nine equal parts by large horizontal and vertical meridians or roads, with ancestral temple in the east, altar of land and grain in the west, imperial court in the front and a market at the back". The findings of archaeological excavations have revealed conformity of the city with these requirements. The Ming-era city, which was later located in the south-western end of the Lu city, had borrowed part of the original section, namely the southern and western moat and walls of its predecessor.

Originated in the State of Song (today Shangqiu city), the ancestors of Confucius were forced to migrate to the State of Lu during the rebellions of Family Hua (*Records of the Grand Historian: House of Confucius*). Confucius' father Shuliang was said to live in Zouyi, the southeast of Lu. He married the daughter of Family Yan and the couple gave birth to Confucius. After the death of his father, Confucius moved with his mother to the south-western part of Lu, where the Temple of Confucius is seated today. Following his travels through various states, Confucius lived in a mansion between the banks of Zhu and Si Rivers, where

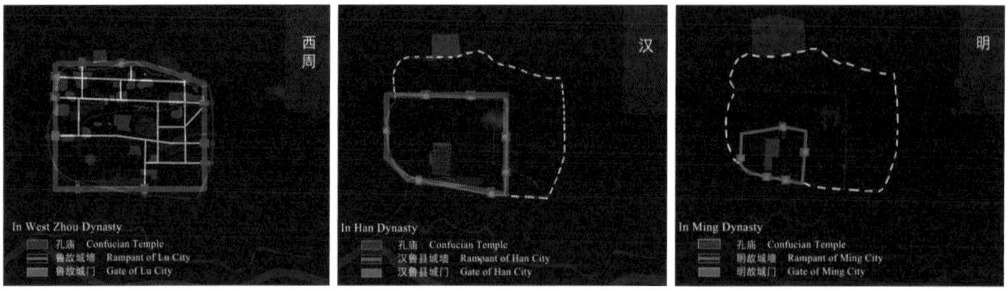

图 2. 曲阜明故城发展图（上海同济城市规划设计研究院）
Fig. 2 the development of Qufu Ming city in the history (Shanghai Tongji Urban Planning and Design Institute)

经九纬，经涂九轨。左祖右社，面朝后市，市朝一夫。”根据对鲁故城的考古发现，可以看到当时的城市建设基本遵从了《周礼 · 考工记》的要求。而后来的明故城在鲁故城西南角，明故城的营造利用了原鲁故城的西护城河、西墙、南护城河和南墙的各一部分作为明故城的西护城河、西墙以及南护城河、南墙。

孔子先祖原居宋国（今河南商丘），因“畏华氏之逼而奔鲁”（《史记 · 孔子世家》），传至孔子父叔梁纥，居鲁城东南尼山昌平乡陬邑，娶颜氏女而生孔子。叔梁纥死后，孔子随颜母迁居鲁城内西南部分今孔庙所在之地，孔子出游列国后居于洙泗之间的“居堂”授徒讲学，但其妻、子及其子孙仍居于此。公元前 479 年 2 月 18 日孔子去世，葬于鲁城北泗上。第二年鲁哀公将孔子生前“故所居堂”立为庙，庙屋有三间。后迁至城内并增扩到三百六十间，历经 2500 年的历史过程，中途从未间断，是我国最古老的庙。

2. 汉鲁故城建设与“孔庙内移”

西汉初，继续实行秦时的郡县制，此地仍名鲁县，隶属不变。汉高祖为了屏卫王室，在消灭异姓王的同时，又将少量的同姓子孙封于各地。汉高后元年（公元前 187 年），以其地封鲁元公主之子张偃为鲁王，即改县为鲁国。景帝三年（公元前 154 年），徙其子淮阳王余王鲁（仍号鲁国），是为恭（共）王。恭王好治宫室苑囿，曾建造当时极为豪华的灵光殿。“坏孔子旧宅，以广其居。闻钟、磬、琴、瑟声，乃不复坏。于其壁中得古文经传。”（《山东通志 · 疆域志 · 封建》）据考证，灵光殿基当大致在今孔府附近。汉鲁城基本是以灵光殿为中心来设计营造的，汉鲁城使用时间不长，到东汉后期城垣即已颓废，而整座城最后维持之下限当不超过东汉末年。

he gave his lectures on classics to his disciples, while his wife and decedents still lived in the original house. When Confucius died in 479 BC, he was buried on the bank of the Si River. Two years after his death, Duke Ai of Lu consecrated his former house as a temple. The three-room house was later removed into the inner city, and expanded into 360 rooms. The temple was further repaired and renovated in subsequent centuries for 2,500 years, among the oldest temples in China.

2.2 The Construction of Ancient Han Lu City and the Relocation of the Temple

In early Western Han Dynasty, the prefecture-county system created by State Qin was continued, and the city remained its name of Lu County. In order to consolidate the power of imperial family, Emperor Gao Zu of Han Dynasty got rid of vassal kings who were not related to the imperial clan and gave lands to a few princes from the family clan. In the first year of the reign of Empress Lu (187 BC), Zhang Yan, the son of her daughter Princess Luyuan was appointed the Duke of Lu, and Lu was upgraded from a county to a state. In the third year of his reign (154 BC), Emperor Jing of Han appointed his son Yu to govern State Lu as Duke Gong. Duke Gong, who was fond of palaces and gardens, built a luxurious Lingguang Palace at the site. "(Duke Gong) destroyed the former house of Confucius for the expansion of his palace until rings of bells and musical instruments were heard, he stopped further destructions and discovered ancient books and scriptures in the walls of the house". (*General Annals of Shangdong Territory Feudalism*) According to research, Lingguang Palace was located around today's Confucius Temple, at the center of Han Lu City. The city had been deteriorating during the late Eastern Han Dynasty and had been totally abandoned by the end of the dynasty.

Since the proposals of "eliminate the hundred schools of thought and respect only Confucianism" were accepted in Han Dynasty, Confucianism was gradually mainstreamed and a lot effort was made to rebuild the Temple of Confucius. In the first year of Yong Xing (153 AD), the emperor gave orders to build Confucius Temple, appointed Kong He the keeper of the temple, and inscribed tablets in the temple. Relocated from the bank of Si River to the former house of Confucius, the three-room temple could hold about one thousand people. The relocation laid a foundation for the construction of the Ming city.

2.3 The Separation of the Temple and the City during the Sui, Tang, Song and Yuan Dynasties and the Expansion of the Temple

From Shi City in the Northern Wei Dynasty to Xianyuan City in the Song Dynasty, Qufu remained a county-level city and was downsized. According to historical records and archaeological findings, the city area had been moved to the highlands around Zhou Gong Temple in the north east of Qufu, thus making a separation of the temple and the city. From Xianyuan County in the Song Dynasty to Qufu County in the Jin and Yuan dynasties, the city retained its status for five hundred and ten years.

With the promotion of Confucianism, the separation did not prevent the momentum of its development. The temples in the Lu city had been rebuilt from time to time since the Wei and Jin dynasties, during which the basic forms dating from the Han Dynasty were maintained. In early Tang Dynasty, the court decreed to build two respective temples for Zhougong and Confucius in the capital city, and ordered prefectures and counties to build Confucius temples, as well as to conduct large-scaled expansion activities. The temple was rebuilt five times during the Tang Dynasty. According to *Que Li Zhi*, "there are five main rooms to consecrated Confucius, who sits southward … more than 20 side rooms to commemorate his 72 well-known disciples, with their pictures painted on the wall; another rear hall at the back to memorize his wife. There are three gates in the front … ". The temple had attained certain scale at that time. During

随着汉代“罢黜百家，独尊儒术”，儒学从此居于统治地位以来，开始重视对孔庙的修建。东汉永兴元年（公元 153 年），皇帝下令修孔庙，并派孔和为守庙官，“立碑于庙”。孔庙由鲁城北泗上迁到鲁城内孔子旧宅，初具规模，庙屋三间，庭院可容千人。孔庙搬迁至鲁故城内为以后明故城的营造打下了基础。

3．隋唐—宋元庙城分离与“孔庙扩建”

从北魏石城到宋仙源城，曲阜的城市级别为县城，因此城市的规模缩小了很多。同时根据史料记载和考古发现，县城已经移至今曲阜城东北的周公庙高地一带，从而出现了庙城分离的格局。宋仙源县治及金元曲阜县治，前后达 510 年。

虽然庙城分离，但是由于儒学思想不断被推崇，孔子的地位进一步加强，使得魏晋以来，鲁城内的孔庙时有修复，但基本维持汉代的形制。到了唐初，除下诏在京城国子监修建“周公、孔子庙各一所”外，又令“州、县皆立孔子庙”，并开始对孔庙进行较大规模的扩建。唐代共修庙 5 次，《阙里志》载：“正庙五间，祀文宣王，南向坐……两庑二十余间，把七十二贤，图绘于壁上。庙后为寝庙，祀其官夫人。前为庙门三间……”此时孔庙已颇具规模。宋代时，孔庙再次扩大，宋真宗时，始建孔庙大成殿、寝殿、藏书楼；后又把大成殿北移重建，于原址筑坛植杏，纪念孔子杏坛讲学。

4．明代“移城卫庙”

明孝宗弘治十二年（公元 1499 年），孔庙毁于雷击，大成殿等主要建筑 123 间“化为灰烬”。明帝朱祐樘下令重修孔庙，历时 5 年，耗银 15.2 万两。

明正德六年（公元 1511 年），刘六、刘七领导的农民起义军攻下曲阜县城，焚烧官衙，闯进孔庙，“秣马于庭，污书于池”。明朝皇帝武宗准奏，“移城卫庙”，开始建设曲阜砖城。至嘉靖元年（公元 1522 年）竣工，历时十年，耗银三万五千八百余两。从此时起县治由古鲁国以东的旧县治所迁往阙里，治所安排在孔庙围墙外。

明朝政府不是只有单纯针对“天灾人祸”的恢复性建设，而是采取了以修建孔庙为中心的整个庙城的发展建设计划。包括：①重修大成殿及其他庑房、牌坊等；②扩建颜庙；③重修并扩建孔府；④修建城池。城周 4.8 千米，占地约 1.5 平方千米，占鲁故城的七分之一。但是这是曲阜历史上第一座砖砌城廓，城墙高 7 米，厚 3.5 米，四周环有约 3.3 米的护城河；⑤在孔府门前留下很大一片空地，在空地之东第一次兴建了鼓楼，鼓楼门东西正对孔庙的东门，直通西门，形成一条东西轴线。

“移城卫庙”并不仅仅意味着围绕孔庙、孔府、颜庙、陋巷建起一座新的砖筑县

the Song Dynasty, the temple was further expanded and enlarged. In the reign of Emperor Zhen Zong, the Dacheng Hall, the rear hall and the library was started to build. Dacheng Hall, which was later moved and rebuilt northward, was replaced with Xing Tan Pavilion (apricot altar) to commemorate the place where Confucius preached.

2.4 The Relocation of the City to Defend the Temple in the Ming Dynasty

In the 12th year of the reign of Emperor Xiao Zong, the Confucius Temple was struck by lightning and destroyed in a disastrous fire. About 123 main buildings including Da Cheng Hall were burnt to ashes. Emperor You Tang decreed to rebuild the temple, which took 5 years and a sum of 152 thousand dollars.

In the 6th year of Zheng De (1511 AD), Qufu County was conquered during the peasant rebellion led by Liu Liu and Liu Qi. They burnt down the administrative office and broken into the Confucius Temple where they "fed horses and smudged books in the pool". The Emperor Wu Zong gave orders to relocate the city to defend the temple, and started to build a brick-walled city. It took 10 years to complete the project (1522 AD), with a cost of more than 30.58 thousand dollars. Hence, the county was removed from the old seat to the east of the former Lu State to Que Li (birthplace of Confucius), with the government office outside the temple walls.

The effort made by Ming government is more than simply a restoration project, but an overall temple-city development plan which was centered with the Confucius Temple. The measures taken included: (1) rebuilding Dacheng Hall and other side rooms and gateways; (2) expanding the Temple of Yan Hui; (3) rebuilding and expanding the Kong Family Mansion; (4) constructing city wall and moat, with a 1.5-square-kilometer area about 4.8 kilometers in circumference, taking one-seventh of the entire Lu State; (It was also the first brick city wall in Qufu, about 7 meter high and 3.5 meter thick surrounded by a 3.3-meter width moat.) and(5) leaving open space in front of the mansion gate, constructing the first drum tower in the east end with the gate facing the east gate of the temple, all the way connected to the west gate, thus constituting an east-westward axis.

The move led to more than a newly-constructed brick county city which was centered with the Confucius Temple, the Kong Family Mansion, the Temple of Yan Hui and various alleys, even more than simply a relocation of the county to Que Li. The effort brought about significant social changes in the functions of the Qufu temple city, integrating the worship function of the temple, the housing function of the mansion with the political, military, economic and cultural function of the county city.

Qufu is called a temple city because of its city pattern, in which the temple is surrounded and defended by a city. With the Confucius Temple in the city center, the layout reflects the key role of Confucianism in the society.

2.5 The Integration of the Temple and the City in the Qing Dynasty

Before the Tang Dynasty, Qufu had been a memorial site for the veneration and pilgrimage of Confucius since the Spring and Autumn period. The temple was rather shabby at that time. The Tang and Song dynasties witnessed the rebuilding and expansion of the Temple and Cemetery, which later attained a size and scale equal to the economic and social status of Confucianism. The city was relocated to surround the temple in the Ming Dynasty, but the city here was merely a concept in the terms of defense and administration. It is not until the Qing Dynasty that the temple and the city fully achieved integration. In addition to an increasingly strengthening of the status of the temple and the mansion at the center of the city, there were another two features worth highlighting.

城，也不仅仅意味着县治由旧县迁往阙里。这一举措使曲阜庙城功能发生了具有历史意义的社会变迁，使以孔庙为中心的祀事功能和孔府的府第功能与县城的政治、军事、经济、文化功能相互融合在一起。

曲阜城因为其以城卫庙的城市布局被称为庙城。孔庙居中的特征，体现了儒家思想在社会中的核心地位。

5．清代“庙城合一”

春秋至唐朝以前，曲阜只是孔子纪念地，孔庙是简陋的。唐宋时期重点建设了孔庙、孔林，使之规模达到与儒学在经济社会发展中的地位相称。明代“移城卫庙”，但这个“城”只是防御设施和管理治所的概念，真正达到“庙城合一”是在清代。这一时期，除了孔庙、孔府在城市中心的地位不断得到加强外，还有两个方面的特点。

首先，东城区聚集了“衍圣公”的胞弟支系府第和商业功能。因为“孔府”是指“衍圣公”所住的府第，即孔子的嫡孙世袭“衍圣公府”。而到清代，不仅因为各代衍圣公的胞弟需另择地建宅，也不仅因为孔家子弟“人才辈出”，名人达官多起来，更因为经济社会的发展和变迁，所以孔氏府第迅速多起来。如建于雍正年间的有二府、慎修堂等；建于乾隆初年的有大府、三府、四府、十府、十二府；建于乾隆末年的有五府、八府、一贯堂等。所有城内孔氏府第都坐落在孔庙、孔府以东的东门大街南北城区。这使东城区既是一个以孔氏府第为主的阔气富裕城区，也是商业集市比较发达的商业城区。据调查清代末年及民国时期，曲阜城内的手工业有 20 个行业，71 家，主要分布在棋盘街、鼓楼大街、南门大街、东门大街，其中最为繁华的是棋盘街。

其次，西城区发展了城市公共机构。主要是衙署、书院、学校、仓储，当然也有饭馆和商业。这说明清代曲阜西城是以县衙办公、学校教育和一般城市居民消费为主的公共建筑和公共管理机构为主的城区。

由以上三个部分城区表明曲阜庙城在清代的发展，实质上已完全形成了“庙城合一”的格局，即中心城区是祭祀功能，东城区是居住和商业功能，西城区是办公和文教功能（图 3）。

◎三、曲阜明故城的历史文化特征及价值

根据曲阜明故城的历史因循以及今日的遗存，我们可以看到其有以下三个方面的重要历史文化特征：

Firstly, the residences of the families of Duke Yansheng's brother and some commercial functions were accommodated in the eastern part of the city, while Duke Yansheng—the first born of every generation in Confucius family who assumed this title—lived in the Confucius' Mansion. With an increasing number of collateral relatives and their thriving status in the government and society, as well as the economic and social development, more and more mansions of the Confucius family rapidly emerged during the Qing Dynasty, such as the Youer Mansion and Shenxiu Mansion in the reign of Emperor Yong Zheng; the You Da, Si, Shi and Shier Mansions in early Emperor Qian Long period; and the You Wu, Ba and Yi Guan Mansions in late Qian Long period. All these residences were located in the Dongmen Street area to the east of the Confucius Temple and the Kong Family Mansion, making the east side a wealthy section with booming markets and fairs. According to the research, there were about 71 workshops from 20 trades in Qufu in late Qing Dynasty and the Republic Period, which scattered along Qipan, Gulou, Nanmen and Dongmen streets, with Qipan Street as the most prosperous one.

Secondly, a number of public institutes were developed in the western side of the city, including government office, academies, private schools and warehouses, and restaurants and commerce as well, making the western city section an area dominated by buildings and institutes oriented towards public functions.

The above three sections of the city area indicate that Qufu had fully achieved an integration of the temple and the city in the Qing Dynasty, with the central area for functions of worship and pilgrimage, the eastern area for housing and commercial functions and the western part for office and cultural functions (Fig. 3).

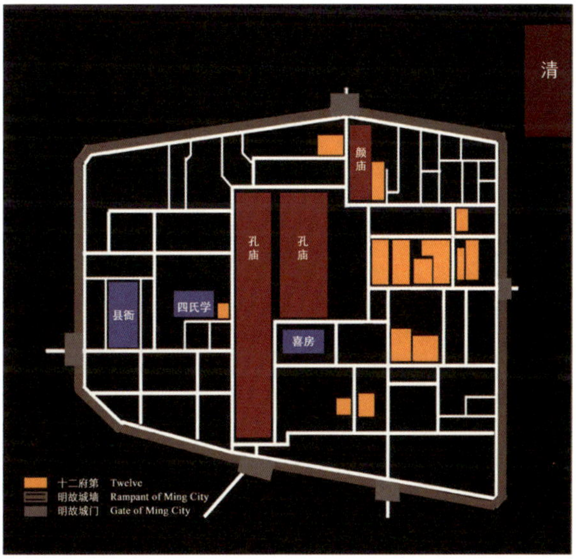

图3. 清代明故城主要功能分布简图(上海同济城市规划设计研究院)
Fig. 3 the functions of different Ming city parts in the Qing Dynasty (Shanghai Tongji Urban Planning and Design Institute)

1．自然基底特征

历史城区处于泗河之南、沂河之北的平原上，城外有护城河围护，城内有古泮池。在春秋战国时期古泮池与鲁国都城宫殿前的水系连成一片，面积巨大，环境优美。自从封建统治者令全国各府、州、县城普建孔庙时起，各地孔庙棂星门内外必有“泮池”和“泮桥”的模拟建筑。曲阜历代不仅对古泮池整修，而且在池西修有出水口（即今之“池门口”）和明暗水道，引池水西行，经新文化街地下水道，至孔庙棂星门前泮桥，又西行出“水门”，注入护城河。这股西行之池即名泮水，至今其水道尚依稀可见。因此，曲阜明故城的自然基底已经具有强烈的文化特质。

2．物质文化特征

（1）历经 3000 多年的聚落历史层积

由于明故城是在周鲁故城、汉鲁故城的基础上营建的，局部城墙直接建在以前城池的基础之上，因此在明故城的范围内外，有着 2500 多年的历史层积。其中鲁故城是先秦时期“营国制度”的典型代表，而明故城的“庙城”是我国城市建设史上的独特案例。

（2）孔庙居中、以城卫庙的城市格局

曲阜明故城的城市格局与传统中国城市最大的不同，是孔子家族对城市的决定性控制作用。在这个城市中，以孔庙孔府为核心的建筑是最重要的，其他建筑的重要程度根据与孔子关系的重要性而定。城市是为了保卫孔庙而修建的，先有孔庙，后有城市。

（3）T 字形为主的街巷格局

由于明故城是以孔庙的轴线为轴线，因此城市的道路街巷也表现出不同于一般明代城池的特色。也就是孔庙将城市分为东西两半，而城市的南北门又在孔庙的轴线上，所以城市没有一条贯通南北或者东西的主街道；而次级街巷多为 T 字形，交通极为不便，但是强调了街巷的对景以及防御的需要。

（4）主次分明的建筑肌理

由于明故城独特的城市功能，其建筑可以分为三大类型：以大型祭祀类公共建筑为主的传统公共建筑、府第型居住建筑与普通民居建筑。

以孔庙、颜庙为代表的大型祭祀类公共建筑由传统的大尺度的院落组合而成。整个建筑群建筑布局沿轴线对称分布，院落组合上空间序列明确，院落规模较大，每个院落主体建筑地位显著，具有独立的功能。如孔庙建筑仿皇宫之制，分九进庭院，贯穿在一条南北中轴线上，左右基本上是对称式排列。有 5 殿、1 阁、1 坛、1 祠、2 庑、2 堂、2 斋宿等 466 间，另有门坊 54 座，占地 327.5 亩，被古建筑学家称为世界建筑

◎ 3. The Historical and Cultural Character and Value of Qufu Ming city

Based on its historical continuation and the remains today, Qufu Ming city has three important characteristics in historical and cultural terms.

3.1 The characteristics of the natural setting

The historic area is situated to the south of the Si River, on the flat land to the north of the Yi River. The city is defended by moats outside. There is an ancient Pan Pond in the city, which was connected with the wider water system in front of the palace in the capital of Lu State during the Spring and Autumn period. Since the feudal rulers decreed the states, prefectures and counties to widely build Confucius Temple, a number of structures as mimics to Pan ponds and Pan bridges were successively built inside and outside the Ling Xing gates of the temples. In addition to the renovation of the pond by each dynasty in Qufu's history, an exit was constructed in the west side the pond (today's Pond Gate) and visible and invisible waterways to navigate the water westwards into the moat through the underground channels along the Wenhua Street, to the Pan Bridge in front the of the Ling Xing Gate and the Water Gate. The westward pond was named Pan Water, whose waterways are still faintly visible today. Hence, the natural setting of Qufu Ming city presented a strong cultural characteristic.

3.2 The Characteristics of Physical Cultural Resources

(1) A Layering of Historical Settlements for More Than 3,000 Years

Built upon the former Zhou Lu city and Han Lu city, Ming city, which was partly constructed on the basis of the original city walls, has a historical layering of more than 2,500 years around the area. The former city of Lu State was a typical example that was constructed by following the city planning system from the Pre-Qin period, and the "temple-city" pattern of Ming city was a unique case in the history of Chinese urban development.

(2) The City Pattern Centered with the Confucius Temple That was Defended Around by the City

The decisive control over the city by the Confucius Family led to the fundamental difference between Qufu Ming city and other traditional Chinese cities. The core complexes of the temple and mansion of Confucius are the most important buildings in the city, while the importance of the rest buildings was largely determined by its connections with the Confucianism. The city was created to defend the temple which was preceded the former.

(3) The "T-shaped" Street Pattern

Ming city was constructed along the axis of the Confucius Temple, thus the alleys and streets in the city had taken on a distinctive feature compared with other cities in the Ming dynasty. The city was divided in half into east and west parts, with the southern and northern city gates right on the axis of the temple; therefore, there was neither south-north nor east-west transportation lines running through the city. Those sub-streets or sub-alleys, mostly T-shaped, caused difficulty in transportation, while highlighting a symmetric street pattern and the need of defense,

(4) The Buildings with Clear Hierarchical Importance

The buildings in Ming city can be divided into three types due to its unique city functions, namely the traditional public buildings for large sacrifice and worship activities, residential buildings of mansions and ordinary residential buildings.

史上的孤例（图 4）。

府第型居住建筑群由 2~3 个传统的大尺度的居住院落组合而成，三进左右。一般情况下主要轴线上为前厅后宅模式，除正房外，还配有东西厢房。两侧辅助轴线设有祠堂、厨房、储藏等院落，同时整个建筑群中一侧或后部设有庭院（图 5~6）。

而普通的民居建筑则由 3~4 个建筑和一个天井组成一个院落，俗称四合院。在曲阜，院落式住宅一般只有一进，与公共建筑相比，尺度小。四合院自成独立的单元，在历史上，一个院落一般住一户人家（图 7）。

（5）对比鲜明的整体色彩

明故城与中国其他传统城市一样，大型祭祀类公共建筑用的颜色较为灿烂，多用琉璃瓦做屋顶。而普通民居用的颜色较为朴素，多用灰色。这一点也体现了中国传统封建思想中严格的等级观念：不同等级的人使用不同的颜色。作为普通民居，朴素的灰色既能衬托出宫殿建筑的金碧辉煌，同时，其本身也给人特殊的美感（图 8）。

图 4. 孔庙大成殿 © 曲阜市政府
Fig. 4 the Dacheng Hall © Qufu government

Public buildings for sacrificing and worship activities, such as the Temples of Confucius and Yan Hui, consisted of large courtyard complexes. With symmetric patterns of buildings along the central axis, the complex was arranged with clear space sequences, featured sizable courtyards and distinctive main buildings of independent functions. The temple of Confucius, copying the layout of imperial palaces, was composed of nine courtyards along a south-north central axis, with symmetric buildings at both sides. There were a total of 466 rooms including five halls, one pavilion, one altar, one ancestral temple, two side rooms, two principal rooms and two rooms for fast, etc., and 54 archways, with a total area of 327.5 mu, known as a unique case in world architectural history by architects in ancient buildings (Fig. 4).

The residential complex was made up of two to three traditional residential courtyards. The complex took a pattern with halls in the front and rooms at back, including a principal room and side rooms in east and west wings. The ancestral temple, kitchen and warehouse were arranged at both sides respectively. There was also open-air courtyard at one side of the complex or at the back (Fig. 5-6).

The ordinary residence was composed of three to four buildings and one courtyard, which was known as Sihe Yuan (quadrangle courtyard). In Qufu, the residence had one courtyard and room surrounding it, thus it was relatively smaller compared with those for public use. As an independent unit, one courtyard usually accommodated one household in general (Fig. 7).

(5) Sharp Contrast of Overall Colors

Similar to other Chinese cities, the colors of large-scaled public buildings for worship and sacrificing functions in the Ming city are brilliant and made of glazed roofing tiles, while the ordinary residences were grey and dark in color. The color design also highlighted the hierarchy system in Chinese feudal society. Each social class had its distinctive color. The palace complex became more contrast against the grey color in ordinary residences and the later also showed its own unique atheistic attraction (Fig. 8).

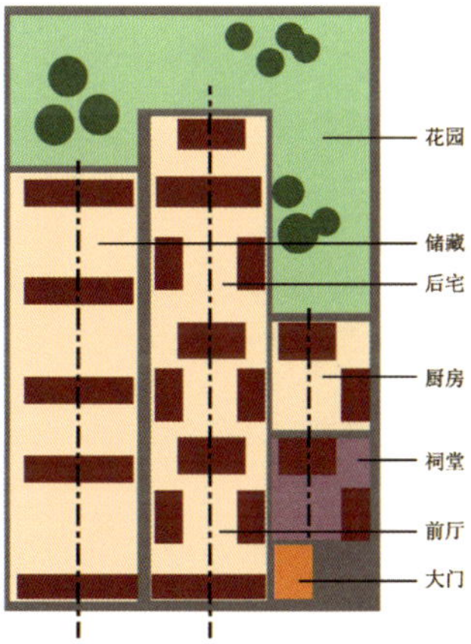

图 5. 府第型居住建筑平面示意
Fig. 5 the plan of mansion-type residential buildings

图 6. 明故城府第分布示意图 © 上海同济城市规划设计研究院
Fig. 6 the plan of the mansions in Ming city © Shanghai Tongji Urban Planning and Design Institute

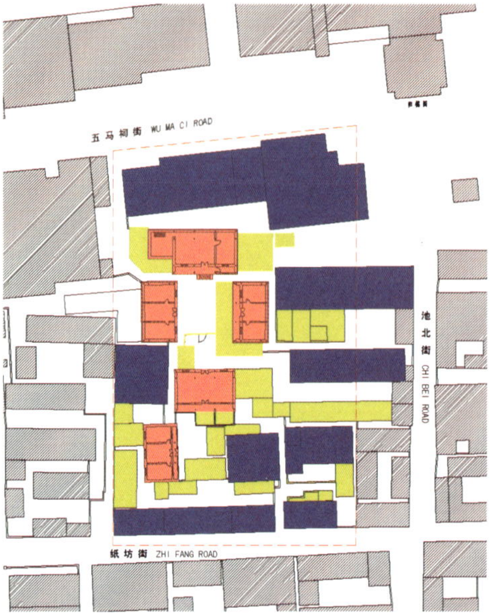

图 7. 商业局诊所（原吴庭玉宅部分）民居测绘图
© 上海同济城市规划设计研究院
Fig. 7 the survey map of the residence in the clinic of Commercial bureau (former residence of WU Tingyu)
© Shanghai Tongji Urban Planning and Design Institute

图 8. 明故城鸟瞰以及色彩关系
Fig. 8 the overview of the Ming city and its overall color design

3．传统人文特征

（1）世界儒家文化的发源地与人文精神的体现地

儒家文化为春秋时期孔丘所创，是在总结、概括和继承了夏、商、周三代尊尊亲亲传统文化的基础上形成的一个完整的思想体系。儒家文化经历代统治者的推崇，以及孔子后学的发展和传承，对中国文化的发展起到了决定性的作用。

曲阜是儒家创始人孔子的诞生地，其后曲阜的发展都与之有着密不可分的关系。孔庙、孔林、孔府是与纪念孔子、推崇儒学紧密联系发展起来的人类遗产，文化积淀丰厚，以历史悠久、规模宏大、文物丰富、科学艺术价值高而著称。

（2）中国仍然“活着”的最古老、最丰富的宗族文化和独特的社区结构

曲阜是“至圣”孔子、“复圣”颜子、“宗圣”曾子、“述圣”子思、“亚圣”孟子的诞育发祥之地，也是“元圣”周公后裔的奉祀之地。在中国两千多年漫长的历史长河里，六大“圣人”受到封建王朝的竟相尊崇，他们的子孙后裔也都蒙朝廷赐爵封赠，钦拨田产，敕建府第，设置属官，优免差徭，籍列儒户，成为不与齐民等同、不受改朝换代的影响而世袭罔替、显赫尊荣的封建家族。因此，形成了曲阜与众不同

3.3 Traditional Cultural Characters

(1) The Birthplace of Confucianism and a Vivid Presentation of Humanism

Created by Confucius during the Spring and Autumn period, Confucianism finally took on a complete ideological system based on the review, summarization and continuation of the traditional culture from Xia, Shang and Zhou dynasties. Through the promotion of rulers in Chinese history and the development and inheritance of the next generations, Confucianism played a decisive role the development of Chinese culture.

As the birthplace of the founder of Confucian culture, Qufu and its development had a close connection with the culture. The Temple, Cemetery and Mansion of Confucius are heritage of all human being that was developed with the commemoration and promotion of the sage and his thought. Dating back into a long cultural history, the heritage is well known for its long traditions, massive scales, rich cultural resources and scientific and artistic significance.

(2) The Oldest and the Most Abundant 'Living' Family Culture in China and its unique Social Structure

Qufu was the birthplace of the Six Sages of Confucianism, namely the Great Sage—Confucius, the Continuator of the Sage—Yan Hui, the Ancestral Sage—Zeng Zi, the Sage of Transmitting—Zi Si and the Second Sage—Mencius. Qufu was also a place where the decedents of the Duke of Zhou were enshrined. Honored by the feudal dynasties in Chinese history for more than 2000 years, the Six Sages and their decedents were granted royal titles and properties, appointed officers, exempted from corvee and registered as members of Confucius family. They became a superior feudal family with prestigious honor that hereditarily continued and was immune to the change of regimes. Thus Qufu takes on a distinctive family culture which has long been a part of its local culture and a significant part of Chinese feudal culture. The decedents of the family are all over the Qufu and made lofty accomplishments in various areas, an indispensible part for the continuation of Qufu culture. The temple complexes, family cemetery, family steles, family archives and genealogical records have been well preserved in Qufu, and serve as the important physical resources for the research on the social, political, economic and cultural changes in Chinese feudal society and for other researches on sociology, demography and genealogy as well.

Above all, Qufu Ming city of significant historical, artistic and scientific values, serves as a unique example among the historical and cultural cities in the world.

◎ 4. Living Heritage—the Concept and Approach for the Comprehensive Conservation of Qufu Ming city

By the analysis above, Qufu Ming city is more than a historic area for sacrificing and worship purposes, but a comprehensive area which also integrates other functions of residence, commerce, education and offices. Meanwhile, the city space is not only about large public buildings for sacrificing and city walls, but also a large number of distinctive streets and residential communities and commercial areas that was developed from the traditional residences. More importantly, about 10,000 residents still live within the Ming city today, most of whom are the family decedents of Confucius, Mencius, Zeng Zi and Yan Hui; therefore, the city is a living heritage! The protection shall extend beyond the physical heritage, such as the Temple and Mansion of Confucius, to develop into a holistic system of protection thoughts (Fig. 9) which is centered by "giving the residents priority". A number of aspects are included in the conservation:

(1) Protecting the natural setting, including the conservation of the moat, Pan Pond, Pan Water and an-

的宗族文化，同时亦延伸浸润于乡土文化中，是中国封建文化的重要内容之一。其后代遍布曲阜各地，各家名才辈出，是曲阜历史文化传承发展的重要组成部分。同时曲阜目前保存有较为完整的庙府建筑群、家族墓地、历代优礼碑刻、家族档案和完备系统的家志谱牒，是研究我国封建社会历史、政治、经济、文化等范畴的因革、演变和社会学、人口学、谱牒学等方面不可多得的典型实例和珍贵的实物资料。

综上，曲阜明故城具有非常重要的历史、艺术和科学价值，在世界的历史文化名城中独树一帜。

◎四、曲阜明故城的整体保护理念与方法——活态遗产

由以上分析可知，明故城不是一个仅有祭祀功能的历史城区，而是一个以祭祀功能为主，集居住、商业、教育、办公等功能为一体的综合的城区。同时，其城市空间也不仅仅只有祭祀类的大型公共建筑与城墙，还有非常富有特色的道路街巷、大量的传统民居形成的居住街坊和商业街市。更加重要的是，今天的曲阜明故城之内还有1万左右的居民，而其中还有大量的孔、孟、曾、颜四姓的后代，是一个活态遗产！因此，曲阜明故城的保护不能仅仅限于物质遗产，更加不能仅仅限于孔庙孔府，而是应该形成整体的保护思想（图9），形成“以居民为核心”的保护思想。因此，在保护内容上应该包括以下几个方面：

（1）保护自然基底。包括对护城河、泮池、泮水、古树名木等自然基底的保护，等等。

（2）保护从殷周时期以来的历史层积物。依托遗址保存现状与整体空间环境，规划提出“宏观控制引导，局部展示利用”的保护利用原则。宏观层面以总体规划为依据，首先控制城市建设区在鲁城范围的蔓延，对于遗址范围及其周边区域景观、环境加以引导。实施整体保护的同时，对于局部重要节点通过考古遗址公园的方式结合绿化景观塑造加以展示利用。

（3）保护独特格局。保护历史城区整体空间格局，包括“以城卫庙”的特色格局，传统轴线关系，道路街巷体系，院落肌理与建筑形态以及重要景观视线。对明故城的空间形态保护需要限制整体高度，保持平缓的空间形态。对色彩关系特色进行保护。

（4）保护街巷体系。虽然曲阜历史城区的建筑大部分已经翻建，但历史街巷格局保留至今。它们大部分保留了历史走向，其中一部分街巷的尺度也维持了历史宽度，与之共同延续的则是历史街巷名所承载的地名历史信息。规划将历史现状具有历史价值的街巷认定为保护街巷。针对保护街巷，应保护其走向、宽度、空间尺度、两侧界

图 9. 明故城历史文化遗存分布图 © 上海同济城市规划设计研究院
Fig. 9 the historic remains in Qufu Ming city © Shanghai Tongji Urban Planning and Design Institute

cient and rare trees and plants.

(2) Protecting the historical layering developed since the Shang and Zhou dynasties. The planning proposes the principle of "macro-level control and guidance and local-level displaying and utilization" based on the state of conservation and the holistic environment. Firstly, efforts should be made to control the spread of urban development within the old city area under the macro-guidance of the Master Plan, and to guide the development of the landscape and environment within and surrounding the property. In addition to a comprehensive conservation, actions should be taken to display and utilize important local nodes through a combination of establishing archaeological parks and greenery landscapes.

(3) Protecting the unique pattern. Efforts should be made to protect the overall city pattern of the historic area, including the distinctive layout featuring "the city defending the temple", the relations of the traditional axes, the street pattern, the layout of courtyards, the building forms and the important landscape view corridors. The height must be limited to protect the overall pattern of the city so as to maintain a flat space. Attention also needs to be paid to the protection of the traditional color arrangement.

(4) Protecting the street system. Though most of the buildings in the historic area have been renovated, the street pattern in the history has been well retained. Together with the direction and scale in the history, the historical information in the street names has also been mostly reserved. According to the planning, those recognized as protected streets due to their historic significance shall be well retained in terms of the direction, width, scale, streetscapes and relevant historical information. Frontage ratio is regulated to maintain the continuity of the street interface, not allowing for change or widening. Old names of the streets will

面风貌、相关历史信息等，要求贴线建设，保证界面连续性，不允许改线或拓宽。建议根据历史信息恢复街道名称。

（5）保护传统民居建筑和肌理。规划将明故城内的建筑分为五类：文物建筑、历史建筑、传统风貌建筑、一般建（构）筑物（与历史风貌无冲突）和一般建（构）筑物（与历史风貌有冲突）。不同类型的建筑应采取不同的保护与更新的方式。

（6）保护非物质文化遗产。非物质文化遗产的保护应从两方面做起：一是保护物，包括有效的、多种方式的保存遗产原物，如民间文学记载、传统音乐乐谱、医药古籍等；针对传统技艺、舞蹈、戏剧等活动，即是在艺人或是匠人制作、表演过程中，将那些“看不见”“摸不着”的非物质文化遗产的“成品”以“有形化”的方式记录或保存下来，主要包括文字记录、照片、影像等。二是将保护重心直接放在非物质文化遗产的传承人身上，如戏剧、舞蹈、传统技艺等，可建立传承人培训体制，保证这些遗产的原真性，鼓励艺人收徒授艺，进行民间艺术传承活动。

（7）保护社会结构和社区复兴。明故城拥有独特的社会结构，至今仍然保留有将近 10 000 人口，其中 25% 左右为孔、孟、曾、颜后代。规划提出着重保护原有的社会结构，并且积极促进社区复兴，在明故城内的四个社区组团中分别设置了社区管理、基础教育、商业服务、社区文化、社区绿地等设施，为明故城内的居民提供便捷舒适的生活环境；同时保留合院的居住模式，改善基础设施，改善居住环境。

◎五、总结

曲阜明故城不仅拥有独特的自然基底、几千年的建设层积，异常丰厚的人文内涵，而且今天仍然是容纳着城市日常生活的、依然处在生长和变化中的活态文化遗产。

发展和变化是城市永恒的话题，在城市日益成为社会和经济发展核心地域的今天，明故城内外进行着持续的城市更新与大规模的地产开发，旅游带来的超容量的游客、环境的污染、过度商业化等，这些都使原本和谐的人—地关系遭到破坏，从而影响到明故城的历史文化价值。

因此，为了更好地保护明故城这类活态遗产，我们很有必要建立整体保护的理念，更加离不开“居民”以社区为单位的参与。保持适当的人口比例，改善居民生活环境，保护居民的利益，建设适宜人居的历史城市至关重要。

be put back into use based on the historical information that has been collected.

(5) Protecting traditional residences and the fabric. According to the planning, the buildings within the Ming city are classified into five categories, namely heritage building, historic building, traditional building, ordinary structure (not conflicting with the historic landscape) and ordinary structure (conflicting with historic landscape). Different measures for conservation and renewal will be taken for each type of the buildings.

(6) Protecting intangible heritage. Measures should be taken from two aspects to protect the intangible cultural heritage. Firstly, we should protect the physical objects, including effective protection of the remains of the heritage, such as the records of folklores, sheets of traditional music scores and medicine literatures. Those intangible heritage with products neither visible nor touchable, such as traditional craftsmanship, dances and operas, should be preserved and filed during the creation and performance process of the craftsmen, including the preservation of transcripts, photos and images. Secondly, emphasis should be put on the inheritors of intangible heritage, such as the opera, dances and traditional techniques. Training systems should be set up for these transmitters to guarantee the authenticity of the heritage and to encourage craftsmen to recruit apprentices for the inheritance of these folk activities.

(7) Protecting the social structure and regenerating the community. With a unique social structure, the Ming city area still accommodates a population of 10,000, 25% of which are decedents of Confucius, Mencius, Zeng Zi and Yan Hui. The plan has proposed to protect the original social structure and to regenerate the local communities. Facilities for community management, basic education, commercial services, community culture and green space have been set up in the four community clusters within the Ming city area for a better and more convenient living environment of the local residents. At the same time, the living style of courtyards has been retained, and infrastructure improved and the living conditions enhanced.

◎ 5. Conclusion

In addition to a unique natural setting, a historic layering dating back to thousands of years ago and the unusually abundant cultural resources, the Ming city today remains as a living cultural heritage where the daily life of the city still continues, evolves and changes.

Development and change are the eternal theme of city. In today's world where cities have increasingly become the key part of social and economic development, the Ming city has also undergone a successive urban renewal and large-scaled development of real estates. Tourism brings polluted environment, excessive tourists and commercialization, which has destroyed the harmonious human-nature relationship and affected the city's historical and cultural values.

Above all, in order to better protect the living heritage like Ming city, it is necessary for us to establish a comprehensive conservation idea, and engage the participation of residents, the individual units of local community. It is essential to maintain the local population at an appropriate ratio, to improve the living conditions and to protect the rights and interests of the residents for the construction of a livable historic city.

基于历史价值与现实条件的曲阜鲁故城遗址保护与展示[1]

郭璐　刘健

曲阜鲁故城遗址的保护与展示是迫切而重要的现实问题。本文以探寻彰显历史价值、适应现实发展的遗址保护与展示途径为目标，首先，挖掘历史价值，认识到鲁故城城市整体空间结构的奠基性和标志性；其次，分析现状条件，发现鲁故城遗址主体结构清晰、片状遗址占压严重；在此基础上，提出重点展示、整体保护、分期推进的保护与展示设想，综合运用多种规划设计手法，形成“两城—三轴—多片区”的空间格局。

曲阜位于山东省中南部丘陵地带与鲁西南平原的交接地带，洙水、泗水、沂水等河流蜿蜒交织，气候温暖湿润、水源丰沛、土地肥沃，适合农业生产，为人类居住提供了良好的自然条件，这一地区在数十万年前即有古人类生存繁衍[2]，至今仍是人口密集、环境适宜的城市地区。

西周至战国末年，诸侯国之一的鲁国建都于曲阜，即通常所说的“鲁故城”。鲁故城遗迹保存至今，位于今曲阜市区及其东、北面，1961 年被列入全国第一批重点文物保护单位，具有重要的历史价值。经过多次考古挖掘，鲁故城遗址的整体空间结构已经较为清晰地呈现在世人面前，而其面临的占压、破坏等现实问题也伴随着大规模、高速的城乡建设进程而日益严峻。探寻一条彰显历史价值、适应现实发展的遗址保护与展示途径，迫在眉睫。

◎一、鲁故城遗址的历史价值：城市整体空间结构的奠基性和标志性

进行遗址保护与展示，首先需要挖掘遗址本身的历史价值，从而厘清应当进行保护与展示的内容。

有关曲阜城市建设历史的明确记载始于西周时期，西周建国以前，这一地区是东夷文化的中心，商时还一度被作为王朝的政治中心，古名“奄”。周王朝建立后，为更好地统治东方遗民，成王八年（公元前 1035 年），封重臣周公旦于曲阜，建立鲁国，

Protection and Display of Relics of Ancient Capital City of Lu State in Qufu Based on the Study of Historical Value and Realistic Conditions[1]

GUO Lu LIU Jian

It is an exigent and important realistic problem to protect and display the relics of Ancient Capital City of Lu State in Qufu. This papers targets at exploring the means of protection and display of the relics that can manifest historical value and adapt it to the realistic development of the modern society. Firstly, the historical value is explored to recognize the fundamental and symbolic role of the overall spatial structure of the Ancient Capital City of Lu State; secondly, the current situations is analyzed to reveal the fact that the Ancient Capital City Relics of Lu State has a clear major structure, while several relics areas are covered and occupied seriously; based on this, this paper puts forward the conception of protection and display by focusing on integrated protection, emphasized display and staging advancement to form the spatial layout of "two cities-three axes-multiple districts" with comprehensively utilization of various planning and design skills and methods

Qufu is located at the junction of the southwest plains and hilly land on the central south of Shandong Province, with the winding rivers including the Zhu River, the Si River and the Yi River. It boasts warm and moist weather, abundant water resources and fertile land, which are suitable for agricultural production, providing favorable natural conditions for human inhabitation. The ancient people survived and reproduced in this area hundreds of thousands of years ago[2]. Now it is still an urban area with intensive population and livable environment.

From the Western Zhou Dynasty (1122 BC–771 AD) to the late Warring States Period (475–221 BC), the Lu State established its capital at Qufu, generally known as the "Ancient City of Lu State". The relics of Ancient City of Lu State, listed into the First National Key Cultural Relics Protection Units in 1961, are still in existence, located at the downtown area and the east and north of present Qufu. Through the archaeological excavation for times, the overall spatial structure of the Ancient City of Lu State has been presented. However, with the large scale and high speed urban and rural construction process, the realistic problems such as occupancy and damages of relics are growing serious increasingly. Hence, it is extremely urgent to explore an approach of protection and display that can manifest historical value and adapt it to the realistic development of the modern society.

◎ 1. Historical Value of the Ruins of Ancient City of Lu State: Fundamental and Symbolic role of the Overall Spatial Structure

To protect and display the relics, the historical value of relics should be excavated to clarify the contents to be protected and displayed.

According to explicit records, the construction history of Qufu dated back to the Western Zhou Dy-

由其子伯禽修筑都城曲阜[3]，城市空间结构的基本构架开始形成。直至鲁顷公二十四年（公元前 249 年）楚国灭鲁，设鲁县，近 800 年间城市建设屡有兴作，踵事增华，形成了东方的繁华大都市，是重要的政治、经济、文化中心。两周以后至今数千年间，曲阜城市均是在这一片区进行建设。鲁故城的历史价值可以从两方面来认识：纵向梳理，鲁故城对此后千年、直至今日的曲阜城市空间发展具有奠基性的作用；横向比较，鲁故城在两周时期的诸侯国都城中地位重要、形制特殊，具有标志性的意义。

纵观历史沿革，鲁故城创造了曲阜城市建设的黄金时期，此后数千年间曲阜城市发展都在这一片区，并依托鲁故城的城市结构而渐次发展。秦至西汉初沿用先秦鲁故城为鲁县治所，西汉中期开始于鲁故城西南角，利用其西墙、南墙修筑汉鲁城，宋真宗时崇尚道教，在鲁城东门外传说中的黄帝出生地寿丘附近建仙源城，将县治东迁，但曲阜城并未荒弃，以鲁故城范围内的孔庙、孔府、周公庙的营建为重点的城市建设依然不绝。明世宗嘉靖元年（公元 1522 年）移县城护庙，重新以孔庙为中心建立曲阜县城，也就是在鲁故城、汉鲁城的南部地区，其南边界与鲁故城南边界重合，城市轴线则延续了自春秋时期渐次形成的孔氏家族墓地孔林的轴线。今天所见的曲阜城市的基本格局则是以明清曲阜城为中心逐渐发展形成的。可以说鲁故城奠定了数千年来曲阜城市空间发展的结构框架。（图 1~ 图 2）

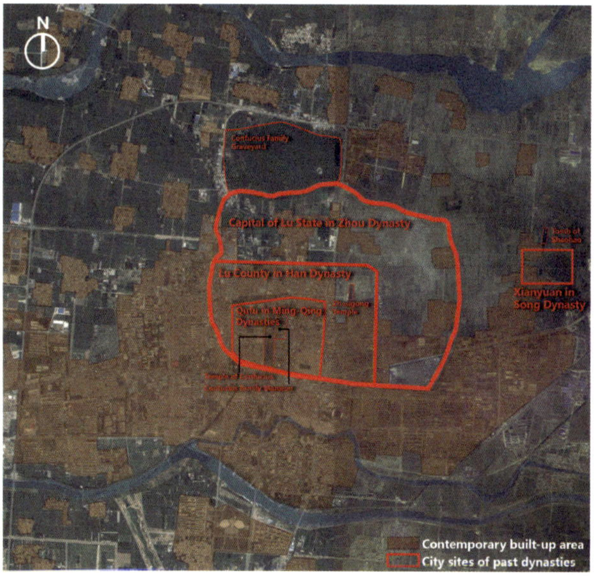

图 1. 历代城址与当代曲阜城市建成区的位置关系
Fig. 1 The positional relation between city sites of past dynasties and contemporary built-up areas of Qufu

nasty. Before the founding of the Western Zhou Dynasty, this area was a center of Dong Yi culture. In the Shang Dynasty (1600— 1046 BC), this area once served as the political center of the state, named as "Yan". After the founding of the Zhou Dynasty, the senior minister Zhou Duke was enfeoffed to Qufu in the 8th year of Emperor Cheng (1035 BC), establishing the Lu State there, so as to better govern adherents of the former dynasty in the eastern areas. His son Bo Qin built Qufu[3]. Then the basic frameworks of the urban spatial structure came into being. This city was basking in the boom of construction and developed into a flourishing metropolis in the east, serving as the important center of politics, economy and cultures in almost 800 years, until the 24th year of Luqing Gong (249 BC), when Chu State destroyed the Lu State and built Lu County. For thousands of years from the Zhou Dynasty to present, Qufu is still built in this area. The historical value of the Ancient City of Lu State could be identified in two aspects: by horizontal analysis, the Ancient City of Lu State has played a fundamental role in the urban spatial development of Qufu for thousands of years and even till present; by vertical analysis, the Ancient City of Lu State played a symbolic role among the capitals of various states in Western Zhou Dynasty and Eastern Zhou Dynasty, with an essential status and special pattern.

Throughout the history, the Ancient City of Lu State created the golden age of the construction of Qufu. Qufu has been located in this area and gradually developed by relying on the urban structure of the Ancient City of Lu State for thousands of years since then. From the Qin Dynasty (221–206BC) to the early Western Han Dynasty (206BC–220AD), the Ancient City of Lu State was still used as the government of Lu County. Since the mid of the Western Han Dynasty, people started to build the Lu City on the southwest corner of the Ancient City of Lu State by using its western and southern walls. Then, as the Emperor Zhenzong of Song Dynasty (960–1279) advocated Taoism, he built Xianyuan City nearby Shouqiu, the legendary birthplace of Huang Emperor outside the eastern gate of Lu City and moved the county government eastwards, but Qufu was not abandoned yet. The city construction was still booming, with a focus on the Temple of Confucius, the Confucius Family Mansion and Zhougong Temple in the range of the Ancient City of Lu State. In the first year of Emperor Shizong of Ming Dynasty (1522), the Qufu County was moved and rebuilt to protect the Temple of Confucius, located on the south of the Ancient City of Lu State and Lu City of Han Dynasty. Its southern border coincided with the southern boundary of the Ancient City of Lu State, and the city axis followed the axis of Confucius Family Graveyard gradually formed since the Spring and Autumn period. The basic pattern that we have seen currently was gradually developed and formed by centralizing on Qufu in the Ming Dynasty. It might say that the Ancient City of Lu State has laid a foundation for structural frameworks of Qufu urban spatial development for thousands of years (Fig. 1~2).

With a broad overview to city construction in the Dynasties of Western Zhou and Eastern Zhou, Qufu, the City of Lu State, boasted an important and special status. Due to Zhou Duke's important political status, the Lu State had a higher status than other kingdoms. It was generally thought that the Lu State integrated the system of Rites of Zhou since its establishment, as the saying goes, "the Lu State possessed the most complete ritural system of Zhou Dynasty".[4] Moreover, it was the most durable state capital among all kingdoms throughout the Dynasties of Western Zhou and Eastern Zhou. Seen from the results of archaeological excavation, imperial palace of the Ancient City of Lu State was located in the middle surrounded by the outer city wall. The axis of the imperial palace was also the south-north central axis of the city. Thus, the overall spatial structure of the city was orderly and in neat formation. While there is no similar city among the ancient cities of pre-Qin period as we knew. It is generally thought that this may reflect several features of the cities, especially the capitals of Western Zhou Dynasty[1][2][3]. This has an extremely significant status under the realistic conditions that Feng, Hao, Luoyi and other capitals of the Western Zhou were not in existence (Fig. 3).

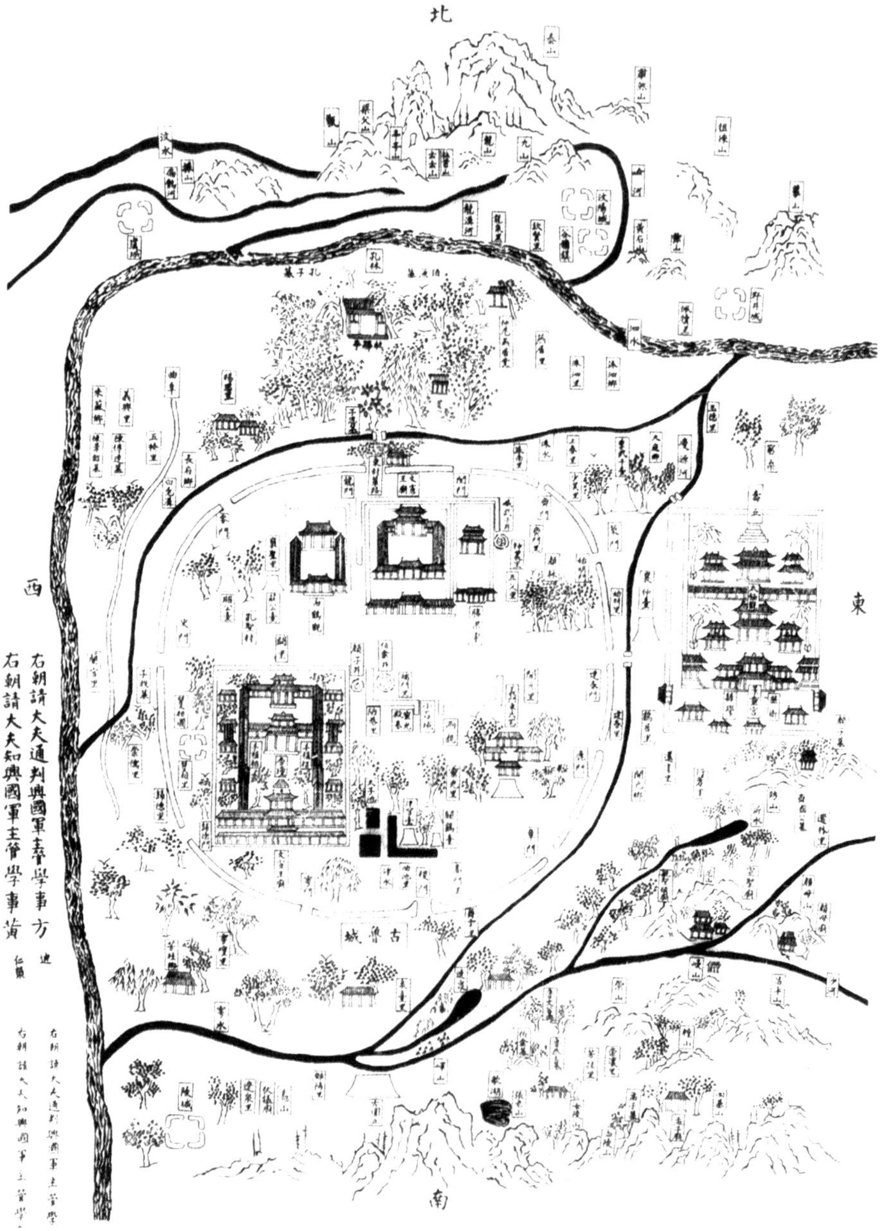

图 2. [宋]《鲁国之图》墨线图。从中可见曲阜周边自然地理条件与历史遗存。
来源：曹婉如编 . 中国古代地图集（战国—元）[M]. 北京 : 文物出版社，1990:51.
Fig. 2 Ink Drawing of *Map of the Lu Statein* Song Dynasty (It revealed the natural geographic conditions and historical relics nearby Qufu). Source: Cao Wanru. An Atlas Of Ancient Maps In China (Warring States–Yuan Dynasty). Beijing: Cultural Relics Press, 1990: 51.

◎ 2. Excavation and Current Preservation Situation of the Relics of Ancient City of Lu State: Clear structure and serious occupancy

Based on the exploration of historical value, the analysis of excavation and current preservation situation of the historical ruins is required to identify the contents to be protected and displayed.

As the city served for several dynasties, some ruins of city walls are still in existence in Qufu area. As early as 1940, Japanese scholars conducted a preliminary survey and reconnaissance[4], proving that this is the location of the Ancient City of Lu State. In 1957–1958, the Institute of Archaeology, Chinese Academy of Sciences made tentative drilling and excavation on the relics of Ancient City of Lu State. In 1977–1978, Shangdong Provincial Institute of Archaeology made comprehensive and systematic reconnaissance and partial excavation, which preliminarily identified the basic situation such as age of construction, scale of city, spatial structure and layout[5]. The existing results of archaeological excavation reveal the overall spatial structure of Ancient City of Lu State clearly, but a great amount of ruins areas are still challenged with serious occupancy and other realistic issues.

First of all, the structural elements forming the overall urban space of the Ancient City of Lu State have been excavated archaeologically, with the eligible conditions for display. (1) The "hollow square" form of enceinte with imperial palace in the middle: The plan of the Ancient City of Lu State is a flat square around 3.6km from east to west and 2.7km from south to north with a perimeter of about 11.8km, covering a total area of about 10.45km^2. On the ground of many sections, there are still clear ruins of ancient city walls, especially in southeast corner. Although a part of sections had been buried underground, the archaeological excavation can still restore the whole circle of this ancient city. There were moats surrounding the city, currently located on the south, west and north as well as the south of the eastern city. Now the river course is still in existence. In the highland area of Zhougong Temple, located in the middle of the ancient city, there are large rammed earth construction sites with a grand scale, nearly 1km from east to west and around 2km from south to north. As estimated, this site was the imperial palace of the Lu State, whose terrain still stands higher than the surrounding areas, as the commanding elevation of the city. Currently, the ancient architectural complex of Zhougong Temple, built in Song Dynasty, is just located in this area[5]. (2) The "T-shaped" urban inner spatial framework formed by the south-north axis and east-west artery: The archaeology unearthed over a dozen inner roads in the city, most of which were connected to city gate. Among them, the most prominent position was the artery from the south of imperial palace straight to the southeastern gate of the Ancient City of Lu State, which extended directly towards the relics of Wuyu Terrace, 1735m off from the south of the ancient city, forming a clear urban central axis—the south-north artery in the urban space. There was a main artery and a channel running east to west of the city, located on the north of the imperial palace. In the past, the ruins of riverbed were still visible on the ground. Although blocked now, we still could discover it easily after drilling[5]27. (3) In the area of the Ancient City of Lu State, there is still another axis running south to north and connecting the Ancient City of Lu State with the Ancient Qufu of Ming Dynasty. Starting from the entrance of Confucius Family Graveyard, this axis passed Wan Gu Chang Chun Memorial Archway (also named the Memorial Archway of the Confucius Family Graveyard), crossed the northern gate of Qufu of Ming and connected Temple of Yanhui, Drum Tower, Temple of Confucius and the Confucius Family Mansion, linking together a series of cultural relics from the Spring and Autumn Period to Ming and Qing Dynasties. This axis should be originated from the late Spring and Autumn Period, serving as the road for sacrifice from the Temple of Confucius to tomb of Confucius. Although the archaeology studies have not discovered any unearthed ruins of roads, research-

横览两周时期的城市建设，鲁都曲阜具有重要而又特殊的地位。由于周公旦重要的政治地位，鲁国地位超出其他诸侯国，一般认为其在建设之初即融入了周礼制度，所谓“周礼尽在鲁矣”[4]，而且其作为国都，贯穿两周始终，是各诸侯国都城中沿用时间最久的。从考古发掘的成果来看，鲁都曲阜宫城与外郭内外相套、宫城居中，经过宫城形成城市南北中轴线，城市整体空间结构严整有序，已知的先秦故城中尚无与其相同者，学术界普遍认为其可能体现了西周时期城市尤其是都城建设的若干特点[1][2][3]，这在丰镐、洛邑等西周都城城址湮没不存的现实条件下，具有极其重要的标志性的地位。（图 3）

◎二、鲁故城遗址挖掘与保存现状：结构清晰，覆压严重

在历史价值挖掘的基础上，需要对历史遗迹的挖掘与保存现状进行分析，从而明确能够进行保护与展示的内容。

鲁故城沿用日久，如今曲阜一带仍有多处城垣等遗迹残存于地表。1940 年代初，日本学者曾进行过初步调查和小规模勘测[4]，证明此处确为鲁都所在。1957—1958 年，中国科学院考古研究所对鲁故城遗址进行了钻探和试掘。1977—1978 年，山东省考古所进行了全面系统的勘察和局部发掘，初步明确了其建设年代、城市规模、空间结构与布局等基本情况[5]。现有的考古发掘成果可以较为清晰地展现出鲁故城的整体空间结构，但大量面状遗址仍然存在占压严重等现实问题。

首先，鲁故城中塑造城市整体空间的结构性要素已经获得了较好的考古发掘，并具备展示的条件。（1）内外两重城垣、宫城居中的“回”字形城廓形态：鲁故城平面略呈扁方形，东西约 3.6 千米，南北约 2.7 千米，周长约 11.8 千米，总面积约 10.45 平方千米，故城城垣的许多地段在地面上仍有清晰的遗迹，尤其是在城的东南角及其两侧，部分地段虽湮没于地下，但是通过考古发掘仍能复原整个城圈，城四面均有濠，今南、西、北三面和东城南部，仍有河道存在；在故城中部周公庙高地一带，有规模宏大的大型夯土建筑基址，东西近 1 千米，南北约 2 千米，据推测为鲁城宫城，至今其地形仍明显高于周边，为全城至高点，现在此范围内有周公庙古建筑群[5]，是鲁故城的核心部分。（2）南北轴线与东西干道形成的“丁”字形城市内部空间主干：考古发现城内道路十余条，多与城门相连，经纬交织，其中最为突出的是宫城南面直通鲁故城南东门稷门的干道，其延长线直指城南 1735 米的舞雩台遗址，构成了一条清晰的城市中轴线，是城市空间的南北主干；宫城以北有横贯城市东西的一条主干道和一条用于给排水的大型水道，以往地面上仍可见河床遗

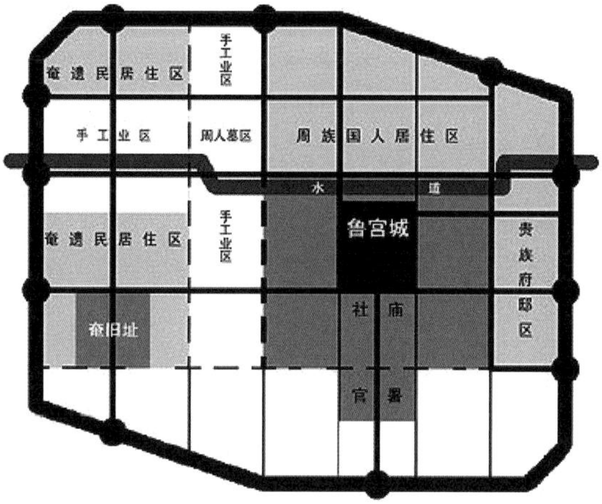

图 3. 根据考古线索规整的鲁国形态图。来源：张悦 . 曲阜城市形态的历史演化研究与当代曲阜的城市设计构想及实践 [D]. 清华大学博士论文 . 2000：42.
Fig. 3 Graph of the Lu State Structured upon Archaeological Clues. Source: Zhang Yue. *Research on Historical Evolution of Qufu Urban Form and Conception & Practices of Modern Qufu Urban Design*. Doctoral Dissertation of Tsinghua University, Beijing, 2000: 42.

ers generally estimated it as an important road running through south to north of the Ancient Capital of Lu State. In the Ming Dynasty, the layout of Qufu was just developed around this axis. This aixs served as a spatial tie connecting the Ancient City of Lu State and the Ancient City of Ming Dynasty. Hence, it boasted a quite special status (Fig. 4).

When the structural elements for overall urban space were excavated and preserved more clearly, the problems of the Relics of Ancient City of Lu State is also obvious. Inside the outer city walls and outside the imperial palace, there are a large number of manual workshops, residence area, tomb areas and other cultural relics. Due to large area and wide range of the relics as well as the accumulative construction of this area over thousands of years, the relics were tightly coupled with the urban and rural life, which led to serious occupancy of a great amount of relics areas. Along with the continuous development of urban and rural construction, that situation is getting serious increasingly. Hence, it is unreachable to display the whole relics in a short time and even the basic safety of the relics is confronted with challenges. The south-west of the Ancient City of Lu State was the city of Qufu in the Ming and Qing Dynasties, which is now still the downtown area with intensive buildings, so that drilling and excavation could not be conducted completely. Many relics nearby the urban built-up areas (mainly located in the range of the city of Lu State in the Han Dynasty) are facing the great pressure of land development and serious extent of occupancy. The relics outside the city area are still confronted with huge threats because of the large scale as well as the increasingly expanded rural construction (Fig. 5).

◎ 3. Planning and Design Conception based on Historical Value and Realistic Conditions: Integrated protection, emphasized display and staging advancement

The excavation of historical value and analysis of current conditions basically determined the major contents that "should" and "could" be protected and displayed in the Ancient City of Lu State. Based on

迹，现已淤塞，但钻探则极易发现[5]27 构成城市空间的东西主干。（3）在鲁故城的范围内还存在一条贯穿南北、联系鲁故城与明故城的轴线，北起孔林入口，沿神道，经万古长春牌坊，穿明曲阜城北门，连接颜庙、鼓楼、孔府孔庙，串联起了从春秋战国直至明清的一系列文化遗迹，这一轴线应当产生于春秋末期鲁人从城的孔庙去往孔子墓地祭祀的道路，虽然考古挖掘尚未有道路遗迹发现，但是研究者普遍推测此为鲁故城南北向的重要道路，明代曲阜城正是围绕此轴线展开城市布局的，可以说是联系鲁故城与明故城的空间纽带，具有非常特殊的地位。（图 4）

在塑造城市整体空间的结构性要素得到较为清晰的挖掘与保存的同时，鲁故城遗址所存在的问题也是显而易见的。在外城垣以内、宫城以外，还分布有大量的手工业作坊、居住遗址、墓葬区等文化遗存，由于遗址面积大、范围广，且数千年来城市在一个地区累加建设，使得遗址与城乡生活结合紧密，大量面状遗址覆压严重，伴随着城乡建设的不断发展，形势日益严峻，不仅短时间内整体展示无法实现，遗址的基本安全都面临着挑战。鲁故城西南部为明清曲阜城所在地，至今仍是建设密集的城市中心区，无法进行充分的钻探挖掘；大量靠近城市建成区的遗址（主要是汉鲁城范围内），面临土地开发等巨大压力，占压覆压情况极为严重；还有城市外围的遗址因为规模尺度大，多为农田所覆盖，部分亦为不断扩大的乡村建设用地所覆压，面临着巨大的威胁。（图 5）

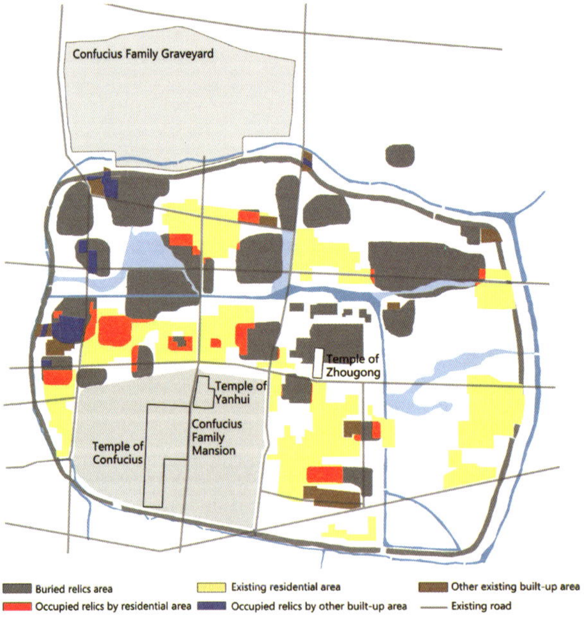

图 4. 鲁故城遗址分布
Fig. 4 Relics Distribution of the Ancient City of Lu State

this, we may come to the planning and design conception for protection and display of the Ancient City of Lu State to show the historical value that "should" be displayed under the realistic conditions that "could" be realized.

3.1 Spatial Pattern of "Two Cities-Three Axes-Multiple Districts"

Seen from the above analysis, we come to a conclusion that the most prominent historical value of Ancient City of Lu State in Qufu is reflected in its neat and orderly overall spatial structure, whether in the construction history of Qufu over thousands of years or in the urban planning of various states in Qing Dynasty. Judged from realistic conditions, the spatial structural elements of the city, such as the relics of city walls, imperial palace, axes and main arteries, are preserved clearly and completely, which are eligible for display. However, other ruins areas are confronted with very complicated situations and have difficulty being displayed thoroughly. Hence, during the planning and design of relics landscape, the display of structural elements that can manifest the overall spatial structure of the Ancient City of Lu State should be highlighted, including the "hollow square" structure formed by outer city walls and imperial palace, the "T-shaped" structure formed by the south-north axis and the east-west main artery, and the axis of Confucius Family Graveyard bridging the Ancient City of Lu State and the Ancient City of Ming Dynasty. With regard to other relics areas with great quantities, firstly, the integrated preservation should be conducted strictly according to the national laws, with special attention to the damages caused by urban and rural constructions; secondly, the environmental governance should be conducted gradually, and the relics area could be excavated and displayed one by one for some time in the future according to the situation of development; finally, the spatial pattern of "Two Cities (outer walls and imperial city) -Three Axes (the south-north axis, east-west artery, and axis of Confucius Family Graveyard) -Multiple Districts" could be

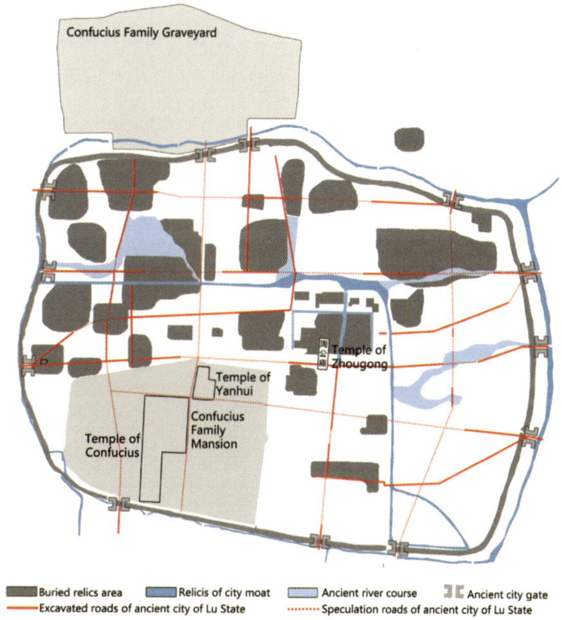

图 5. 鲁故城遗址占压现状
Fig. 5 Occupancy Situation of the Ancient City of Lu State

◎三、基于历史价值和现状条件的规划设计设想：整体保护、重点展示、分期推进

历史价值挖掘和现状条件分析基本明确了鲁故城“应当”及“能够”进行保护与展示的主要内容，在此基础上，可以得到鲁故城保护与展示的规划设计设想，在“能够”实现的现实条件下，彰显“应当”展示的历史价值。

1．“两城—三轴—多片区”的规划格局

通过上文分析可以看到，不管是在数千年的曲阜城市建设史中，还是在先秦各诸侯国都城的城市规划中，曲阜鲁故城最为突出的历史价值体现在其严整有序的城市整体空间结构；而从现实条件来看，城市空间的结构性要素，如城垣、宫城、轴线、主干道等遗址保存得清晰、完整，具备良好的展示条件，而其他片状遗址情况复杂，全面展示尚存在不少困难。故而在曲阜鲁故城保护与展示中，可以主要围绕能够体现出鲁故城整体空间结构的结构性要素开展遗址景观规划设计，进行重点展示，包括鲁故城外郭与宫城形成的“回”字形结构、城市南北轴线与东西主干道形成的“丁”字形结构、联系鲁故城与明故城的孔林轴线。对其他量大面广的遗址片区，首先遵照国家法律，加以严格的整体保护，尤其注意严防城乡建设所带来的破坏；进而逐步开展环境治理，根据发展状况，在未来一定时期内逐片加以发掘与展示，最终形成“两城（即外郭与宫城）—三轴（城市南北轴即周公庙轴线、东西干道与水道、孔林轴线）—多片区”的规划格局。

这种重点展示、整体保护、分期推进的保护与展示思路，可以恰如其分地体现鲁故城最具历史价值的特征，即城市严整有序的整体空间结构；同时，充分尊重现实的发展条件，在短时间内较易实现；此外，为未来的发展留有余地，城乡发展的需求在不断变化，对鲁故城的考古挖掘和学术研究也在不断深化，这些都可能为鲁故城遗址保护与展示提出新的要求、提供新的启发。（图 6）

2. 历史遗存与农业景观交相辉映的规划设计手法

整体的规划格局需要具体的规划设计手法加以实现。在历史文化遗产的保护与展示中，当前国际上通常采取建设遗址公园或博物馆等形式，根据遗址本体与周边环境的特征等，采用不同类型的规划设计手法。对于鲁故城遗址而言，遗址本体尺度大、范围广，主要分布在建设密度较低的农村地区，局部在建设质量较差的城市边缘区，大量遗址就处在农田之中，有条件将遗产保护与展示同城乡居民生活环境整治、农业生态景观建设结合起来，创造历史遗存与农业景观交相辉映的大型郊野遗址公园。

established.

By following this protection and display concept of integrated protection, emphasized display and staging advancement, the features of the Ancient City of Lu State with the most historical value, namely, the neat and orderly overall spatial structure of this ancient city could be reflected appropriately. This concept could also be easily realized in a short time because it gives full respect to the realistic development conditions. Additionally, this concept allows for the future development. As the needs of urban development are changing increasingly, the archaeological excavation and academic studies on the Ancient City of Lu State are also deepened accordingly, which are likely to impose new requirements and also new enlightenment for protection and display of the Relics of the Ancient City of Lu State (Fig. 6).

3.2 Planning and Design Techniques for Complementary Enhancement between Historical Relics and Agricultural Landscapc

The overall spatial pattern needs to be realized via specific techniques of planning and design. Relics Park or museum construction is a common technique worldwide in the protection and display of historical and cultural heritages, while the planning and design techniques may vary depending on the features of relics and surrounding environment. The relics of the Ancient City of Lu State, with a large scale and a widc rangc, mostly distributcd in the rural areas with a low construction density and partially stand at the urban fringe with low construction quality. Quite a few relics are just situated in the farmland. Hence, it is eligible to integrate the protection and display of relics with the living environment governance and agricultural landscape construction, and thus create a large outer suburb park where the historical relics and agricultural landscape add radiance and beauty to each other.

Based on this goal, the mode of "Reduction-based Increase" could be adopted in the planning strategy. The so-called "Reduction" means the appropriate relocation and environmental governance based on the objective of relics protection and urban-rural environmental improvement. In the near future, factories, rural residences and tombs occupying the relics in the range of relics could be relocated, especially those occupying and surrounding the important structural elements such as two cities and three axes. For a long run, along with the transformation of land usage, natural migration of population and other variation tendency in the area of the Ancient City of Lu State, population size and construction intensity should be controlled based on maintaining the appropriate agricultural production. The so-called "Increase" is to conduct the landscape design and appropriately develop the cultural and leisure activities suitable for the features of relics park based on the objective of relics display and urban-rural environmental improvement, including the groups of relics display and small museum, memorial forest, landscape footpath and tourism service facilities, etc.

For each specific part of the Ancient City of Lu State, a specific position should be determined and different techniques of planning design should be adopted in allusion to different relics and its surrounding environmental conditions and resources.

The imperial palace in the "Two Cities", namely the highland of Zhougong Temple, can be built into the archaeological relics park which integrates agricultural characteristics and sense of history. This area boasts abundant buried relics including large-scale temple ruins with great value of display, while the architectural complex of Zhougong Temple built in Song Dynasty is still in existence. The abstract restoration and display of the relics could be adopted to make people feel the "Sadness of Nostalgia" by integration of archaeological experience and educational functions.

The outer city walls in the "Two Cities" could be designed into the unique encircling landscape belt which integrates cultural heritage and ecological landscape. Firstly, the scope of protection and planning

基于这一规划设计目标，可以在规划策略上采用“先减后加”的模式。所谓“减”，即以遗址保护与城乡环境治理为共同目标，进行适当的搬迁与环境整治：近期重点考虑搬迁遗址范围内的工厂、覆压遗址的农村居民点和墓区，尤其是两城、三轴等重要结构性要素之上及周边的住宅、坟墓等；远期，伴随着鲁故城范围内用地性质的转化、人口的自然迁移等变化趋势，在维持适当的农业生产的基础上，控制人口规模与建设强度。所谓“加”即以遗址展示与城乡环境提升为共同目标，进行景观规划设计，适当发展符合遗址公园特征的文化休憩活动，包括：遗址展示群与小型博物馆、纪念林、景观步道、旅游服务设施等。

针对鲁故城遗址的每一特定部分，需要根据遗址本体与周边环境条件与资源的不同，确定具体定位，采取不同的规划设计手法。

“两城”中的宫城即周公庙高地一带，可以形成兼具农业特色与历史沧桑感的考古遗址公园。这一片区历史埋藏丰富，且为具有较强展示价值的大型宫庙建筑，现有始建于宋的周公庙建筑群，可以对遗址进行抽象复原展示，结合考古体验、教育等功能，使人感受到“黍离之悲”的凭古之境。

“两城”中的鲁故城外郭可以成为文化遗产与生态景观兼容的特色环城景观带。城垣与城河遗迹斑斑可循，蔚为体系，可以作为一个整体进行规划和展示。首先，划定保护与规划范围，优先搬迁工厂及占压城垣的陵墓、民宅等，清理、整治遗址周边地区环境，对河道进行清淤与生态治理；其次，建设环城景观带，以绿化廊道、人行步道串联，在适当位置设置供休憩、观眺的景观节点；第三，采用现代景观设计手法，标识各城门遗迹。同时，由于城垣尺度较大，不同区段特点不同，需要根据遗址现状及可利用资源进行分段，有针对性地确定每一区段的具体功能、节点分布及设计手法。（图 7，表 1）

“三轴”中的鲁故城南北轴（周公庙轴线）可以成为视线通畅的景观性、礼仪性轴线。这是两周时期曲阜城市最为重要的礼制性轴线，贯穿宫室、宗庙、城门与城外的祭坛，气势壮阔。今天这条轴线部分为城乡建设用地所覆压，建议清理从周公庙高地到稷门遗址轴线上的覆压建筑，建设成为绿化景观良好、视线通畅的道路，控制道路两侧建设密度与高度，重现历史上的恢弘轴线；在城门遗址处与城墙遗迹结合，建设与周公庙“遗址公园”呼应的具备“城市公园”性质的节点，并设登高观景之处，实现与城外舞雩台[6]的视线联系。

“三轴”中的鲁故城东西轴，可以成为串联各遗址的览古之路。这一轴线在两周时期包括道路与水道两部分，与现有的贯穿鲁故城南北的道路走向大体一致，局部重合，在其南北两侧的农田中分布有大量遗址区。对道路两侧的遗址片区进行逐步发掘，

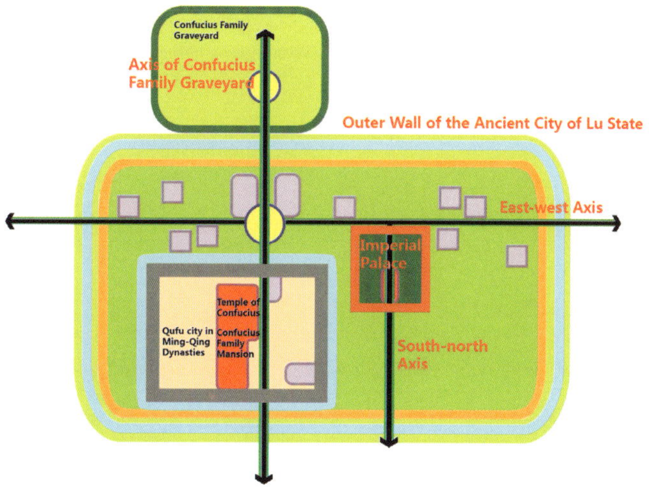

图 6. "两城—三轴—多片区"规划格局示意
Fig. 6 Schematic Diagram of Spatial Pattern of "Two Cities–Three Axes–Multiple Districts"

should be determined, factories and those tombs and residences occupying city walls should be relocated, and then clearance and governance of the surrounding environment and the dredging and ecological governance against the river course could be conducted; secondly, the landscape belts around the city could be constructed, linked by greening corridors and pedestrian ways, at the appropriate positions of which landscape nodes could be set up for rest and sightseeing; thirdly, modern techniques of landscape design could be adopted to identify the relics of all city gates; meanwhile, as the city wall is in a large scale with distinct features in different section, it should be divided into several segments according to the situation of relics and available resources, and thus the specific functions, distribution of nodes and design techniques could be determined in allusion to each segment (Fig. 7, Table 1).

Among the "Three Axes", the south-north axis (axis of Zhougong Temple) of the Ancient City of Lu State could serve as a landscape and etiquette axis with smooth vision. As the most important axis of ritual system of Qufu in the period of Western and Eastern Zhou Dynasty, this axis ran through palaces, temples, gates and altars outside the city, with magnificent momentum. However part of this axis is covered and occupied by urban and rural construction currently. In this instance, the buildings occupying the axis from highland of Zhougong Temple to Jimen Relics (the southeastern city gate) should be cleared and a street with beautiful landscape and smooth vision could be built to reproduce the magnificence of historical axis, while the density and height of buildings on both sides of the street should be controlled strictly. In the junction between relics of city gate and city walls, it is suggested constructing the nodes which not only correspond to the "Relics Park" of Zhougong Temple but boasts the features of "City Park"; meanwhile, the viewing decks could be built to make a visually link with Wuyu Terrace[6] outside the city.

The east-west axis among the "Three Axes" can function as the road to visit several historic relics. In the period of Western and Eastern Zhou Dynasty, this axis included road and waterway, with the direction similar to the current road running east to west of the Ancient City of Lu State, but some parts were over-

表 1：鲁故城外郭城垣分段环境整治与设计设想

分段	功能定位	控制范围	具体手法
A-B	城市生活性的小尺度滨水空间	城河内侧 30 ~ 40 米，外侧 15 米	1. 整治周边民房，搬迁厂房 2. 结合周边民居特色，创建小尺度的连贯沿河步道 3. 设近水驳岸及供城市居民使用的小型开放空间
B-C	新阙里： 作为孔庙的入口空间的城市公园	城河外侧 100 米	整治入口空间环境，提升空间品质，在有效集散的基础上，塑造肃穆的氛围
C-D	城市中心绿地	静轩路南侧至南东门遗址南 30 米	1. 清理占压房屋 2. 建设绿化带 3. 以南东门遗址为中心进行放大节点，强调周公庙轴线
D-E	景观丰富的城墙遗址公园	城河外侧 20 米至城墙内侧 20 米	1. 清理环境，搬迁范围内厂房 2. 利用北端城墙遗址、荷花池、林木，创建景观节点 3. 根据现有条件对城墙内侧进行分段特色景观设计 4. 城墙与城河间保留农田
E-F	田野间的景观步道	城墙轴线内侧 10 米，外侧 20 米	简单整治路面
F-G	遗迹与田园风光结合的特色历史景区	城墙内侧遗址范围，城河外侧 15 米	1. 适当发掘展示遗迹 2. 设计网状路网，形成多角度感知 3. 局部设置上城脚架
G-A	孔林林墙	城墙外侧 30 米	保持现状农田

Table 1: Environmental Governance and Design Concept for Subsection of Outer City Walls

Subsection	Functional Orientation	Scope of Control	Specific Techniques
A-B	Small-scaled waterfront space with urban life characteristics	30-40 m off from inner side of city moats and 15 m off from outer side	1.Renovate the surrounding residences and relocate the plants 2.Create the small-scale continuous walkways along the river with features of surrounding residences 3.Set up waterside revetment and small-sized open space for citizens
B-C	New Que Li City park at the entrance space of the Temple of Confucius	100 m off from outer side of city moats	Improve the spatial quality of the entrance and the surrounding area , and create the solemn atmosphere as well as effective distribution of the flow of people
C-D	Central green space of the city	South side of Jingxuan Road to 30 m south of relics of southeastern gate	1.Clear up the houses occupying the relics 2.Construct the greenbelt 3.Enlarge nodes by centralizing on the relics of the southeastern gate and emphasize the axis of Zhougong Temple
D-E	City Wall Relics Park with rich landscape	20 m off from outer side of city moats and 20 m off from inner side of city walls	1.Clear up environment and relocate plants in the scope 2.Create landscape nodes by virtue of relics of city wall on the north end, lotus pond and woods 3.Conduct the landscape design inside city walls by subsection according to the existing conditions 4.Maintain farmland between city walls and city moats
E-F	Farmland landscape walkway	10 m off from inner side of the city wall axis and 20m off from outer side	Simply renovate the road
F-G	Featured historical scenic spot integrating relics and rural scenery	In the range of relics of inner side of city walls and 15 m off from outer side of city moats	1.Excavate and display the relics appropriately 2.Design net-shaped road system to create the multi-dimension perception 3.Build foot stand in partial positions
G-A	Wall of Confucius Family Graveyard	30 m off from the wall	Maintain farmland

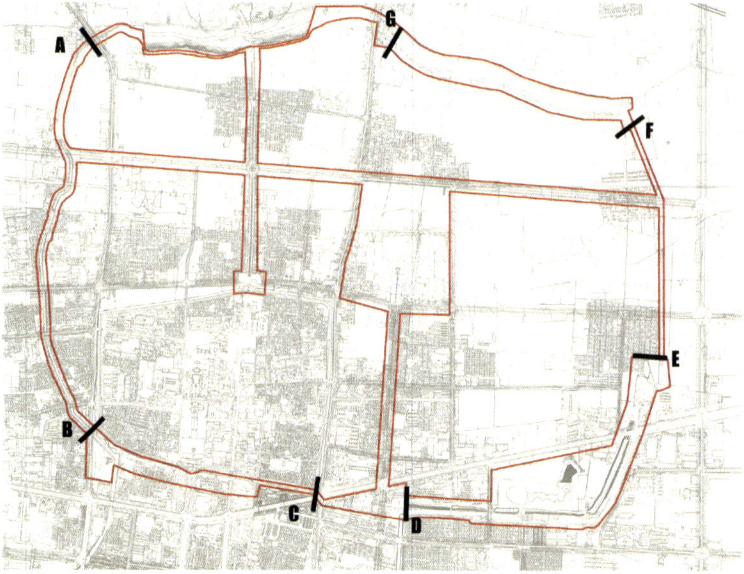

图 7. 鲁故城遗址保护控制范围与外郭城垣分段示意
Fig. 7 Subsection Diagram for Protection & Control Scope of Outer City Walls

并选择适宜方式展示遗址本体与考古发掘现场，形成一系列各具特色、具有野趣的历史遗址展示群；对现有东西向道路进行简单整治，局部恢复旧有水系，在道路周边与重要遗址位置有较好交通、视线联系处，设置数个停靠点，提供必要的旅游服务设施和视野开阔的观景点，串联各遗址片区；伴随着考古发掘的不断推进，这一轴线也必将更为充实。

“三轴”中的孔林轴线，可以成为具有神圣感和文化性的儒学之路。这一轴线自北向南串联起了从春秋战国直至明清的一系列文化遗迹，轴线两端分别为孔氏家族墓地孔林和孔府、孔庙，既是儒学文化的圣地，也是游客众多的世界文化遗产，这条轴线两侧建设密度较高，人流密集。首先，整治轴线两侧环境，特别是既有建设，确定控制范围，保证轴线景观；其次，沿轴线从明城墙到孔林入口，创造不同特色、具备儒学文化意义的开放空间，营造空间上登堂入室的序列感，其中重点设计孔林入口、万古长春牌坊及鲁城墙遗址、汉城墙遗址、明城墙与轴线的交点处的开放空间。(图 8)

◎四、结语

我国是一个历史悠久的文明古国，在广阔的国土上分布着数量众多的历史文化遗产；与此同时，1970 年代末改革开放以来，中国经历了大规模、高速度的城镇化进程，

lapped. There are a large number of relics distributed in the farmland on the southern and northern of this axis. It is suggested that the relics on both sides could be gradually excavated and displayed in an appropriate way, so as to form a series of featured and delightful exhibition groups for historic relics. The current east-west road could be simply renovated, while the ancient water system could also be restored partially. Several docking points could be built at the sites with a good traffic and visual linkage with important relics to provide necessary tourism service facilities and sightseeing points with wide vision. This axis is bound to be more enriched with gradually advanced archaeological excavation.

The axis of Confucius Family Graveyard among the "Three Axes" can serve as the road of Confucianism with the sacred and cultural sensation. This axis links together a series of cultural relics from the Spring and Autumn Period to Ming and Qing Dynasty. Temple and Confucius Family Graveyard and the Confucius Family Mansion respectively stand on the two ends of this axis, which is not only the holy land of Confucian cultures but also the world cultural heritage. On both sides of this axis, the building density is high and population is intensive. Firstly, the environment on both sides of the axis, especially the existing buildings, should be improved and controlled, so as to guarantee the landscape along the axis. Secondly, it is suggested that open space with different characteristics and significance of Confucian cultures could be built from the city wall of Ming Dynasty to the entrance of Confucius Family Graveyard to create a sense of spatial sequence. Specially, the design emphasis is the open space at the entrance of Confucius Family Graveyard, Wan Gu Chang Chun Memorial Archway as well as the junctions between the axis and relics of City Wall of Lu State, relics of City Wall of Han Dynasty and relics of City Wall of Ming Dynasty (Fig. 8).

图 8. 鲁故城遗址保护与景观规划设计设想
Fig. 8 The Conception of the Relics Protection and Landscape Planning and Design of the Ancient Capital City of Lu State

城乡建设的重点地区往往也就是文化遗产密集的地区，历史遗产与城乡建设之间的矛盾不可避免。如何既保护与展示珍贵的历史遗产，又与现实的发展条件相适应，是一个重要而迫切的科学问题。

本文对鲁故城保护与展示规划设计的研究即是尝试提出应对这一问题的一条可能途径：首先，通过对历史文献和考古资料的研究，深入挖掘历史遗产最为重要的历史价值，作为"应当"展示的内容；其次，考察考古发掘和城乡建设的现状，分析现实具备的条件和问题，得到"能够"展示的内容；综合以上两方面的研究分析，可以得到与遗址的历史与现实相匹配的规划设计设想，确定规划格局，进而综合运用各领域的规划设计手法，在"能够"实现的现实条件下，彰显"应当"保护与展示的文化遗产的历史价值。

1. 本文是在《区域文化视角下的曲阜城市发展构想及城市中轴线城市设计研究》（清华大学建筑学院，2009）中"鲁故城遗址保护与景观设计"部分的基础上开展的研究。

2. 考古挖掘已经发现了旧石器和新石器时代的若干古人类生存遗迹，详见：刘振清编．齐鲁文化．济南：山东美术出版社，（香港）商务印书馆，1997：18. 文献也记载传说中的人文始祖黄帝、炎帝、少昊、颛顼等都曾在这一地区活动乃至建都，如《史记正义》引《帝王世纪》云："炎帝陈营都于鲁曲阜，黄帝自穷桑登帝位，后徙曲阜。少昊邑于穷桑，以登帝位，都曲阜。颛顼始都穷桑，徙商丘。"《史记正义·周本纪》云："穷桑在鲁北，或云穷桑即曲阜也。又为大庭氏之故国，又是商奄之地。"

3. 据《史记·周本纪》《史记·鲁周公世家》载，周武王灭商后，封其弟周公旦于鲁，周公不就封，留佐武王。武王死后，又相成王，而使其子伯禽代就封于鲁。《史记·鲁周公世家》记载，周武王"遍封功臣同姓戚者。封周公旦于少昊之墟曲阜，是为鲁公。"

4.《左传·昭公二年》。

5. 周公庙占地75亩，历经宋、元、明、清6次修建。1977年，被列为山东省第一批省级重点文物保护单位。

6. 舞雩台遗址至今仍清晰可见，台基东西120米、南北125米，残高7米，目前已有栏杆维护、标识牌、绿化等基本的保护、展示。

参考文献：

[1] 张学海．浅谈曲阜鲁城的年代和基本格局[J]. 文物，1982（12）:13-16.

[2] 曲英杰．春秋时期鲁都城复原试探[J]. 孔子研究,1988（03）:106-114.

[3] 张悦．曲阜城市形态的历史演化研究与当代曲阜的城市设计构想及实践[D]. 清华大学博士论文．2000.

[4] 驹井和爱．曲阜鲁城の遗蹟．东京大学文学部考古学研究室，1951.

[5] 山东省文物考古研究所，山东省博物馆，济宁地区文物组，曲阜县文管会编．曲阜鲁国故城[M]. 济南：齐鲁书社，1982.

◎ 4. Conclusion

China is an ancient country with a long history, numerous historical and cultural heritages distributed in its vast territory; meanwhile, since the reform and opening in the late 1970s, China has experienced large-scale and high-speed urbanization. The key regions of urban-rural construction are generally located at the regions with intensive cultural heritages. The conflict between historical heritages and urban-rural construction is inevitable. Hence, how to protect and display the precious historical heritage while meeting the realistic conditions of development is an urgent and significant scientific problem.

This paper studies the planning and design for protection and display of the Ancient City of Lu State, which is just a tentative approach to solve this problem. Firstly, the most important historical value of historical heritage has been excavated by studies on historical literatures and archaeological materials to determine the contents that "should" be displayed; secondly, the realistic conditions and existing problems have been analyzed by surveys on actuality of archaeological excavation and urban-rural construction to conclude the contents that "can" be displayed; in combination of the above studies and analysis in two aspects, a planning and design conception is suggested matching history and reality of the relics, including an overall spatial pattern and comprehensive utilization of various planning and design techniques, to the historical value of cultural heritages that should be protected and displayed in realistic conditions.

---

1. This paper conducts the research of "Protection and Landscape Design of the Ancient City Relics of Lu State", a part of the project Conceptual Planning for Qufu's Urban Development in Regional and Cultural Perspectives and Urban Design for Qufu's Central Axis (School of Architecture, Tsinghua University, 2009).

2. The archeological excavation has discovered the several survival relics of ancient people at the age of the Paleolithic Period and the Neolithic Age Liu Zhenqing. Culture of Qi-Lu. Shanghai Far East Press, Jinnan: Shandong Fine Arts Publishing House, The Commercial Press (Hong Kong), 1997: 18. Literatures also recorded that the first ancestor of Han Chinese—Yellow Emperor, Yan Emperor, Shaohao and Zhuanxu in the legends took activities and even established capital in this area. As said in the Age of Kingscited in Zhengyi, "Yan Emperor built the capital in Qufu; Yellow Emperor moved to Qufu after he came to crown in Qiongsang. Shao Hao established a city in Qiongsang for becoming the emperor and set up the capital in Qufu. Zhuanxu established the capital in Qiongsang and afterwards moved to Shangqiu.""Qiongsang was located on the north of Shandong, so Qiongsang was named as Qufu. Qufu was also the former capital of Datingshi (the name of a clan in the ancient times of China) and also the capital of Shang Dynasty." (Historical Records·Records of Zhou Dynasty·Zhengyi)

3. As recorded in the Historical Records of Zhou Dynasty and Records of Family of Zhougong of Lu State, Emperor Wu enfeoffed the Lu State to his younger brother Zhougong after he threw away Shang Dynasty, but Zhougong rejected it and continued to assist Emperor Wu. After the death of the Emperor, Zhougong served as prime minister of Emperor Cheng. The son of Zhougong set up a capital in the Lu State.

4. Chronicle of Zuo—The 2nd Year of Shaogong.

5. Zhougong Temple covered a land area of 75mu, totally rebuilt for six times in Song Dynasty, Yuan Dynasty, Ming Dynasty and Qing Dynasty. In 1977, Zhougong Temple was listed as the first provincial important heritage sites under state protection of Shandong Province.

6. The relic of Wuyu Terrace is still visible clearly, 120 m from east to west, 125 m from south to north, with a height of 7 m. Currently, the terrace is protected and displayed basically with handrails, identification labels and afforestation.

第三章 有生命力的活态城市，可持续发展与合作

Section 3 Living City, Sustainable Development & Cooperation

亚洲现有历史名城保护中城市政策可持续和平衡发展的新台阶：中国曲阜案例研究[1]

林志宏

本文以世界文化遗产地之一和中国历史文化名城曲阜（孔子诞生地）为例，分析当前文化遗产评估的现状 / 问题和未来对城市保护、重建和发展的规划。本文旨在通过问题探讨和反思为选择合适的方法论（策略）和方法 / 工具（规划 / 任务 / 行为）制定指导意见，来评估历史名城中文化遗产的价值和文化影响，这也是文化发展规划的一部分。本文作者提出对跨专业的方法和发展规划文化的需要，号召跨专业城市研究领域研究员和专家的参与：城市规划、交通运输、住房建筑、地域研究、旅游业、文化遗产保护、历史学、社会学、经济学、考古学、建筑学、人类学、博物馆研究、艺术 / 美学研究等，使亚洲历史名城保护中城市政策可持续和平衡发展上一个新台阶。

◎引言

就当代中国和山东省的规模而言，曲阜可谓是一个相当小的城市：占地总面积 895 平方千米，总人口 70 万。曲阜位于山东省西南部，距山东省会城市济南市 160 千米。曲阜被认为是远东亚洲文明和城市规划中的一个重要例子。其大部分建筑都与孔子、孔子弟子或后裔有关。1982 年，曲阜被列为全国首批 24 个最重要的历史文化名城之一。

随着中国历史朝代的更迭，在原有面积不变的基础上，曲阜城市的面貌不断发生着变化，成就了曲阜的历史。事实上，曲阜承载着城镇土地使用的历史记录（图 1）。如今依然可以看到几乎长达 25 个世纪的历史下的不同城市阶层，这赋予了曲阜独特的城市形态学遗产和与孔子哲学相关的珍贵的无形遗产。25 个世纪前的曲阜鲁城的考古遗迹代表了最古老、最本真的中国三纵三横的方形 / 矩形城市形态学（10.45 平方千米，东西横距超过 3.7 千米，南北纵距超过 2.7 千米；这种城市形态如今依旧在北京和西安的城市建设中使用）和具有历史意义的城市土地征用。在 16 世纪，为了纪念孔子，一群气势恢宏的纪念标识拔地而起，旨在“建造一个以保护古庙为己任的城市——为了

A New Step for a Sustainable and Balanced Urban Policy in an Asian Living Historic City Conservation Context: The Case of Qufu[1], China

Roland Lin Chih-Hung

Taking the case of Qufu (birthplace of Confucius), China, a world cultural heritage site and Chinese living historic city, the author analyses the current situation/issues of culture heritage assessment and the foreseen future planning of urban conservation, renew and development. The objective of this article is to explore issues and reflection to generate guidance for selecting appropriate methodologies (strategies) and principles/tools (planning/tasks/action) to assess cultural heritage values and cultural significance in the living historic city context as part of integrated culture for development planning. The author calls for the necessities of interdisciplinary approaches to this reflection and the need of culture for development planning, with the participation of researchers and specialists from interdisciplinary areas: city planning, transportation, housing, territory studies, tourism, cultural heritage preservation, history, sociology, economy, archaeology, architecture, anthropology, museum studies, art/aesthetic studies, etc. for a new step for sustainable and balanced urban policy in an asian living historic city conservation context.

◎ Introduction

On the scale of modern-day China and of Shandong Province, Qufu is a rather small agglomeration. The city occupies an administrative territory of 895 km^2 for a population of 700,000. In the southwest of Shandong, located 160 km from Jinan, the provincial capital Qufu is considered to be an important example of civilisation and of city planning in Far East Asia. Most of its buildings are linked to Confucius, to his disciples or to his descendants. Qufu is one of the first series of 24 most important historical and cultural towns in the country as classified by the Chinese government in 1982.

The history of Qufu is derived from the successive relocation of urban implantations, to the inside of a same boundary, throughout the Chinese dynasty eras. In reality, Qufu is home to the history of successive urban land uses (Fig. 1). The different urban strata of almost 25 centuries of history can still been seen; it provides Qufu a unique heritage of urban morphology and an intangible heritage related to Confucius philosophical scarceness. The ancient archaeological remains of Lu City in Qufu dated 25 centuries ago represents the most ancient and most authentic Chinese city morphology of square/rectangular in shape with 3 north-south and 3 east-west big axes (10.45 km^2, extending over 3.7 km from east to west and over 2.7 km from north to south; this Chinese urban morphology is still duplicated and seen in Beijing and Xi'an today), and the latest historical urban land uses with high-quality of group of Confucian monu-

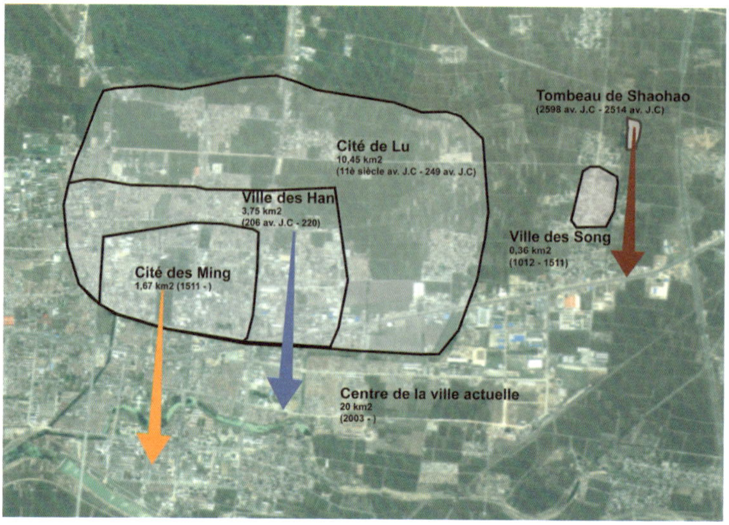

图 1. 曲阜的城池及历史变迁图 © 林志宏教授—法国欧亚印象顾问公司
Fig. 1 Qufu Sucessive Urban Land Uses © Prof. Roland Lin - ISASES Consultants

避免乡民损坏古庙，特别是 1521 年农民起义对孔庙、佛寺和道观的毁坏”[2]，此城如今被称为曲阜明故城（中央面积缩减为 1.64 平方千米）。（图 2）

◎现代城市化进程中的曲阜变迁

16 世纪，为护卫曲阜孔庙，始建曲阜明故城（图 3），占地 1.64 平方千米，之后少有变动。直至文化大革命时期（1966—1969），许多建筑物被拆除，并代之以当时材料和样式的公共建筑。1978 年，明故城城墙也难以幸免，于 2003 年得以重建（只有北部的部分残垣和南北门得以保留）。

18 世纪 70 至 80 年代，曲阜城区占地已接近 3.1 平方千米，以明故城为中心向外围发展。第一个城市规划可以追溯至 1980 年。20 世纪 80 年代提议的规划方针让曲阜以明故城为中心向东南西北四个方向全面扩张（图 4）。东部，鲁故城和城市扩展，作为旅游景区；西部，大学和研究区；南部，新居住和行政区；北部，孔子文物，作为历史保护区。规划以“三孔”为线，重点强调旅游、文化和历史。其后的数次保护

图 2. 曲阜孔庙和孔府 © 曲阜市政府
Fig. 2 Qufu Cofucius Temple and Confucius family mansion © Qufu City Government

ments dated 16th century with the notion "*build a city to protect the temples—in order to avoid pillaging by people from the countryside, following the peasant riot of 1521 against the house of Confucius, Buddhist and Taoist temples*"[2] , called as today Ming City in Qufu (reduced into the very centralized territory of 1,64 km^2) (Fig. 2) .

◎ Qufu throughout the modern urbanisation

The Ming City of Qufu (Fig. 3), with its 1,64 km^2 after built during the 16th century to protect the related Confucian monuments in Qufu, saw few modifications, until the Cultural Revolution (1966–1969). Many buildings were destroyed during this period, and major public buildings were constructed with contemporary material and form during this period. The fortifications of Ming City were also destroyed in 1978 and were reconstituted in 2003 (only a few original fragments remain in the northern corners as well as the north and south gates).

During the 1970s-1980s, the urban area of Qufu was around 3.1 km^2, developing mainly around the Ming City. The first urban planning dates from 1980. The proposed 1980s guidelines establish an urban development in the shape of a four-petal flower (Fig. 4), with the Ming City at the heart; East: City of Lu

图 3. 明时期曲阜城 © 曲阜市政府
Fig. 3 Qufu Ming City © Qufu City Government

计划和总体规划继续遵循四面扩张的方针，突出以下三点：①城市保护与经济发展的关系；②城市发展与建筑、城市及景观遗产保护的关系；③遗产保护与旅游发展的关系。1999 年制定了新的适应中国社会主义市场经济的城市规划项目。这些新的指导方针旨在让曲阜成为具有国际声誉的历史名城。2003 年制定了新的总体规划（图 5），其目的之一是为了让这座历史名城发展成为集历史、传统和现代化为一体的南部新城，计划总面积为 895 平方千米。2008 年，随着“欧亚城乡合作计划”的圆满结束，明故城战略计划呼之欲出，主要有以下几个方面：提高历史名城的质量；推动社会经济发展；保护有形和无形资产；突出城市自身特点，以及提高城市宜居性。

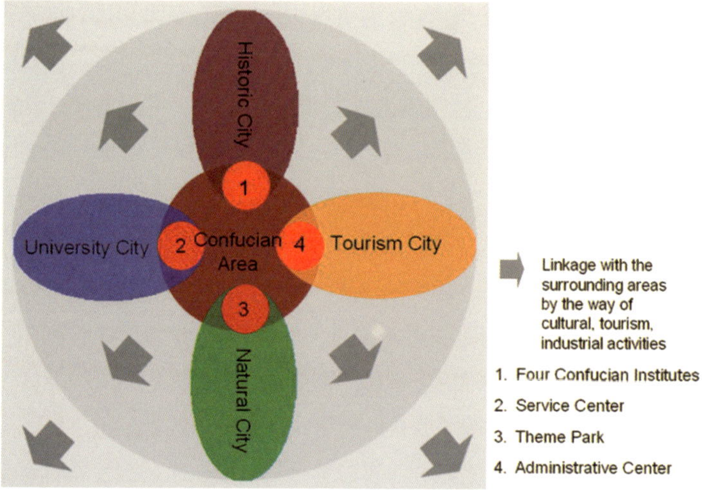

图 4. 曲阜城市发展指南——“十字花瓣”式空间格局 © 吴良镛教授
Fig. 4 Qufu Urban Development Guidelines—four- petal flower © Prof. WU Liangyong

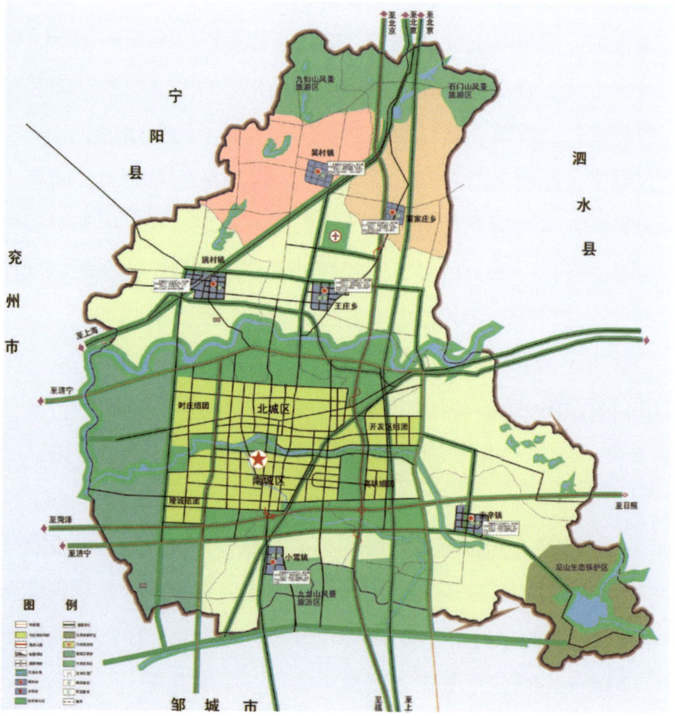

图 5. 2003 年曲阜总体规划图 © 曲阜市政府
Fig. 5 Qufu 2003 Master plan © Qufu City Government

◎反思可持续发展均衡城市政策的研究方法

自 1994 年“三孔”被列为世界文化遗产，1999 年新的城市规划计划将曲阜打造成一座具有国际声誉的历史名城，曲阜政府在近 20 年来就一直想加强遗产保护，同时建立发展机制。在未来几年发展机制将会得到进一步加强，并将曲阜的可持续发展纳入考虑。

有了上述动机，一些法国专家纷纷响应，与曲阜进行合作。2003 年和 2004 年，他们分别寻找适合曲阜政府重点关注的项目，尤其是可持续发展基础上的遗产保护。[3]

如前所述，随着中国历史朝代的更迭，在原有面积不变的基础上，曲阜城市的面貌不断发生着变化，成就了曲阜的历史。而曲阜明故城是城市扩张考虑的对象。在共同遗产方面，曲阜似乎优先考虑人口和生活质量，而负责发展的专家们则寻找大量的补充方案来鼓励和开发对遗址的利用，以便吸引游客来曲阜逗留数日，而不是短暂地只在被列为世界文化遗产的“三孔”停留半日。例如，可以让游客参观当代儒学研究中心和其他相关的城市历史文物。曲阜的城市旅游还未落实到位，然而，构成它框架的文物和景观已经存在。

总而言之，曲阜的文化景观和遗迹应予以保护。曲阜在很多方面堪称世界著名遗址：孔子出生地，直接与人类历史相关；文化景观和文物所在地，见证了中国的历史发展；鲁故城、明故城、当代的曲阜和儒学朝圣者的聚集地。

在注释中前述的三位专家（孟毅大使，克莱蒙建筑师及作者本人）把曲阜作为自己的研究案例，并为研究反思可持续性均衡城市政策确定了如下实验研究法：①将曲阜看成区域系统的一部分；②考虑经济发展和遗产保护之间的协同作用；③推进儒学特色的曲阜；④将居民和利益相关者置于城市发展的中心。

◎中欧合作欧盟亚洲城市复兴项目（Asia Urbs）：“2005—2007 曲阜遗产”雷恩—曲阜—圣地亚哥

2004 年，中欧合作欧盟亚洲城市复兴项目（Asia Urbs）同意将亚洲城市（中国曲阜）和两个欧洲城市（法国雷恩和西班牙圣地亚哥）作为发展对象开展为期三年的项目。[4] 该项目名为曲阜城市遗产的保护和发展：中欧合作欧盟亚洲城市复兴项目 Asia Urbs：“2005—2007 曲阜遗产”雷恩—曲阜—圣地亚哥。[5]

这个为期三年的项目在以下几个方面取得了成功：①提供完善的曲阜遗产知识，加强政府和百姓保护遗产的意识；②鼓励使用城市管理工具保护遗产；③从文化旅游

and urban extension for tourism; West: university and research zone; South: new town for habitation and administration and North: cemetery of Confucius for historic zone. The emphasis is placed on tourism, cultural and historical development, in liaison with the Confucian monuments. Several Conservation Plans and Master Plans afterwards following the four-petal flower guideline highlighting three key points: (1) The link between protecting the city and economic development; (2) The link between urban development and protecting architectural, urban and landscape heritage; (3) The link between protecting heritage and tourism development. In 1999, a new urban planning programme was produced to fall into step with the Chinese socialist market economy. These new guidelines were with the objectives of making Qufu a historic city with an international reputation. A new Master Plan was updated in 2003 (Fig. 5), one of the desires of this plan was to turn the historic city into a vast garden by integrating history, tradition and modernity. This 2003 plan concerns a surface area of 895 km^2. In 2008, as a result of the Qufu Sino-European Asia Urbs programme, a Ming City strategic plan has been prepared with the following orientations: improving the quality of the historic city; promoting socio-economic development; protecting the tangible and intangible assets; highlighting the specific identities and features of the city and improving comfort for residents.

◎ Methodology for reflection on a sustainable and balanced urban policy

The Qufu Government, after the inscription of the World Heritage property in 1994 and the ambition for making Qufu a historic city with an international reputation, since these recent twenty years, seeks the way to reinforce its heritage's protection, as well as the establishment of a corpus, which would be enforced in the years to come and would take into consideration the sustainable development of the territory.

With all a forementioned motivations, some French experts agreed to respond Qufu's request for a qualified cooperation. From years 2003/2004 they accordingly looked for a programme which could fit the immediate preoccupations of Qufu Government, in particular on heritage protection in its connection with sustainable development.[3]

As mentioned, the history of Qufu is derived from the successive relocation of urban implantations, to the inside of a same boundary, throughout the Chinese dynasty eras. The City of Ming in Qufu is the object of an extensive urban re-think. The municipality appears to be giving priority to the population and its quality of life in respect of common heritage. In parallel, the technicians in charge of development envisage adequate, complimentary solutions for encouraging and developing the use of heritage sites as a means of persuading visitors to spend several days in the town, not only a short half day visit for the three World Heritage inscribed monuments. This could be, for example, a visit to the Contemporary Centre for Confucianism Research as well as the other related urban historical spaces and monuments. Urban tourism in Qufu has not yet been put in place, however, the monuments and landscapes which will frame this development already exist.

In conclusion, the importance of the cultural landscape and memories of space and sites in Qufu should be preserved. Qufu is a multi-facetted world famous site: birthplace of Confucius, directly linked to the History of Humanity; cultural landscape and place of memories, recurrent witness to the History of China; ancient City of Lu, City of Ming, Modern Qufu and centre for Confucian Pilgrims.

Convinced Qufu as a case, the aforementioned three experts (Ambassador Menguy, Architect Clément and the author) have identified an experimental methodology for the reflection on a sustainable and bal-

的角度参与发展曲阜遗址；④加强参与该项目的政府部门之间的关系，以及中欧之间的关系。[6]

该项目启动之初先是通过城市遗产名录认识和熟悉曲阜的各个遗址。然后，针对明故城和鲁故城分别从建筑保护和地景保护的角度进行研究。当地团队使用 IT 工具对收集的信息进行分析，思考城市项目，包括对地域规模和曲阜的整体了解。在这样的工作基础上确定遗址保护和开发的方向。项目同时也使用案例分析来检查所制定的研究方法。

旅游业的开发被视为遗址城市化开发和促进的自然产物，尽管它仍为当地居民保留了中心地带。该项目努力通过文物展示、遗产日、新闻和网页提高居民保护遗产的意识。最终，历史建筑得以修复原貌，项目开展获得的体验得以落到实处。如今的曲阜拥有开放的各类遗址和一个信息中心，可供当地居民和游客参观。

◎曲阜历史保护的现状，面临的问题和挑战

曲阜保护强调中国规划方面两个重要和根本的观念：一方面，在 2500 年前“鹿城”建立之后，城市化现象一直持续，地理位置未有变化；另一方面，当保存和更新“明城历史遗址”时，四合院——四面建有房屋中间为庭院的结构——依然是理想的建筑模型，不仅仅是保护而且是重建。[7]

根据《周礼》（周朝的习俗）所描述的中国城市模型，当时鲁故城的占地面积为 10.45 平方千米，这着实令人震惊。建筑的特色为：城墙、道路、大门、屋檐，虽然已经化为废墟，但仍依稀可见，因为鲁故城有 2500 年历史。如何根据《周礼》来保存中国城市模型中依稀可见的建筑风格？鲁故城目前是农村地带，这为大规模地保存遗迹、城市的脉络带来问题。毫无疑问的是，更加丰富的考古遗产埋藏在鲁故城城下。

曲阜明城历史遗迹（中央面积缩减为 1.64 平方千米），最初是为了护卫曲阜孔庙——孔庙和孔子的后代，目前也面临着挑战：保护遗迹和城市发展之间的冲突。长期以来，遗迹的保护重点在孔庙。所以，围绕孔庙和孔子居所的旅游业蒸蒸日上，而老城的经济日渐衰落，环境恶化，人口边缘化。正如其他中国古城一样，曲阜明城存在一个共有的问题，如何保存整个城市的面貌，全面考虑历史中心的过去、现在和将来？这为曲阜的管理提出了挑战，目前的管理系统并没有使曲阜的历史遗迹得到保护。并且，历史中心和历史遗迹的监督有时沦为不假思索的仓促决定，全面保护并没有纳入考虑范围，比如说加建了尺寸不协调的新型建筑和拆毁了一些具有历史和本地特色的建筑。[8]

为了缓解曲阜正在面临的问题和挑战，我们可以学习雷恩（法国），圣地亚哥·德·孔

anced urban policy by: (1) Regarding the city as involved in a territorial system; (2) Considering the synergy between the economic development and the protection of heritages; (3) Promoting Confucian identity of the City; and (4) Associating the population and related stakeholders in the heart of urban development.

◎ A Sino-European cooperation Asia Urbs Programme: "Heritage for Qufu 2005–2007" Rennes–Qufu–Santiago de Compostela

In 2004, European Programme Asia Urbs gave its assent to a three year programme of cooperation involving an Asian city (Qufu, China) and two European counterparts (Rennes, France, and St. Jacques de Compostelle, Spain).[4] The programme was called *Protection and enhancement of the urban heritage of Qufu: A Sino-European cooperation Asia Urbs Programme: "Heritage for Qufu 2005–2007" Rennes–Qufu–Santiago De Compostela.* [5]

The three years programme implementation has succeeded in (1) Providing improved knowledge on the Qufu heritage and increasing the awareness of the authorities and local population in preserving it; (2) Encouraging the implementation of urban management tools for the preservation of this heritage; (3) Participating in enhancing the sites of Qufu from a cultural tourism standpoint, which is an engine for sustainable economic developments; and (4) Strengthening the ties between the authorities that are participating in the project, and more generally between Europe and China. [6]

The project began with becoming aware of and familiar with the urban heritage sites in the field, through the work of urban heritage inventory. An architectural approach was employed for the City of Ming, while a landscaped one was used for the City of Lu. Mastery of IT tools and analysing the information that was collected made it possible to establish a diagnosis that led to the local team giving thought on the urban project, including the territorial scale and an overall view of the town. This work allowed directives to be developed concerning the protection and enhancement of the heritage sites. Case studies were used to check the methodologies that were formulated.

The development of tourism was apprehended as an accompaniment in the process of urban development and enhancement of the heritage sites, while still reserving a central place for the local residents. Efforts to heighten awareness were made through exhibitions, heritage days, newsletters and an internet website pages dedicated to the project. Rehabilitating a historical building made it possible to put the experience that was acquired during the project into practice. Today, this historical building accommodates classes on heritage sites and an information centre for the local residents and visitors.

◎ Actual situation of the historical preservation in Qufu, the problems and challenges it is facing

Qufu highlights two important and fundamental ideas of Chinese planning: on one hand, for the city itself, the long duration of the urban phenomenon since its settlement establishment "City of Lu" twenty-five centuries ago and its persistence in the same territory; and on the other hand for housing and the persistence of an ideal model of courtyard housing "Siheyuan — a house with four wings surrounding a courtyard" which is still the architectural model when it comes to thinking of how the "Ming Historical Heritage City" can be preserved and renewal, not just as element of protection but also of regeneration.7

It is surprising for us to see that the City of Lu covering a vast territory of some 10.45 km^2, according to

波斯特拉（西班牙）和巴黎圣安东尼街区的保护和全面整修的经验。

雷恩（法国）

法国雷恩城市政策可持续和均衡发展的经验要从 1906 年开始。雷恩将历史市区作为一个完整的遗址，采取了当代的城市发展方案来开发。城市遗址政策将住房、交通、公共设施和公共场所的城市政策作为一个框架，刺激雷恩经济的快速发展。如今，城市遗址政策对城市的更新和城市的可持续发展具有深远的影响，尤其是雷恩 4 个关键的策略，分别是城市公共控制、城市均衡发展、城市中心形象和与市民沟通。城市遗址被作为均衡和可持续发展的工具来达到城市更新和可持续发展的目的。（图 6~ 图 7）

圣地亚哥 · 德 · 孔波斯特拉（西班牙）

西班牙的圣地亚哥 · 德 · 孔波斯特拉（以下简称圣地亚哥）认为保存历史城市中心是必要的。在城市更新和整合的背景下，需要两个重要目标：住宅区的使用和公共场所环境的再生。任何城市的更新都必须提升市民的生活品质，整合和提升公共空间。城市中既有建筑又有空地。城市的振兴需要提升和保存公共空间，不仅仅是建筑和纪念碑。[9]

图 6. 雷恩街景 © 林志宏教授
Fig. 6 Rennes Street Shape © Prof. Roland Lin

the Chinese city model described by Zhouli (Ritual of Zhou Dynasty), the trace of the structure: ramparts, eaves, roads, gates, although in ruins, are still visible, as it has lasted for 25 centuries. How to deal with this large archaeological reserve to preserve the only still visible Chinese city model in line with Zhouli? This City of Lu, currently inhabited by villages and country-dwellers, itself poses a very specific problem for the large-scale preservation of a territory, of major landscapes, urban fabric and traces, as well as without doubt the richness that important relics that are buried under the ground.

Ming Heritage Historical City in Qufu (reduced into the very centralized territory of 1.64 km^2), was intentionally constructed to protect sites related to Confucius: the Temple and the residences of the different lines of Master Confucius. Within this small territory, we are facing the contradictions between protecting the heritage sites and urban development. For a long time, importance was given only to the Temple. So, while tourism was being developed on the sites of the Temple and the Residence of Confucius, the economy of the old town declined, the environment was becoming deteriorated and the population was marginalized. This Ming Heritage Historic City poses a very common problem, as other Chinese historic cities, how to preserve the whole city setting, with thorough considering the past, present and future of historical centre as a whole. The managing issue is also important challenges for Qufu, it seems the historical area and the historical relics have never benefited from a overall management system on a daily basis or any concrete principles to monitor the historic centre and heritage relics which has sometimes ended up in decision being made without much thought concerning the construction of unharmonised structures or tearing down the historical and vernacular building.[8]

Here, for seeking some mitigation of the problems and challenges Qufu is facing, it seems that we can

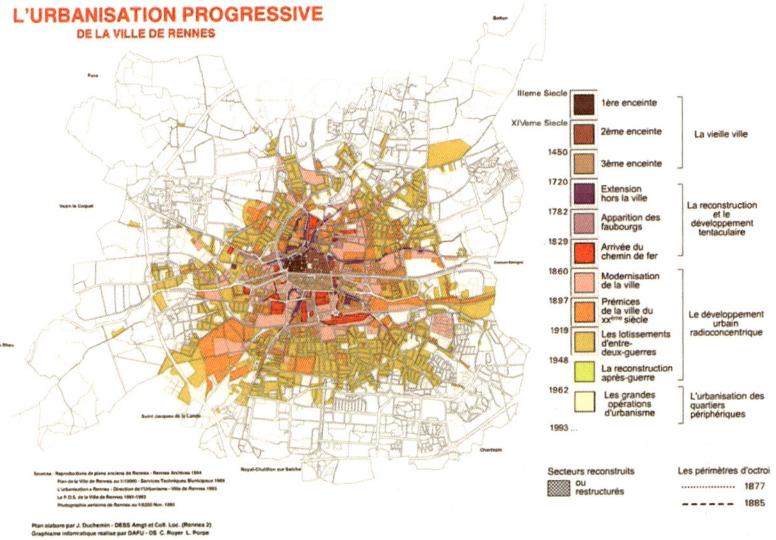

图 7. 雷恩城市化状况 © 雷恩市政府
Fig. 7 Rennes City Urbanisation © Rennes City Government

为了保存历史遗迹和制定城市政策，圣地亚哥城市更新工作由国家、地区和当地行政机构共同承担责任。经验表明，有效的跨部门合作可以增进城市更新项目中的互信，这在居民的参与中是不可或缺的。

简而言之，圣地亚哥的保护世界遗产策略——世界遗产城市和朝圣中心以及大教堂被认为是人类创造的杰作，也是世界遗产的里程碑，这也就使得技术方面对历史经典的保护成为必然。另外，优化的城市政策使居民融入到城市更新工程中，尤其是利用公共空间来提升生活条件及品质，这并不意味着建造新的建筑，而是组织市区活动和居民友好型的节日。城市更新的目的是继续发展或巩固城市，并且值得记住的是，城市首先需要的是合作、团结和理解。城市需要宽容和管理，需要团结和多样化，需要时间。历史中心将一直会处在不断的更新、变化和发展中。（图 8~ 图 9）

巴黎的圣安东尼街区

自罗马帝国以来，圣安东尼街区就是通往巴黎城东的唯一道路，是中世纪法国国王往来巴黎与东郊文森城堡的必经地，在巴黎的城市结构上有其独特的意义。同时，

图 8. 圣地亚哥市中心 © 圣地亚哥市政府
Fig. 8 Santiago City Centre © Santiago City Government

take the experiences of protection and comprehensive renewal from Rennes (France) ; Santiago de Compostela (Spain) and Paris historical area of Faubourg Saint Antoine.

Rennes (France)

Taking experiences of the Sustainable and Balanced Urban Policy in Rennes, France, after 1906, Rennes took its urban region as a whole spatial heritage and took contemporary urban development as a new heritage approach. Urban heritage policy combined urban policies of housing, transportation, public facility and public space into a whole framework which has motivated Rennes' rapid development. Nowadays, urban heritage policy has great influence on urban renewal and urban sustainable development, especially on four key strategies in Rennes. They are urban public control; urban balanced development; urban centre's image and the communication with citizens. Urban heritage has been taken as the balanced and sustainable tool to achieve urban renewal and urban sustainable development. (Fig. 6~7)

Santiago de Compostela (Spain)

Taking Santiago de Compostela in Spain (here after Santiago) as an example, the designation of World Heritage statue backed the idea of preservation of historical city setting of Santiago is a must. In the context of a complex urbanistic policy of urban renewal and integration, two essential objectives are required: the recovery of residential uses and the environmental regeneration of the public space. It is desirable that the

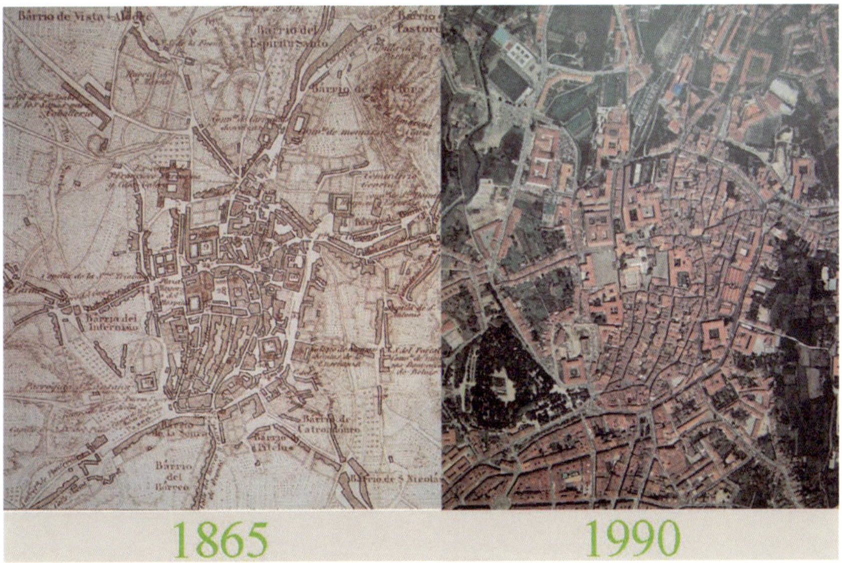

图 9. 圣地亚哥历史中心城区城市化状况 © 圣地亚哥市政府
Fig. 9 Santiago City Urbanisation © Santiago City Government

街区比邻塞纳河，通过水路运输木材极为便利。后来，其自然而然地发展成为木质家具的制造和供应中心，为皇室提供优质家私。之后，该街区又发展成为巴黎的手工艺品中心。在法国大革命期间，街区曾经是中层和低层工人阶级反抗统治者的大本营。在 20 世纪 90 年代初，圣安东尼街区的新老建筑遥相呼应，道路经过加宽之后，先前的城市结构已消失远去。巴黎是如何梳理复杂的城市脉络，保留自己的文化底蕴的，这是一个值得我们学习的成功案例。

巴黎的圣安东尼街区并不是一个具有纪念性质的独特建筑，也不是特别保护的对象。巴黎倾向于保护的是城市的空间布局——狭长的庭院和小径，高耸的烟囱，18 世纪的街道和工厂车间，以及精致的木质家具工业。在 20 世纪 90 年代初，最早建立的独特公共庭院和过道日渐分割，因为追求利益最大化，形成了支离破碎的住宅区。在一些热心人士、专业团队和人民代表的努力下，巴黎城市委员会于 1994 年 1 月通过保护传统社区的提议。在界定了项目的范围后，巴黎城市委员会部分修订了该地区的土地使用法规。

该提议有三个目标：

(1) 新老建筑之间取得平衡；

(2) 继续住宅区和商业区混合的传统；

(3) 记录所有街区、庭院、后院和单一建筑的历史和文化特色，并收录入库，从而保护这些建筑和满足城市发展的需要。

圣安东尼街区的保护工作遵照以下 4 个措施：

(1) 在街区研究中修改城市用地的条款和起草一套适合圣安东尼街区的法律法规，来保护城市的历史面貌，并在住宅、商业功能和用途之间达成平衡。

(2) 编纂公共空间指导原则——任何街区范围内的公共领域的整修工程在规划和建造中须遵循保护指导原则，来确保新或翻新的道路、人行道和小广场能够和受保护的传统社区和平共处。

(3) 巴黎、巴黎工商保护和促进基金会共同合作制定具体的措施，来保护和开发传统街区内的手工艺和商业活动。

(4) 通过激励措施和综合性的新政策来提升老住宅区内人们的生活质量。（图 10~ 图 11）

从曲阜（中国）、雷恩（法国）、圣地亚哥（西班牙）和巴黎的实践经验来看，中国和欧洲之间的差异关键在于历史城市中心保护的理念和方法，具体如下所示：

(1) 中国的历史城市中心保护在保护之前大多着重技术层面。而与此同时，欧洲似乎将城市翻新下的跨领域合作作为重点来考虑，其中包括公共交通、住房、公共领

object of any process of urban renewal must be that of improving the living condition of citizens, as well as integrate and promote marginalized free spaces in which the urban act of coexistence is played out. The city is with construction and with empty space; its revitalization could depend on promoting and preserving empty space, not only the physical structures and monuments. [9]

To well establish the historic city preservation and urban policies, its urban renewal should be considered as a shared responsibility by national, regional and local administrations. Experience has also shown that efficient inter-administrative coordination generates trust in the urban project and is indispensable for the necessary involvement of residents.

In short, Santiago, with its double World Heritage statute: a World Heritage city and piligrim centre and its cathedral listed as a masterpiece of the human creation also World Heritage monument, the technical preservation of the monuments and historical setting are the must to do. Additionally, an optimized urban policy involves the residents for urban renewal projects, particularly using the empty space for improving the living condition, not necessary adding new construction, but often organizing urban event and residents' friendly festivals. The aim of urban renewal today is continuing or consolidating cities and it is worth bearing in mind that the city, first and foremost, is and requires cooperation, solidarity and understanding. It requires the generosity and management, it requires integration and diversity and it requires time. The historical centre in its complex dynamics is, and always has been, constant renewal, adaptation and renovation. (Fig. 8~9)

Faubourg Saint-Antoine in Paris

Since the time of Roman Empire, Faubourg Saint-Antoine has been the only path that leads to the city east. As a must path for the French kings in Middle Ages to shuttle between Paris and Château de Vincennes, this block has a unique meaning in the city texture. Meanwhile, it is near the river Seine, which gives it the convenience to transport timbers by water, naturally this area became a manufacturing and supplying hub for fine wooden furniture made for the royal families. Later it became the handicraft centre in the city of Paris. Around the time of French Revolution, it was once the camp for protests organized by middle and lower-class workers against the rulers. In the early 1990s, the new and old buildings in Faubourg Saint-Antoine formed a sharp contrast and the newly-widened roads led to the disappearance of the former square vision. How the city of Paris has sorted its complicated urban texture and rehabilitated its cultural identity is a successful case worth to study.

The Faubourg Saint-Antoine block, was neither a special single building monument nor a special protected area within Paris. The objects and elements the city of Paris intended to protect were its spatial layout—the long and narrow courtyards and paths, the high towering chimneys, the 18th century streets and workshop-floors, and the exquisite wooden furniture creative industry. In the early 1990s, the original and unique public courtyards and passages gradually became segmented and broken residual space due to the pursuit of maximum profit. Under the advocacy of enthusiasts, professional teams and people's representatives, the council of Paris city passed the proposal for the protection of traditional neighborhood in Jan. 1994. After identifying the programme boundary and the scope, it agreed to partially modify land-use regulations special for this area.

The proposal has three goals:

(1) To achieve a balance between new buildings and old neighborhood.

(2) To continue the tradition of a mixed block for both residential and commercial purposes.

(3) Keep a record and inventory of all the historical and cultural elements of the streets, courtyards,

图 10. 巴黎圣安东尼街区鸟瞰 © 巴黎市政府都市规划工作室
Fig. 10 Paris St Antoine Aerial View © APUR

图 11. 巴黎圣安东尼街区保护规划 © 巴黎市政府都市规划工作室
Fig. 11 Paris St Antoine Conservation Plan © APUR

backyards and single buildings for protection purpose as well as urban development need.

The conservation of Faubourg Saint-Antoine was carried out following the four measures below:

(1) Modification of the land-use regulations in the block—study and draft a set of laws and regulations special for Faubourg Saint-Antoine to protect historic urban landscape and to keep a balance between residential and commercial function and use.

(2) Compilation of public space guidelines—any public space improvement projects within the boundary and scope of this block should follow the conservation guidelines in planning and construction to make sure that the new or restored streets, pedestrians and small squares exist in harmony with the protected traditional neighborhood.

(3) Joint development of specific measures to conserve and develop the handicraft industry and commercial activities in the traditional block by the city of Paris and Paris Industry and Commerce Protection and Promotion Foundation.

(4) Improvement of the quality of living in old residences through incentive and comprehensive renewal policies. (Fig. 10~11)

Seen from the practice in Qufu (China), Rennes (France) and Santiago de Compostela (Spain), and Paris, it seems the key differences between China and Europe in terms of the ideas and methodologies of historic preservation could be listed as below:

(1) Previously, the Chinese historical preservation is focusing majorly on technical aspects. Meanwhile, the European seems focusing more interdisplinary aspects of urban renew context, including public transportation, social housing, open spaces and economical sustainability.

(2) It seems the Chinese historical preservation programme is usually very short time scale, within a

域和经济可持续性发展。

(2) 中国历史城市中心保护的保护项目似乎耗时短。保护的项目须在一个规定的时间内完成。而欧洲的保护项目通常时间跨度长。

(3) 欧洲的地方、地区和国家组织通常投入充足的公共预算到历史城市中心保护项目中（鉴于时间跨度较长）。中国当地政府需要为短期的历史城市中心保护项目找到一个筹资的渠道。

(4) 欧洲的历史城市中心保护进程更加重视跨领域咨询。中国在保护历史城市中心方面，由于重点强调技术层面，并没有足够的跨领域咨询或沟通。

(5) 欧洲历史城市中心保护的目标更多的是为市民和居民服务，来创建更加适宜居住的生存环境。中国保护的目的似乎更注重当地政府文化和服务业的创收。

(6) 欧洲保护进程中非政府组织和当地社区的更多参与，更多是自下而上的过程。而中国更多的是政治方面的决策，是自上而下的过程。

◎曲阜历史文物未来发展的建议

通过这些欧洲的案例和为期 3 年曲阜 / 圣地亚哥 / 雷恩之间的中欧合作，曲阜市应该积极地推进传统社区的保护工作和市区的综合翻新；同时，曲阜应该将新文化、娱乐产业和住宅需要纳入考虑范围。曲阜市要调动所有方面——政府、市民、学术方面和建筑领域来创建一个适宜其市民生活的环境。

著名的历史和文化景点的规划和打造需要考虑到城市的历史和现状，保护其结构和环境、平衡保护和城镇化之间、继承和发展之间的关系。更为重要的是曲阜应该加强城市历史和文化的保护。在实现全面保护的同时如何有效地强化城市丰富的文化内涵已经成为历史城市中心保护方面的最大挑战。城市中心的保护不仅仅是复制或翻修文化遗迹，也应该注意无形的文化遗产，比如口口相传的文化、艺术、社会习俗、礼节、节日和传统手工艺品的制作。

城市面貌革新的目标和方法即强化城市发展的整体面貌和保留城市的文化和自然底蕴。但是，我们需要注意的是不要将传统的风貌强加于新的建筑上，这可能和“城市结构”相违背。我们需要注意的不是将新建筑上装饰一些传统的特色，而是应该保护和更新具有城市发展价值或历史、文化意义的建筑和领域，特别是那些“城市结构”的重要组成部分。先前提到的建筑和领域包括普通的小建筑，小组建筑群（小社区和乡镇），公共活动地点和多用途地点。在保护历史城市中心结构的完整性中，我们也要同时思考近邻历史城市中心结构现有的马路和公共领域的结构，同时思考设计街道

very limited time scale, a preservation programme should be delivered and finished. As for European preservation programme, it is often quite long time scale.

(3) It seems European local, regional and national authorities could put enough public budget for the historical preservation programme (since the time scale is longer). And the Chinese local authorities need to find a financial way to carry out the short time scale historical preservation programme.

(4). The Inter-services consultation is more emphasized in European historical preservation process. In Chinese historical preservation, due to focusing on technical aspects, there is not enough inter-services consultation nor coordination.

(5) The objectives of European historical preservation are more focusing to serve the citizen and inhabitants to create more pleasant living environment. The Chinese objectives for preservation seems to focus to create the cultural and tourism income for the local government.

(6) More involvement of NGOs, local communities in the European preservation process, more bottom-up process. In Chinese experience, it seems more like a political decision and up to bottom process.

◎ Suggestions for the future development of historical preservation in Qufu

Through these European cases as well as the three years' Sino-European collaboration between Qufu/Santiago/Rennes, it is desirable for the city of Qufu actively pushed forward the conservation of traditional neighborhoods and comprehensive urban renewal; meanwhile, it also took into consideration the development of new cultural and recreational industries as well as residential need. It mobilized resources from all directions—the government, the citizen, academic circle and the construction industry to create an ideal living environment for its citizens.

The planning and development of famous historical and cultural cities should pay due respect to the city's history and current status, protect its structure and texture and balance the relationship between conservation and utilization and that between inheritance and development. What's more important is that it should intensify the protection of the city's history and culture. How to effectively highlight the city's rich cultural heritage while realizing overall protection has now become the greatest challenge in the conservation of historical cities. Conservation of historical cities is not to simply copy or restore cultural relics; it should also pay attention to intangible cultural heritage such as oral heritage, performing arts, social customs, etiquette, festivals and traditional handicraft.

Stressing the overall image of the urban development and keeping the city's cultural and natural identity have been the targets and methods of urban renewal. However, we have to be cautious not to impose upon the new buildings a traditional look that does not fit in with the "urban texture". Instead of dotting the new buildings with traditional elements, we need to pay attention to the conservation and renewal of many buildings and space that are considered to have an urban value or historical and cultural meanings, especially those that are used to constitute the key elements of the "urban texture". The aforementioned buildings and space include ordinary small buildings, small groups of premises (small communities and towns), space for public activities and transitional space for mixed uses. While keeping the urban texture intact, we can comprehensively extend the existing roads and the structure of public space, redesign the street corridor structure, redesign the proportion of road width to the building height and set up new buildings and space outside of the protected zone in harmony with the existing neighbouring old towns

走廊的结构，重新思考设计路宽和建筑高度之间的比例。在保护区外建造新的大楼，也应同时思考与近邻现有的老城镇或历史地点相协调，共同促进城市和经济发展并满足现代需要。除了城市发展的需要外，还需要对社会和人类经济变革进行深入的研究，来使土地规划符合城市的结构。当制定新的城市发展政策时，我们应该强调新老元素的和平共处，保护历史遗迹和城市的历史风貌。土地规划、城市规划和城市翻修的总规划也应该反映这一概念。随着遗迹和古迹保护的发展，人们开始意识到除了雄伟的城堡和大厦外，其他形式的历史古迹也是我们记忆中的一部分。工厂、城市的历史面貌、乡村、农场和公共场所，任何具有历史和文化意义的地方都可能是值得保护的文化遗迹。

在曲阜遗产保护和开发领域我们强调三个重点：

(1) 保护重点——规划必须完全和历史、文化遗产的价值在各层面上相匹配，并必须允许遗产在所有角度有所提升；

(2) 提升可持续发展——有赖于功能的合理分配，我们应该能够推动曲阜在各层面全面而和谐地发展；

(3) 以人为本——当地的居民和游客的兴趣和经历必须给予应有的重视。这需要将以下内容纳入考虑范围：建立一个合理的道路系统和交通网络——历史景点交通设施及其安全，尤其是人行道网络和公共交通系统；创建一个高质量的生存环境，绿色植被和公共区域相得益彰，重新设计用户友好型的区域，方便当地人口的社会生活和创建具有竞争力的服务设施。总之，曲阜市将会成为引人瞩目的城市中心。[10]

目前的中国，历史和文化城市的决定性因素在发生变化。先前只针对物质文物的保护，现在更应用到了社会和经济领域。曲阜市在中国来说是一个小规模城市，必须创建具有代表性和榜样性的保护方法。为了可持续发展，曲阜市必须寻找一个管理的良方，将传统文化和现代生活结合起来。当考虑到曲阜道路和水域交通及其同周边地区的交通便利程度时，在地方、省和社区层面开展研究可以提供一些必要的信息——在开始着手城市发展项目之前需要考虑城市的特质。一方面，要保护一个多样性的历史遗产和朝圣之地，另一方面满足当地和地区发展的需要，两者需要中和。需要执行城市保护项目。著名历史和文化城市的旅游和保护、发展的关系非常紧密。但是，旅游不能被认为是唯一的来源。旅游业的发展应该带来城市结构的优化，随之促进多样化经济的发展。应从城市保护、旅游业、城市结构优化、多样性经济这四个方面共同发力来确保曲阜市的可持续发展。总之，曲阜具有文化和纪念意义的景点应该得到保护。

曲阜，一个多姿多彩的 举世闻名的历史城市中心的保护；

曲阜，孔子之乡，直接跟人文历史密切相关；

or historic area to facilitate urban and economic development and meet modern needs. Other than the need for urban development, in depth research on social and human revolution should also be conducted to make the land planning fit into the urban texture and structure. When making new urban development policies, we should emphasize the harmony of new and old elements and the protection of historical relics and historic urban landscapes. Land planning, urban planning and master plans for urban renewal should also reflect this concept. With the advancement of protection of relics and antiques, people started to realize that other than magnificent castles and mansions, other forms of historical remains were also part of the collective memory. Factories, historic urban landscape, villages, farmhouses and public space, any space that has special historical and cultural textures is all possible cultural relics worth protecting.

We can then emphasize three priorities in protecting and developing of heritage area in Qufu:

(1) Priority for protection: planning must fully comply with the value of the historical and cultural heritage at all levels, and must also allow the heritage to be enhanced from all standpoints,

(2) Promotion of sustainable development: thanks to distributing functions rationally, we should be able to promote complete and harmonious development for Qufu, at all levels;

(3) Priority for man: the required degree of importance must be given to the interests and experience of local residents and visitors. This has to take following into account: setting up a rational road system and transportation network: transportation facility and safety in the historical area, particularly concerning the pedestrian network and the public transportation system; setting up a good-quality living environment with comfortable green and public areas, redesigning use-friendly areas allocated to social life for the local population and creating facilitates with compete services. In sum, the city of Qufu can become an urban centre that attracts people locally and from outside.[10]

In China, the determining factors for the conservation of historic and cultural towns are changing today. Protection which has previously been put in place for material objects is now being applied to social and economic aspects. The city of Qufu, which is only a small scale city in China, must establish representative and exemplary conservation. For its sustainable development, it must find a method of governing which combines traditional culture with modern day life. Carrying out studies at local, provincial and neighbouring area levels, will provide the information required when considering the issues of road and river access to Qufu and how it is regionally connected: The exceptional character of the town is the first issue for consideration, before embarking upon the broad lines of the development projects in hand. It is in this perspective of reconciliation between the important issues of conserving a diverse heritage and pilgrimage destination with the needs for local and regional development that an urban protection programme should be implemented. The relationship between tourism and the protection and development of this famous historic and cultural town is very close. However, tourism should not be considered as its only resource. Development of the tourist sector should itself bring about an improvement in the urban infrastructure which in turn should encourage the development of a diverse economy. These four elements— urban protection, tourism, improvement in the urban infrastructure, development of a diverse economy, should work together to ensure the sustainable development of our town. In conclusion of this section, the importance of the cultural landscape and place memories in Qufu should be preserved.

Qufu, a multi-facetted world famous site: Qufu, birthplace of Confucius, directly linked to the History of Humanity;

Qufu, cultural landscape and place of memories, recurrent witness to the history of China;

Qufu, ancient city of Lu and City of Ming as well as Modern Qufu; Qufu, centre for Confucian Pilgrims….[11]

曲阜，文化景点和纪念圣地，中国历史的见证者；

曲阜，鲁故城和明城，现称曲阜；

曲阜，孔学文化的中心……[11]

◎"曲阜友谊协会"民间团体——发展规划的文化智囊团

为了进一步加强上述所倡导的亚洲历史名城城市政策的可持续和均衡的发展，前述的三个专家表示，除了上述 Asia Urbs 之外，还可通过其他渠道，进一步咨询和联系中欧专家，来调动更大范围的参与。

首先，在亚洲历史名城追求城市政策可持续和均衡的发展中，曲阜被作为一个案例在中国同中国的专家分享和讨论。就城市化和曲阜地区规划来讲，中国专家和经验丰富的建筑工程师[12]可以侃侃而谈。就孔学和跨文化来说，每次到北京，我们欧洲专家同中国专家之间就有了进一步的沟通，跨文化联合咨询机制又有了进一步的深化。[13]

保护历史名城的运营团队来自同济大学（上海）和山东大学（济南）的建筑学教授们。他们为我们提供了城市和建筑保护方面的技术支持，并介绍当地特色。我们的工作跟两位法国著名的学者的贡献分不开。[14]

历时 3 年（2005—2007）的同中欧专家的咨询和沟通为建立"曲阜友谊协会"民间团体奠定了坚实的基础（以上提及的中欧学者均为曲阜友谊协会的开拓者）。多亏曲阜友谊协会，两个国际论坛"相约曲阜"分别于 2008 年和 2010 年在曲阜和同济大学（上海）召开，来探索文化遗产价值和文化意义评估方面的问题、方法、原则和反思。两个论坛也为挑选适合的方法（战略）和原则 / 工具（计划 / 任务 / 行动）提供了指导意见，使得亚洲历史名城城市政策可持续和均衡的发展成为发展规划文化不可或缺的一部分。

第一次"相约曲阜"大会于2008年5—6月份在中国曲阜召开。会议的主要议题是"文化和空间"，分为四个主题供中欧专家展示和讨论：①曲阜、空间和文化、环境；②法律、精神和空间；③曲阜：地方的记忆；④遗产和城市管理。值得注意的是中欧学者在三年的沟通和咨询中双方一直积极参与。大会的结果在北京大学编辑的《跨文化对话》杂志（中文版）的"文化传统和空间发展"专栏得以分析和出版。[15]

第二次"重构曲阜"大会于 2010 年 9 月在中国上海同济大学召开。除了紧跟第一次会议的主题，中欧对城市研究和规划战略进行跨文化反思之外，我们试图将人 / 文化的可持续发展纳入主题中，分为三个主题，供中欧专家展示和讨论：①人性化空间；②从人 / 文化角度来谈可持续发展；③以文明作为工具来更好地了解跨文化在城市研

◎ "Friends of Qufu" civil society as thinking tank of Culture for Development Planning

For advancing the above-mentioned methodology for the reflection of sustainable and balanced urban policy in the Asian living historical city conservation context, the three experts have convinced the need of further consulting and networking the Sino-European scholars in order to motivate a great number of actors, even if through other platforms in addition to the above-mentioned Qufu Asia Urbs Programme.

Firstly, our reflection of sustainable and balanced urban policy in the Asian living historical city conservation context, Qufu as a case, was shared, discussed and advised during our every mission to China with Chinese counter partners. For urbanism and Qufu regional planning reflection, the Chinese academics and experienced architects[12] were very informative. For Confucianism and Transculture, during each of ourBeijing mission, we have the opportunity to reinforce the 90's European Association Transculture already established networking and consultation with the Chinese academic experts. [13]

The historic city preservation operational team from Tongji University (Shanghai) and the young professors in Architecture department of Shangdong University (Jinan) are providing us with the technical and local aspects of the urban and architectural conservation. Here we need to add the valuable contribution of two well-known French scholars to our work. [14]

During this three years' process (2005–2007) of consulting and networking, the Sino-European scholars provided a very solid foundation in establishing a "Friends of Qufu" civil society (all the above-mentioned Chinese and European scholars were founding members of "Friends of Qufu"). Besides, thanks to this "Friends of Qufu", two international forums "Rencontres de Qufu", have been organized in Qufu in 2008 and in Tongji University (Shanghai) in 2010, to explore issues, methodologies, principles and reflection on cultural heritage values and cultural significance assessment, as well as to generate guidance for selecting appropriate methodologies (strategies) and principles/tools (planning/tasks/action) to formulate the need of sustainable and balanced urban policy in the Asian living historic city conservation context as part of integrated "Culture for Development Planning".

The first "Rencontres de Qufu" took place in May-June 2008 in Qufu, China. The main topic was "Civilisation and Space" with four sessions of Sino-European presentations: (1) Qufu, space and civilisation, the context; (2) Law, spirituals and space; (3) Qufu: memory of place; and (4) Heritage and urban governance. It is worthwhile to note the active participation of the Sino-European scholars, resulted from the above-mentioned three years process of consultation and networking the Sino European scholars. The results of this meeting were analysed and published in the special section of "Cultural Tradition and Spatial Development" of the Magazine *Tanscultural Dialogues* (in Chinese) edited by Peking University. [15]

The second "Rencontres de Qufu" was held in September 2010 in Tongji University, Shanghai, China. Besides following the theme of the first "Rencontres de Qufu" on the Sino-European transculture reflection in urban studies and planning strategy, we tried to put the human/cultural dimension of sustainable development into our main topic, with three sessions of Sino-European presentations and discussion: (1) Humanised Space; (2) Human/cultural dimension of sustainable development; and (3) Civilisation as a tool to better understand this transculture reflection in urbanism studies and planning strategy. The results together with the adopted "Shanghai Manifesto" were analysed and published within the magazine *China Ancient City*.[16]

究和规划战略中的影响。结果连同“上海宣言”在《中国名城》杂志上分析和出版。[16]

希望中欧合作，Asia Urbs 项目开展三年、中国举办两次国家论坛之后，“曲阜友谊协会”可以继续作为曲阜案例中的智囊团，来探讨研究历史名城中城市政策可持续和平衡发展的问题、方法、原则和反思。其目标是为挑选适合的方法（战略）和原则 / 工具（规划 / 任务 / 行动）制定指导意见，来评估历史名城中文化遗产的价值和文化影响，这也是文化发展规划的一部分。

◎亚洲历史名城保护中城市政策可持续和平衡发展的新台阶

通过曲阜案例研究，我们了解到，如今城市遗产政策对于城市可持续发展有深远的影响，尤其是四个主要的战略和挑战，分别是城市公共控制、城市均衡发展、城市中心形象和与市民对话。城市遗产被作为均衡和可持续发展的工具，来实现城市保护、更新和可持续发展的重任。最后，作者提出对跨专业的方法和发展规划文化的需要，号召跨专业城市研究领域的研究员和专家的参与：城市规划、交通运输、住房建筑、地域研究、旅游业、文化遗产保护、历史学、社会学、经济学、考古学、建筑学、人类学、博物馆研究、艺术 / 美学研究等。希望曲阜作为一个案例，可以引发我们思考亚洲历史名城保护中城市政策可持续和平衡发展的新方向。

---

1. 孔子诞生地曲阜由于其杰出的普世性价值被联合国教科文组织根据第一、四和六条标准列入世界遗产名录：

标准（1）：曲阜文物古迹群具有其杰出的艺术价值，原因是中国两千多年以来历代君王对其给予了充分的支持，为孔子而建的建筑和景观由最好的设计师和工匠进行创作和重建。

标准（4）：以曲阜为代表的杰出建筑群反映了中国在相当一段时间内物质文化的变迁。

标准（6）：对两千年来的东方国家以及 18 世纪和 19 世纪的西方和欧洲而言，孔子在哲学和政治理论方面的贡献一直是影响现代思想和政府管理演变的最深刻的因素之一。

孔庙是纪念、祭祀孔子的祠庙建筑。孔林是孔子及其后裔的墓地。孔府是封建帝制下孔子的男性直系后代建造的贵族府邸。孔子，伟大的思想家、哲学家、教育家和儒家创始人，是世界上杰出的文化人物之一。由孔子创立的儒家思想被视为中国两千多年封建社会的正统思想。在其他国家，如韩国、日本、越南等也是如此。儒家思想对欧洲的启蒙运动有着积极的影响。目前，许多发达国家都在研究和探索如何利用孔子思想，纠正现代文明陋习。中国和其他亚洲国家建有超过两千座祭祀孔子的庙宇。孔子故里的曲阜孔庙是其中最大的一个……

孔庙始建于公元前 478 年，占地 14 公顷，共有 104 座建筑，分别建于金至清朝，主建筑有大成殿、奎文阁和兴坛等。庙内有 1250 多棵古树，寺庙内还保存着 1000 多块不同时期建成的石碑，以及刻有描绘孔子生活图画的汉画石像和明清的石雕龙雕刻等贵重物品。广泛分布于东亚和东南亚国家的所有孔庙均以此庙为原型，特别是在布局和风格方面加以借鉴。

It is hoped that through the initiation of the three years' Sino-European AsiaUrbs programme, as well as the two international forums held in China, "Friends of Qufu" civil society can continue, as a thinking tank, through the case of Qufu, to explore issues, methodologies, principles and reflection for a sustainable and balanced urban policy in the Asian living historic city conservation context. Its goal is to generate guidance for selecting appropriate methodologies (strategies) and principles/tools (planning/tasks/action) to assess cultural heritage values and cultural significance in the living historic city context as part of an integrated Culture for Development Planning.

◎ A new step for sustainable and balanced urban policy in the Asian living historic city conservation context

Through the case of Qufu, we understand, nowadays urban heritage policy has great influence on urban sustainable development, especially on four key strategies and challenges. They are urban public control, urban balanced development, urban centre's image and the communication with the citizens. Urban heritage can be taken as the balanced and sustainable tool to achieve urban conservation, renew and sustainable development. Finally, the author calls for the necessities to have the interdisciplinary approaches for this reflection and the need of Culture for Development Planning, with the participation of researchers and specialists from interdisciplinary urban studies areas: Planning; Transportation, Housing, Territory Studies, Tourism, Cultural Heritage Preservation, History, Sociology, Economy, Archaeology, Architecture, Anthropology, Museum Studies, Art/Aesthetic Studies, etc. It is hoped that Qufu could be a case as reflection for a new step for sustainable and balanced urban policy in the Asian living historical city conservation context.

1.Birthplace of Confucius, Qufu was inscribed on the UNESCO World Heritage List on the basis of criteria i, iv, and vi of Outstanding Universal Values:

Criterion (i) : The group of monumental ensembles at Qufu are of outstanding artistic value because of the support given to them by Chinese Emperors over two millennia, ensuring that the finest artists and craftsmen were involved in the creation and reconstruction of the buildings and the landscape dedicated to Confucius.

Criterion (iv) : The Qufu ensemble represents an outstanding architectural complex which demonstrates the evolution of Chinese material culture over a considerable period of time.

Criterion (vi) : The contribution of Confucius to philosophical and political doctrine in the countries of the East for two thousand years, and also in Europe and the west in the 18th and 19th centuries, has been one of the most profound factors in the evolution of modem thought and government.

The Temple of Confucius was built to commemorate and offer sacrifices to Confucius. The Cemetery of Confucius was the place where Confucius and his descendants were buried. The Kong Family Mansion was the aristocrat mansion built by male direct descendants of Confucius under imperial orders, all of them concerned to the great thinker, philosopher, educator, the founder of Confucianism—Confucius, one of the outstanding cultural figures in the world. Confucianism created by him was regarded as the sovereign ideas of the feudal society for the past over 2000 years. So was in other countries such as Korea, Japan, Vietnam etc. It had influenced the Enlightenment of Europe positively. Today, many developed countries are studying and exploring how to use the thought of Confucius to correct the abuse of modern civilization. There were more than 2000 temples for offering sacrifices to Confucius built in China and other Asian countries. The Temple of QuFu, the native place of Confucius was the largest one of them.......

孔林距曲阜城北 1100 米，占地 183 公顷，拥有超过 10 万个墓冢，在 2400 多年间一直被不断使用，成为在世界上使用时间最长的家族墓地。到目前为止，孔林拥有墓碑累计超过 4000 块，是中国拥有墓碑最多的墓地。

孔府位于孔庙东侧，是孔子嫡长子孙的府第，旧称衍圣公府，占地 7 公顷，共有约 170 座建筑。府内有 10 余万件馆藏文物，其中最著名的有商周时期的十件礼器，不同时期的孔子画像，明清时期的衣服和帽子等。此外，从孔府收集到的明清时期的 60 000 多份文件和档案，不仅提供了孔府 400 多年各类活动的可靠记录，而且对明清历史（尤其是该时期的经济史）研究具有相当高的价值。因此，孔府也被认为是中国最大、历史最悠久的私人档案室。

2. 参考文献 [3]，42.

3. 代表性人物包括孟毅大使（前法国外交官，其与中国的业务始于共同外交时期，作为欧洲协会 Transcultura 的一员其在与中国合作伙伴沟通时获得了很多经验）、在中国经验丰富的建筑师皮埃尔·克莱蒙教授和本文作者（林志宏）。孟毅大使是一名会说中文的前外交官，在完成其在中国的外交使命后并没有终止与中国的联系，后成为亚洲大使。退休后，孟毅加入了 1990 年代由 Umberto Eco 成立的欧洲协会 Transcultura，该协会由从事跨文化工作的现代人类学家 Alain le Pichon 主持。Transcultura 的宗旨是促进欧洲机构（高校和企业）和对应的中国机构的“和解”。该协会已与一些中国大学建立了密切联系，其中包括北大。协会有一个目标是成立一座“没有墙的大学”。如果这个项目不幸在布鲁塞尔被中断，此举所激发的精神将继续鼓舞大量参与者加入，即使是通过其他平台。目前曲阜中欧平台算得上是一个很好的例子。

4. 由于孟毅大使的努力，法国雷恩市市长 Edmond Hervé 热情响应了该项目，并指导开始的所有准备工作，包括寻找另一个欧洲城市（因需要两个欧洲城市与曲阜合作）。西班牙的圣地亚哥市接受了该项目。

5. 见参考文献 [3]，103.

6. 预算总额达 1 052 249 欧元，其中 71.27% 资金由欧盟提供，11.10% 由法国雷恩市政府提供，10.25% 由中国曲阜市政府提供，7.38% 由西班牙圣地亚哥市政府提供。参考文献 [3]，18.

7. 见皮埃尔·克莱蒙在曲阜城市遗产保护最终报告中的文章，参考文献 [3]，26.

8. 见邵甬在上述最终报告中的文章，参考文献 [3]，95.

9. 见安杰·帕内罗·帕多在上述最终报告中的文章，参考文献 [3]，32.

10. 见邵甬在上述最终报告中的文章，参考文献参考文献 [3]，96.

11. 见林志宏在上述最终报告中的文章，参考文献 [3]，25.

12. 清华大学（北京）吴良镛教授及其同事刘健教授。

13. 北京大学教授汤一介教授和乐黛云教授及其同事李中华教授。

14. 莱昂·汪德迈教授和玛丽亚娜·巴斯蒂德教授。

15. 详见参考文献 [2]

16. 详见参考文献 [1].

The Temple of Confucius was built in 478 B.C, covering 14 hectares, with 104 buildings dating from Jin to Qing dynasties, such as main buildings like Dacheng Hall, Kuiwen Pavilion and Xing Altar and over 1250 ancient trees. The Temple also houses more than 1,000 steles made in different times, and precious objects such as Han stone reliefs, carved pictures depicting the life of Confucius, and the stone dragon carvings of Ming and Qing dynasties. The Temple is the prototype and model for all the Confucius temples widely distributed in countries in East Asia and Southeast Asia, particularly in terms of layout and style.

Located 1,100 meters to the north of Qufu City, the Cemetery of Confucius covers an area of 183 hectares, with more than 100,000 graves, and has been in constant use for more than 2,400 years, making it the longest functioning family graveyards in the world. Now there are more than 4,000 gravestones accumulated so far, making it the largest gravestone forest in China.

Lying to the east of the Temple, the Kong Family Mansion is the place where the eldest direct male descendants of Confucius, who were bestowed the title "Duke Yansheng", covering 7 hectares with a total of some 170 buildings. Over 100,000 collections are kept in the Mansion, among them the ten ceremonial utensils of Shang and Zhou dynasties, the portraits of Confucius made in different periods and clothes and caps dating to the Ming and Qing dynasties are the most famous. Furthermore, the more than 60,000 files and archives of the Ming and Qing dynasties collected in the Mansion not only provide credible record of all kinds of activities in the Mansion for more than 400 years, but are highly valuable for studying the history of Ming and Qing, particularly the economic history of that period as well. This collection also makes the Mansion the largest and most time-honoured private archive in China.

2.See Final Report of Protection and enhancement of the urban heritage of Qufu: A Sino-European co-operation, Asia Urbs Programme: "Heritage for Qufu 2005–2007" Rennes–Qufu–Santiago De Compostela, Rennes, France, March 2008. p.42.

3.These steering personalities were Ambassador Marc Menguy, a former diplomat whose services in China dated from the mutual diplomatic era, who had acquired experience in dealing with Chinese partners as a member of the European Association Transculture, an architect with great experience in China, Professor Pierre Clement, and the author (Roland Lin Chih-Hung). Ambassador Marc Menguy, a Chinese speaking former diplomat, did not end its relations with China after the completion of his mission, serving later in Asia as an ambassador. After his retirement, he joined in the 90's the European Association Transcultura founded by Umberto Eco, presided by a modern anthropologist, Alain le Pichon, who was engaged in a "transcultural'"process. Transculture's objective was to promote a "rapprochement "between European structures—universities, enterprises—and their Chinese counterparts. This Association had established most close contacts with some Chinese universities, including Peking University and had an objective to create a "University without Wall". If this project unfortunately was interrupted in Bruxelles, the spirit which had inspired by this action continues to motivate a great number of actors, even if through other platforms. The current Qufu Sino-European platform could be regarded as the good example.

4.Thanks to Ambassador Menguy, the Mayor of Rennes in France, Edmond Hervé responded with enthusiasm to this opportunity and gave instructions to start all preliminaries, including the search of another European town, since two European cities were needed to work together with Qufu. St Jacques de Compostelle, in Spain, accepted to join this project.

5.See Final Report of Protection and enhancement of the urban heritage of Qufu: A Sino-European co-operation, Asia Urbs Programme: "Heritage for Qufu 2005–2007" Rennes–Qufu–Santiago De Compostela, Rennes, France, March 2008. p.103.

6.The total amount of the budget was 1,052,249 Euros, of which 71.27% was financed by the European Union, 11.10% by the City of Rennes (France), 10.25% by the City of Qufu (China) and 7.38% by the City of Santiago de Compostela (Spain). See Final Report ibid. p. 18.

7.See Pierre Clément's article in Final Report ibid, p.26.

8.See Shao Yong's article in Final Report ibid, p. 95.

9.See Angel Panero Pardo's article in Final Report ibid,p. 32.

10.See Shao Yong's article in Final Report ibid, p. 96.

11.See Roland Lin Chih-Hung's article in Final Report ibid, p. 25.

12.Professor WU Liangyong of Qianghua University (Beijing), together with his colleague Professor LIU Jian.

13.Prof. TANG Yijie, Prof. YUE Daiyun of Peking University together with their colleague Prof. LI Zhonghua.

14.Prof. Léon Vandermeerch and Prof. Mariamme Bastid.

15.See "Cultural Tradition and Spatial Development"

参考文献：

[1] 段晶坤 . 中法专家对话可持续发展（"文明、空间和可持续发展"中法国际研讨会摘要)[J]. 中国名城，2010(12)：26-29.

[2] 北京大学跨文化研究中心 . 跨文化对话："文化传统和空间发展"专题 . 2009，北京大学，凤凰出版传媒集团，江苏人民出版社，2009（25）：81- 146.

[3] 曲阜城市遗产保护最终报告：中欧合作，欧盟 Asia Urbs 项目："曲阜文化遗产 2005 --2007"雷恩 --曲阜 -- 圣地亚哥 . 法国：雷恩，2008：103.

[4] 林志宏 . 曲阜历史文化名城的可持续发展 [M]// 林志宏 . 世界文化遗产与城市 . 上海：同济大学出版社，2012：248-275.

[5] Roland Lin Chih-Hung. A New Step for a Sustainable and Balanced Urban Policy in the Context of Asian Living Historic City Conservation: The Case of Qufu, China, in Towards a Sustainable Ecology & Sustainable Cities : Global Challenges and Local Responses in Africa and Asia - 55 Years after 1955 Bandung Asian-African Conference. co-published by GRIC-University of Le Havre (France), OISCA (Japan), Afrique Challenge (Morocco), Yayasan Pondok Eakyat (Indonesia), Brawijaya University Press, Malang, Indonesia, 2012: 189 -198 .

[6] 林志宏 . 对世界文化遗产与城市的思考——巴黎和曲阜 . 中国名城，2010（11）：9-16.

[7] Roland Lin Chih-Hung. Projet urbain et identité patrimoniale en Chine : le cas de Qufu, caractéristiques,spécifiques, difficulté et solutions, in Espaces urbains à l'aube du XXIè siècle : patrimoine et héritages culturels. Paris: Presse Universitaire Paris Sorbonne. 2010: 279 -288.

[8] 林志宏 . 曲阜历史文化名城的可持续发展 [M]// 林志宏 . 世界遗产与历史城市 . 台湾：商务印书馆，2010：188-207.

[9] 林志宏，顾乃安 . 文化景观与地域记忆——论曲阜及世界遗产 . 跨文化对话："文化传统和空间发展"专题，2009（25）.

[10] Roland Lin Chih-Hung. L'exemple de Qufu, lieu de naissance de Confucius : intégrer les notion de "tradition" et de "civilisation" au développement durable. Paris: La revue PASSAGES, 2009, no. 160, pp. 50 -54.

[11] Roland Lin Chih-Hung. Qufu, ville natale de Confucius, un espace sacré face aux défis de la modernité. // Roland Lin Chih-Hung, Jocelyne Fresnais-Vaudelle, Sylvie Guichard-Anguis. Le Nouvel Age de Confucius. Paris: Presse Universitaire Paris Sorbonne, 2007: 277 -294.

[12] Roland Lin Chih-Hung. Rapport de mission à Qufu, Asia Urbs Programme: "Heritage for Qufu 2005 -2007", Paris/Rennes, 2005: 15, 25.

[13] Roland Lin Chih-Hung. Rapport de fin d'étude sur la faisabilité de programme européen pour la Mairie de Qufu. Paris, 2003: 46.

section of the "*Tanscultural Dialogues – Dialogue Transculturel*". Peking University, Phoenix Publishing & Media, Jiangsu People's Publishing House, 2009: 81-146.

16.See "Summary of the Sino-French Forum « Civilisation, Space & Sustainable Development », International Forum, Tongji University, Shanghai, China, Sep, 2010", inww *China Ancient City*, only in Chinese, Special n°, March, 2011, Beijing & Yangzhou, p.p. 26–29.

难忘的经历：2004—2010 年在曲阜的欧洲人

前法国大使马克·孟毅

中国历史城市曲阜的案例最早在谈到可持续发展及遗产合作时被提及。在曲阜近期的发展历程中，继欧盟三年亚洲城市复兴计划（2005—2007）出台后，曲阜市通过与民间协会合作（由联合国教科文组织顾问林志宏博士和我共同设立的曲阜友谊协会），致力于维系合作各方间的信任及友好关系。这也是正与曲阜开展合作的诸多合作伙伴及曲阜市市长的期望。为进一步拓展合作，各方一致赞同以会谈和研讨会的形式开展交流，让中欧各合作方能共同探讨曲阜这座历史城市所无法回避的主题，如文化空间和有关文明的问题（2008 年曲阜研讨会）。此外，2010 年 9 月，合作各方以“曲阜会谈”为主题，共同探讨了可持续发展、环境及人文建设等问题。公元前 5 世纪，孔子出生在山东省曲阜市，曲阜因而成为了中华文明的奠基地之一，在历史进程中传播了儒家学说的“箴言”汇编。这些有关人类及社会的整体性思考构成了一个社会道德体系。直至 20 世纪，皇权及整个中国社会都建立在这个体系之上。在汉民族统治者们的努力下，尽管曲阜并非一成不变，却保留了其建筑古迹的精华，成为了重要的传统所在地。中国非物质文化遗产的历史组成部分之一、中国国家主管部门所称的“儒家学说”源于曲阜。1994 年，曲阜被列为世界文化遗产，地方领导们因而致力于结合可持续发展这一首要任务，按照全国纪念场所保护项目的要求，寻求保护这份遗产的途径及方式。曲阜市领导班子采纳了城市规划家和建筑师的建议，间接找到我们。他们希望借鉴在遗产保护领域享有盛誉的欧洲方面的经验，与欧洲开展遗产保护及开发方面的合作，从而让曲阜在中欧合作欧盟亚洲城市复兴项目（Asia Urbs）的框架下，符合联合国教科文组织制定的遗产保护标准。我们建议曲阜市领导向法国雷恩市（Rennes）寻求合作——雷恩市所在的布列塔尼大区早已与山东省缔结友好关系——西班牙圣地亚哥·德·孔波斯特拉市（Saint Jacques de Compostelle）与雷恩市也有合作。2005 年至 2007 年间，这两座城市始终伴随着曲阜的发展。资金方面主要由欧盟出资，曲阜、雷恩和圣地亚哥·德·孔波斯特拉市提供少部分资金。三方的合作建立在“遗产和发展”这两个研究领域之上，并提出相应的方案。合作目的更多是为了让合作各方（包括曲阜地方领导在内）都参与其中，共同开展工作（遗产清点、比较研究、培训专家及年轻的教育界人士、让欧洲人适应文化差异、受传统启发制定试点项目、制图、起草文献汇编等），而非传递知识。由这三所城市共同成立的“联合合作体”，其工作目的并非为了消除旅游形态与遗产保护及可持续发展之间无法避免的矛盾(这是曲阜市领导们最关心的问题)，而是为了让大家重新认识优先顺序、现实和结果。正如一直以来如果没有对中国发展前景的探讨，我们就无法真正做出决策。无论是在由中欧专家们组成的“联合合作体”，还是在其中某个组织的内部，这一方法论所引发的思考将让各个城市在合作时采取新颖而又具体的形式：让群众获得利益、改善居住环境、内部协商等——中国本身的环境好像就是这样的。我们将根据 Asia Urbs 项目举办的曲阜研讨会上讨论的热烈程度，以及由“曲阜友谊协会”在这座儒学名城举办的研讨会上各位权威人士（如

Une Expérience Inoubliable: Des Européens à Qufu 2004-2010

Ambassadeur Marc Menguy

Le cas de Qufu – ville historique de la Chine- s'est inscrit initialement dans le contexte à la fois du développement durable et de la coopération en patrimoine. Dans son évolution la plus récente, à l'issue d'un projet trisannuel non renouvelé avec l l'Union européenne (2005-2007), la coopération décentralisée avec ce site s'est engagée, dans un cadre de société civile (la Société des Amis de Qufu, créée par le Dr Roland Lin Chih-Hung, consultant à l'UNESCO et moi-même), à maintenir les liens de confiance et d'amitié que de nombreux de partenaires en coopération et notamment le Maire de Qufu ne souhaitaient pas voir disparaitre. Dans l'attente d'élargir cette coopération, les échanges s'accordent au niveau de rencontres et de colloques qui permettent d'évoquer entre partenaires européens et chinois les thèmes que le site historique de Qufu ne peut manquer de susciter, tels que l'Espace culturel, les questions de civilisation (Colloque de 2008). A cette thématique, s'ajouteront en septembre 2010, au titre de ces « rencontres de Qufu », des échanges entre partenaires sur les questions ayant trait au Développement durable, à l'Environnement, à l'Etablissement humain. La Ville de Qufu, dans le Shandong, lieu de naissance de Confucius au Vème Siècle av. JC, est l'un des sites fondateurs de la civilisation chinoise, d'où s'est répandu au fil des siècles un corpus de «préceptes », le message confucéen. Cet ensemble de réflexions sur l'Homme et la Société, en harmonie, est devenu le système moral et social sur lequel s'est appuyé jusqu'au XXème siècle le Pouvoir impérial et la Société chinoise toute entière. Consacré par les empereurs Han, ce lieu a préservé non sans de multiples variations l'essentiel de son patrimoine architectural, espace de haute tradition, d'où s'est dégagée l'une des composantes historiques du patrimoine immatériel de la Chine, aujourd'hui reconnue comme telle par les autorités nationales : le Confucianisme. Le site de Qufu ayant été inscrit en 1994 au Patrimoine de l'Humanité, les autorités locales se sont préoccupées de rechercher les voies et moyens de protéger cet héritage, conformément programme national de préservation des hauts lieux de mémoire, non sans y associer leurs préoccupations essentielles en matière de développement durable. Les autorités de Qufu, conseillées par des urbanistes et architectes, nous ont approché indirectement pour rechercher en Europe – réputée dans ce domaine - une coopération en patrimoine et en développement qui permettrait à ce site de répondre aux critères de l'Unesco , dans le cadre du Programme Asia Urbs. Nous leur avons suggéré de faire appel à la ville de Rennes - déjà engagée dans le Shandong, avec la Région Bretagne-- à laquelle s'est associée la ville de Saint Jacques de Compostelle. Ces deux cités ont ainsi accompagné Qufu de 2005 à 2007 dans une démarche financée pour l'essentiel par l'Union européenne et à moindre degré par les trois cités concernées. Patrimoine et Développement, tels ont été les champs de recherche et de propositions sur les quels cette coopération s'est établie, dans un contexte où il s'agissait moins de transmettre un savoir que d'impliquer l'ensemble des partenaires – y compris les autorités locales - dans un travail commun (inventaires, études comparatives, formation d'experts et de jeunes universitaires, nécessaire adaptation des Européens aux différences culturelles, projets pilotes inspirés des traditions, cartographie, élaboration de corpus…) . Cette entreprise conjointe avait en effet pour objectif, non pas de résoudre les contradictions inéluctables entre Préservation du Patrimoine et Développement durable dans sa forme touristique - préoccupation majeure des autorités locales -, mais bien de rechercher les moyens de vivre ces contradictions dans une prise conscience nouvelle des priorités, des réalités, des finalités, avec comme toujours en Chine la perspectives de débats, sans lesquels rien ne peut être réellement décidé. Tant dans la mise en œuvre de cette entreprise conjointe entre experts européens et chinois qu'au sein même des structures locales, les réflexions suscitées par cette méthodologie auront permis à cette coopération de prendre une forme originale et concrète - intéressement des populations, modification de l'habitat, concertations internes - ce qui semble-t-il aura été perçu dans l'environnement chinois lui-même. On en jugera par la

诸多中欧教育界人士等）的讨论成果，来做出评判。结语：在这一始于2004年的合作进程中，我们首先是发起者，之后是调解者。曲阜地方领导及监管人士应尽可能去聆听，自由做出选择和决策，并具备高度的合作适应能力。我们在撰写报告时充分考虑了以下项目进展趋势：从项目大纲出发，在实施过程中再讨论项目草案的各项条款。

◎第一部分　中欧合作欧盟亚洲城市复兴项目（Asia Urbs）

联合国教科文组织专家兼巴黎索邦大学（Université Paris-Sorbonne）研究员林志宏，曾与曲阜（被列为世界人文遗产）市领导有过接触，希望促进在曲阜这个孔子诞生地及中国名城开展中欧合作欧盟亚洲城市复兴项目。林志宏知道汉学家与前法国大使孟毅（Marc Menguy）大半的职业生涯位于亚洲，有国际合作方面的丰富经验。林志宏与前法国大使孟毅会面商谈此项目。

林志宏向孟毅简要描述了欧盟委员会的 Asia Urbs 项目在亚欧城市开展城市遗产方面合作所提供的机会，同时向他咨询是否有哪座法国城市可以与期望参与城市遗产复兴项目的曲阜开展合作。

孟毅知道法国布列塔尼大区（Bretagne）向来对开展国际合作感兴趣。他在经过深思熟虑之后，向林志宏表示将联系法国布列塔尼大区首府雷恩市市长。1985年，布列塔尼大区与曲阜市所在的中国山东省缔结友好省区关系。自此，雷恩市就与中国保持着非常良好的关系。2002年，雷恩市还与山东省省会济南缔结了友好城市关系。在平等互利的基础上，这两座城市商议将共同推动文化、经济和旅游活动的开展。所有这些活动都将拉近布列塔尼大区与山东省的友好关系。

雷恩市市长雷蒙·贺伟（Raymond Hervé）在得知项目规模、实施条件及合作开展的框架后，经过几次必要的工作会议，更为清晰地认识到雷恩市在合作中将提供哪些助力。他毫不迟疑地原则上同意了这次合作，并签署了最终协议——据悉，在与曲阜签订合作协议之后，雷恩市就会在亚洲城市复兴项目中作为带头城市，负责向欧盟委员会提交涵盖遗产保护和可持续发展的整体性项目文件，以及项目的融资方式。

林志宏和孟毅作为非官方项目指导委员会的成员，从2003年起来到曲阜，让曲

vigueur des débats ouverts à l'occasion des colloques qui furent organisés à Qufu par le Programme Asia Urbs, mais aussi par le réel intérêt que les autorités locales comme de nombreux universitaires chinois et européens portent aux séminaires que les Amis de Qufu organisent dans cette Cité marquée encore par le confucianisme. Remarque finale: tout au long de cette coopération initiée en 2004, à laquelle nous avons participé en tant qu'initiateur puis de modérateur, les autorités locales et de tutelle auront su faire preuve d'une grande capacité d'écoute, d'une liberté de choix et de décision, d'une remarquable faculté d'adaptation. Les rapports ne s'en sont pas moins déroulés à un rythme qui tenait compte d'une tendance qui mérite d'être citée: accepter au départ les grandes lignes d'un projet, quitte à en rediscuter les termes en cours d'exécution.

◎ Première Partie: Le Projet Asia Urbs

Le projet Asia Urbs sur Qufu – lieu de naissance de Confucius et ville prestigieuse de la Chine - fut initié lors d'une rencontre entre Roland Lin Chih-Hung, expert à l'UNESCO et chercheur de l'Université Paris-Sorbonne et Marc Menguy, ancien ambassadeur. Roland Lin Chih-Hung avait eu des contacts avec les autorités de Qufu, cité inscrite au Patrimoine de l'Humanité, et connaissait les expériences en Asie de Marc Menguy, sinologue, où il avait servi une grande partie de sa carrière.

Après l'avoir briefé sur les opportunités qu'offraient au sein de la Commission européenne les programmes d'Asia Urbs en matière de coopération en Patrimoine urbain entre villes asiatiques et européennes, Roland Lin Chih-Hung lui a demandé s'il connaissait une ville française qui serait susceptible d'entrer en coopération avec cette cité, qui souhaitait s'engager dans un programme de réhabilitation de son patrimoine urbain.

Marc Menguy, après un temps de réflexion, averti de l'intérêt historique de la Bretagne pour la coopération internationale, a indiqué à Roland Lin Chih-Hung qu'il allait prendre contact avec le Maire de Rennes. Cette ville entretenait avec la République populaire de Chine des relations privilégiées depuis 1985, suite à un accord officiel de coopération signé entre la Région Bretagne et la province du Shandong, où était justement située la Ville de Qufu. En 2002 Rennes s'était jumelée avec Jinan, capitale de cette province chinoise. Sur une base d'égalité et de réciprocité les deux villes étaient convenues de promouvoir les activités culturelles, économiques et touristiques, toutes activités participant au rapprochement entre les deux régions.

Après s'être informé de la dimension de ce projet, des conditions dans lesquelles il serait mis en œuvre, et du cadre dans lequel allait se situer cette coopération, le Maire de la Ville de Rennes, M. Raymond Hervé, n'a pas tardé à donner son accord de principe suivi d'un accord final, après quelques séances nécessaires de sensibilisation de ses services: Il était entendu que dans la présentation à Asia Urbs, Rennes serait désignée, après accord de Qufu, en qualité de ville pilote, chargée de soumettre un document de projet global recouvrant Protection du Patrimoine et Développement Durable, ainsi que ses modalités de financement. La ville espagnole de Saint Jacques de Compostelle acceptait de son côté de participer au projet en matière de développement touristique.

阜市领导在签署正式协议之前了解未来欧洲合作伙伴们的具体安排，从而向欧洲委员会下属的亚洲城市复兴项目办公室提交项目文件。该办公室在2004年最终通过将在2005年、2006年及2007年实施的合作项目。

(1) 欧洲方面清楚地知道这样的协议会为曲阜带来什么技术支援，而曲阜领导们也毫不迟疑地表达了想与欧洲开展合作的热忱。这在欧洲和亚洲的历史进程中是重要的一步。对雷恩市而言，欧洲专家团队第一次在中国儒家学说的文明土地上，自由地表达他们对遗产保护及可持续发展的看法，具有历史参考意义。这些专家学者并没有忽略，曲阜是整个亚洲远东地区（越南、韩国、朝鲜、日本）亚洲文化传承最重要的地方。而对曲阜市而言，市领导可能未曾访问过欧洲，他们从不掩饰想与雷恩市长开展合作的意愿，后者将带头开展合作。雷恩市市长本身也在物色第二个亚洲城市复兴项目框架内的欧洲城市，推荐及选定了和雷恩市都属于大西洋弧城市联盟（Atlantic Arc Cities）的西班牙圣地亚哥·德·孔波斯特拉市（Saint Jacques de Compostelle）。

(2) 不是由我们欧洲方面提出项目开展的总体清单。简言之，欧洲方面应按照合作协议中列出的准备工作，主动了解曲阜原汁原味的城市遗产。如果对“明故城”（曲阜世界文化遗产中的三处位于“明故城”）的研究从建筑角度出发，那么对“鲁国古都”的研究应从更为广阔的文化景观角度出发。采集的数据可以借助信息工具进行分析诊断，随后从曲阜的地域及城市整体视角反思这个城市项目，并通过案例分析来验证这些假设。

在深入探讨之后，我们认为在城市遗产保护及开发时，应将旅游业的发展考虑在内，从长远角度实现可持续发展。中方对于城市遗产的看法、城市遗产的发展及面向未来所做出的选择，有时也同样引发了热议——我们由此发现这一发展目标对中方的重要性。这类与欧洲开展的合作的亮点之一，毫无疑问在于将曲阜传统性场所转变为未来曲阜的文化遗产中心。而这就需要重塑泮池附近的文昌庙遗址的价值并进行开发（曲阜市领导们很有眼光地选择了这里的一座民宅，据亚洲城市复兴项目中一位中国项目的负责人说这里很早以前曾是一个小型耶稣会的聚集地）。这里将接纳曲阜文化遗产研究中心。

项目总预算略超100万欧元，其中的71.27%由欧盟出资，雷恩市、曲阜市和圣地亚哥·德·孔波斯特拉市分别出资11.10%、10.25%和7.38%。项目于2005年1月1日启动，2007年12月31日结束。

(3) 这项合作最吸引人的地方在于其创造性。一位年轻的法国建筑师被派驻到当地研究工作团队，并基于其在亚洲工作的经验，他成功地将当地的专家团队带入了工作。这些专家们个性相异，但都愿意并希望尝试冒险。他们中大部分人都表示希望这

Constitués informellement en comité de pilotage, Roland Lin Chih-Hung et Marc Menguy, se rendent dès 2003 à Qufu pour faire connaître aux autorités de cette cité les dispositions des futurs partenaires européens avant que des accords formels n'interviennent en vue de la présentation d'un Document de projet à Asia Urbs. Cette Agence de la Commission européenne allait donner son accord final en 2004, pour un projet portant sur les années 2005, 2006 et 2007.

(1) Si les Parties européennes étaient conscientes de ce qu'allait représenter une telle intervention à Qufu, les autorités de cette ville historique n'hésitèrent pas pour leur part à manifester leur enthousiasme pour une coopération avec l'Europe. De part et d'autre il s'agissait bien d'un pas dans l'histoire entre l'Europe et l'Asie. A Rennes, on était conscient que pour la première fois sur une terre de civilisation, marquée par le message confucéen et la référence historique des équipes d'experts européens allaient pouvoir librement s'exprimer en terre chinoise sur des questions de patrimoine et de développement durable. Ces techniciens n'ignoraient pas que ce site représentait pour toute l'Asie extrême orientale le plus haut lieu de la culture asiatique, qu'il s'agisse du Vietnam, de la Corée et du Japon. Quant à Qufu, dont les autorités n'avaient sans doute jamais visité l'Europe, elles ne cachèrent à aucun moment leur désir de coopérer avec le Maire de Rennes, qui allait piloter cette coopération. C'était celui-ci qui s'était lui-même préoccupé d'identifier la deuxième ville européenne imposée par Asia Urbs. Saint Jacques de Compostelle, laquelle appartenait comme Rennes à ce contexte des Villes de l'Arc Atlantique.

(2) Notre propos n'est pas de faire un inventaire global du déroulement de ce projet, vu du côté européen. En bref, il s'agissait bien pour la partie européenne de se familiariser avec un patrimoine urbain, in situ, via un travail préalable d'inventaire qui fut effectuer dans les règles. Si l'approche fut architecturale pour la cité Ming – où sont situés les trois sites inscrits au Patrimoine Mondial, elle fut paysagère pour le *Pays de Lu*, d'une plus vaste dimension. Des outils informatiques alliaient permettre l'analyse des données collectées et d'établir un diagnostic, plus une réflexion sur le projet urbain, incluant l'échelle territoriale et une perception globale de la ville, avec des études de cas pour vérifier les hypothèses.

Un développement touristique fut intégré dans ces réflexions et suggestions, après avoir fait l'objet de discussions approfondies, s'agissant de la mise en valeur du patrimoine, dans la perspective à long terme d'un développement durable. Les vues chinoises sur le patrimoine urbain, son développement et les choix pour l'avenir ont ainsi donné lieu à des échanges parfois animés – nous verrons ultérieurement l'importance que cette objectif devait revêtir pour la partie chinoise. L'un des points forts de cette coopération européenne fut incontestablement la réalisation d'un lieu traditionnel en futur centre du patrimoine de la Ville de Qufu. Il s'agissait de réhabiliter et de mettre en valeur du site du *Temple Wenchang* près du lac *Panci* (les autorités eurent le bon gout de choisir une residence qui fut dans un passé lointain celle d'une petite communauté de jésuites - confidence reçue d'un directeur de projet chinois associé à Asia Urbs). Il serait destiné à accueillir le Centre d'études de Qufu en patrimoine.

Le montant total du budget fut un peu plus de 1 million d'Euros, financé à 71,27% par l'Union Européenne, 11,10% par la ville de Rennes, 10,25% par la ville de Qufu, 7,38% par Saint Jacques de Copostelle. La phase opérationnelle a commencé le 1er janvier 2005 et s'est achevée le 31 décembre 2007.

(3) L'un des aspects les plus fascinants de cette coopération, fut la création, à Qufu même, d'une cellule de recherche et de travail, au sein de laquelle se trouvait un jeune architecte français. Envoyé en terra incognita, après une expérience asiatique dans un autre contexte, il réussit à impliquer une équipe d'experts locaux, une équipe formée d'individualités différentes, tous disponibles et désireux de tenter l'aventure. La plupart se montrèrent désireux de conserver à ce « haut lieu culturel d'Asie » son caractère d'un lieu

个“亚洲文化胜地”能保留其本身的人文精神特性。他们开展调查，实地收集数据，从而更好地了解曲阜 2005 年的人口结构、地块片区和建筑结构。这些信息都将被整理成数据库，成为曲阜市制定未来发展方案的重要依据。我们在简要提及这些专家们的默默付出时，不能夸大法国和西班牙专家们通力协作所取得的成果，中国的团队也做出了巨大贡献，包括项目主任刘海涛先生和孔涛先生。此外，在城市规划方面，同济大学的邵甬教授也做出了卓著贡献，为欧洲团队开展下一步工作奠定了基础。

我们应当特别提到中国方面的举措。中国政府对文化遗产有一些“原则上”保护策略，将部分中国城市列为“历史城市”，而曲阜是最早获益于该举措的城市之一。此后，1983—1984 年间，中国建设部审核颁布了一项历史保护方案，将遗产保护与经济发展间的关系、城市发展与建筑遗产保护间的关系以及城市与景观间的关系考虑了进去。方案最终还将遗产保护与旅游业发展的关系也纳入其中。

(4) 1994 年，为适应社会主义市场经济，让曲阜成为国际性历史城市的全新城市发展规划于 1995 年经山东省政府审核通过并实施。2003 年，全新的指导方案制定完成，制定了曲阜市的主要保护区域，而全新的明故城“战略计划”方案则由同济大学根据亚洲城市复兴项目来制定。全新的发展规划旨在改善曲阜这座历史城市的品质、促进曲阜的社会经济发展、保护曲阜市的物质及非物质文化遗产和提高曲阜居民的生活舒适度。我们预计曲阜市政府在未来几年实施的指导性方案，将深化明故城和鲁国古都之间的关系，延伸曲阜的城市轮廓，改善曲阜市的交通和基础设施，大力发展旅游业，保护并开发鲁国古都。

(5) 由于亚洲城市复兴项目要求的文化传递同与欧洲开展合作的整体目标一致，专家、建筑师和城市规划师们在 2005 年曲阜专题讨论会和 2006 年雷恩专题讨论会期间展开了史无前例的交流。对我而言，我从未出席过比 2005 年曲阜讨论会更具批判性和积极性的交流活动。来自中国各地的专家们出席了这次的讨论会。我唯一的遗憾是如此高规格的交流活动没能被记录下来。最后，我要提到一个无法被忽略的趋势，那就是在合作开展过程中，政府领导们似乎越来越重视发展的必要性和迫切需要。

◎第二部分　亚洲城市复兴项目续篇：跨文化研究方式

2006 年，孟毅和林志宏意识到，曲阜 Asia Urbs 项目超越了严格的行政意义上的合作框架。他们两位作为项目发起者，始终致力于推动项目发展：孟毅负责协调，而林志宏则担任技术顾问。他们与曲阜市领导、项目的中欧技术人员开展讨论和交流。

他们两人发现，很多同样面临城市发展和古迹开发问题的其他中国历史城市，

spirituel de l'Humanité. Ils mirent en place des fiches d'enquête, des données furent collectées sur le terrain, pour mieux appréhender la structure de la population; du parcellaire et du bâti pour l'année 2005 – toutes informations qui furent structurées en base de données, qui devraient servir à la Municipalité de la Ville de Qufu dans ses futures approches. On ne peut dans un rappel aussi bref soit-il passer sous silence, outre les efforts conjoints des experts français et espagnols l'immense contribution de l'équipe chinoise et de ses directeurs de projet M. Liu Haitao et M. Kong Tao, et d'autre part les contributions d'une urbaniste remarquable, Mme Shao Yong, professeur à l'université Tongji de Shanghai, qui aura permis aux équipes européennes de tracer leurs contributions.

Les approches chinoises méritent d'être relevées. En dépit d'un certain «a priori» sur le traitement par la Chine de son patrimoine culturel, le Gouvernement central de la RPC prit la décision de qualifier un certain nombre de villes en Chine au titre de «Ville historique». Qufu fut parmi les premières à bénéficier de cette approche officielle. Suite à cette inscription, un plan de conservation historique fut réalisé en 1983-84, validé par le Ministère de la Construction de la Chine. Ce plan d'ores et déjà prenait en compte le rapport entre la protection du Patrimoine et le développement économique, le rapport entre le développement urbain et la protection du Patrimoine architectural, urbain et paysager; enfin le rapport entre la protection du Patrimoine et le développement touristique.

(4) En 1994, afin de s'accorder à l'économie de marché socialiste, une nouvelle planification urbaine fut réalisée, validée par le gouvernement provincial du Shandong en 1995 : faire de Qufu une ville historique d'envergure internationale. Si un nouveau schéma directeur fut élaboré en 2003, circonscrivant des espaces de préservation majeurs, un nouveau «Plan stratégique » fut élaboré dans le cadre d'une mission confiée à l'Université Tongji de Shanghai, document réalisé - il y a lieu de le signaler – en lien avec le projet Asia Urbs. Son objectif : améliorer la qualité de la ville historique, promouvoir le développement socio-économique, protéger les patrimoines matériel et immatériel, améliorer le confort des habitants. Il est prévu que dans les années à venir la Municipalité de Qufu mettrait en œuvre un Schéma directeur qui devrait approfondir les rapports entre la cité Ming et le Pays de Lu et les extensions urbaines de Qufu, les transports, les infrastructures, le développement touristique et la mise en valeur du Pays de Lu.

(5) S'agissant des transferts culturels prescrits par Asia Urbs, conformément aux objectifs intégrés de toute coopération européenne, des échanges sans précédent ont eu lieu tant à Qufu qu'à Rennes, entre experts, architectes, urbanistes, à l'occasion de symposium organisées tant à Qufu, en 2005 qu'à Rennes, en 2006. Pour ma part, je n'avais jamais assisté à des échanges aussi critiques et positifs qu'à cette conférence de 2005, en présence de spécialistes venus de toute la Chine. Je n'eus qu'un regret, c'est que ces échanges d'un si haut niveau n'aient pas été enregistrés. Je terminerai mes remarques sur une tendance qui ne pouvait nous échapper, c'est qu'avec le temps qui passait en parallèle, les autorités ont paru mettre de plus en plus l'accent sur les impératifs du développement, facteurs de priorité.

◎ Deuxième Partie: Les suites d'Asia Urbs : Une approche transculturelle

En 2006, Marc Menguy et Roland Lin Chih-Hung sont conscients que le projet Qufu Asia Urbs dépasse le cadre même d'une coopération stricto sensu. Tous deux ont été à l'origine de ce programme et continuent de s'y attacher, l'un en qualité de régulateur, le second en tant que consultant technique. Ils participent aux discussions et échanges avec les autorités de la Ville comme avec les techniciens chinois et européens

对亚洲城市复兴项目中由中欧合作方实施的项目章程也非常感兴趣。两场研讨会期间，专家们互相交流，评估合作成果。同济大学和清华大学高水准的城市规划师团队对此做出了很大贡献。曲阜市市长也积极主动参与合作事宜，倾力付出。更何况这些文化合作伙伴间多样化的交流已经远远超出了合作的范畴，成为了真正的“跨文化”交流 ：合作各方并没有将个人意愿强加于他人，而是在真正团结和理解的基础上，实现真正意义上的意见交流，在具体操作过程中充分考虑他人的意见。

对所有人来说，“曲阜空间”以其浓厚的历史及和谐的环境，赋予来自不同背景的现代工匠们创新的灵感，就像教堂赋予其建造者灵感一样。这是真正意义上的灵感延续。没有创新，曲阜可能就不是曲阜，丧失了其独特性。

1．曲阜友谊协会

曲阜市委书记张术平、市长江成分别毕业于山东大学哲学系和文学系。他们积极支持建立曲阜友谊协会，希望在合作基础上拓展彼此的交流。2006 年，曲阜友谊协会（ADAQF）在巴黎成立，成为联结欧洲合作伙伴们的新纽带，同时加入了其他教育界的专家学者。协会随后吸引了几个杰出的中国合作伙伴的加入。

在协会的各项计划中，大家一致认同举办专题讨论会不仅能让中欧合作方深入地交流对于合作的看法，更是引入合作以外的新想法的契机。古往今来，曲阜这座历史名城不断激发着创新。曲阜的寺庙古建及其周边区域形成了一个人文空间，在孔子及其后人们影响下成了一方文明的胜地。几个世纪以来，中国及其他部分亚洲国家都打上了这种文明的烙印，社会和政治结构受到了很大影响，在哲学研究方式方面的影响尤其深远，正如同时代的希腊城市一样。

在中国开展各类活动时，我们以往认识的或者在既定会谈时碰到的几位中国教育界人士都非常赞同上述观点。举办专题讨论会符合他们的关注点，也让我们有机会能与他们进行探讨。双方因而成立了科学委员会，负责确定讨论会的主题和框架。

我们因此曾多次与以下这些中国教授碰面：中国儒家学说方面最具权威的专家之一汤一介教授和他的妻子、北京大学教授乐黛云，以及清华大学建筑系教授吴良镛。

在诸多繁复的任务中，对曲阜文化整理具有极高的权威性的儒家学说研究和学习中心在曲阜成立——这是第一所致力于传播中国伟大圣人学说的全国性研究所。

曲阜友谊协会主席孟毅和秘书长林志宏，法国最具权威的中国哲学专家莱昂·汪德迈（Léon Vandermeersch），巴黎建筑学院主任、中国建筑方面的专家、法国教育界人士皮埃尔 · 克莱蒙（Pierre Clément），以及巴黎索邦大学远东研究中心教授顾乃安（Antoine Gournay），曾多次在北京及曲阜与中国合作方进行非正式会谈，商

du Projet.

Ils constatent que les programmes de ce projet Asia Urbs, mis en œuvre par les divers partenaires chinois et européens, intéressent les autres villes historiques de Chine, confrontées elles-mêmes à des problèmes équivalents dans leurs plans de développement et de mise en valeur de leur patrimoine. Les échanges intervenus lors des deux séminaires d'experts ont permis d'évaluer le niveau atteint par cette coopération. Celle-ci allait bénéficier de la contribution d'une équipe urbanistes de haut niveau de l'Université Tongji de Shanghai et de l'Université Qinghua de Pékin. Enfin le Maire de Qufu lui-même avait à cœur de témoigner par ses initiatives de l'intérêt qu'il portait à cette coopération. Ces divers échanges entre partenaires de cultures si différentes ne pouvaient pas ne pas transcender cette coopération, désormais placée dans un véritable contexte de «transculturalité»: Il s'agissait plus d'imposer son point de vue que procéder à de réels échanges d'opinion, afin de l'appliquer sur une base de réelles solidarité et compréhension.

Personnes ne diraient que cet Espace de Qufu, riche pour son histoire et par son harmonie, agissait sur ces artisans modernes d'origines si diverses, et, leur donnait tout comme aux bâtisseurs des cathédrales, le souffle nécessaire pour une nouvelle création, véritable prolongement de cette inspiration sans laquelle Qufu ne serait pas Qufu, dans sa singularité.

A. La Sociéte des Amis de Qufu

Le Secretaire-général du PCC et le Maire de Qufu, M. Zhangh Shuping et M. Jiang Cheng, anciens diplômés en Philosophie et en Littérature de l'Université du Shandong, avaient réagi très positivement à l'idée d'une association des amis de Qufu dont l'objet serait de prolonger les échanges intervenus sur le terrain de la coopération. Instituée à Paris en 2006, la Société des Amis de Qufu (ADAQF), allait créer un nouveau lien entre les partenaires européens, auxquels allaient ensuite se joindre d'autres personnalités des milieux universitaires, avant que n'y adhèrent spontanément quelques éminents les partenaires chinois.

Parmi les projets de cette structure associative, il fut convenu que l'organisation d'un colloque permettrait de transcender les vues des partenaires européens et chinois sur cette coopération sino-européenne. Un tel symposium serait l'occasion d'introduire de nouvelles réflexions au-delà de ce contexte, cette ville historique ayant été un lieu où des vues visionnaires ont puisé leur inspiration au cours des âges. Il s'agissait en effet d'un espace humain, avec ses temples et espaces géographiques, transformé par Confucius et ses successeurs en haut lieu de civilisation, laquelle allait marquer la Chine et une partie de l'Asie au cours des siècles, influencer les sociétés de ces pays au plan de l'organisation sociale et politique, mais surtout les marquer en profondeur dans leur approche philosophique, à l'instar des villes grecques de la même époque.

Ces messages furent parfaitement entendus par les universitaires que nous connaissions ou que nous avions été amenés à rencontrer lors de diverses missions en Chine. L'idée d'un colloque répondait à leurs propres préoccupations, et nous eûmes l'occasion d'en discuter, ayant de part et d'autre former un comité scientifique, chargé d'en définir les thèmes et contours.

C'est ainsi que nous rencontrâmes à plusieurs reprises les professeurs Tang Yijie, l'une des plus hautes autorités de Chine en matière de Confucianisme, son épouse, la professeure Yue Daiyun, de l'Université de Pékin, le Professeur Wu liangyong, Directeur à l'Université QingHua du Faculté d'Architecture, et entre autres, une haute autorité sur l'aménagement culturel de Qufu, où il fit construire un Centre de recherches et d'études sur le confucianisme : le premier Institut national consacré au message du grand sage de la Chine.

议 2008 年第一届主题研讨会的筹备工作。这次的研讨会受曲阜市领导支持，是中欧双方首次开展的主题研讨会。法国驻中国大使 Hervé Ladsous 和公使衔参赞（Nicolas Chapuis）为会谈的开展提供了极大帮助。

2．曲阜案例：举办两场中法研讨会

曲阜研讨会，2008 年 5 月 31 日至 6 月 1 日——空间和文明

本次研讨会是在北京与合作高校（北京大学及清华大学）商讨后的结果。这些合作高校成为了曲阜友谊协会的成员，这有利于各方交流彼此的看法并在会谈时开展讨论。在与曲阜市领导商议之后，研讨会的日期就确定了下来。

法国及中方两个科学委员会负责研讨会的准备工作，确定主题。研讨会主题应围绕两条互补的研究主轴：社会文明及其被社会文明物化的城市空间。本次研讨会旨在研究城市空间如何带有社会文明的烙印，以及这种社会文明无论多么久远，如何仍在继续影响着城市发展的进程。

因此，曲阜在中国民族性形成方面所扮演的角色可以作为所有与会人员的案例分析。用以研究一种特定城市空间 / 土地区域如何被儒家思想所规范，并能反过来促进它长久流传下去。

研讨会之余，与其他带有某种思潮烙印并成为文明中心的文化胜地（尤其是欧洲）近距离接触，也会促进与会人员互相交流——了解后续情况、清楚地知道那些可以观察到的普遍现象以及物质和非物质文化遗产的特性。

中国政府非常赞赏的是，从曲阜案例开始，汉学家们的研究成果能针对具有纪念意义的场所和生活类场所作为补充。尤其是那些在中国哲学和儒家思想方面具有渊博知识的中方与会者，他们的贡献更大。至于汉学以外的研究成果，就跨文化而言，都针对特殊案例。从制度和人文角度来看，它们标志着欧洲经历的历史、政治、社会、司法和宗教等变革。与会者们一致赞同建筑遗产和建筑空间在人民和社会不间断的历史进程中起到了重要作用。

这些研究成果展现了法方在建筑、历史、空间和文明方面的法规起草、城市景观规划、遗产对照方式——这要归功于布鲁盖荷（Bastid-Bruguière）、苏皮奥荷（Alain Supiot）（如今在法兰西公学院 <Le Collège de France>）、皮埃尔 · 克雷蒙和林志宏等。对中方而言，这些研究成果则展现了曲阜的“文明”和“空间”之间的关系。我们要特别感谢汤一介、吴良墉、谢安庆教授和曲阜市市长刘森等。北京大学教授乐黛云的想法非常棒，她在法方与会者孟毅、林志宏、玛丽亚娜 · 巴斯蒂德（Marianne Bastid-Bruguière）、皮埃尔 · 克莱蒙（Pierre Clément）、顾乃安（Antoine Gournay）、苏皮

De façon informelle, Marc Menguy et Roland Lin Chih-Hung, président et secrétaire général de la Société des Amis de Qufu, Léon Vandermeersch, la plus haute autorité française sur la philosophie chinoise, Pierre Clément, directeur d'une école d'architecture parisienne et spécialiste de l'architecture chinoise, l'universitaire français, M Gournay, professeur au CREOPS (Centre de Recherche Extrême-Orient de Paris-Sorbonne), allaient rencontrer plusieurs fois à Pékin ces partenaires chinois, pour s'entendre sur la préparation d'un premier colloque qui allait se tenir en 2008, le premier symposium jamais organisé entre Européens et Chinois, sous l'égide des autorités de Qufu. Ces rencontres il convient de le dire furent facilitées par l'Ambassadeur de France en Chine, M. Hervé Ladsous, et le Ministre conseiller, M. Nicolas Chapuis.

B. Le Cas Qufu: organisation de 2 colloques franco-chinois

Le colloque de Qufu du 31 mai au 1er Juin 2008 – Espace et Civilisation

Ce colloque fut le résultat de ces consultations tenues à Pékin avec les partenaires universitaires, eux-mêmes devenus membres de la Société des Amis de Qufu, ce qui rendait plus faciles les échanges de la rencontre, dont la date fut interrompue après consultation des autorités de Qufu.

A propos de la thématique envisagée, deux comités scientifiques furent chargés de la préparation de la rencontre. Le thème du colloque devait s'articuler autour de deux axes de recherche complémentaires: l'approche des sociétés en termes de Civilisation, et leur concrétisation matérielle dans l'aménagement de l'Espace. L'objectif de ce colloque devait être en effet de montrer comment l'espace aménagé porte l'empreinte des systèmes de civilisation, mais aussi comment loin d'en être le reflet, il participe en même temps de leur façonnement et de leurs mutations.

Dans ce contexte, le rôle joué par Qufu dans la formation de l'identité chinoise pourrait apparaître comme un cas d'école pour tous les participants. Comment un type particulier d'espace urbain, de territoire avait pu être régi par des normes issues du Confucianisme, normes que ces aménagements ont contribué à définir et à pérenniser.

En arrière plan, le rapprochement avec d'autres hauts lieux marqués par une pensée et devenus aussi des centre de civilisation, notamment en Europe permettrait à ces échanges – le cas échéant ultérieur, de mettre en lumière des phénomènes communs observables, mais aussi des spécificités, qu'elles relèvent du patrimoine matériel ou immatériel.

Il fut agrée à Pékin que les contributions sinologiques, partant du Cas de Qufu, porteraient sur les complémentarités entre lieux de mémoire et lieux de vis, notamment du côté des participants chinois, forts de leur connaissance en matière de philosophie chinoise et confucianiste. Quant aux contributions extra-sinologiques, en termes de transculturalité, elles porteraient sur des cas d'espèces, marquant les évolutions intervenues en Europe dans leur perspective institutionnelle et humaine – historique, politique, sociale, juridique, religieuses…. tous les participants s'accordant sur l'importance majeure de l'espace et du patrimoine architectural, dans cette marche ininterrompue de l'histoire de nos peuples et sociétés.

Comme l'ont démontré les contributions, celles-ci ont évoqué du coté français les approches architecturales et historiques, de l'élaboration du Droit en terme d'espace et civilisation, du paysage urbain, des patrimoines comparés – Madame Bastid-Bruguière, Alain Supiot (aujourd'hui au Collège de France), Pierre Clément, Roland Lin Chih-Hung.... Du côté chinois, les liens entre civilisation et Espace à propos du site de Qufu, tout particulièrement, les professeurs Tang Yijie, Wu Liangyong, Xie Anqing et le maire de Qufu, Liu Shen … La professeure Yue Daiyun, de l'Université de Pékin a eu la bonne idée d'assembler certaines contributions au symposium de Qufu en 2008 dans le volume n° 25 de la revue *Dialogue Trans-*

奥荷（Alain Supiot）以及中方与会者吴良墉、谢安庆和刘森的帮助下，将 2008 年曲阜研讨会的部分成果汇编在了《跨文化对话》第 25 辑的“跨文化传递和土地发展”栏目中。这个栏目是为了纪念这次的讨论会（参见《跨文化对话》第 25 辑 . 2009：81-146.）

上海研讨会，2010 年 9 月 29 日——文明、空间及可持续发展

继 2008 年曲阜研讨会之后，曲阜友谊协会的成员们及合作方，尤其是同济大学（建筑和城市规划方面中国最好的大学之一），经过两年时间的深思熟虑，于 2010 年再次举办研讨会。亚洲城市复兴项目的专家之一，同济大学的高级城市规划师邵甬教授，对曲阜贡献卓著。曲阜友谊协会秘书长林志宏也是同济大学的老朋友，他在同济大学担任客座教授。

鉴于曲阜讨论会的主题“空间与文明”本应该加入更多“可持续发展”相关的内容，中法方的组织者决定将研讨会的主题扩展为“文明、空间及可持续发展”，但没有像在北京开展讨论时那样侧重人文科学。同济大学的教授们在同济大学和巴黎索邦大学的大力支持下，参与了上海研讨会的筹办工作。参与筹办的还包括曲阜友谊协会（SDAQF）、巴黎索邦大学远东研究中心（CREOPS）、巴黎建筑城市规划和社会研究学院（IPRAUS），以及法国驻上海总领馆。法国驻上海总领事 Thierry Mathou 和同济大学副校长伍江为举办本次研讨会提供了帮助。

部分出席过 2008 年曲阜研讨会的法国教授再次接受邀请，参与本次中法会谈。需要指出的是，本次研讨会是 2008 年曲阜研讨会的延伸。这些专家学者包括汪德迈、玛丽亚娜·巴斯蒂德、林志宏、皮埃尔·克莱蒙（他为与会听众再现了一些创建城市空间的图表）、顾乃安和 Guillaume Giroir 等教育界人士，以及雷恩市的城市规划师 Bertrand Guidon。同济大学的几位教授即上海研讨会的负责人（潘海啸、蒋大和、张松、诸大建和于一凡教授）也参与了本次对话形式的会谈。与这些正式会议相比，本次研讨会的创新之处在于组织方同与会者达成协议，将最终讨论成果以“上海倡议书”为题刊登出版。[本次研讨会的简介和“上海倡议书”用中文刊登于《中国名城》，2010（12）：26-29.]

culturel, dans une section «Transmission de la culture et le développement du territoire» consacrée à ce colloque notamment avec l'aide des participants français Marc Menguy, Roland Lin Chih-Hung, Marianne Bastid-Bruguière Pierre Clément, Antoine Gournay, Alain Supiot, ainsi que les participants chinois Wu Liangyong, Xie Anqing et Liu Shen (voir revue *Dialogue Transculturel*, Volume n° 25, 跨文化对话，第 25 辑 , Beijing : 2009, 11: 81 – 146).

Le Colloque de Shanghai, 29 septembre 2010 – Civilisation, Espace et Développement Durable

Ce colloque succède en 2010 au Colloque de Qufu de 2008, après deux années de réflexion des membres de la Société des Amis de Qufu, conjointement avec des partenaires notamment de l'Université de Tongji, l'une des grandes universités chinoises en matière d'architecture et d'urbanisme. L'une des hautes participantes au Projet Asia Urbs était la professeure Shao Yun, urbaniste de haut niveau, de l'Université Tongji; sa contribution à Qufu fut une contribution majeure. Roland Lin Chih-Hung, secrétaire général de la SDAQF, est également un familier de Tongji, où il lui arrive d'enseigner en tant que professeur invité.

Considérant que le thème Espace et Civilisation, qui était celui du colloque de Qufu, aurait pu insister davantage sur le Développement durable. Les organisateurs français et chinois décidèrent d'ajouter cette dimension au concept Espace et Civilisation : le colloque s'intitulerait dès lors Civilisation, Espace et Développement Durable. Ses organisateurs étaient moins portés sur les sciences humaines qu'à Pékin. Sous le haut patronage de l'Université Tongji et de l'Université Paris-Sorbonne, des professeurs de Tongji allaient participer à l'organisation de cette manifestation, aisni que la SDAQF, le CREOPS, l'IPRAUS (Institut Parisien de Recherche Architecture, Urbanistique et Société) et en arrière plan le Consul général de France à Shanghai. Ce colloque fut facilité par le consul général de France à Shanghai, M. Thierry Mathou et le président adjoint de l'Université de Tongji, professeur Wu Jiang.

Un certain nombre de professeurs français présents à Qufu avaient accepté de participer une nouvelle fois à cette rencontre franco-chinoise, qui était considérée comme un prolongement du Colloque de Qufu de 2008. On citera Léon Vandermeersch, Marianne Bastid-Bruguière, Roland Lin Chih-Hung, Pierre Clément (qui a reproduit pour les auditeurs un certain nombre de schémas sur la fabrication d'un milieu urbain), des universitaires Antoine Gournay et Guillaume Giroir ainsi que Bertrand Guidon, urbaniste de la Ville de Rennes. Quelques professeurs de Tongji et responsables de la ville de Shanghai (professeurs Pan HaiXiao, Jiang DaHe, Zhang Song, Zhu DaJian et Yu Yifan) sont également intervenus dans cette rencontre qui prit la forme d'un dialogue. La novation, par rapport à ces conférences, fut qu'un accord intervint entre les personnalités organisatrices et les participants pour qu'à la fin des travaux un manifeste soit publié, au titre du colloque intitulé «Manifeste de Shanghai» (Le résumé de ce colloque ainsi que le Manifeste de Shanghai ont été publiés en chinois dans *Chinese Famous Cities*, 中国名城 , 2010/12: 26-29).

面对永续发展的挑战：西班牙圣地亚哥市与曲阜市的环境、建设施工技术、宜居性能源以及城市遗产保护与改善的日常平衡

安杰·帕内罗·帕多

2005 年到 2007 年间，法国雷恩市、欧洲西班牙圣地亚哥市和亚洲中国曲阜市曾在中欧合作欧盟亚洲城市复兴项目（Asia Urbs）框架内，共同实施过一个城市合作与交流项目。我有幸代表圣地亚哥市参与了此项目。这三座历史城市有着截然不同的文化背景，但就城市而言，尤其是历史城市特有的方面则有着共通之处，我将在本文一开始综合阐述通过本项目所吸取到的大量经验教训，除此之外在此项目中我还发现以下特点：

（1）这三座历史城市面临的问题与全球其他地方的历史城市几无差别，或者说十分类似；

（2）历史城市具有非凡的潜力和资源，能够成功解决城市发展面临的问题；

（3）最后，了解历史范畴有助于面对这些问题，如果我们把历史城市面临的问题视为在历史长河中，为了实现城市效能与成功，使人与周边环境和谐共存而伴生的必然结果，则历史城市保护工作远不止是外观的考古保护，而是要解决复杂的永续性改造和持续改变的问题。

我专业从事文化遗产保护工作已有 20 多年，我极为重视历史城市的保护，也长期参与保护工作。历史城市圣地亚哥和“朝圣之路”都已被联合国教科文组织列为世界文化遗产。高效能城市结构具有持续改变和永续性改造特征，在这一动态发展过程中去探索遗产保护方法是相当激动人心的想法。像我一样从事文化遗产保护的建筑师，肯定也会对此倍感兴奋。本文中阐述的历史城市恢复方法，是基于我在圣地亚哥·德·孔波斯特拉古城修复过程中积累的经验，并结合了在参与欧盟亚洲城市复兴曲阜项目期间取得的跨文化工作经验。本文认为历史城市发展所具有的可持续性已经过时间的证明，因此要把历史城市保护作为城市发展的参照模型。

本文将试着阐明历史城市得以留存下来的一些原因，首先从进化论的观点开始，指出这部分取决于历史城市及其建筑的容量，进而随着居民日常生活的变化过程而演化调整以适应这些变化。另外，重要性远远高于可持续发展问题的是，历史城市的永续存在是其自身不断完善的结果，也就是说历史城市具有自我完善的能力。

我曾说过，历史城市保护的问题是，要想在不破坏遗产价值的情况下提高生活水平，怎样的改造速度才合适呢？在我看来，答案毫无疑问与城市能源因素相关，或许首先会通过维护的

The Challenge of Retaining Permanent Change: Environment, Construction Technology, Energy for Livability, and Everyday Balance for the Protection and Enhancement of the Urban Heritage in the Cities of Santiago de Compostela (Spain) and Qufu (China)

Angel Panero Pardo

Once upon a time, between 2005 and 2007, three cities, Rennes (France) and Santiago de Compostela (Spain) from Europe, and Qufu (China) from Asia, had the opportunity to develop a project of urban cooperation and exchange within the framework of the European programme ASIA URBS. I had the fortune to participate on behalf of the city of Santiago, and in urban terms, especially in relation to historic cities even in very different cultural contexts, aside from the many lessons learned, which are at the origin of many of the ideas that I would like to develop synthetically in this article, I found what is next:

(1) The problems with cities that we must face are the same or quite similar ones anywhere around the world,

(2) the potential and resources of historical cities to tackle them successfully are extraordinary and, ultimately,

(3) that historic category is a great help to face them just if we manage it as the result of a process of efficiency and urban success through time to accommodate properly the coexistence of humans in neighborhood that, far from be linked to archeological conservation of appearance, has to do with a complex phenomenon of permanent transformation and continuous change.

For someone who, like me, has more than 20 years professionally engaged in conservation and put in value of historic cities with huge significance, both the historic city of Santiago and the Pilgrims Path, have been recognized by UNESCO as world heritage site, the dramatic idea of searching for the keys to conservation in this dynamic of continual change and permanent transformation characteristic of efficient urban structures, has been really exciting. In connection with the rehabilitation of historic cities, based on the experience developed in the process of rehabilitation of Santiago de Compostela and the cross-cultural experience lived during the ASIA URBS programme, this article is going to claim historic cities as urban reference models by its proven sustainability over time.

It tries to point some of the reasons of that urban success of historic cities starting from the *Darwinist* idea that it is partly the result of the capacity of historic cities and their architecture, to evolve and adapt to changes of everyday life of its inhabitants. And even much more, and more important than a question of sustainability, that permanence of historical cities is at last, the product of its perfectibility. That means, their ability to change to better.

And once I said that, the question is, what is the pace appropriate to change while improving living standards without damage of heritage values? In my opinion and without doubt, the response has to be with the item of energy, and maybe could be found first based on reflections on the culture of the maintenance

文化而不是恢复的文化得以反映出来。此外，它还与容易进行改造的建设智能化相关，也和在历史城市改造过程中创造就业机会，推动当地经济蓬勃发展的能力联系在一起。

本文将简要介绍历史城市保护策略的转型，最后一部分建议摒弃我们常用的现行管理规范，因为在这些规范的管理下，我们在世界各地的城市遗产保护工作并未取得多大成功。应该把重点重新放回对居民日常生活的干预准则，除了宜居性和环境外，这在很大程度上取决于能源因素。

◎一、物竞天择：历史中心地区建筑的演变与适应过程

就 21 世纪全球经历高速城市化的发展，人类所面对的一系列挑战，主要应从城市区划的协调与修复改造领域入手。事实上，从一开始城市就是人类迅速进化的产物，但也许这是我们第一次认识到，城市面临的其中部分挑战对人类存亡起着举足轻重的作用。近 50 年来城市的发展让我们很不满意，这不仅仅是因为我们没能突破高质量城市化与多样性共存的窘境，最主要的原因在于我们没能处理好城市文脉的传承问题。我们没能像自己的前辈们一样，在持续改变和调整以适应居民日常生活的自然过程中，解决好这些问题。这些问题对于历史城市尤为突出，近 30 年，关于历史城市遗产价值保护与认定方面的理论和论述层出不穷，但结果却是这些遗产遭到破坏和废弃。更糟糕的是，历史城市的居民遭到驱逐，这虽然没有直接对城市社会的结构造成不可逆转的破坏，但这种对居民不公的行为，变成了城市核心一触即破的毒瘤。我们白白浪费了原本成熟、高效能的城市，忽视了在全球城市化背景下，对这些城市的长久使用本身已经是其作为模范城市有效性的最佳证明。我们过于重视历史城市的外观，但外观并不是某个具体城市改造项目的结果，而是每个年代持续改造，并使之与居民日常生活相适应这一过程的产物。这种顺应性解释了文化遗产是如何形成的，在我看来这也是其得以作为历史城市流传至今的关键所在。

位于历史城区中心地区那些工业化之前的传统建筑都经过了漫长、稳定的演变过程。经过一系列的试验和对错误的纠正，各种技术和施工解决方案在对环境的适应过程中被及时地改正更新，其实施也逐渐得到简化，以最低的经济和能源成本提高了历史城市的宜居性。

more than on the culture of rehabilitation, and also it has to be with the intelligence of the construction to allow change easily, or the ability to create jobs and boost the local economy of the processes of urban transformation.

The article tries to present a concise reformulation of strategies for the rehabilitation of historic cities, at last proposing to abandon the dogma of current regulations that we usually use without much success to preserve urban heritage around the world, and recovering the focus of intervention criteria on everyday life of inhabitants, having very much present the item of energy after livability and the environment.

◎ I. The natural selection: evolution and adaptation of architecture in historic centres

It seems that the challenges of humanity in the 21st century, with the intensely urbanized planet, should be addressed in the area of metropolitan coordination and rehabilitation of the consolidated city. In fact, cities have been, from the beginning, the scenario of the exponential evolution of homo sapiens, but, perhaps for the first time, we know that some of these challenges, are even crucial to the survival of our species. we cannot be satisfied with what has happened in the cities during the past 50 years, not only because we have not been able to resolve the dilemma of coexistence quality urbanism in diversity, but, mainly, because we have failed to handle the inherited cities. We have not been able to deal with them as those who preceded us, in a natural process of continuous change and adaptation to the daily life of its inhabitants. And especially in the case of historic cities, in which, after a prolific last third of the 20th century in terms of theories and statements of protection and recognition of their heritage value, the result is that their deterioration and abandonment, and what is worse, the eviction of residents, when directly not destroyed irreversibly its structure, has become them unfairly in a conflictive cyst in the heart of the cities. We have squandered their proven efficiency urban, ignoring that his tenure in the nonsensical context of global urbanization, was the best proof of its validity as a model urban. Their appearance, which we probably value in excess, is not the result of a concrete urban project, but the result of the process of continuous transformation, and adaptation in each era, to the everyday life of its inhabitants. This resilience explains the heritage built up, and in my opinion is the key to his success as city.

The pre-industrial architecture of historic centres comes from a slow and steady evolution. Technology and constructive solutions have been debugged in time through sequences of trial and error, in a process of adaptation to the environment that gradually has also been simplifying its execution and increased livability at the lowest economic and energy cost.

This accumulation of intelligence in time, knowledge of materials and their characteristics, economy of construction processes, accuracy in the answer to the everyday problems of the people, no doubt, is the reason for their survival and constructive force. And this physical reality of our historic centres, in

智慧随着时间的推移不断累积，包括对材料及其特性的认知、经济高效的施工过程、解决民众日常问题的准确性和针对性，毫无疑问，这些都构成了历史城市存续和建设的动力。从进化论的观点看，历史城市对持续改造的积极适应同时滋润着它们的现实状况，而这些持续改造则源于居住其间的居民对文化与社会的变革与适应。物质环境建设的演进，及其为适应持续变化而发生的功能方面的改进是历史城市成功存续的关键条件。无论在哪个年代，这两点都是保持城市与居民日常生活平衡关系的所在。

1．持续变化

如果我们认为城市本质上是持续变化的，那么我们就必须承认：历史城市的复原过程须尊重这种微妙的永续改造的节奏和连续性。建筑亦是如此。所以我认为对历史城市采取干预方法时，除了考虑文化遗产的价值外，还务必使干预方法融入历史城市及居民的日常生活中，使之调整以适应复杂的持续变化情况。这样做并不容易，但在我看来这才是历史城市改造真正要面临的挑战，而且将是十分不易的事，虽然城市科学在 20 世纪有了长足的发展，但事实证明这些科学似乎不足以处理城市复杂的日常问题。城市治理文化无边无界，但我认为必须认识到城市化的体系和过程是远远不够的。不管是具有充足资金支持的密集型项目，还是城市规划、甚至较不具标准化的管理模式，都无法安然适应城市演化的自然节奏。我们都知道，采用既着眼于整个城市，又兼顾特定领域具体问题的方法才是关键所在，但这还不够，因此我们重视涉及地域体系的曲阜和圣地亚哥这两座城市。在具有特殊文化价值的历史城市中，20 世纪最后 30 年的保护政策偏离了城市日常现实情况，更为糟糕的是，更偏离了居民的日常生活状况，严重阻碍了保护目标的实现，但所幸，这些政策尚未成为保护的对立面，成为破坏整个城市遗产和自然演化过程的因素。为此，我们迫切需要重新制定历史遗产地的保护和改善策略，通过提升城市治理水平来实现上述目标。

2．隐身化

我认为可以继续用进化论的并行性来解释为什么许多现代建筑师在历史城市中从事项目时会感到不安。现代建筑师主要是在建筑学院接受教育，目的是成为一名创造者，而不是演化者。为了实现独特性和差异性的目标，我们不得不作为建筑师来有意地培养自身的创造才能，同时，20 世纪上半叶开展的现代建筑运动始终武断地对历史建筑采取一概蔑视的态度，我认为这两方面的原因导致了专业义务论的产生，坦白说，使我们无法从对历史城市中发现的基本问题的思考出发来采取行动。为此，我认为在历史城市中开展建筑和住宅的修复项目的核心在于建筑师身份。建筑师匿名者的

darwinist key, is enriched with its proven adaptation in time to the constant transformations derived from the cultural and sociological changes of those who inhabited them. Both, fisico-constructiva evolution and functional adaptation to permanent change, are main keys to the success of the urban condition. Both, in every age, have been due of the usual daily balance of the city and its inhabitants.

1. The continuous change

If we admit that city, as nature, is continuously changing, we must admit that urban rehabilitation processes must respect the rhythm and continuity of this subtle and permanent transformation. And also with architecture. So I think that in historic cities, even aside from its heritage value, methodologies for intervention must be necessarily diluted in the daily reality of the city and its inhabitants to adapt to this complex scenario of continuous change. It is not easy, but this is in my opinion the real challenge of urban renovation, and is not small, because urban science, as it has developed during the twentieth century, seems to me that has proved incompetent to handle the simple complexity of everyday in the cities. Unbound still a culture of urban governance, I believe that we must begin to think that the systems and procedures of urbanism are not enough. Neither intensive projects, amply financed, nor urban plans and its even less standard management formulas, have been able to fit peacefully in that natural rhythm of cities evolution. We know that an approach from the perspective of the entire city to the specific problems of certain areas is essential, and so we regard both, Qufu and Santiago, involved in a territorial system, but it is not enough. In the historical centres with special cultural value, protection formulas in the last third of the 20th century, divorced from everyday reality of cities and what is definitely worse, of its inhabitants, have reached dimensions of extraordinary ineffectiveness on the goal of conservation, when they have not become contrary by a factor of destruction of heritage and the natural evolution of the city as a whole. That is why it is so urgent to reformulate strategies of conservation and enhancement of the historical sites by means promoting good urban governance.

2. Anonymity

I believe that it is possible to continue with the darwinian parallelism to explain the discomfort of many contemporary architects when working in historic cities. We, modern architects, have been mainly trained in the schools of architecture to be creationist, rather than to be evolutionist. The aim of uniqueness and distinction that requires the creative genius that we are forced to cultivate as architects, together with dogmatic disdain for the past that ran the modern movement during the first half of the 20th century, is over in my opinion to produce a professional deontology frankly unable to act from consideration of elementary problems that we find in the historical centres. I advocate that the tessitura of the architectural project in the rehabilitation of buildings and homes in historic centres is the anonymity. An anonymity intensely committed to construction, technology, and to inhabitants of each site, which, ultimately, should serve to chain our intervention in the evolutionary sequence of the architecture on which we act.

3. Best perfectible than sustainable

Since historic cities have demonstrated ability to survive in very difficult circumstances and, lately, in downright inhospitable urban contexts, we could admit its essential condition of sustainability in the sense we have given to the term nowadays. However, that permanence is best explained from the capacity of adaptation and change, than from proven sustainability. And in fact, we can say that historic cities have

身份致力于为建设、技术和遗产地居民的服务行动中，并最终使我们将对所改造建筑演化过程的干预融合到一起。

3．完善性优先于可持续性

历史城市向人们展示了自身在极艰难环境中生存下来的能力，但近年来，历史城市变得完全不适合居住。在这种背景下，如今谈到历史城市，我们得承认可持续发展是基本条件。但是，相对于久经证实的可持续性，更能说明城市永续性的是城市的适应和变化能力。事实上，我们可以说，历史城市具有可完善性，而不是可持续性，前者更严谨地说明了其所具备的不断完善的能力。这种为了完善而不断演化的能力才是提升城市效能的关键因素。

4．维护优先于修复

尽管不愿承认，但城市修复并不是我们这个时代的新发明。但事实上，比起那些已在历史城市发生或即将发生的行动，我们现在所做的一切既不是前无古人，也非后无来者。事实证明，在近50年间，保护与改造的自然过程已受到很大程度的干扰。目前，我们似乎得启动持续改变的引擎，这也解释了在许多情况下要对历史城市寻求采取大量行动的原因。我们要认识到，真正支撑城市永续性发展的已经不再是修复，而是维护，这也是保证城市以适当节奏持续改变的要素。对建筑物与公共空间进行规范化维护不仅能保证稳定的持续改变，也能保证经济与社会的效益。

◎二、建筑智能化

建筑语言越来越国际化，并且在20世纪下半叶我们能够随意运用智能技术，这让我们在面对历史城市的建筑物与公共空间的环境状况和建筑特征时，逐渐缺乏思考。很多时候我们往往会觉得这是一种释放创造力的表现，但很遗憾，正是这一切造成了古建筑逐渐消失，不仅包括其所在的环境，还有我们建造这些建筑所掌握的特定技术，这在建筑发展史上是从未出现过的情况，我认为这已在历史城市干预过程中产生了毁灭性的后果。建筑的产生要严格服务于经济因素，这导致了历史城市中破坏古建筑遗产与城市规划之间的一个死循环。我认为历史环境中的建筑物与住宅恢复，必须通过建设的智能化进行控制管理。这不仅是为了使干预措施与城市背景相适应，也避免了建筑可能会中断良性的持续性改造过程（这我前面提到过）。采用建筑智能化的依据有下面五点：

been, rather than sustainable, perfectible, that means strictly capable of improving. This ability to evolve to improve, is the key to urban efficiency in time.

4. Better maintenance than rehabilitation

It's hard to admit that urban rehabilitation is not an invention of our time. But our actions are neither the first, nor will be the last of all those that have happened and will happen in historical cities. What is proven is that during the past 50 years, the natural sequence of conservation and transformation was largely interrupted. And now it seem as if we were to start the engine of continuous change, what explains why historic cities requires intensive actions in so many cases. It is necessary to recognize that the true support of physical permanence of the cities, the guarantee of continuous change at proper pace, has not been there habilitation, but maintenance. The culture of normalized maintenance of buildings and public spaces guarantees not only the stability of continuous change, but its economic and social profitability.

◎ II. Intelligence of Construction

The internationalization of the architectural language and the possibilities that technology put at our disposal during the second half of 20th century, contributed to the gradual lack of consideration of environment conditions and the constructive characteristics of the building sand public spaces in historic cities. Those circumstances, unfortunately so many times presented as liberating from the point of view of creativity, has resulted in a progressive uprooting of architecture, not only with the environment, but also with own specific technology that produces it, something which never before happened in the history of architecture and, in my opinion, has had catastrophic consequence in the processes of intervention on the historical centres. The production of architecture at the service of strictly economic factors, closed the circle of destruction of the built heritage and the urban landscape in our historic cities. In my opinion, the rehabilitation of buildings and homes in historical sets, must be governed by the intelligence of construction. Not only in order to contextualize interventions, but also to avoid that architecture could break the desired sequence of continuous transformation that already I have referred. Intelligence of the construction can be formulated on the basis of five ideas:

(1) Construction is a formidable supportive, cooperative and participatory process in which resulting architecture can be enriched with the circumstances arising from the process of construction.

(2) The logistics of construction determines the architecture. Determining aspects of the logistics of the building have to do with technology, the location and the cooperative organization of the different trades involved in the process. The success of the construction process, certainly also its economic profitability, depends on the use of appropriate technology and the successful organization of persons involved in the implementation, taking advantage of synergies and support that can be produced with the aim of better to fix the production of the work. If this is indisputable during the strict phase of commissioning work, also must be during the project phase, which, no doubt, would result in interventions more contextualized, consistent with the everyday reality of historic cities.

(3) Construction intelligence requires technological compatibility. Coherent technology is common in

(1) 建设是有力的支持、合作和参与过程，最终产生的建筑可以通过建设过程中不断发生的各类状况得以充实巩固。

(2) 建设施工的后勤准备对建筑有着决定作用。建设过程能否成功，取决于建筑施工的后勤准备与技术以及过程中所涉及的不同行业的地点及合作机构的积极的参与性。当然还包括建设能否盈利，都取决于是否运用了相应的技术，实施过程中的各参与人员是否组织得当，充分利用协同和支持，从而更好地解决工程生产问题。如果在严格的工作委托阶段以及项目执行阶段，这些决定性因素全部落实到位，则无疑干预措施能更好地融入城市发展，与历史城市的日常现实状况更加一致。

(3) 建筑智能化要求技术兼容性。技术兼容性在其他一些行业中很常见，例如造船业或汽车制造业，但令人惊讶的是，若在建筑施工中考虑采用技术兼容性，人们会认为限制了创造力。技术兼容性要求具备法律知识，了解实施方所干预的建筑物的建筑特征，以及建筑在适应过程中的演化。技术兼容性与历史城市的日常经济息息相关，因此必定要求技术具有人文的一面，能根据人的尺度进行调整，1973 年英国经济学家舒马赫（E.F. Schumacher）的著述《小即是美》中就已谈到过这一点。

(4) 建筑智能化要求循环和再利用。历史城市的修复也需要循环和再利用。与大众的普遍认知相反，对修复工作的全面理解必定会带来节约。当然这肯定有利于社会福祉，有助于提升经济效益。事实上，假设用维护取代修复思想，效益甚至会好得多。所以，始终要做的不仅是建筑物与住宅的维护，还有公共空间的维护。

(5) 建筑智能化涉及可逆转性。可逆转性是效益、改变与改造的保证。

◎三、就业与小企业以及修复经济学

历史城市的修复可以也应当被视为是建筑业转型的良机。建筑业的预期变革并不包括只占很小比例的营收增长，该部分资金会记入与修复工作关联的账目中，而是在此之前，必须对企业、劳动力、技术、行政管理、财政和物流文化建设及其配套行业进行深入的结构性改革。相对于建设新建筑，修复工作更多的是需要大量技术娴熟的工人，能在中长期实现资金节省，控制好成本。除了节省资金外，维护工作还能及时稳定几乎所有目标投资，从而创造就业机会，形成稳定、合格的就业市场。就世界各地众多历史城市目前的社会经济形势而言，很难想象能开出比这更好的良方了。

1. 城市更新与就业

城市更新能够强烈刺激当地经济发展，有利于雇佣当地劳动力，在工作当中工人

other sectors, such as the naval construction or the cars construction, but in the construction of buildings, surprisingly, it has come to be considered even as a limitation to creativity. Technological coherence requires knowledge of law and characteristics of construction of buildings on which the operator intervenes, and also of its evolution in the adaptation process. Technological coherence is linked with the everyday economy of historic centres, and necessarily requires the technology with a human face, adjusted to the right size of the man, which already spoke in 1973 E.F. Schumacher in "Small is beautiful".

(4) Construction intelligence requires recycling and reuse. Rehabilitation requires recycling and reuse. Against the widespread popular feeling, well understood rehabilitation necessarily generates savings. It is certainly socially profitable, but also it is in economic terms. Indeed much more if we imagine a scenario in which the maintenance culture replaces the rehabilitation. So it was always, maintenance of buildings and houses, but also maintenance of the public space.

(5) Construction intelligence involves reversibility. Reversibility is a guarantee of profitable change and transformation.

◎ III. Employment and Small Business, Economics of Rehabilitation

The rehabilitation can and should be understood as an extraordinary opportunity to transform the building sector. Change expected in the sector does not consist of a mere percentage inflation of the turnover which is billed to linked to rehabilitation work, and before much more, has to produce a deep structural reformulation of business, labor, technical, administrative, fiscal and logistical culture construction and its auxiliary industry. Against the construction of new buildings, rehabilitation required intensive skilled labor, and generates in the medium and long term, savings and cost containment. Maintenance in addition to savings, stabilized in time entirely virtually intended investment to create jobs, stable and qualified employment. It is difficult to imagine better medicine for the present socio-economic situation in so many cities around the world.

1. Urban renewal and employment

Urban rehabilitation can strongly stimulate the local economy, employ local workers, and generates self-esteem because it allows workers to develop their skills and knowledge. The success of the policies of urban recovery has to endure about this circumstance. In every city, in every neighborhood, it is necessary to boost the army of the rehabilitation, in which all agents of the sociological spectrum must be integrated. This army is responsible of promoting the collective cultural change that is necessary to make rehabilitation an opportunity for all.

2. Training for qualified employment

It is essential therefore to educate workers, entrepreneurs, technicians, officials, politicians, owners or tenants. In particular, it is urgent to promote strategies of training and retraining of construction workers. Training for qualified employment should also aim to generate jobs. The success of rehabilitation also depends on our ability to foster small businesses able to reconstruct, sensibly, the productive small structure of everyday economy of cities.

们能够磨炼技能、积累知识、建立自尊。历史城市修复政策的成功与否有赖于对这一情况的包容度。在每一座城市、每一个社区，都有必要发展历史城市修复的队伍，其中必须囊括社会各个方面的所有主体。这支在地的历史城市修复队伍负责提高集体文化的正面改变，这对于把修复变成有利于各方的机会来说是必要的。

2. 培训合格就业人才

面向工人、企业家、技术人员、政府官员、政治家、业主或租客开展宣传至关重要。尤其是，对建筑工人进行培训和再培训，提高相应技能刻不容缓。合格的就业还应包括就业机会的创造。修复能否成功还取决于我们培养小企业的能力，使这些企业有能力合理地为历史城市富有成效地重建小范围的日常经济结构。

◎四、反思历史中心修复的战略标准

下面我想简要说明几点与历史城市修复实施方案相关的一些理念，我相信这些理念对于圣地亚哥市和曲阜市也同样有用。我认为，要解释城市遗产保护与改善政策显而易见的失败，可以站在“遗产保护信条”的角度进行分析。这一信条自相矛盾的一点是，一方面遗产保护是由行动力弱、官僚性强的专家委员会进行管理，另一方面又要求“规范信条”具有活力，而前者恰恰抑制了后者的活力。这两方面是发达社会过度热情导致的结果。再者，还有特定文化问题以及与防范与安保相关的法律问题。这两者都会损害居民利益，造成历史城市保护没有可持续发展能力，而只能靠大量捐助和当局拨给的公共资金进行维持。我能肯定的是，依托遗产概念实施的传统历史城市保护方法效率十分低下。话虽如此，我还是视其为备用方案（或许有些夸大其辞）。我提出的战略重组建议基于以下各点：

(1) 城市与居民的日常平衡。从全世界范围看，历史城区中的居民在周边环境保护与改善过程中被边缘化，这绝不是夸大之辞。当局不遗余力地向居民们宣传他们不能对自己的住宅和街道进行改造的方面，但没有任何人向居民说明他们能改造哪些地方，也没有人解释如果能改造的话，该如何改造以及为什么要改造。因此，我们必须依据城市或邻近区域居民既简单又复杂的日常生活，着眼于过程与处理程序。这意味着减少专家委员会的数量，刹住官僚主义作风，取而代之的是在邻近地区开展更多工作，直接为居民送去关怀。

(2) 宜居性能源。在历史城市中，显而易见遗产破坏、建筑能源价值破坏与城市化是并存的。建筑形式的消失，比如明清四合院建筑形式的消失，不仅仅是建筑的损失，

◎ IV. Rethinking Strategic Criteria of Rehabilitation in Historic Centres

I would like to point very briefly some ideas relating to the operational formulation of urban rehabilitation that I am sure may be useful both for Santiago and Qufu. In my opinion, the contrasting failure of policies of protection and enhancement of urban heritage, can be explained on the basis of what can be called "the dogma of heritage protection". Paradoxically this dogma, managed with slowness and bureaucracy from the committees of experts, collides in paralyzing dynamics with "the dogma of regulations". Both are the result of excess zeal of developed societies. In a case with certain cultural issues, and on the other, with legal issues related to safeguards and security. Both at the expense of citizens, have made unsustainable the conservation of city centers, by many grants and public investment that authority wants to offer. I am convinced that the traditional approach to urban protection by mean heritage concepts is very inefficient. Having said that, I synthesize, maybe in excess, an alternative. My proposal of strategic reformulation is based on these headings:

(1) Everyday balance of the city and citizens. All over the world, citizens who live in historical areas have been literally marginalized in the process of protection and enhancement of its immediate surroundings. Authorities shown them vehemently from what they could not do in their homes or streets, and however, no one has explained to them what they could do, or how and why could do it. Therefore we must focus intensely procedures and processing based on complex but simple everyday life of the inhabitants of cities or neighborhoods. That means less committees of experts and bureaucracy and instead much more work in proximity and direct care to residents.

(2) Energy for livability. It can be shown a clear parallel between the destruction of the heritage and the destruction of the energy values of architecture and urbanism in historic centres. The disappearance of models, for instance the "si he yuan" in the Ming city, is not only the loss of an architecture, but a way of living wisely adapted to the environment. Instead of rehabilitation, it seems advantageous to talk about livability. The history of the improvement of conditions of livability is the story of evolution of cities. And livability requires energy. The construction, rehabilitation and maintenance can also be made in energy terms. The production of building materials has also aspects closely linked to the discourse of energy. The pre-industrial architecture today is a model of efficiency and economy in search of basic livability in homes and public spaces. Livability of all buildings constructed (approx.3.500 million square meters) is responsible for 20% of the total energy consumption in Spain.

It is not possible to deal with commitments on the reduction of consumption and emission of greenhouse effect gases without reviewing the lessons involved in architecture and urbanism in historic cities. The approach to the rehabilitation and conservation of the urban heritage is certainly possible and strategically smart from aspects relating to energy, the energy for the livability and construction. I think if we formulate the inventory of architectural elements with energy value in the historical centres, it is possible to not be very different from the traditional listed to protect its historical and artistic value. Energy and preventive maintenance for the preservation of the historic city policies can only be managed from the active involvement of users. This is another reason for hope, because we need to urgently engage citizens in the preservation of heritage. It is necessary to replace the subsidy culture by a culture of commitment.

(3) Praise of vacuum. Often has been granted excessive importance to the stone. After the vortex in soil consumption we have experienced, we have to be aware of the importance of keeping the vacuum. Urban voids, gap areas which remained unbuilt in our cities, are decisive in the process of urban recovery. These

也是一种巧妙地适应环境的生活方式的消失。不讨论修复工作，而只讨论宜居性似乎很有利。改善宜居条件的历史也是城市演化的历史。宜居性需要能源。建设、修复和维护也可以从能源角度实施。建筑材料的生产也与能源使用密切相关。如今，工业化之前的传统建筑成为一种效能和经济模型，可帮助在住宅和公共空间中寻找到基本宜居性。在西班牙，所有建成建筑（约 350 万平方米）的宜居性占到国家总能耗的 20%。

要想在历史城市中致力于减少能耗、降低温室气体排放，不吸取建筑与城市化的相关经验教训是不行的。城市遗产的恢复与保护方法当然是可行的，从能源（宜居性能源和建设能源）方面来说，在战略上也是明智的。我认为，如果在历史城市中，按能源价值开列建筑要素清单，则与把历史城市列入历史和艺术保护对象的传统方法无甚差别。通过能源和预防性维护措施来保护历史城市的政策只能在民众积极参与的情况下进行管理。我们希望这样做的另外一个原因是我们迫切需要居民积极参与遗产保护工作。把补贴文化变成参与文化十分必要。

(3) 重视留空。石料建筑往往受到过分重视。脱离了用地漩涡后，我们必须认识到留存空地的重要性。城市空地，即城中未建的间隙区域对于历史城市复原有着举足轻重的作用。这些间隙不仅是理解历史城市城市平衡的关键，也与地域更新紧密联系在一起。它们也意味着有开发机会，有利于改进平衡、连贯的历史城市复原政策。历史城市保护不仅要留出绿地作为居民休闲场所，更多是为了能够构建统一形象，巩固当地综合历史城市修复进程，直面各种待解决的环境问题，例如水资源循环与管理、生物多样性、城市土地生产率以及土地对小范围的当地日常经济的贡献。

总之，不管是亚洲的中国曲阜市还是欧洲的西班牙圣地亚哥市，除外观以外，城内的一切几乎全是城市保护的基本要素。通过呆板的方式来了解自己所在城市的现状，会错误地以为建筑是缓慢、稳定地在演变。如果我们希望面对永续变化的挑战，则必须在这两个城市中到处走走，了解第一手资料，吸取相应的教训。

gaps not only contain the keys to understanding the urban balance of historic centres and its relationship with the territory. They are also always spaces of opportunity to promote balanced and coherent policies of urban recovery. Its conservation not only leaves green spaces for citizens leisure, and much more, it allows build coherent arguments to reinforce a process of locally integrated urban rehabilitation, pending environmental aspects, as the cycle and management of water, biodiversity, or the productivity of urban soil and its contribution to the small local everyday economy.

I would like to conclude by saying that almost everything both in Qufu (China, Asia) or Santiago de Compostela (Spain, Europe) have basis beyond the appearance. Who read their urban realities just in a formalistic way, joins himself wrongly into the slow, steady and alive evolutionary process of their architectures. And if we want to face the challenge of retaining permanent change, this is the lesson we must learn while walking around in both cities from the hand of air.

作者简介

玛丽亚娜 · 巴斯蒂德

布鲁盖尔院士，法兰西道德与政治科学学院成员、教授、导师、法国国家科学研究中心。历史学家，毕业于高等师范大学和国立东方语言与文明学院，从事历史和地理研究，并获历史学博士学位。1966 年于国家科学研究中心担任研究员。现为该研究中心名誉主任，现代和当代中国研究中心成员。1972—2008 年，任教于巴黎第七大学和高等社会科学研究院博士班。1988—1993 年曾任法国高等师范大学副校长、1992—1996 年欧洲汉学研究协会会长。2001 年获选为法兰西道德与政治科学学院成员。获颁阿伯丁大学和俄罗斯科学院荣誉博士学位，并于中国担任数所大学的名誉教授。著作专长探究 19 世纪和 20 世纪中国的政治，社会和文化问题。

皮埃尔 · 克莱蒙

建筑师、城市规划师，法国建筑学院院士，巴黎贝拉维拉全国高等建筑学院名誉教授，arte-chaptentier 建筑师事务所主席， 毕业于法国建筑学院与东方语言和文明学院，并获民族学博士学位。他自 1980 年代初参与中国工作，专业为亚洲城市研究。他参与了该机构中最重要的建筑和城市项目，例如巴黎流星线的圣拉扎尔站、位于莱茵兰普法尔茨的苏伊布鲁克空军基地再转变、柬埔寨暹粒 / 吴哥的城市规划、阿尔吉耶港湾的装配规划，他也是塞纳河都市之大巴黎团队中的一员。他参与多项上海城市重大项目如上海歌剧院、中央广场、世纪大道、万里新区……其著作包括：与索菲 · 克莱蒙和新 · 扬海合著：《远东地区的景观建筑》，巴黎国立高等美术学院；与弗朗索瓦 · 盖德、齐湾合著：《上海住房转型——建筑设计》；与克莱尔 · 奈隆和安东尼 · 弗拉乌斯托合著：《建设城市，创造城市性》，巴黎。

郭璐

清华大学建筑学院博士后，英国李约瑟研究所劲牌学者。2014 年于清华大学获城乡规划学博士学位，主要研究方向为中国古代城市规划与设计，以及中西古代城市的比较研究，已发表相关领域中英文论文十余篇。

林志宏

城市规划师，教授、博士生导师，联合国教科文组织（UNESCO）总部世界遗产中心亚太区专员。于法国巴黎索邦大学（Sorbonne）艺术史和考古学专业取得艺术史博士学位（研究主题：景观表现的意向）。同时是在“城市规划及东方城市研究”和“花园、景观及区域研究”领域获得法国巴黎拉维莱特建筑学院（La Villette）建筑高等证书的城市规划师。现任联合国教科文组织（UNESCO）总部世界遗产中心亚太区专员，执行国际遗产保护等项目。在中国受聘担任同济大学（上海）建筑规划学院、天津大学（天津）建筑学院客座教授、博士生导师。林先生也是法国巴黎索邦大学（Paris IV—Sorbonne）远东研究中心（CREOPS）的研究员、法国巴黎 Belleville 建筑学院的“巴黎城市、建筑与社会研究中心—IPRAUS ”与巴黎 La Villette 建筑学院 “城乡发展研究中心—ATELAB”及德国 Aachen 工业大学遗产保存与调查研究中心（ACDC）的研究员。法国籍华人，1967 年生于台湾宜兰市，曾任台湾大学建筑与城乡发展研究基金会规划师、台湾文化大学景观系讲师及台湾乐山文教基金会主任。他在 2004—2007 年间以专家和顾问身份，参与中国曲阜“中欧合作欧盟亚洲城市复兴项目”（Asia Urbs）。目前已出版三本专著：《景观表现的意向、乾隆的玉山》（法文）、《世界遗产与历史城市》和《世界文化遗产与城市》（中文）。他发表了许多关于文化遗产和历史城市的中、英、法文文章，编著过十多本书籍，包括“中亚丝绸之路世界遗产系列和跨境遗产申遗文本”（Almaty，2014，英/俄），并参与了 80 多篇关于保护亚洲世界文化遗产需求论文的攥写。研究范围：世界遗产、活态历史城市、城市更新、丝绸之路、文化总体规划、文化景观。

刘健

注册城市规划师，清华大学建筑学院副教授，加拿大不列颠哥伦比亚大学人居中心、法国文化部建筑遗产中心当代中国建筑观察站访问学者。长期主持或参与小城镇总体规划、城市设计教学，讲授中外建筑与城市文化比较、20 世纪巴黎城市规划实践评介、中国当代城市规划与设计等课程。担任亚洲规划院校联盟副主席，世界人居学会副主席，中国城市规划学会国际城市规划学术委员会、乡村规划与建设学术委员会委员，中国城市规划协会女规划师委员会委员，《城市规划（英文版）》、《国际城市规划》编委会委员，《城市规划（英文版）》编辑部主任。主持或参与北京、绍兴、南通、济宁、张家港、曲阜等多地城市和城镇的规划设计，并有多本学术专著和数十篇学术文章在国内外出版发表。

马克 · 孟毅

前法国大使、曲阜友谊协会主席、国际合作顾问。在法国巴黎大学（东方语言和文化学院法律系）和剑桥大学国王学院（中越机构比较研究）毕业后，孟毅成为法国外交部亚洲事务专家。他曾是法国香港领事馆的中国政治观察员（1960—1963），曾参与中法建交后北京法国大使馆的设立过程（1967 年以前）。之后，他又被派驻几个国家的大使馆，并成为华盛顿法国大使馆参赞，负责亚洲事务。之后，1977 年，他又前往河内参与了法国驻越南大使馆的设立。1979 年，他在休假年期间从越南前往哈佛大学，从事一项有关中越关系的学术项目。之后，他又相继担任驻瓦努阿图和老挝大使，最终派驻台湾成为台北法国研究院的主任。1993 年退休以后，他成为 ASIE21 智库的成员，包括在 Umberto Eco 创立跨文化联盟，从事研究中国相关的文化工作，并在 2003 至 2010 年间，担任法国雷恩和曲阜间的中欧合作欧盟亚洲城市复兴项目 Asia Urbs 的协调人。孟毅作为曲阜友谊协会的主席，曾组织了一系列关于曲阜空间和发展的研讨会。1960 年代，他曾撰写了一篇有关“NATIONAL MINORITIES OF PEOPLE' S CHINA”（中国国家少数民族）的论文（DOCUMENTATION FRANCAISE）、*QUE-SAIS-JE, EDITIONS, PARIS, on THE ECONOMY OF PEOPLE'S CHINA*（我所知道的中国经济）一书（FRENCH UNIVERSITY PRESS，1965& 1971）、以及 HARVARD CENTER FOR INTERNATIONAL AFFAIRS PUBLICATIONS 有关 1979 年中越冲突的文章（1981）以及 *L' ASIE DEMAIN*（明日亚洲）(L' HARMATTAN, 2003) 等。

安杰 · 帕内罗 · 帕多

建筑师、城市规划师、城市更新和历史建筑改造方面的专家。自 1994 年起在西班牙圣地亚哥的一所国家、地区和地方政府的公共合作机构担任建筑师（1989 年马德里理工大学建筑和城市规划学院），该机构于 1993 年成立，旨在发展以保护世界遗产圣地亚哥 · 德 · 孔波斯特拉为重点的城市开发项目。该项目被授予 1996 年的欧洲联盟文化遗产奖、1996 年的古比奥奖、1997 年的欧盟地方规划奖、2002 年的迪拜联合国人居国际最佳实践案例等。2006 至 2012 年间，帕内罗曾担任圣地亚哥 · 德 · 孔波斯特拉技术办事处的首席建筑师，负责该世界遗产地历史建筑和公共空间的维护项目、城市基建管理的总体规划、城市的绿色战略以及城市更新和建筑改造信息中心的筹建。帕内罗也是自由建筑师，并获得了诸多建筑竞赛的奖项。他现为各类欧洲项目和国内国际机构的外部专家，包括联合国教科文组织世界遗产中心、西班牙合作开发机构（AECID）、西班牙城市和区域联盟（FEMP）等。他发表了众多有关城市更新、历史城市和世界遗产问题的文章，并在不同的大学担任客座教授，讲解研究生课程和组织研讨会，包括 2014 年基多第 19 届泛美洲建筑双年展。研究领域包括：世界遗产、活态历史城市、城市更新、能源改造、文化景观、遗产对发展的促进作用等。

邵甬

同济大学建筑与城市规划学院教授，博士生导师。法国夏约学校访问学者。1990 年代初至今主持了中国大量的历史城市、村镇、世界遗产等的保护与发展规划，包括平遥、丽江、曲阜、上海、天津、苏州、青岛、宁波、南通等城市和周庄、角直、慈城、查济等历史文化名镇名村；参与编制国家《历史文化名城保护规划规范》和《历史文化名镇名村保护规划规范》；二十多次获得国家和建设部优秀规划设计奖，三次获得“联合国教科文组织亚太地区文化遗产保护奖”；完成数十篇相关领域的科研论文；参与编写《江南古镇》和《欧洲城市史纲》，主编《城市遗产研究与保护》和《历史文化村镇的保护规划与实践》，完成专著《法国建筑、城市和景观遗产保护与价值重现》。2000 年至今参与多项联合国人居署、联合国教科文组织的重要课题；2005—2007 年作为国际专家参与欧盟项目“欧亚城乡合作计划：曲阜的遗产保护与发展”；2008 年负责“十一五”国家科技部支撑项目《历史文化村镇保护规划技术研究》子课题；2010 年负责国家自然科学基金项目《中国人居型世界遗产资源的保护与利用研究》等。

莱昂 · 汪德迈

汉学家，法兰西学院通讯院士（自 1992 年起），国际孔夫子研究协会顾问（自 1999 年起），北京师范大学荣誉教授（自 2015 年起），法国荣誉军团勋章骑士，学术界棕榈叶勋章官员，日本瑞宝章金银星获得者。曾在法国国家东方语言机构培训，获得中文文凭（1948）和越南语文凭（1950），曾在巴黎哲学大学学习（于 1950 年获得高等研究文凭），并获得法学博士学位（1950），曾在实践研究工作机构学习汉学（1962）并获得文学博士学位（1975）。他曾于西贡做一位中学教师（1951—1954），曾担任河内 - 京都 - 香港法国远东研究机构研究员（1956 — 1965）。他曾于法国埃克斯马赛大学（1966—1973）、巴黎第七大学（1973—1979）和高等研究实验学校（1979—1993）担任汉语文化教授，并曾任法国 - 日本之家的法国主任（1981—1984），以及法国远东学院主任（1989—1993），并于 1993 年退休。出版关于汉语和中国文化多国语言书籍，包括法语、中文、英语、日语、越南语。

吴良镛

中国科学院和中国工程院院士，清华大学建筑与城市研究所所长，清华大学建筑学院建筑和城市规划与设计教授，著名的建筑学家、城乡规划学家和教育家，中国人居环境科学的创建者。自 1940 年代起，长期致力于中国建筑与规划教育事业，曾于 1996 年获颁国际建筑师协会让·屈米奖。主持大量城市规划、城市设计和建筑设计的研究和实践项目，例如人居环境科学研究、京津冀地区城乡空间发展规划研究、桂林中心区保护城市设计、中央美术学院校园规划设计、孔子研究院规划设计、国家图书馆规划设计、天安门广场扩建规划设计，并曾多次获得国际和国内重要奖项，包括国家最高科学技术奖、陈嘉庚奖、世界人居奖、亚洲建筑师协会金奖等。北京市菊儿胡同危旧房改建试点工程获得亚洲建筑师协会金质奖，在联合国总部获世界人居奖。长期在中外学术和职业领域担任要职，发起成立中国建筑学会、中国城市规划学会、中国城市规划协会等重要机构。在国内外出版和发表大量有关建筑和规划的学术专著和文章。

Author's Short Biography

Marianne Bastid-Bruguière

Historian of modern and contemporary China, is academician at the Académie des Sciences morales et politiques (Academy of Humanities, Social and Political Sciences) of the Institut de France, and Emeritus Research Professor at the National Center for Scientific Research (CNRS) in Paris. She was trained at the Higher Normal School, the School of Oriental Languages, the Faculty of Letters in Paris, and Peking University History Department. She taught and was Ph.D. Student Director at Paris 7 University and at the School for Higher Social Sciences Studies (EHESS). She was Deputy-Director of the Higher Normal School, and President of the European Association of Chinese Studies. She holds an honorary doctorate from the Russian Academy of Sciences and from the University of Aberdeen, honorary membership of the Institute of Modern History at the Chinese Academy of Social Sciences, and honorary professorships from various Chinese universities. She has published widely in French, Chinese, English and Japanese on Chinese political, social and cultural history since the 19th century.

Pierre Clement

Architect & Urban Designer, Member of the French Académie d'Architecture, Honorary professorat the Architecture School of Paris-Belleville, Chairman of the Board of Arte Charpentier Architectes. Architect D.P.L.G at the Ecole Nationale Supérieure des Beaux Arts de Paris, Degree at the Institut National des Langues et Civilisations Orientales de Paris, Ph.D. in Ethnology, Paris La Sorbonne Université. Pierre splits his time between research, teaching and practice. He has been professor at the Architecture School of Paris Belleville since 1984 where he manages the research department: Institut Parisien de Recherches Architecture Urbanistique et Sociétés IPRAUS and a specialized program on Asian-Pacific Metropolis.

He is part of the most important architectural and urban projects of the agency, such as the Saint-Lazare station of the Météor line, in Paris, the reconversion of the air base of Zweibrucken in Rhénanie Palatinat, the urban plan of Siem-Reap/Angkor in Cambodia, the fitting plan of the Algier's Bay, or Grand Paris in Seine Métropole Team. He also worked on many Chinese projects: Shanghai Opera House, Nankin Road, the Century Avenue in Shanghai as well as the new cities of Wanli, Zengzhou, and the New CBD at Wuchang (Wuhan), and the reconversion of Kaohshiung waterfront area. He published extensively in French, English and Chinese about Architecture and City Planning.

GUO Lu

Postdoc research fellow in the School of Architecture, Tsinghua University, China; Jing Brand Fellow in the Needham Research Institute, Cambridge, UK. She received her doctoral degree on urban and rural planning from Tsinghua University in 2014 with the thesis "Regional Design of the Human Settlement of Chinese Capital: Chang'an Region and Contemporary Enlightenment". Her research mainly focuses on the history of urban planning and design in ancient China, as well as the comparative study of ancient cities in China and Europe. She has published a dozen of papers in academic journals and international conferences.

Roland Lin Chih-Hung

City planner and art historian, Programme Specialist at the Asia–Pacific Unit of the World Heritage Centre at UNESCO headquarters in Paris. He is in charge of UNESCO cultural heritage protection projects in Central and South Asia as well as the World Heritage Silk Roads serial nomination Central and Southern Asian section. In addition, Lin is a Ph.D., Professor and Ph.D. Student Director, Faculty of Architecture and Planning, Tianjin University, Tianjin, China; Visiting Professor, Faculty of Architecture and Planning, Tongji University, Shanghai, China; Research Fellow, CREOPS (Centre de Recherche en Extrême-Orient de l'Université Paris-Sorbonne), Paris, France. Lin has published prolifically, authoring three academic books on landscape, historiccities, and World Heritage issues in English, French and Chinese, edited over ten books including *Silk Roads World Heritage Serial and Transnational Nomination in Central Asia 2011–2014* (Almaty, 2014 in English/Russian) and contributed over eighty specialized papers on the need for safeguarding world and cultural heritage in Asia. Research Area: World Heritage; Living Historical Cities; Urban Renew; Silk Roads; Culture Master Planning; Cultural Landscape.

LIU Jian

City planner, associate professor of urban planning & design at the School of Architecture at Tsinghua University, and visiting scholar at the Center for Human Settlements at University of British Colombia and l'Observatoire d'Architecture de la Chine Contemporaine of the Cité d'Architectue et du Patrimoine, Ministère de la Culture et de la Communication de la France. LIU chairs studios of town planning and urban design, as well as seminars on Comparison of Architectural and Urban Culture between East and West, Contemporary Urban Planning and Design in China, and Urban Planning & Development of Paris Region in the 20th Century. She serves or served as Vice President of Asian Planning School of Association, Vice President of the World Ekistics Society, member of the Academic Committees of Rural Planning & Development and International Urban Planning of the Urban Planning Society of China, member of the Female Planner Association of China Association of City Planning, Editorial Board member of *China City Planning Review* and *Urban Planning International*, and Managing Editor of *China City Planning Review*. She has been involved in the practical projects of urban planning and design of many Chinese cities, towns and villages including Beijing, Shaoxing, Nantong, Jining, Zhangjiagang, Qufu and so on. She has published several books and her papers are also frequently seen in some well-known journals of urban planning both at home and abroad.

Marc Menguy

Former Ambassador; President, Society of Friends of Qufu; Advisor for International Cooperation. After studied at French Paris University (Institute of Oriental Languages and Civilizations; Faculty of Law, Paris) and King's College, Cambridge (Comparative studies on Chinese and Vietnamese institutions), Marc H. Menguy became a specialist on Asian affairs at the French Ministry of Foreign Affairs. He served as a political observer in the French Consulate general, Hong Kong (1960–1963), and took part in 1964—after the France-China diplomatic Recognition—in the opening process of the French Embassy, Beijing, up to 1967. After being assigned to a few countries embassies in Asia, he became Councilor with the French Embassy, Washington, in charge of Asian affairs. Following his assignment to the opening of the French Embassy in Hanoi 1977, Vietnam, he was sent from Vietnam to Harvard University in 1979 on a sabbatical year, to work on an academic project related to Vietnam and China relations. Sent as Ambassador respectively to Vanuatu and Laos, he later was assigned to Taiwan as director of the French Institute in Taipei. Retired, in 1993, he became a member of ASIE 21 think tank, Paris, and engaged in some cultural projects with China: a few years with TRANSCULTURA Association, founded by Umberto Eco, and then from 2003 to 2010, was assigned as the moderator in an European Asia Urbs Heritage Project between the City of Rennes (France) and the City of Qufu, birth place of Confucius. Marc Menguy, President of the Society of Friends of Qufu, organised a few seminars with this historical city on space and development. He wrote in the 60's an essay on the National Minorities Of People'S China (Documentation Francaise); *a QUE-SAIS-JE on THE ECONOMY OF PEOPLE'S CHINA*, 1965 & 1971 (French University Press); Harvard Center For International Affairs Publications, a paper on the 1979 Sino-Vietnamese Conflict, 1981; *L'ASIE DEMAIN* (L'HARMATTAN), Paris, 2003.

Angel Panero Pardo

Architect, city planner, urban renewal and historic buildings retrofitting specialist. Architect (1989 ETSAM. School of Architecture and city Planning of the Polytechnic University of Madrid, Spain) since 1994 in the Consorcio de Santiago (Spain), a Public Institution of cooperation between National, Regional and Local Governments, created in 1993 to develop an urban project with special emphasis on protection of the Word Heritage Site (WHS) of Santiago de Compostela. The work was awarded by *Europa Nostra* Prize 1996, *Gubbio* Prize 1996, *European Union Local Planning* Prize 1997, *Dubai UN-HABITAT International Best Practice* Prize 2002 etc. Between 2006 and 2012, Panero was Head Architect of the Technical Office of Consorcio de Santiago, promoting the Maintenance Program of historic buildings and public spaces in the WHS of Santiago de Compostela, the Master Plan of urban infrastructures management, the Green Strategy for the city, and the Reference Center of formation in urban renewal and building retrofitting etc. Panero eventually worked also as a free-lance architect, obtaining some prizes in architecture competitions. He works as external expert of European projects, National and International Institutions, including UNESCO World Heritage Centre, the Spanish Agency of Cooperation for development (AECID), the Spanish Federation of Cities and Regions (FEMP). He published articles and papers about urban renewal, historic cities and world heritage issues, and lecturer as guest professor at different universities, postgraduate courses and specialized symposiums, including XIX Bienal Panamericana de Arquitectura de Quito 2014. Research Area: World Heritage; Living Historical Cities; Urban Renew; Energy retrofit; Cultural Landscape; Heritage for development.

SHAO Yong

Urban planner, Professor in the College of Architecture and Urban Planning of Tongji University, National Research Center of Historic Cities, China. She is the expert member of ICOMOS-ISCEAH, ICOMOS-CIAV, and National Committee of Historical and Cultural Cities Conservation of China. She got the Doctor diploma at 2003 from College of Architecture and Urban Planning, Tongji University, and followed the training of French State Architects and Urban Planners (AUE) in the Ecole de Chaillot and Ecole Nationale des Ponts et Chaussées in France in 1999 and 2006. From 1990 to now, Dr. Shao has worked a lot for the conservation of historical cities, towns and villages, World Cultural Heritage sites, such as Lijiang, Pingyao, Qu Fu, Shanghai, Tianjin, Suzhou, Qingdao, Ningbo, Nantong, Zhouzhuang, Luzhi, Cicheng and Zhaji, etc. These planning have achieved awards at Chinese State, provincial and municipal level. Dr. Shao's project "The Water Town Conservation" has got the Conservation Distinct Award of Asia-Pacific region of UNESCO in 2003, and "Community-based Conservation Project of World Heritage Lijiang" has got the Merit Award in 2007. She is the author of "Ancient Town in Jiang Nan" and "Equilibre et Harmonie: protection et mise en valeur du patrimoine architectural, urban et paysager en France", in charge of the edit of *Urban Heritage Conservation and Research on Conservation Plan of Historical and Cultural Towns and Villages*, and published many articles about urban and rural heritage conservation in professional journals. She joined several international conservation projects as an expert, including Project Asia UrbS, Sino-French cooperation of architectural, urban and landscape heritage conservation, UNESCO Chair of Environment and Landscape Design, UN-Habitat program for "historic quarter for all", and the activities of ISCEAH and WHEAP, etc.

Léon Vandermeersch

Sinologue, Correspondent of the Academy of Inscriptions and Belles—Lettres of the Institut de France (since 1992), Councilor of the International Association of Confucian Studies (since 1999), Honoris Causa Professor of the Beijing Normal University (since 2015), as well as Knight of the Legion of Honors; Officer of the Academic Palms; Gold and Silver Star of the Sacred Treasure of Japan. He was trained at the INALCO (National Institute for Oriental Languages) Diplomas in Chinese (1948) and in Vietnamese (1950); at Paris University in Philosophy (DEA—High Studies Diploma, 1950) and PhD in Law (1950); as well as in EPHE (Institute for Research Work Practice) in Sinology (1962) and Doctoratès Lettres (National Ph.D. in Literature, 1975). After being Middle School teacher in Saigon (1951–54); researcher of the EFEO (French Institute for Far-Eastern Studies) in Hanoï –Kyôto – Hongkong (1956–1965); he was Professor and Ph.D. Student Director of Chinese Language and Civilization in several Universities (1966–93): University of Aix-en-Provence; University of Paris 7 and EPHE (Institute for Research Work Practice). Also he was French Director of Tôkyô French-Japanese House (1981–1984) and Director of EFEO (French Institute for Far-Eastern Studies, 1989–1993), before his retirement in 1993. He has published widely in French, Chinese, English, Japanese and Vietnamese on Chinese Language and Civilization.

WU Liangyong

Well-known architect, planner and educator, academician of both Chinese Academia Sciences and Chinese Academia of Engineering, Director of Institute of Architectural &Urban Studies of Tsinghua University, professor of architecture and urban planning and design of the School of Architecture at Tsinghua University. WU has dedicated most of his lifetime to architectural and planning education in China since the 1940s, being awarded the Jean Tschumi Prize by UIA in 1996. He has led a great number of research and practical projects of urban planning, urban design and architectural design, including research on Sciences of Human Settlements, research on Rural and Urban Spatial Development Planning for Greater Beijing Region, urban design for the Conservation of the Central Area of Guilin, Campus Planning and Design of the National Academy of Art, Planning and Design of the Research Institute of Confucius, planning and design of the National Library in Beijing, planning and design of the Enlargement of Tian An Men Square, and so on. Many of his projects have been awarded both at home and abroad, including the National Grand Prize for Science and Technology of China and the Tan KahKee Science Award for the research on Sciences of Human Settlements, the Gold Medal for Architecture of ARCASIA and the World Habitat Award for the project of rehabilitating Beijing and New Courtyard House Complex Development at Ju'er Hutong. WU has played a significant part in academic and professional circles both nationally and internationally. He had worked in founding national professional bodies such as the Chinese Architectural Society, the Urban Planning Society of China and the Chinese Society for Urban Studies. He has published widely in Chinese and English on architecture and urban planning.

图书在版编目（CIP）数据

孔子故里 · 曲阜：迈向可持续城市 / 林志宏主编 . -- 上海：同济大学出版社，2018.7
（亚洲文化遗产系列丛书）
ISBN 978-7-5608-7842-3

Ⅰ . ①孔… Ⅱ . ①林… Ⅲ . ①城市—文化遗产—保护—曲阜②城市—文化遗产—可持续性发展—曲阜
Ⅳ . ① K295.24

中国版本图书馆 CIP 数据核字 (2018) 第 089548 号

亚洲文化遗产系列丛书

孔子故里 · 曲阜
迈向可持续城市

林志宏　主编

出 版 人：华春荣
策　　划：秦蕾 / 群岛工作室
责任编辑：李　争
责任校对：徐春莲
平面设计：张　微
版　　次：2018 年 7 月第 1 版
印　　次：2018 年 7 月第 1 次印刷
印　　刷：上海安兴汇东纸业有限公司
开　　本：787mm × 960mm　1/16
印　　张：15
字　　数：300 000
书　　号：ISBN 978-7-5608-7842-3
定　　价：128.00 元
出版发行：同济大学出版社
地　　址：上海市四平路 1239 号
邮政编码：200092
网　　址：http://www.tongjipress.com.cn
经　　销：全国各地新华书店

the Serie of Asian Cultural Heritage

QUFU, BIRTHPLACE OF CONFUCIUS
Towards a Sustainable City

Edited by: Roland Lin Chih-Hung

ISBN 978-7-5608- 7842-3
Publisher: HUA Chunrong
Initiated by: QIN Lei / Studio Archipelago
Editor: LI Zheng
Proofreading: XU Chunlian
Graphic Design: ZHANG Wei
Published in July 2018, by Tongji University Press,
1239, Siping Road, Shanghai, China, 200092.
www.tongjipress.com.cn